THE "MAGIC" BACKGROUND OF PEARL HARBOR

OF

PEARL HARBOR

VOLUME II
(May 12, 1941—August 6, 1941)

DEPARTMENT OF DEFENSE   UNITED STATES OF AMERICA

For sale by the Superintendent of Documents, U.S. Government Printing Office
Washington, D.C. 20402 (8-part set; sold in sets only)

Stock No. 008–000–00233–9

THE "MAGIC" BACKGROUND OF PEARL HARBOR

TABLE OF CONTENTS
CHAPTER II

APPENDIX

DoD Comment:

The reader will note that beginning with Volume II an additional Part was added to each of the original Volumes. This new part covers Japanese intelligence activities as reflected in their diplomatic messages. Of particular interest, no doubt, will be the references to espionage in the continental United States and in the Hawaiian Islands.

Following the usual format for the series, the textual portion is based on the Japanese messages. An Appendix contains the actual messages themselves.

OUTLINE OF VOLUME II

Part A

Hull-Nomura Conversations.
   (a) Secretary Hull's Reports.
   (b) Ambassador Nomura's Reports.

Part B

Japanese Intelligence Reports in Diplomatic Messages.
   (a) Japanese Reports from the United States.
   (b) Japanese Reports from the Panama Canal.
   (c) Japanese Reports from Cuba.
   (d) Japanese Reports from the Philippine Islands.
   (e) Japanese Reports from the Hawaiian Islands.

Part C

Japanese Diplomatic Activities Throughout the World.
   (a) Japanese-American Relations.
   (b) Japanese-Mexican Relations.
   (c) Japanese-South American Relations.
   (d) Japanese-British Relations.
   (e) Japanese-Axis Relations.
   (f) Japanese-Russian Relations.
   (g) Japanese-French Relations.
   (h) Japanese-Chungking Relations.
   (i) Japanese-Nanking Relations.
   (j) Japanese-Dutch Relations.
   (k) Japanese-Thaiese Relations.

CHAPTER II

(May 12, 1941 – August 6, 1941)

PART A—HULL–NOMURA CONVERSATIONS

Consideration of the Japanese Proposal of May 12, 1941 and Interruption of Conversations Following the Movement of Japanese Troops into Indo-China[1].

1. Hull-Nomura Conversation (May 12, 1941).

(a) *Secretary Hull's Report.*[2]

The Japanese Ambassador called at Secretary Hull's apartment in a very disturbed state because on the preceding day he had given some documents to Mr. Hull by mistake. Requesting that these documents be returned, the Ambassador delivered other papers which contained his official instructions.

To Secretary Hull's inquiry about the change of the provision in the original proposal which had spoken of Japan's keeping out of the South Pacific in a military way, Ambassador Nomura replied that the original statement had restrained Japan alone, but that the proposed modification was designed to impose equal restrictions on all countries. Furthermore, Ambassador Nomura insisted that Japan would not use force in the South Pacific since its sole desire was to keep war out of that whole area. The Secretary of State then inquired whether the three principles expressed by Prime Minister Konoye in December 1938 were the basis for the "New Order" in eastern Asia.

Indicating that both documents which he had just given to Secretary Hull were official, the Japanese Ambassador explained that they had been submitted separately to permit eventual transmission to the press of only the main document, with the explanatory manuscript omitted. Secretary Hull commented that he would receive the papers unofficially and would study them informally before coming to any decision.[3]

One of the two documents handed to the Secretary of State by Ambassador Nomura had already been deciphered in its several versions by United States cryptanalysts; first, when the original Japanese version had been sent to Tokyo for approval on April 13, 1941; second, when sent in English to Tokyo on April 30;[4] third, when it was returned from Tokyo to Washington on May 9;[5] fourth, when it was re-submitted by Ambassador Nomura to Tokyo on May 12;[6] fifth when the final text of the proposal was transmitted in its approved form from Tokyo to Washington.[7]

The other document was an "Oral Explanation" for proposed amendments to the original draft. This had been deciphered by American experts on May 12, 1941.[8] The reader will note the difference between the text of the "Oral Explanation" presented to the American State Department by Ambassador Nomura and the text of the deciphered secret dispatch from

---

[1]Chapter title taken from the divisional arrangement of the State Department documents in *S.D.*, II, 332.

[2]"Memorandum by the Secretary of State", May 12, 1941, *S.D.*, II, 418–419.

[3]*Ibid.*

[4]Appendix I, 54.

[5]Appendix I, 55–59.

[6]Appendix II, 1–7. Hereafter referred to as II, 1–7.

[7]II, 8–9.

[8]*S.D.*, II, 423–425, II, 10–12.

Foreign Minister Matsuoka to Ambassador Nomura.[9] The submitted "Oral Explanation", outlining Japanese activities in the Southwest Pacific area, did not emphasize Mr. Matsuoka's statement that Japan sometimes found it necessary to use armed force in achieving peace. Although stating that Japan desired to settle international questions peacefully, the Foreign Minister said:

> In the future developments of the international situation, the Imperial Japanese government, should it ever be provoked beyond endurance, will not be able to avoid exercising military force and that she give a guarantee not to do so would be very difficult. However, regardless of the future developments of this situation, it is very clear that Japan alone could not determine such a course.[10]

The Japanese insisted on making a specific reference, in Section II of the proposal, to Japan's obligations under the Tripartite Pact of military assistance to Germany and Italy. Another proposed change in Section III, dealing with the China affair was said to be in perfect agreement with the ideas expressed by the United States. It referred to the three principles of Prime Minister Konoye:

1. Neighborly friendship.
2. Joint defense against communism;
3. Economic cooperation—by which Japan does not intend to exercise economic monopoly in China nor to demand of China a limitation in the interest of Third Powers.[11]

It was further explained that these principles implied the following:

1. Mutual respect of sovereignty and territories;
2. Mutual respect for the inherent characteristics of each nation cooperating as good neighbors and forming a Far Eastern nucleus contributing to world peace;
3. Withdrawal of Japanese troops from Chinese territory in accordance with an agreement to be concluded between Japan and China;
4. No annexation, no indemnities;
5. Independence of Manchukuo.[12]

According to the Japanese proposal, the United States was to promise secretly to discontinue aid to Chiang Kai-shek, if he refused to enter into negotiations for peace with Japan. Furthermore, the Japanese wished to delete the prohibition against a large-scale Japanese immigration into Chinese territory on the grounds that the Japanese people might consider that America was dictating Japanese immigration policy concerning China, as it had always done with reference to the United States. However, despite its demand for the deletion of this clause, the Japanese government fully understood and accepted its true meaning and purpose.

The Japanese proposal left naval, aerial, and mercantile marine relations in the Pacific for further discussion until an "understanding" had been reached and the diplomatic situation had become clear. The suggestion that naval squadrons from each country pay a courtesy visit to the other nation would be considered in the future as a separate proposal. Another Japanese change would omit, until a full "understanding" had been reached, the proposal that the United States grant Japan a gold credit.

An important deletion was made by the Japanese of a phrase indicating that Japan would carry on activities in the Southwestern Pacific by peaceful means "without resorting to arms". This was deleted as inappropriate and unnecessarily critical because, according to the Japanese, the peaceful policy of Japan had long been evident.

---

[9]II, 10–12.
[10]II, 11.
[11]*S.D.*, II, 423–425, II, 12.
[12]*Ibid.*

An agreement to restrict future transfers of territories in the Far East was omitted because Japan claimed that it would involve military and treaty obligations requiring complicated legislative procedure in both countries. For the same reason, a statement referring to the independence of the Philippine Islands was also altered. The phrase—"and to the Southwestern Pacific area"—was omitted from a discussion of Japanese immigration because the Japanese felt that this question should be solved by direct negotiations with authorities in that area. Japan desired the proposal for the holding of a conference to be deleted since it felt that it would be more desirable to estimate first the effects of the "understanding". Announcement of the joint acceptance of the "understanding" would be drafted in Tokyo and cabled to Washington for approval.[13]

(b) *Ambassador Nomura's Report.*[14]

Ambassador Nomura's secret report of this interview recorded Secretary Hull's request for a formal explanation of the three basic principles of Prime Minister Konoye. The Japanese Ambassador asked Tokyo to modify his instructions so as to permit him to explain these principles advantageously.[15]

Ambassador Nomura mentioned his efforts to assure Secretary Hull that Japan had no aggressive ambitions in the Southwest Pacific. When asked by Mr. Hull why one of the provisions of his original document had been changed, Ambassador Nomura had replied that the modification had been made simply to avoid restrictions on Japan alone, since the original proposal permitted other countries to act freely in that area. This statement agreed with Secretary Hull's report of Ambassador Nomura's reply.[16] The Secretary of State then remarked to Ambassador Nomura that every precaution was being taken to ensure the secrecy of their conversations.[17]

2. Revisions of the Japanese Proposal.

For a day or two after Foreign Minister Matsuoka had sent to Washington the final, approved version of Ambassador Nomura's original proposal, suggestions for interpretation of the meaning and changes in the document kept arriving from Tokyo. One message requested that it be made clear that the attitude of the United States government toward the European War, as stated in the proposal, merely represented a declaration of attitude on the part of the American government and was not to imply Japanese approval of that attitude.[18]

Changes in important passages,[19] coding mistakes,[20] and omissions of important sentences[21] indicated that Foreign Minister Matsuoka had some reasons for claiming that Tokyo could not proceed as hastily as Ambassador Nomura had desired.

Ambassador Nomura was disturbed at the many requests from Tokyo for minor and major changes in the so-called approved version of the proposal which he had already handed to Secretary Hull, for he now asked Mr. Matsuoka to limit all further instructions to only major matters and to permit him to exercise his own discretion on all minor details.[22] Stressing the

---

[13]*S.D.*, II, 423–425, II, 10.
[14]II, 13.
[15]*Ibid.*
[16]*S.D.*, II, 418–419, II, 8.
[17]II, 14.
[18]II, 16.
[19]II, 17–18.
[20]II, 19, 22.
[21]II, 23–25.
[22]II, 26.

gratitude of all Japanese diplomats in Washington for the support given by the Foreign Minister to the "understanding", Ambassador Nomura stated that since only President Roosevelt, Mr. Hull, and Postmaster General Walker were aware of the contents of the negotiations, it would be disadvantageous to create the impression that Japan had not entered the discussions well prepared. Ambassador Nomura remarked:

> If we continue to submit minor revisions from time to time, I am afraid that the United States may get the impression that we have entered into this business without being too well prepared. This naturally, reflects upon my integrity and may give rise to doubts in the other parties concerned as to my sincerity. This could lead the negotiations into a failure.[23]

Foreign Minister Matsuoka, replying two days later that he had carefully noted Ambassador Nomura's request, proceeded to order several more changes in the proposal. However, he did grant to the Japanese Ambassador permission to make the changes whenever a favorable opportunity arose.[24]

3. Ambassador Nomura Attempts to Restrain Mr. Matsuoka.

A bluntly worded telegram from Foreign Minister Matsuoka was received by Ambassador Nomura on May 13, 1941. Intended for delivery to Secretary of State Hull, it stressed that Japan had entered the current negotiations only on the premises that, first, the United States would not enter the European war, and second, that the United States would agree to advise Generalissimo Chiang Kai-shek to make peace with Japan as quickly as possible.[25]

Ambassador Nomura replied that no official negotiations had begun as yet, since all discussions that had occurred so far were "off the record" private conversations. Pointing out that he had directed all his efforts to achieving the two points mentioned by Foreign Minister Matsuoka, the Japanese Ambassador warned that the presentation of this dispatch to Secretary Hull would interfere with the establishment of the "understanding". Ambassador Nomura asked that the Foreign Minister approve of his withholding the message since he intended to bring up the subjects mentioned by Mr. Matsuoka at an opportune moment during one of his conversations with Mr. Hull.[26]

4. Hull-Nomura Conversation (May 14, 1941)

(a) *Secretary Hull's Report.*[27]

Ambassador Nomura called at Secretary Hull's hotel apartment on May 14, 1941 to deliver a proposed amendment to the original draft under discussion.[28] The Japanese Ambassador had nothing to say about the points at issue except to stress that there was no danger to the United States from a war in Europe. When Secretary Hull emphasized the necessity of self-defense on the part of the United States, Ambassador Nomura replied that the United States, in the opinion of Japan, would not be in danger.

Repeating some points from his speech of April 24, 1941 to the American Society of International Law, the Secretary of State declared that the United States would be in great jeopardy if Chancellor Hitler's plan to attack South America proceeded unimpeded. According to Mr. Hull, the Japanese Ambassador was impressed with his statements since Ambassador Nomura responded that only a few individuals and small groups among the Japanese wanted war with the United States.

---

[23]*Ibid.*
[24]II, 27–28.
[25]II, 29.
[26]II, 30.
[27]"Memorandum by Secretary of State", May 14, 1941, *S.D.*, II, 425–426.
[28]*S.D.*, II, 426.

6

Ambassador Nomura brought up the difficult problem of reconciling the attitude of the United States towards the European war with Japan's obligations to Germany and Italy under the Tripartite Pact. Commenting that Ambassador Nomura was probably aware from newspaper stories that Ambassador Grew had called upon Mr. Matsuoka, who had been rather offensive during the visit in his references to the United States,[29] Mr. Hull said that he knew Mr. Matsuoka was a politician, who was addicted to the use of bluffing language. However, there was still some uncertainty as to whether or not the Foreign Minister would hinder or defeat further conferences in regard to peace. Ambassador Nomura agreed that Mr. Matsuoka was very much a politician, but denied that the Foreign Minister was powerful enough to defeat the purpose of their conversations.[30]

(b) *Ambassador Nomura's Report.*[31]

According to Ambassador Nomura, the conversation of May 14, 1941 was quite pleasant throughout. Secretary Hull implied that a preliminary understanding with China and England would be necessary before the China affair could be settled.

In a discussion of American self-defense, the Japanese Ambassador stated that since America was completely safe from invasion, it was difficult for the Japanese people to understand why so many in the United States desired to enter the war. The Secretary of State answered that his speech to the American Society of International Law, on April 24, 1941, expressed his own views concerning the dangers to America. An attack on South America would be one of Chancellor Hitler's first objectives after he had successfully conquered the rest of Europe. Chancellor Hitler would have to control the seas to do this, but there was always a possibility that an English Quisling would surrender the British navy to the Germans.

Ambassador Nomura reminded Secretary Hull that England had promised not to turn over its navy to the Germans under any circumstances, but Mr. Hull countered by recalling that though France had made similar promises, Darlan and Laval seemed to be ready to transfer the French fleet to Germany. Since there was a possibility of the British navy being turned over to the Germans, it was absolutely necessary for the United States to aid the Churchill government, not merely to protect democracy as a whole, but to protect the United States itself. According to Secretary Hull, it seemed to be Japan's policy to prevent the United States from aiding Britain, even if this meant war, for Foreign Minister Matsuoka had actually threatened war in his conversation with Ambassador Grew.

Ambassador Nomura then asked if the flight of Rudolph Hess to Scotland had any implications of peace, but Secretary Hull, replying that he knew of no such motives, stated that the flight was an indication to him of the German government's deterioration. (See *Part C—Japanese-Axis Relations, Section 134.*)

Despite the assurances of Ambassador Nomura, Secretary Hull was not convinced that the Japanese had given up hope of a southward expansion. The Secretary of State pointed out that Chancellor Hitler had been signing treaties only to break them ever since 1933, and many another treaty-makers in history had broken pacts to suit his convenience.

Ambassador Nomura concluded his report by urging the Japanese government to make every effort to convince Secretary of State Hull of its sincere intentions. Ambassador Nomura's position at this point in the negotiations is best expressed in his own words:

---

[29] See Section 5—(*Ambassador Grew Interviews Mr. Matsuoka*).

[30] *S.D.*, II, 426.

[31] II, 31–33.

I firmly believe that we should enter into this Understanding while the United States is interested in the proposition and before any outside interference enters into it. Towards this end, I am making every possible effort. All the persons concerned in this matter are of the same opinion.[32]

5. Ambassador Grew Interviews Mr. Matsuoka.[33]

The interview of Ambassador Grew with Mr. Matsuoka had been marked by the belligerent attitude of the Japanese Foreign Minister who insisted that America's convoying of ships to Great Britain would certainly lead to war with Germany. According to Mr. Matsuoka, a neutrality zone in the Atlantic or any other ocean was contrary to international law, and Chancellor Hitler, who desired to avoid war, so far had shown great "patience and generosity" in not declaring war on the United States. Mr. Matsuoka doubted, however, that the German leader could exercise patience indefinitely.

If Germany sank American ships in the Atlantic, and if the United States then attacked German submarines, this would be an act of American aggression which would call into question the application of the Tripartite Pact. There was no doubt in Mr. Matsuoka's mind that war would then ensue between Japan and the United States. According to the Japanese Foreign Minister, the issue was exclusively in the hands of President Roosevelt, and he felt that the "manly, decent, and reasonable thing" for the United States to do was to declare war openly on Germany, instead of engaging in actual war under cover of neutrality.

When Ambassador Grew emphatically resented this statement concerning the "decent thing" to do, Mr. Matsuoka agreed to withdraw it, and when Mr. Grew reminded him that Japan had attacked China without a declaration of war, the Foreign Minister, remarking that the situations were entirely different, changed the subject. Each allegation of Mr. Matsuoka was answered in turn by Ambassador Grew who reminded him that far from breaking international law, the United States was determined to maintain the freedom of the seas against Germany's illegal submarine warfare. However, both Mr. Matsuoka and Mr. Grew finally agreed that further debate was useless, since a meeting of minds was impossible.

Mr. Grew discussed Japan's policy in the South Pacific, and stressed the fact that despite the assurances of Japan concerning its peaceful intentions, many highly placed Japanese were openly advocating the use of force. Mr. Matsuoka, deploring the use of a policy of force as well as anti-foreign agitation in Japan, stated that his government was about to ban publication of this type of propaganda for Japan was determined to carry out the southward advance by peaceful measures, "unless circumstances render this impossible". Answering a query concerning the circumstances he had in mind, the Foreign Minister indicated that the British were concentrating troops in Malaya. Though assured that this movement was simply a defense measure by the British, Mr. Matsuoka replied that the Japanese people considered the action provocative. If the Japanese public became further disturbed, pressure might be brought on the government to act.

Ambassador Grew explained that the United States was determined to support Great Britain; therefore, it could not complacently watch the destruction of the British lifeline from the East. In view of this, there was potential danger in the statement that Japan's peaceful intentions depended on "circumstances". Ambassador Grew regretted the negative aspect of current Japanese-American relations since he had hoped to establish something constructive, but the recent change of Japanese policy had made this impossible. Mr. Matsuoka replied that he was hopeful of establishing strong relations in the future, but that everything now depended on one man, President Roosevelt. Ambassador Grew ended the conversation by saying that, henceforth, Japan's relations with the United States would depend upon Japanese actions rather than words.

---

[32]II, 33.

[33]"Telegram: Ambassador to Japan (Grew) to Secretary of State", May 14, 1941, 5 P.M. (Received May 14, 9:55 A.M.), *S.D.*, II, 145–148.

8

Immediately after the interview Ambassador Grew received a personal letter, written in the Foreign Minister's own hand, apologizing for his misuse of an English word in referring to America's aid to England. Intending to say "indiscretion", instead he had said "indecent" in remarking that he hoped the American government would be more cautious and careful in its actions.[34]

6. Hull–Nomura Conversation (May 16, 1941).

(a) *Secretary Hull's Report.*[35]

The Japanese Ambassador, accompanied by Colonel Hideo Iwakuro, Assistant Military Attache, and Mr. Katsuzo Okumura, Second Secretary of the Japanese Embassy, called at Secretary Hull's apartment on May 16, 1941 at his request. Mr. Hull outlined the main points of an informal and unofficial oral statement, which he later handed to Ambassador Nomura.[36]

This oral statement declared that though there had been no time for a careful study of the proposals of the Japanese government, certain preliminary comments could be made. The American government understood that the purpose of the discussions with the Japanese Ambassador was to work out a formula whereby both countries would pledge themselves to preserve peace in the Pacific. In regard to the European war, the United States considered aid to Great Britain as an essential part of its program for self-defense. It was expected that a formula satisfactory to both Japan and the United States could be achieved for the European area, and certain suggestions for accomplishing this agreement were made.

Expressing the opinion that a treaty based on the principles of the submitted proposal could be arrived at by China and Japan, the oral statement suggested that the points contained in the official Japanese explanation of the proposal be included in the proposal itself. A request was made by the State Department that President Roosevelt be allowed to give Generalissimo Chiang Kai-shek, in confidence, advance notice of the basic terms by which China and Japan might agree to a peace settlement. Another provision, making Section V of the proposal applicable to both Japan and the United States in limiting their economic activities to peaceful penetration, was acceptable to the American government.[37]

During the course of the conversation on May 16, 1941 Ambassador Nomura asked Secretary Hull whether the United States might enter the European war, even if its territory were not attacked. Secretary Hull replied that it would be necessary for any country to act in self-defense against an aggressor who followed its announced purpose of unlimited conquest of other nations. Aid to Britain was an act of self-defense on the part of the United States, and any other actions would depend upon the measures of defense considered essential by the military authorities of the United States.

Ambassador Nomura emphasized Japan's desire for peaceful relations with the United States, though he indicated that it might be called upon to perform certain obligations to the Axis. Secretary Hull reiterated his remarks concerning the attitude of the United States in the matter of self-defense, and indicated that the Japanese would feel the same as the American people under similar circumstances.

---

[34] *Ibid.*, 148.

[35] "Memorandum of a conversation", by Joseph W. Ballantine, Foreign Service Officer, detailed to the Department on special consultation, *S.D.*, II, 427–428.

[36] "Informal and unofficial oral statement handed by the Secretary of State to the Japanese Ambassador (Nomura)", on May 16, 1941, *S.D.*, II, 428–434.

[37] *Ibid.*, 430.

Ambassador Nomura requested that the United States suggest to China at the earliest possible moment that it enter into negotiations with Japan for peace. Secretary Hull remarked that once the preliminary points had been cleared, the remainder of the proposal could be considered very rapidly. Concerning the question of Japan and China's joint defense against communism and the recognition of Manchuria, Mr. Hull declared that if China and Japan could reach an agreement on the other points, there would be little trouble in solving these difficulties.

The Secretary of State, mentioning the revision of Section V of the Japanese proposal, expressed the hope that other countries could be brought in to develop the economic activity of the Southwest Pacific area in a manner similar to the free trade program in South America. Then Mr. Hull, suggesting that Ambassador Nomura might wish to study the newly received American oral statement, stated that he would be ready to see the Japanese Ambassador at any time. Neither Ambassador Nomura nor his companions said anything concerning the oral statement, since they had had no opportunity to examine it.[38]

(b) *Ambassador Nomura's Report.*

Either no specific report of this meeting was transmitted by Ambassador Nomura, or such a dispatch was not intercepted. However, Ambassador Nomura's report on the conversation of May 28, 1941 mentions a meeting on May 16, 1941. (See Part A—Section 15(b)).

7. Axis Nations Notified of Hull-Nomura Conversations.

Ambassador Nomura was notified by Foreign Minister Matsuoka, on May 15, 1941, that since Germany and Italy would be affected by the proposed "understanding" between Japan and the United States, the German and Italian Ambassadors in Tokyo had been told of the Hull-Nomura conversations in a general way.[39] The utmost secrecy had been sought because of the delicate nature of the negotiations, which Japan declared had been originated by the United States, and the Axis Ambassadors had been warned to divulge this information only to Chancellor Hitler, Premier Mussolini, and their Foreign Ministers. The Japanese Ambassadors in Germany and Italy had also been told of the nature of these discussions, and all those informed had been requested to exercise every precaution in guarding against publicity leaks. (See *Part C—(e) Japanese-Axis Relations, Sections 137–139.*)

Mr. Matsuoka told Ambassador Nomura that it was necessary to put in writing the Japanese requests to the United States to stay out of war and to promote peace between China and Japan.[40] This had been the subject of a previous exchange between Foreign Minister Matsuoka and Ambassador Nomura.[41]

8. Mr. Matsuoka Disavows Threats to Ambassador Grew.

It will be recalled that Secretary Hull had discussed with Ambassador Nomura a report of a meeting between Foreign Minister Matsuoka and Ambassador Grew,[42] who had commented on the truculence of the Foreign Minister's remarks in declaring that Japan would enter the war, if America attacked Germany. Mr. Matsuoka now sent word to Ambassador Nomura that he had neither the intention nor cause to threaten or intimidate Ambassador Grew, and, in addition, he had replied to Ambassador Grew's questions in a conversational tone. According

---

[38]*Ibid.,* 428.
[39]II, 34.
[40]*Ibid.*
[41]See Section 3—*(Ambassador Nomura Attempts to Restrain Mr. Matsuoka).*
[42]See Section 5—*(Ambassador Grew Interviews Mr. Matsuoka).*

to Mr. Matsuoka, the American Ambassador was easily excited and quite hard of hearing, and possibly he had misunderstood the Foreign Minister. The Japanese Ambassador was asked to explain this matter to Secretary Hull.[43]

9. American Newspaper Divulges Points of Hull-Nomura Conversations.

Ambassador Nomura reported to Tokyo on May 16, 1941 that the *New York Herald Tribune* of this date carried an article from Tokyo with the headline "Japan Asks the United States to Mediate Sino-Japanese Conflict". It revealed that a Japanese-American "understanding" had been presented to American authorities in Washington.[44]

According to Ambassador Nomura's report, the article stated that the United States was to help settle the China incident; America recognized Japanese leadership in China; Japan guaranteed the non-use of military force in the Southwest in return for American recognition of Japan's right to carry on economic activity in that area; Japan would agree to deal with Generalissimo Chiang Kai-shek, contrary to its previous declaration, and would permit a third power to mediate the China incident; Japan was to clarify its intentions with regard to its place in the Southwest Pacific, and promised not to take hostile measures against the United States. The article declared that the China incident probably would be settled, but because of various circumstances an "understanding" between Japan and the United States was impossible.[45]

Foreign Minister Matsuoka promptly confirmed the accuracy of the report, and ascribed the publicity leak to Japanese inhabitants of New York who had reported their suspicions to financial circles in Tokyo. Mr. Matsuoka emphasized his desire to check these leaks, and requested Ambassador Nomura to do likewise.[46]

10. Hull-Nomura Conversation (May 20, 1941).

(a) *Secretary Hull's Report.*[47]

Ambassador Nomura, accompanied by Colonel Iwakuro and Mr. Tadao Wikawa, an officer of the Cooperative Bank of Japan, visited Secretary Hull at his apartment on the evening of May 20, 1941. Mr. Ballantine and Mr. Maxwell M. Hamilton, Chief of the Division of Far Eastern Affairs for the State Department, were also present. To a question from Secretary Hull concerning the prospects of the proposal under discussion, Ambassador Nomura replied that since the Japanese Army, Navy, Foreign Office, and Cabinet had approved the document, it had been referred to the Emperor.

Stating that if the proposal failed he would be very much embarrassed, Ambassador Nomura implied that he had assured his government of the United States' agreement to the proposal. Asking that the proposal be viewed in a general way rather than criticized for its technicalities, Ambassador Nomura pointed out that there was no essential difference between his original proposal and the draft which had been finally approved by his government.

The Secretary of State remarked that there were two points in regard to China which would have to be discussed; first, the "joint defense against communism", and second, the stationing of Japanese troops in certain parts of Chinese territory. He did not wish to discuss the merits of the two points but would like to know on what basis Japan proposed to negotiate so that when

---

[43]II, 35.
[44]II, 36.
[45]II, 37.
[46]II, 38.
[47]"Memorandum of a conversation", May 20, 1941, by Joseph W. Ballantine, *S.D.*, II, 434–437.

the United States approached Gerneralissimo Chiang Kai-shek with its proposal for peace with Japan, some information could be given to the Chinese government.[48]

Colonel Iwakuro expressed his surprise at this question since he believed that the objective of the discussion was peace in the Pacific between the United States and Japan, with the China affair concerning only China and Japan. Mr. Hull agreed that the principal objective was peace in the Pacific, but emphasized that a treaty between Japan and China was essential to this peace. Mr. Hamilton remarked that public opinion was necessary for the success of all treaties, and if it were first agreed that Japanese troops would be withdrawn from China, and then another provision allowed Japanese troops to remain for "defense against communism", unfavorable publicity would arise.

Denying that troops would be retained all over China, Colonel Iwakuro foresaw no difficulty with Chinese authorities in keeping Japanese troops along the northern border since Generalissimo Chiang Kai-shek would be very willing to cooperate in restraining Chinese Communists. Furthermore, the term "joint defense against communism" had been a slogan in Japanese-Chinese relations for years, and, consequently, it would be impossible for Japan to abandon it in its negotiations with China. In dealing with the United States, however, Japan might agree, after further study, to use broader language in discussing this point.

As for the wording of Section III of the proposal, the Secretary of State pointed out that if the principles of Prime Minister Konoye were enumerated as the Japanese desired, the term "joint defense against communism" would have to be included. On the other hand, Colonel Iwakuro remarked that if no specific principles were mentioned when accepting Prince Konoye's ideas, the proposal would thereby endorse the destruction of Generalissimo Chiang Kai-shek and the creation of a "New Order in East Asia", which Prince Konoye had also desired. However, the Japanese agreed to study the whole question further when the suggestion was made that "inimical foreign ideologies" could be substituted for the phrase "joint defense against communism".

Referring to Section V, *"Activities of the Two Countries in the Southwest Pacific Area"*, Mr. Hull asked whether it would not be helpful from a Japanese point of view to recognize the right of a country to protect itself under international law, though qualifying the right to permit no occasion for acts of aggression. Colonel Iwakuro rejected this suggestion as merely confusing.

According to Mr. Hull, the proposed agreement would be strengthened if it emphasized that its central purpose was peace in the Pacific. When the Japanese pointed out that the first section of their proposal already conveyed this impression, Secretary Hull suggested that for the sake of emphasis all references to peace in the Pacific should be gathered together in one place in the document. This would impress the people of all nations with the fact that peace was to reign in the Pacific; thus, businessmen would feel confident in commencing financial and commercial operations in the Southwest Pacific. The Japanese agreed to study this matter, and the meeting was adjourned until the following evening.[49]

(b) *Ambassador Nomura's Report.*[50]

On May 19, 1941 Ambassador Nomura sent an interim report to Mr. Matsuoka which stated that while trying to discover the American government's intentions through undercover channels, he was continuing his conversations with Secretary Hull. Declaring that the current diplomatic situation revolved around aid to Britain by the United States, Japan's relations to

---

[48]*Ibid.*

[49]*Ibid.*

[50]II, 39.

its Axis partners, the China incident, and the southward expansion of Japan, Ambassador Nomura indicated that there were considerable differences of opinion between the two nations and that there was no room for too much optimism.[51]

In his report on the conversation of May 20, 1941, Ambassador Nomura stressed his belief that Japan should support fully Secretary Hull's economic policy for the Far East, since Japan would profit from such economic development. According to the Japanese Ambassador, after the flight of Herr Rudolph Hess to England, talk of peace had cropped up in Paris and in Vichy, and also among the anti-war minority in the United States. Furthermore, Secretary Hull had remarked that if the "understanding" pact were established, it would be a step in the direction of permanent peace in the Pacific, and it would lead to the achievement of world-wide peace.[52]

11. Hull-Nomura Conversation (May 21, 1941.)

(a) Secretary Hull's Report.[53]

Ambassador Nomura, accompanied by Colonel Iwakuro and Mr. Wikawa, called at Secretary Hull's apartment on the evening of May 21, 1941 to continue the conversation which had been adjourned on the preceding evening. Mr. Hamilton and Mr. Ballantine were also present.

Secretary Hull outlined his experience of eight years in dealing with Latin American countries. A long tradition of distrust had to be dispelled by the determined effort of the United States to build up the good will and confidence of its neighbors without the use of force; thus, in a similar manner, Japan could exert a similar influence for good in the regions of Asia.

As for evacuating Japanese troops from China over a period of time, Secretary Hull thought that it would be feasible to utilize the seasoned troops of Generalissimo Chiang Kai-shek in protecting areas where the interests of foreigners were involved. Mr. Hull emphasized that he was not urging the merit of this proposal, but was only raising the question for consideration.

The Secretary of State again asked that the document under discussion be so phrased that its central purpose of peace in the Pacific could not be misinterpreted by anyone. It should be so clear and unequivocal that it would necessitate no explanation by its sponsors. A tentative draft of Section VI, which spoke of peace in the Pacific, was then drawn up to meet the approval of both sides after the Japanese had objected, on the grounds that it indicated American suspicion of Japan, to a previous provision which stated that action taken to protect national interests under international law was not to be made the occasion for aggression.

At the suggestion of Mr. Hull, the Japanese oral statement of May 12, 1941 was now labelled "Annex and Supplement". When the Japanese were asked for permission to incorporate excerpts from Mr. Hull's speech of April 24, 1941 into the "Annex and Supplement" to clarify the United States' interpretation of self-defense, Mr. Wikawa expressed his belief that the American government's oral statement in which Mr. Hull's speech was included had been withdrawn.

After Mr. Hamilton replied that the oral statement had not been cancelled, Colonel Iwakuro asked why such a simple "understanding" had to be so elaborately documented. Mr. Hull answered that it would be helpful to both sides to clarify the American attitude on the question of self-defense, adding that Mr. Matsuoka had commented favorably to Ambassador Grew on the speech. The Japanese reached no decision in the course of this conversation as to whether or not they would object to the insertion of Secretary Hull's remarks in the "Annex and Supplement".

---

[51]II, 40.
[52]"Memorandum of a conversation", May 21, 1941, by Joseph W. Ballantine, *S.D.*, II, 437–439.
[53]*Ibid.*

Mr. Hamilton then questioned a reference in Section III to the Wang Ching-wei treaties, remarking that the United States had not recognized this regime and pointing out that the treaties mentioned were inconsistent with the principles which both the United States and Japan were ready to accept in the "understanding". Colonel Iwakuro declared that the Wang Ching-wei treaties were a practical application of the Konoye principles; thus, references to them clarified the position of the Japanese nation. Non-recognition of the Wang Ching-wei regime should not militate against a reference to the treaties, and in any case the "understanding" was a confidential document to which the United States would not have to refer in discussing the affair with the Chinese.

Mr. Hamilton pointed out, however, that the United States could not enter into any secret arrangements since such matters would be bound to be known after a few weeks. It was then decided to allow further study on the part of all concerned so that differences could be reconciled at the next discussion.[54]

Two days later, Ambassador Nomura delivered to the Secretary of State some changes which he desired to have made in his confidential memorandum of May 12, 1941.[55] It will be recalled that Foreign Minister Matsuoka sent these revisions to Ambassador Nomura shortly after the delivery of the principal document on May 12, 1941, but Ambassador Nomura had requested permission to withhold them until an opportune moment occurred.

(b) *Ambassador Nomura's Report*

Ambassador Nomura made no special report on this conversation. However, on May 29, 1941, he submitted a composite report of several talks with Secretary Hull, including the conversation of May 21, 1941, which the reader will find in *Section 15(b)*.

12. Foreign Minister Matsuoka Rebukes Ambassador Nomura.

Ambassador Nomura was reprimanded severely on May 24, 1941, by Foreign Minister Matsuoka. Unfortunately, most of the dispatch from Tokyo was not intercepted by American cryptanalysts so that all the reasons for Mr. Matsuoka's displeasure could not be ascertained. However, it appeared that Foreign Minister Matsuoka had received secret intelligence to the effect that Secretary Hull believed Mr. Matsuoka to be hostile toward the American-Japanese discussions for peace. According to Mr. Matsuoka, there were indications that Secretary Hull had received this impression in part from a conversation with the Japanese Ambassador. The Foreign Minister ordered Ambassador Nomura to reassure Secretary Hull immediately of Mr. Matsuoka's great desire for amity between Japan and the United States, and of his purpose to devise some method of stopping the horror of war which threatened to lead civilization into chaos.[56]

In his reply, Ambassador Nomura expressed his shocked surprise at the reprimand from his Foreign Minister, which he considered to be baseless.[57] Judging from his response to Mr. Matsuoka, some parts of the rebuke must have dealt with a discussion of Japanese diplomatic procedure, for Ambassador Nomura gave the details of his statements to President Roosevelt and Secretary Hull concerning the operations of Japanese diplomacy. According to Ambassador Nomura, Japanese diplomacy was the responsibility of the Foreign Minister, although important army and navy questions having great bearing on diplomatic policy were handled

---

[54]*Ibid.*

[55]"Statement handed by the Japanese Ambassador (Nomura) to the Secretary of State on May 23, 1941", *S.D.*, II, 439–440.

[56]II, 41.

[57]II, 42.

in cooperation with the army and naval ministers. The Prime Minister of Japan also had a great deal of influence, and many Japanese officials and citizens of great ability advised the Foreign Minister. Both the Foreign Minister of Japan and the Secretary of State in the United States held similar positions.

Summing up the situation, Ambassador Nomura disavowed the intelligence in the hands of the Foreign Minister by stating:

> Now, should I have voiced erroneous statements which in themselves are incredible, then by that fact alone I deserve punishment. Had I, as a military man, made any such statement, after it be proven, I believe that I should not be permitted to continue my existence. I am convinced that I have absolutely made no such statement. And as far as the Secretary of State is concerned, I do not believe by any stretch of the imagination that he labors under any misunderstanding. However, as you have requested in your wire, I shall outdo myself in extending my best efforts.
>
> Regardless of the impressions imparted by newspaper dispatches from Japan, I am quite cognizant of Your Excellency's fundamental feelings with regard to the Japan-American question, and do not entertain a single doubt with regard to it. I have even told the Secretary of State as much one or two times.[58]

Mr. Matsuoka seemingly accepted Ambassador Nomura's explanation as to the part played by newspaper dispatches from Japan in creating the erroneous impression that the Foreign Minister was hostile to America. In asking Ambassador Nomura to clear up the matter as quickly as possible, Mr. Matsuoka requested also that the Japanese Ambassador try to ascertain the source of this misinformation.[59]

Though Ambassador Nomura stated that he had informed Secretary Hull of Foreign Minister Matsuoka's friendly feelings with regard to the Japanese-American question, Secretary Hull's memorandum concerning his conversation with the Japanese Ambassador records his impression, received from Ambassador Nomura, that Mr. Matsuoka was a politician who frequently spoke in reckless fashion to evoke popular support of his policy.[60]

13. Japan Seizes American Goods En route to Chungking.

Ambassador Nomura reported to his superiors on May 28, 1941 that American newspapers were publicizing the Japanese seizure of American goods in China, which had been destined for Generalissimo Chiang Kai-shek. The American press believed that the Axis nations were about to exert economic pressure in unison, and so Ambassador Nomura now inquired concerning the procedure which the Japanese government intended to follow.[61]

14. Radio Address of President Roosevelt (May 27, 1941).[62]

President Roosevelt's speech of May 27, 1941, had been very mild in its treatment of Japan. No direct reference was made to Japan by name and the China affair had been touched upon very lightly. Since the Japanese Ambassador knew that there was considerable difference of opinion among the American Cabinet members concerning the contents of this speech, which had been conveyed to them before its delivery, he reported his conviction that President Roosevelt, despite his determination to carry out every essential measure of self-defense, was anxious to avoid provocation and desired to have the Japanese-United States negotiations continue.[63]

---

[58]*Ibid.*

[58]*Ibid.*

[59]II, 43.

[60]*S.D.*, II, 391, 412–413, 416. "The Ambassador not only did not take issue with anything I [Secretary Hull] had said, but I felt that he was really in harmony with the statements I made about Matsuoka".

[61]II, 44.

[62]Printed in *Department of State Bulletin.* May 31, 1941, (Volume IV, No. 101), 647.

[63]II, 45.

15. Hull–Nomura Conversation (May 28, 1941).[64]

(a) *Secretary Hull's Report.*

The Japanese Ambassador called at Secretary Hull's apartment on the evening of May 28, 1941. According to Secretary Hull, the Japanese Ambassador was misinformed in considering that Secretary Hull had spoken in a derogatory manner of Mr. Matsuoka's position in the Japanese government. Mr. Hull denied saying anything of this nature to any one. It will be recalled that Foreign Minister Matsuoka had just severely reprimanded Ambassador Nomura because he had learned from a secret source that Secretary Hull had an unfavorable impression concerning him.

Speaking of the difficulty arising from the divergent attitude of Japan and the United States toward the European war, Secretary Hull pointed out that Mr. Matsuoka had continually stressed Japan's obligations under the Tripartite Pact to support Germany in the event of America's entry into the war. Thus, unless Japan cleared up this difficulty, American critics of the "understanding" could point out that there was no assurance as to Japan's position toward Hitler, if the United States went to war to maintain the freedom of the seas.

Ambassador Nomura replied that though Mr. Matsuoka talked principally for home consumption in Japan, the Foreign Minister wanted peace with the United States. Once the "understanding" was achieved, the influence of Japanese extremists would be weakened, since the Japanese people were desirous of trading with the whole world. American embargoes had made the Japanese seek the control of an economic bloc, but normal trade relations would be more desirable.

Secretary Hull agreed that Ambassador Nomura and many of his associates were anxious for friendly relations, but he asked the Japanese government to clarify officially the points he had raised. Ambassador Nomura pointed out that it would be extremely difficult for the Japanese government to add anything to the submitted proposal, since the Japanese government had to deal with Germany and Italy as well as with the pro-Axis group at home. However, Japan would make independent decisions in interpreting the Tripartite Pact.

To Secretary Hull's inquiry concerning Japan's plans for withdrawal of its troops from China, Ambassador Nomura, answering that this would have to be negotiated by the Japanese and Chinese governments, indicated that two years would pass before complete evacuation would be effected. However, Japanese troops retained in China for joint defense against communistic activities would not be evacuated, and he did not know the number of troops that would be involved or the areas in which they would operate.

Remarking that the retention of Japanese troops in China would be detrimental to Chinese-Japanese friendship, Secretary Hull suggested that the experience of the United States in South America ought to convince Japan that a more profitable arrangement could be worked out to protect its interests without the use of troops. Ambassador Nomura agreed with Secretary Hull that the presence of Japanese troops in China would lead to provocative incidents, but he did not think it feasible at the present moment to carry out complete evacuation, since Japanese public opinion would not permit it. Ambassador Nomura then cited the severe Japanese criticisms of Prince Konoye for his moderate handling of the Chinese question in the face of the sacrifices Japan had made in that area.

Secretary Hull announced his plans to talk over the situation with the Chinese government in strict confidence before entering into any negotiations, and stated that he had raised the question of evacuating Japanese troops only because the conversations with the Japanese Ambassador were still in an unofficial and exploratory stage. However, Ambassador Nomura said he did not

---

[64]"Memorandum of a conversation", May 28, 1941, by Joseph W. Ballantine, *S.D.*, II 440–443.

expect the American government to negotiate this question with the Chinese, since America would serve sufficiently the cause of world peace by merely bringing the Chinese and Japanese together into direct negotiations as it had done in 1895 and in the Russo-Japanese negotiations of 1905. When Secretary Hull inquired concerning the Chinese government's reactions to the proposed stationing of troops for joint defense against Communism, Ambassador Nomura replied that the Chinese government had become very much weakened as a result of the war, and that, if America would discontinue its aid, China would be forced to come to terms.

To Secretary Hull's request that the Japanese government consider the two points which he had raised, Ambassador Nomura replied that he believed his government would be unwilling to further clarify the relations of Japan and the United States toward the European war, but as for the second point concerning Japanese troops in China, he promised to consult further with Colonel Iwakuro. The conversation ended with Secretary Hull repeating his plan to talk to China about the proposals since the conversations were still in an entirely informal stage. This fact had also permitted him to discuss unofficially the question of Japanese troops in China.[65]

(b) Ambassador Nomura's Report.[66]

Ambassador Nomura reported to Foreign Minister Matsuoka that he had held conversations with the Secretary of State on May 16, 20, 21 and 27,[67] 1941 but had not as yet come to any concrete agreement. According to Ambassador Nomura, Mr. Hull wanted to have all doubts eliminated from the minds of the people concerning the maintenance of peace in the Pacific. Stating that on one occasion Secretary Hull had expressed a desire to maintain the status quo in the Pacific, Ambassador Nomura had advised that this would be unacceptable to Japan since it hoped to take the leadership in the development of the southwestern area with the cooperation of the United States. However, he was able to report that the Americans wished to give both countries equal opportunities in this region.

Ambassador Nomura had also informed Secretary Hull that Japanese authorities saw no need for the clarification of the meaning of Article III of the Tripartite Pact. The Japanese Ambassador remarked to Foreign Minister Matsuoka that Secretary Hull and his colleagues were reluctant to place Generalissimo Chiang Kai-shek in a difficult situation, and for this reason the United States was demanding Japan's peace terms before acting as a mediator in the China affair. The United States refused to refer to Japan's treaty with Wang Ching-wei's government or to the Tripartite Pact, but, according to the Japanese Ambassador, it was willing to make considerable concessions.

The questions of joint defense against Communism and the stationing of troops in China were to be negotiated directly by China and Japan, though the Japanese Ambassador desired the United States to suggest mediation to Generalissimo Chiang Kai-shek as Dunn and Denby had done in the Sino-Japanese war and Theodore Roosevelt in the Russo-Japanese war. Mr. Hull explained that the United States did not want to use the word "Communism" in the texts because of its relations to Russia and China, but that some expression such as "subversive" would be acceptable.

Ambassador Nomura commented to Mr. Hull that they had held seven discussion, lasting from one to two hours, and although they had talked "off the record" and informally, they seemed to be repeating the same things over and over without achieving results. When Ambassador Nomura asked Secretary Hull for any further suggestions, and was told that two or three minor ones would be forthcoming in a few days, the Japanese Ambassador received the

---

[65]*Ibid.*

[66]II, 46.

[67]The State Department's Memorandum, *S.D.*, II, 440, indicates that this last conversation was held on May 28, 1941.

impression that Secretary Hull was trying to estimate the effect the "understanding" would have upon other Cabinet members and American officials.

Emphasizing that the real purpose of the "understanding" was to change the psychology of both peoples from one of war to that of peace, Ambassador Nomura warned of the great danger that an incident might occur, while they were discussing technicalities, which would make an agreement impossible.

Ambassador Nomura considered it natural for the United States to estimate the actions of Japan in planning political or militaristic moves, and said that President Roosevelt's recent speech indicated the American government's concern about Japan's movements.[68]

16. Mr. Matsuoka Requests American Pressure on China.[69]

On May 31, 1941 Foreign Minister Matsuoka criticized Ambassador Nomura's report of May 29, 1941 [See Section 15(b)] for having lessened the dignity of modern Japan by requesting American mediation as had been done in the Sino-Japanese and Russo-Japanese wars. Claiming that Japan's position in the modern world was much different from that of earlier days, he stated:

> The only thing that this Minister would have the United States do with regard to mediating in the China affair, would be for her to tell Chiang Kai-shek: "Negotiate with Japan. If you refuse, we shall stop all aid to you."

17. Publicity Leaks Concerning the Hull-Nomura Conversations.

On May 30, 1941 Tokyo sent an urgent dispatch to Ambassador Nomura, indicating that a Domei message of May 26, 1941 had quoted several American Senators to the effect that President Roosevelt's recent speech had not referred to Japan because Japan was moving away from the Tripartite Pact, and was about to restrict the use of military force in penetrating the South Pacific. The story had not been publicized in Japan because of its potentially bad effect on the Japanese extremists, but Mr. Matsuoka's message indicated that he was more indignant because the alleged facts were not true rather than because they had been publicized in America.[70]

It was evident that many persons in Japan of varying degrees of importance had become aware by now that Japanese-American negotiations were under way.[71] Both Foreign Minister Matsuoka and Ambassador Nomura, though differing in their viewpoints, knew that this knowledge would be a disrupting factor in the current conversations, since the pro-Axis military extremists of Japan would not remain quiescent in the face of a possible Japanese-American understanding.

Another news leak occurred on June 6, 1941, when Hallet Abend in the *New York Times* stated that Japan was considering a neutrality pact with the United States similar to the one she had contracted with Russia.[72] Ambassador Nomura, having called together the correspondents of the Associated Press, the United Press, the *Tribune*, Domei and Asahi to deny that there was any truth in this article, conferred also with Secretary Hull and advised him to take measures to counteract this report. As a result, President Roosevelt stated in his press

---

[68]II, 46.

[69]II, 47.

[70]II, 48.

[71]II, 49.

[72]II, 50, for complete text which is recorded here to demonstrate how much was known of the conversations in semi-official circles.

18

conference on June 6, 1941 that he knew nothing about the matter, and pointed out that though the Japanese Ambassador and the Secretary of State occasionally had interviews, they discussed only ordinary affairs.[73]

18. Special Committee Meeting (May 30, 1941).[74]

Mr. Hamilton met with Colonel Iwakuro and Mr. Wikawa to discuss one of the two points in the Japanese proposal which the American government had found difficult to accept. This was the proposed joint Chinese-Japanese defense against communistic activities. Colonel Iwakuro outlined the Japanese government's plans concerning this point by briefly reviewing Japan's efforts to keep communism out of Manchuria and Japanese territory. Drawing a rough map of the general region of North China, Mongolia, Manchuria and Siberia, he indicated the strategic problems involved in stationing Japanese troops for protection against communistic elements from Outer Mongolia, and for the maintenance of interior lines of communication.

Replying to a question concerning the number of Japanese troops to be kept in China, Colonel Iwakuro declared that one-tenth to one-fifth of the present number—a military secret—of Japanese soldiers in North China would be necessary. These troops would not interfere with Chinese internal affairs, nor would they be stationed in any other areas outside Inner Mongolia or North China. As to the length of time these troops would be maintained in China, Colonel Iwakura stated that they would be there only as long as necessary for protection against Communism. Since there was a possiblity of war between Japan and Russia, the situation might be altered.

Stressing the views of the American government that no discussion of the merits of the question was to take place, Mr. Hamilton remarked that the American people would expect their government to follow its declared principles in presenting the Japanese proposal to the Chinese government. He discussed a possible formula wherein there would be no reference to stationing of Japanese troops in Chinese territory, but in which the withdrawal of Japanese troops from China would be arranged to have the troops of North China and Inner Mongolia evacuated last. Then, just before the Japanese were scheduled to evacuate completely, Tokyo could consult with Chungking concerning the measures necessary to suppress current communistic activities. The Japanese were anxious to have Mr. Ballantine and Mr. Hamilton write a tentative draft, but Mr. Hamilton, paying tribute to the knowledge and frankness in discussion of Colonel Iwakuro, urged further consideration of this point by each side.[75]

19. The United States Submits a Proposal to Ambassador Nomura (May 31, 1941).

It will be recalled that on April 9, 1941 an informal and unofficial proposal had been presented to the State Department through the medium of private American and Japanese individuals, with the approval and collaboration of Ambassador Nomura.[76] It had then been sent to Tokyo for the consideration of Foreign Minister Matsuoka who finally returned it, after considerable delay, with various revisions for submission to the Secretary of State.[77] On May 12, 1941 Ambassador Nomura had presented it to Mr. Hull, who then submitted the American draft on

---

[73]II, 51–52.
[74]"Memorandum of a conversation", May 30, 1941, by Joseph W. Ballantine, *S.D.*, II, 444–445.
[75]*Ibid.*
[76]*S.D.*, II, 398–402.
[77]*S.D.*, II, 420–422.

May 31, 1941.[78] Various differences between the two versions of the proposal were to be the topic of several conversations in June.[79]

The United States again informed Ambassador Nomura, on May 31, 1941, that it would talk over in strict confidence with the Chinese government the general subject matter involved in the Hull-Nomura conversations, especially as related to China.[80]

20. Hull–Nomura Conversations (June 2, 1941).

(a) *Secretary Hull's Report.*[81]

Ambassador Nomura called at Secretary Hull's apartment on June 2, 1941 to say that he and his associates disagreed with nothing in the American proposal of May 31, 1941 with the exception of some of the phraseology which could be discussed by their representatives while he went to New York.

Deliberately asking Ambassador Nomura whether his government really desired to enter into a settlement for peace in the Pacific, Secretary Hull remarked that he raised the question because of the doubts created by the loud talking of Foreign Minister Matsuoka. The Japanese Ambassador replied that his government was anxious for a fair settlement of the American-Japanese difficulties. Although Mr. Hull expressed the hope that Japan was reconsidering its policy of stationing troops indefinitely in China, Ambassador Nomura offered no encouragement that Japan would change its course.[82]

(b) *Ambassador Nomura's Report.*

It is believed that Ambassador Nomura made no specific report on this conversation, which lasted only a few minutes, since his report on June 8, 1941 summarized several conversations. (See *Section 22(b)*).

21. Special Committee Meeting (June 4, 1941).[83]

Associates of Secretary Hull and Ambassador Nomura met at the Wardman Park Hotel, on the afternoon of June 4, 1941 to discuss unofficially various points of the Japanese and American drafts of the proposal which was first presented to Secretary Hull on April 9, 1941, the last version of which was returned to Ambassador Nomura on May 31, 1941. Mr. Kanome Wakasugi, Japanese Minister-Counselor, Mr. Koto Matsudaira, Second Secretary of the Japanese Embassy, Mr. Hamilton, and Mr. Ballantine were the conferees, and the American draft of May 31, 1941 was the basis for their discussion.

Many minor points involving translations of various phrases were discussed and noted for future decision. The Japanese requested the deletion of one important sentence in the first paragraph of Section II, which read, "Obviously, the provisions of the Pact do not apply to involvement through acts of self-defense." According to Mr. Wakasugi, Japan did not want to be bound by the United States' interpretation of "self-defense", and Japan could not commit herself in advance to future acts of other countries.

Mr. Hamilton said that it was understood from certain sources that the Japanese government desired to disassociate itself gradually from its Axis connections, and that one of the propositions

---

[78]"American draft proposal handed to the Japanese Ambassador (Nomura)", on May 31, 1941, *S.D.*, II, 446–454, II, 58.
[79]The text of this proposal with various Annexes and Supplements was sent to Japan on June 9, 1941; II, 60–69.
[80]*S.D.*, II, 454.
[81]"Memorandum by the Secretary of State", June 2, 1941, *S.D.*, II, 454–455.
[82]*Ibid.*
[83]*S.D.*, II, 455–464.

of the proposed "understanding" was to facilitate Japan's movement in this direction. Mr. Wakasugi stated that this was a false impression since Japan, fully intending to discharge its obligations under the Tripartite Pact, desired to remain free to decide whether the actions of the United States in Europe would cause Japan to carry out its obligations.

Colonel Iwakuro agreed that Japan was not intending to drift away from the Tripartite Pact, and said, furthermore, that, if the United States entered the European war under circumstances which Japan interpreted as obliging her to act, Japan would take up arms against the United States. However, the "understanding" would solve the difficulties in the Pacific, although trouble might still arise from the actions of the United States in the European war. It was hoped that the improved relations resulting from the "understanding" might lead both countries to collaborate in working for world peace.

The Japanese also requested the deletion of an American "Annex", containing excerpts from Secretary Hull's speech of April 24, 1941 which outlined the United States' position in regard to self-defense. They based their claim on the grounds that if these excerpts were retained, Mr. Matsuoka would desire to include his statements in regard to Japanese obligations under the Tripartite Pact. Answering Mr. Hamilton, who declared that the excerpts would clarify the American position on self-defense, Colonel Iwakuro proposed that Mr. Hull's statement be sent separately to the Japanese government. Various other proposals for revisions in the draft were made at this meeting.[84]

22. Hull–Nomura Conversation (June 6, 1941).

(a) *Secretary Hull's Report.*[85]

Ambassador Nomura, with Colonel Iwakuro and Mr. Wikawa, called at Secretary Hull's apartment on the evening of June 6, 1941. When the Japanese Ambassador had first examined the American draft of May 31, 1941 he had felt that both parties were in close agreement, and that the "drafting committee" would be able to work out the details. Both Ambassador Nomura and Colonel Iwakuro stressed the sincere desire of their government to achieve an "understanding" as speedily as possible, and pointed out that despite the misunderstanding of the American government, Foreign Minister Matsuoka also was anxious for peace. Replying that he had no doubt of the sincerity of Ambassador Nomura and his associates, Mr. Hull indicated the desire of the United States to have peace in the Pacific, but emphasized his position in regard to self-defense against control of the seas by the Nazis.

To the suggestion of Ambassador Nomura that President Roosevelt request the Chinese government to negotiate with Japan, Secretary Hull replied that it would be advantageous for President Roosevelt to have an "understanding" with Japan as a basis for his discussion with the Chinese. There was a great need for clear cut and unequivocal terms in the proposed agreement so as to permit the document to speak for itself, and to allow no one to suspect the bad faith of either party.

Mr. Hull then handed Ambassador Nomura an informal and unofficial oral statement, outlining the reaction of the American government to the revisions proposed by the Japanese members of the "drafting committee" which had met on June 4, 1941. The Secretary of State referred specifically to the sections relating to China and the Pacific area where the Japanese proposed to omit clear cut provisions relating to non-discrimination in international commercial affairs.[86]

---

[84]*Ibid.*

[85]*S.D.,* II, 465–467.

[86]"Informal and unofficial oral statement handed by Secretary of State to Japanese Ambassador (Nomura)", on June 6, 1941, *S.D.,* II, 467–468.

Secretary Hull mentioned his disappointment in noting a vast difference between the proposal as revised by the Japanese and the original document on which earlier discussions were based, since the revisions stressed Japan's alignment with the Axis, resisted the placement of Japan's relations with China on a basis which would contribute to a lasting peace, and avoided clear cut commitments in regard to policies of peace and non-discriminatory conduct in the Pacific. Changes of phraseology were not important, but it was essential "that there be a meeting of minds and mutual understanding of the underlying purposes of the proposed understanding" before proceeding any further.[87]

When Ambassador Nomura and Mr. Wikawa had read the American oral statement and had informed Colonel Iwakuro of its gist, the Japanese Military Attache expressed surprise that the American representatives felt the absence of a meeting of minds. Ambassador Nomura, remarking also that he and his associates were in perfect agreement with Secretary Hull as to the principles involved, stated that they would immediately review their proposed revisions in the light of Secretary Hull's oral statement. In a side remark to Mr. Ballantine, Colonel Iwakuro referred to Mr. Wakasugi's presence at the meeting on June 4, 1941 and mentioned Ambassador Nomura's part in bringing Mr. Wakasugi out of retirement. Mr. Ballantine gathered the impression that Colonel Iwakuro thought that Mr. Wakasugi's presence had not been helpful.[88]

(b) *Ambassador Nomura's Report.*[89]

Ambassador Nomura commented that after presenting Japan's final draft to the State Department he had conferred several times a week with Secretary Hull until an American plan had been offered unofficially. Since there were several questions concerning the China incident left unanswered in this new document, Ambassador Nomura had decided to appoint a committee of associates to handle the problem, but several conflicts had arisen in the meeting.

Ambassador Nomura had then gone to see Secretary Hull on Saturday afternoon, June 7, 1941.[90] Secretary Hull informed him that the primary purpose of the "understanding" was maintenance of peace in the Pacific. This point was not to be glossed over or disguised, and when peace was effected, plans could be made for Japanese and American industrial, financial, and economic cooperation. In solving the difficult Pacific situation, the United States wished to keep the friendship of China to ensure free relations between the United States, China, and Japan. As Secretary Hull had stated in his report,[91] Ambassador Nomura suggested that President Roosevelt advised China to make peace, but Secretary Hull responded that this would depend upon the conclusion of the "understanding".

In repeating Secretary Hull's ideas on the question of America's right to self-defense against the encroachment of Hitlerism, Ambassador Nomura hastened to assure Foreign Minister Matsuoka that he was conscious of his superior's views concerning the necessity of keeping the United States out of the European war. According to Ambassador Nomura, the time was not ripe to try to change American thinking on this matter, nor was it an opportune moment to discuss a negotiated peace in Europe since President Roosevelt had denied the peace rumors emanating as a result of the return of Ambassador Winant to Washington. He also warned that the United States regarded the principle of commercial non-discrimination as of primary importance in the

---

[87] *Ibid.*

[88] *S.D.,* II, 467.

[89] II, 53–56.

[90] The State Department documents do not record a conversation on June 7. It is probable that Ambassador Nomura either was mistaken in referring to Saturday, instead of Friday, or he was using Tokyo time in this report.

[91] *S.D.,* II, 465.

Pacific, since Secretary Hull had declared that if Japan were unwilling to adopt this point there could be no "understanding".

Ambassador Nomura summarized his conversations with Secretary Hull up to this point as follows:

> Well, I feel that it will be very difficult to get anywhere by outright dealings and feel the need of conducting some other sort of activities which might be more direct. Well, I and my associates are certainly not optimistic, but on the other hand, we are not pessimistic. We will do our very best to carry out your instructions. Unless something unforeseen happens within the next ten days, I think that the points now pending will so crystallize that I will be able to let you know something more or less definite. I do not doubt his zeal in the matter at all. I call on him two or three times a week. We confer until late at night and when I leave he always says, "Come back to see me anytime you wish."[92]

23. Tokyo Grows Impatient at the Delay of the United States' Answer.

Ambassador Nomura received a message from Tokyo, on June 7, 1941, complaining of the unreasonable delay of the United States in replying to Japan's revision of the "understanding". However, though Tokyo was anxious for a speedy answer, it warned Ambassador Nomura not to rush the United States authorities.[93] Two days later, on June 9, 1941 Ambassador Nomura was requested to telegraph the entire text of the so-called "unofficial American proposal" which he had received on May 31, 1941.[94] Complying with this request, Ambassador Nomura stated that though there were many points unacceptable to him in the proposal just transmitted to Tokyo, the United States authorities were willing to discuss the objectionable parts before submitting it to Japan.[95]

The Japanese Ambassador desired to eliminate references in the proposal to the right of self-preservation, and also Secretary Hull's speech from the Annex to the proposal. In regard to China, he was anxious to work out a mutually satisfactory clause regarding the desire of both countries for peace, and to substitute a clause regarding peace in the Pacific in place of the statement asking for justice and non-discrimination. Stipulations relating to the prevention of the spread of the European war, and to mutual efforts for future world peace and peace in the Pacific would be desirable.

From Ambassador Nomura's viewpoint, the United States should have recognized Japan's national aspirations in the Far East, and Japan should have accepted those of America in the Western Hemisphere, with neither country acquiring military bases in the territory of the other's particular interest.

Ambassador Nomura also reported that Secretary Hull had been ill for two days, but that various delays would soon be ended.[96] Though a preliminary American proposal was already in the hands of Tokyo authorities on June 9, 1941 Ambassador Nomura pointed out that the answer of the United States to the Japanese proposal would probably be forthcoming in a few days.[97]

24. Luncheon of Japanese–American Diplomats (June 9, 1941).[98]

On June 1941 Mr. Ballantine lunched with Colonel Iwakuro and Mr. Wikawa. Colonel Iwakuro attempted, by seemingly casual questions, to ascertain the attitude of the State Department

---

[92]II, 56.

[93]II, 57.

[94]*S.D.*, II, 446–454; II, 58–69.

[95]II, 70–72.

[96]II, 72.

[97]II, 73.

[98]*S.D.*, II, 468–470.

towards the Japanese proposal and its eventual outcome. Informing Colonel Iwakuro that the Secretary of State spoke for the American government in matters of foreign policy, Mr. Ballantine replied that he had nothing to add to Secretary Hull's statement of June 6, 1941 to Colonel Iwakuro and Ambassador Nomura. However, Mr. Ballantine offered to be of assistance, if any points were not clear, and promised to notify Secretary Hull of anything the Japanese diplomats might wish to say to him.

Colonel Iwakuro stated that they understood Secretary Hull's statement very well, but would like to delete the proposed sentence in the first paragraph of Section II which read, "Obviously, the provisions of the Pact do not apply to involvement through acts of self-defense". The Japanese did not intend to imply non-recognition of the American right of self-defense, but the phrase cited above seemed superfluous and would raise difficult questions at home for the Japanese government.

According to Colonel Iwakuro, the relations of Japan and the United States to the European war would have little effect on their relations to each other, and Japan's interpretation of its obligations under the Tripartite Pact would be influenced by the "understanding". Though Japan could not provide in any agreement for all possible situations where the United States might act in self-defense, the Japanese took no exception to the attitude of the American government in this matter.[99]

As for the section of the proposed "understanding" dealing with peace in the Pacific area, the Japanese intended to accept the American draft. Furthermore, they desired to place the mutual pledges of peaceful actions in the Pacific in the preamble of the "understanding" rather than in Section V as found in the American draft. Mr. Ballantine gathered the impression that the Japanese would agree to retain mutual pledges of non-discrimination in international commercial affairs in the Pacific, but would substitute the phraseology of Prince Konoye under caption three Section III in referring to Japanese peace terms for China.

In regard to the Japanese suggestion that President Roosevelt urge China to make peace with Japan, the Japanese pointed out that with Japanese-American difficulties about to be settled, only the Japanese-Chinese difficulties remained to disturb peace in the Far East. For this reason, the President, on his own initiative, should propose that China seek a settlement with Japan.[100]

Japan would not agree to limit the retention of its troops in China to one or two years, though the troops would be withdrawn as soon as the need for resisting communistic activities ceased to exist. The luncheon ended on a very cordial note, with Colonel Iwakuro expressing his determination to speak frankly on any difficulty, and Mr. Mikawa indicating that a newly revised Japanese draft would soon be ready for American approval.[101]

25. Dissension Among Japanese in Washington.

Tokyo issued a strong reprimand to its diplomatic representatives in the Japanese Embassy at Washington because of the disharmony existing between several of the members stationed there. The Foreign Office felt particularly concerned because Ambassador Nomura, a naval man and not a career diplomat, had found such a disconcerting state of affairs in the midst of a national crisis.[102]

A request from Tokyo that something be done to clarify messages sent from the Japanese Embassy added to the woes of the Japanese in Washington, who promised to do better in the future.[103] It is interesting to note that the obscurity of the messages, transmitted from the

---

[99]*Ibid.*, 469.
[100]*Ibid.*, 470.
[101]*Ibid.*
[102]II, 74.
[103]II, 75–76.

24

Japanese Embassy to Tokyo, was probably due to Ambassador Nomura's own phraseology. The Japanese telegraph officials reported that they were sending the messages in as close conformity as possible with the original draft in order to convey accurately the feelings of Ambassador Nomura, who had discussed matters with the Secretary of State.[104] Incidentally, American experts, translating the deciphered dispatches of Ambassador Nomura, also complained of the difficulties involved in rendering good translations of Ambassador Nomura's badly phrased reports.[105.]

Some of the difficulties mentioned above undoubtedly arose because the Japanese were attempting to do too many things with an insufficiency of trained personnel. The usual consular work was suffering because additional men had to be assigned to handle the greatly increased volume of telegraphic work stemming from the intensified Japanese-American negotiations. An urgent call was sent to Tokyo for well trained diplomatic secretaries.[106]

26. Mr. Matsuoka Reaffirms Japanese Allegiance to the Tripartite Pact.

Foreign Minister Matsuoka administered another sharp rebuke to Ambassador Nomura on June 10, 1941 when he learned that Secretary Hull and the Ambassador had agreed to submit a proposal to a "drafting committee" representing both countries.[107] Mr. Matsuoka declared that it was necessary first for both countries to come to an agreement before any discussion on important points of disagreement took place.

The Foreign Minister emphasized that such discussions should have been handled by Tokyo rather than by Ambassador Nomura, and he feared that commitments had already been made which would be difficult to explain away. Therefore, all committee meetings were to be stopped at once until the full text of the unofficial American proposal could be discussed in Tokyo, and until further instructions could be issued for the guidance of Ambassador Nomura.

According to Mr. Matsuoka, good relations between the United States and Japan, though important, were not so important as the duty of the Japanese, under the Tripartite Pact, to keep the United States from entering the war, or to prevent any further anti-Axis measures. Reminding Ambassador Nomura of his conversations with him before the Japanese Ambassador's departure for Washington, Mr. Matsuoka expressed his regrets that there were any outsiders who unfortunately believed that Japan would not fight, even if the United States did so.

Since this erroneous belief seemed to be gaining strength as a result of the Japanese-American negotiations, Mr. Matsuoka stated that it was important for the Japanese to disavow it, especially since President Roosevelt and Secretary Hull were scheming to use the "understanding" to heighten this impression. Mr. Matsuoka's summary may be of interest:

> Summing all this up, if the United States fights Germany, no matter what sort of agreement exists, after all it will inevitably have to be broken. That is clearer than the light of day. The important thing today is for us to maintain a relentless attitude. Even though it is beyond our power to make the United States feel friendly toward Germany, we must keep her from making an outright attack. Compared with this, any advice that the United States might give Chiang Kai-shek to make peace with us is of secondary importance. I think we all know that by now.[108]

A few days later, however, Mr. Matsuoka, having received Ambassador Nomura's explanation of the activities of the committee,[109] was somewhat mollified, and apparently agreed to permit

---

[104] II, 77.
[105] II, 78–79.
[106] II, 80.
[107] II, 81–83.
[108] II, 83.
[109] II, 70–73.

similar meetings of expert assistance to take place. But he did remind Ambassador Nomura that the preliminary proposal should have been telegraphed to the Foreign Office without delay, since it was useful for translation purposes as well as discovering the workings of the minds of President Roosevelt and Secretary Hull.[110]

27. Hull-Nomura Conversation (June 15, 1941).

(a) *Secretary Hull's Report.*[111]

Ambassador Nomura, Colonel Iwakuro, and Mr. Wikawa called at Secretary Hull's apartment to assure Mr. Hull that the Japanese government sincerely desired an "understanding" with the United States, and to certify that there was no hostile feeling among higher Japanese army and navy officials against the United States. Ambassador Nomura stated that it was necessary for him to report to his government just how matters stood at this time, and he would like to confer with Secretary Hull as to the points in the Japanese proposal to which the United States would either agree or disagree.

Replying that such procedure on his part might lead to a misunderstanding with the Japanese government, Mr. Hull suggested that the Japanese Ambassador submit a report concerning his own estimate of the situation. Since Mr. Hull and his associates had conversed a number of times with Japanese representatives, the American attitude on certain points should be very clear. When Mr. Hull referred to the sounding out of the Chinese government with regard to peace before any final move was made, Ambassador Nomura indicated that the weak Chungking government was maintained only by American help, and that if this were withdrawn Generalissimo Chiang Kai-shek would be obliged to accept Japanese terms.[112]

(b) *Ambassador Nomura's Report.*[113]

Ambassador Nomura reported to Tokyo that he had talked, on June 15, 1941, with Secretary Hull, who was sick in bed. Because of the unavailability of Secretary Hull on the preceding day, June 14, 1941, owing to sickness, Ambassador Nomura had talked to Assistant Secretary Welles about an espionage case on the West Coast.[114] According to Ambassador Nomura, Secretary Hull had stated that influential people in Japan did not wish to have an "understanding" between Japan and the United States, and, therefore, he desired Ambassador Nomura to find out whether his government was really in favor of effecting peace between the two countries.

Ambassador Nomura replied that the concessions made by the American government were not really worth consideration, and until the United States offered a concrete and fair proposal, it would be useless to request further instructions on the basis of what had been offered.[115] However, despite this statement of Ambassador Nomura concerning the lack of concessions by the United States, he knew that both Secretary Hull and the State Department, in the face of a number of influential Americans who were advocating a general oil embargo against Japan, were exercising restraint because of the delicate nature of Japanese-American relations. They had also advised the press to remain calm during this period.[116]

---

[110]II, 84.

[111]"Memorandum of a Conversation", June 15, 1941, by Joseph W. Ballantine, *S.D.*, II, 471–472.

[112]*Ibid.;* II, 78–79.

[113]II, 78–79.

[114]II, 85.

[115]II, 78–79.

[116]II, 86.

28. Special Committee Meeting (June 15, 1941).

Later, on this same day of June 15, 1941, Mr. Hamilton and Mr. Ballantine met Colonel Iwakuro, Mr. Wikawa, and Mr. Matsudaira to continue their discussions. The Japanese offered as a basis for discussion a revision of the Japanese draft of June 8, 1941 which had not been previously seen by the American experts.[117] In view of this, a request was made, and agreed to by the Japanese, that discussion be deferred until American authorities had studied its provisions.

The conversation then turned to Japanese discriminatory commercial relations in China, e.g., Japanese special companies monopolizing the system of exchange and currency, and Japanese trade and traveling controls imposed in North China which interfered with the trade of any other nation. Although the Japanese contended that these companies were not monopolistic, since foreigners could purchase shares of the companies, the American diplomats pointed out that Japanese attempts to prevent trade competition of other nations were discriminatory. The Japanese maintained that the difficulties experienced by American firms in obtaining raw silk in China could be attributed to the preferential treatment accorded Japanese-supported companies, mines, and other economic enterprises which the Japanese had paid for in North China. However, the Japanese felt that these firms were not monopolistic and they stated that their operation should not preclude American participation in the Chinese silk industry. The Japanese added that because these businesses provided raw materials vital to their country and since Japan had paid for these supplies, they hoped that their retention would not be considered a discriminatory practice. Since Japan had paid for essential supplies, hoped that their retention by the Japanese would not be considered a discriminatory practice. With this exception, there would be no discrimination favoring Japan in the rest of the Chinese trade. This question was left for future discussion by the committee.

As for Japanese troops in North China, Colonel Iwakuro finally stated that they would definitely remain there without any time for their withdrawal. This answer was to be presented to China as a part of the general settlement between Japan and the United States, and Colonel Iwakuro hoped that some formula could be devised which would offset criticism from the United States. In addition, a tentative formula covering the relations of Japan and the United States with the European war was offered by Colonel Iwakuro. The Japanese stated that the restrictions presently imposed on goods would disappear as soon as hostilities ceased, and they insisted that, in times of peace, there were no general restrictions on American trade. Arrangements were then made to have another meeting on the following day.[118]

29. Special Committee Meeting (June 16, 1941).[119]

Five American and Japanese experts met on June 16, 1941 to continue the discussion of the previous evening. Those present were Mr. Hamilton, Mr. Ballantine, Colonel Iwakuro, Mr. Wikawa, and Mr. Matsudaira. Discussing exchange and currency control, Colonel Iwakuro stated that this would be the responsibility of the Chinese government after the peace settlement, though the Japanese would redeem the military script it had issued in North China.

When asked to interpret a provision of paragraph four of the "Agreed Terms of Understanding" which stated that China's control of foreign trade must not affect Sino-Japanese economic cooperation, Colonel Iwakuro replied that Japan would operate the studied Japanese proposal.[120]

---

[117]"Draft document received informally from associates of the Japanese Ambassador", June 15, 1941, S.D., II, 473–476.

[118]"Memorandum of a Conversation", June 15, 1941, by Joseph W. Ballantine, S.D., II, 472–473.

[119]"Memorandum of a Conversation", June 16, 1941, by Joseph W. Ballantine, S.D., II, 476–478.

[120]*Ibid.*

30. Special Committee Meeting (June 17, 1941).[121]

Mr. Hamilton, Mr. Ballantine, and Mr. Max W. Schmidt, of the Division of Far Eastern Affairs, met with Colonel Iwakuro, Mr. Wikawa, and Mr. Matsudaira on June 17, 1941. Mr. Ballantine suggested the inclusion of the word "unprovoked" in a rewording of a provision of the "understanding" to make it read:

> The Government of Japan maintains that the purpose of the Tripartite Pact was, and is, designed to contribute to the prevention of the unprovoked extension of the European war.

According to Mr. Ballantine, this suggestion was made tentatively, since it was already part of a general idea which the United States wished to discuss. Furthermore, it was suggested that excerpts from the Secretary of State's speech, already objected to by the Japanese as part of the Annex and Supplement presented by the United States on May 31, 1941 should be incorporated in an exchange of letters between the Secretary of State and the Japanese Ambassador to clarify the attitude of the United States toward the European war.

Colonel Iwakuro replied that Japan would not favor the publication of Secretary Hull's statement in either an exchange of letters, or as an annex and supplement to an agreement, since the Japanese government had been fully informed of the attitude of the United States toward the European war. The question should be left for further discussion until after an agreement had been reached between the two countries.[122] Answering a query of Mr. Wikawa as to the type of reply to be expected, Mr. Hamilton said that it could not be treated as secret, but that it would not necessarily be published. To Mr. Hamilton's suggestion, corresponding to that of Secretary Hull's, that Japan indicate its understanding of the attitude of the United States toward the European war in regard to self-defense, Colonel Iwakuro asked whether the United States would accept Japan's own views on self-defense. Mr. Hull (*sic*) replied that the question would not have arisen except for Japan's attitude toward the European war as expressed in the Tripartite Pact. When Colonel Iwakuro responded that Japan in turn might want to send a letter incorporating statements by Japanese leaders, Mr. Hamilton pointed out that this would probably not lead to a meeting of minds.[123]

Discussing the satisfactory relations of the United States with Japan before the signing of the Tripartite Pact, Colonel Iwakuro said that the attitude of the United States left Japan with no other alternative but to join the Axis. Thus, before specific controversies could be solved, it would be necessary first to improve general American-Japanese relations. To a question raised concerning Japanese special companies, such as the North China Development Company and the Central China Promotion Company, Colonel Iwakuro replied that American companies would be allowed to operate in China, with the exception of certain enterprises, which, under Chinese law, must necessarily have more than fifty per cent Chinese ownership.

When Mr. Hamilton remarked that continual complaints were being received from American businessmen, who were suffering from Japanese restrictions of trade in China, Colonel Iwakuro replied that this situation was due to war conditions, and that, when peace arrived, all restrictions in trade and banking would be removed. Equal treatment would be accorded to the nationals of all other powers without any discrimination.

Concerning relations between the government at Chungking and the government of Wang Ching-wei after the proposed peace settlement between China and Japan, Japan desired representatives from both Chinese sections to be present at the peace negotiations, since it believed that both governments would eventually coalesce to form the Chinese government and to sign the peace treaty. This topic was left for future discussion.

---

[121]"Memorandum of a Conversation", June 17, 1941, by Max W. Schmidt, *S.D.*, II, 478–483.

[122]*Ibid.*, 479.

[123]*Ibid.*

To the suggestion of Colonel Iwakuro that Japan and the United States mutually recognize the defensive position which each country had in East Asia and in the Western Hemisphere, Mr. Hamilton commented that the "Good Neighbor" policy in the Western Hemisphere might be jeopardized, because this suggestion might offend some of the American republics. Mr. Hamilton recommended that this suggestion be excluded from the final proposal.[124]

The Japanese then asked the United States to state that it had no ambitions for new military or political bases in East Asia. After Colonel Iwakuro pointed out that there was no mention of military bases in Section VI, which declared that neither government had territorial designs in the Pacific, Mr. Hamilton indicated that the raising of the question of military bases at this time would create new issues, which could be left for discussion until after the "understanding" had been achieved.

Colonel Iwakuro suggested that the United States emphasize its peaceful intention by announcing that no new bases would be acquired, but Mr. Hamilton commented that since Japan had planned to establish bases in Thailand, Indo-China, Hainan, and other areas of the Southwest Pacific, the American public would object to restrictions on the United States' freedom. Furthermore, if Japan considered the question of military bases as separate from the acquisition of new territory, other questions would arise concerning Japan's plans for the South Pacific. When Japan claimed that it did not have territorial designs, did it intend to acquire military bases there?

Colonel Iwakuro replied that Japan did not intend to acquire military bases, but that this decision would be governed by the actions of the United States, for example, the acquisition by the United States of a military base in Singapore.

Though the Japanese urged all possible speed in the discussions so that they could inform Tokyo, Mr. Hamilton reminded them that four important questions were still outstanding:

1. Economic non-discrimination in China.
2. Stationing of Japanese troops in China.
3. Attitude of the two governments toward the European war.
4. The statement regarding military bases.

Because these points would have to be discussed with Secretary Hull, another meeting was arranged for the near future.[125]

31. Hull-Nomura Conversation (June 21, 1941).

(a) *Secretary Hull's Report.*[126]

Ambassador Nomura called at Secretary Hull's apartment at the latter's request to receive a completely revised American draft of the proposal.[127] Secretary Hull also handed the Japanese Ambassador an oral statement which he asked him to read.[128] Accompanying the oral statement and redraft were two annexes and supplements, one in regard to the China incident which would be published as coming from the Japanese government, and the other concerning commercial relations as coming from the United States. In addition, there were the suggested texts of letters to be exchanged in outlining the attitude of the two countries toward the Euro-

---

[124]*Ibid.,* 481.

[125]*Ibid.*

[126]"Memorandum of a Conversation", June 21, 1941 by Joseph W. Ballantine, *S.D.,* II, 483–484.

[127]"Draft proposal handed by the Secretary of State to the Japanese Ambassador (Nomura)", on June 21, 1941, *S.D.,* II, 486–489.

[128]"Oral statement handed by Secretary of State to Japanese Ambassador (Nomura)", on June 21, 1941, *S.D.,* II, 485–486, II, 87–89. This oral statement was returned to American authorities by Ambassador Nomura on July 17, 1941, *S.D.,* II, 511–514.

pean war, and a suggested letter from Secretary Hull to Ambassador Nomura regarding non-discriminatory economic cooperation between China and Japan.[129]

The oral statement expressed the appreciation of Secretary Hull for the efforts of Ambassador Nomura and his associates in bettering American-Japanese relations in the Pacific. However, though many Japanese leaders shared the views of the Japanese Ambassador concerning the desirability of peace, the United States had received reports from many world-wide sources that some Japanese officials were definitely committed to the support of Nazi Germany, and would fight on the side of Hitler should the United States enter the European war as a matter of self-defense.[130] (See *Part C—e, Japanese-Axis Relations*)

Since official spokesmen of the Japanese government were emphasizing Japan's obligations under the Tripartite Pact in an effort to influence Japanese opinion, Secretary Hull asked whether the adoption of the proposed "understanding" would achieve the desired results. The decision of Japan to retain troops in Northern China was also another source of difficulty since it conflicted with America's liberal policy of not interfering with the sovereign rights of another power. The United States desired a clearer indication than had yet been given of the Japanese government's wish to pursue a course of peace.[131]

After Ambassador Nomura had read this oral statement, Secretary Hull reminded him of Foreign Minister Matsuoka's announcements that any resistance to the aggression of Chancellor Hitler would call for action by Japan under the Tripartite Pact. As for American intentions concerning military bases in the Pacific, the United States had been gradually withdrawing from that region, and in 1922 had agreed not to fortify its territory in the western Pacific. In addition, the United States had been willing to renew this treaty in 1936.

In Secretary Hull's opinion, the Japanese government would be controlled in the future either by the pro-Nazi elements or by those opposed to a policy of aggression, and for this reason, the United States would gladly consider a program for cooperation along peaceful lines. Since both he and Ambassador Nomura shared the belief that an "understanding" at this time of world crisis was most important, Mr. Hull announced that though he would leave for the country to recuperate from his recent illness, his associates would be available for consultation with the Japanese Ambassador and his colleagues at any time.[132]

(b) *Ambassador Nomura's Report.*[133]

Ambassador Nomura notified Foreign Minister Matsuoka that he had received from Secretary Hull the oral statement and revised draft of the proposal which were mentioned above. Expressing his dissatisfaction with this latest American proposal, since it was far from being in accord with Mr. Matsuoka's instructions, Ambassador Nomura announced that he was sending the documents to Tokyo. He was convinced that the Japanese government would not accept some of the American terms in regard to the United States' interpretation of self-defense and non-discriminatory commercial relations in China.

In another interview with Secretary Hull on June 23, 1941, Ambassador Nomura had told him frankly that he could not submit this proposal to his government.[134] Despite this last

---

[129]*S.D.*, II, 489–492.

[130]*Ibid.*, 485.

[131]*Ibid.*, 486.

[132]*Ibid.*

[133]II, 78–79.

[134]On several occasions Ambassador Nomura dated his meetings with Secretary Hull one day ahead of the date given by Secretary Hull in his official documents; e.g., II, 78–79, in which Ambassador Nomura speaks of a meeting on June 22, noted by Secretary Hull, as taking place on June 21, and a meeting on June 23 which Secretary Hull recorded as occuring on June 22.

statement, Ambassador Nomura sent the texts of both documents to Tokyo on June 24, 1941,[135] and other messages, clarifying obscure points, were transmitted on the next day.[136]

On June 24, 1941 Ambassador Nomura summarized the current American-Japanese diplomatic situation by indicating three important discrepancies in the demands of both sides:

1. When it comes to the European war, Anglo-American self-defense rights, and the Tripartite Pact, they will not yield to anything we advocate.

2. When it comes to the question of our stationing of troops for protection against Communists, they strangely enough declare that they cannot interfere with Chinese-Japanese peace terms, but in the same breath show considerable ire, declaring that this interferes with the sovereignty of a third power.

3. Secretary Hull's pet principle is that of commercial non-discrimination. He repeats that the Pan-American policy of the United States consists of this. He often says that if we applied the principle of non-discrimination to China and all the Pacific, we would have nothing to lose, and it would, as a matter of fact, be to our material interests.[137]

According to Ambassador Nomura, the United States would negotiate despite these discrepancies, if it were absolutely certain that Japan earnestly desired peace. However, the United States would not support Japan in its desire to station troops in China, nor in its ambition to exercise economic domination in the Pacific area. Yet, since Japan had been exempted from the freezing of foreign assets, the West coast espionage case involving Japanese naval officers had been settled in a friendly fashion, and Secretary Hull, despite illness, had received him three times, Ambassador Nomura believed that President Roosevelt and his immediate associates were anxious to achieve a peaceful settlement. On the other hand, reports from the American Embassy in Tokyo and from financial circles in New York indicated that many American officials doubted the sincerity of the Japanese government.

In view of all this, Ambassador Nomura believed it would be advantageous, despite the difficulties, to continue negotiations, since the freezing of Japanese credit and additional trade restrictions would follow the rupture of relations.[138]

32. Hull–Nomura Conversation (June 22, 1941).

(a) *Secretary Hull's Report.*[139]

Ambassador Nomura called at Secretary Hull's apartment on June 22, 1941 to announce his intention of sending to Tokyo Secretary Hull's oral statement of the preceding day. He could not account for the disagreement among Japanese authorities to which the American State Department had referred, because from the very beginning he had been conforming to the instructions of his government. Secretary Hull asked whether Mr. Matsuoka, as his recent message to Premier Mussolini had indicated, was using the United States to force China to agree with Japan, and at the same time was leaving Japan free to come into the European war.

Ambassador Nomura replied that though Japan did not want war with the United States, it did not wish to bind itself in advance to some future action. Ambassador Nomura then asked Mr. Ballantine to read to Secretary Hull a Japanese oral statement which suggested that the proposed exchange of letters between Secretary Hull and himself, as described in the documents submitted by Secretary Hull on June 21, 1941, be either omitted or modified.[140] Secretary Hull commented that he did not wish to embarrass the Japanese government, nor did he think the Japanese

---

[135]II, 87–92.

[136]II, 84–97.

[137]II, 79.

[138]*Ibid.*

[139]"Memorandum of a conversation", June 22, 1941, by Joseph W. Ballantine, *S.D.*, II, 492–494.

[140]"Informal and unofficial oral statement handed by the Japanese Ambassador (Nomura) to the Secretary of State", on June 22, 1941, *S.D.*, II, 494.

government would want to embarrass the United States; his purpose had been to clarify the attitude of the Japanese government so that public opinion in America would not oppose the "understanding".

In reply to Secretary Hull's question whether Germany's entrance into war against Russia might not make it easier for the Japanese government to come to an "understanding", Ambassador Nomura replied that the Japanese government did not desire to repudiate its obligations under the Tripartite Pact. However, the matter would be referred to his government for further study.

The Japanese Ambassador also objected to the draft letter in regard to non-discrimination in international commercial relations, on the grounds that this matter would involve too many details for the present "understanding", and could be treated at a later time. As for the Japanese proposal that the question of troops in China be left for settlement between Japan and China, Secretary Hull pointed out the possible danger of the United States and Japan reaching an agreement which might not be followed by a similar concord between Japan and China, thus embarrassing the United States. According to Ambassador Nomura, this question would be studied further by his government despite Japan's long-established policy of keeping its troops in China for defense against Communism.

Secretary Hull did not offer to withdraw the exchange of letters, but it was decided to have the Japanese Ambassador refer the essential points of the letters to his government for study under an agreement that another alternative from the Japanese Ambassador might be acceptable. In view of the importance of the "understanding", Secretary Hull asked that Ambassador Nomura and his associates remain in touch with Secretary Hull's associates, who would keep him advised.[141]

(b) *Ambassador Nomura's Report.*

It appears that no specific report concerning this meeting was transmitted to Tokyo by Ambassador Nomura. If he did so, the dispatch is not available.

33. Ambassador Nomura Defends His Actions.

It will be recalled that Foreign Minister Matsuoka had severely rebuked Ambassador Nomura for exceeding his authority in discussing certain details of the proposal which the Foreign Office considered part of its own province. On June 25, 1941 Ambassador Nomura replied that he had never transcended the limits of Mr. Matsuoka's instructions, but had devoted all his time to the betterment of Japanese-American relations as an important phase of Japanese national policy. Since there was sufficient reason to believe that the United States doubted the good faith of Japan, Ambassador Nomura had investigated the reasons for this attitude.[142]

Having discovered that two or three members of the American Cabinet, as well as some of the State Department officials, were not in favor of the proposed "understanding", the Japanese Ambassador remarked that groups in both America and Japan were not in sympathy with his actions and were doing their best to wreck the negotiations. Reminding Mr. Matsuoka that Secretary Hull had asked him on several occasions whether it was not true that certain influential groups in Japan were opposed to the "understanding", Ambassador Nomura indicated that he had strongly denied this charge, and had also refuted the impression that his views did not represent those of the Japanese Government.

The Japanese Ambassador appealed to his past record of friendship with the Foreign Minister and the trying circumstances under which he had assumed his present duties as evidence of his good faith and excellent motives in the current conversations.[143]

---

[141]*Ibid.*
[142]II, 98.
[143]*Ibid.*

34. Ambassador Nomura Urges the Adoption of the "Understanding".

On June 29, 1941 Ambassador Nomura reported to Tokyo that he was still awaiting instructions in regard to the documents presented to him by the Secretary of State, but meanwhile, he would offer his opinion as to the action Japan should take. Reiterating his former pleas for a speedy decision, Ambassador Nomura pointed out that though the United States was feverishly preparing to meet any eventuality, it was unlikely to enter the war for some time to come. Therefore, an "understanding" between Japan and the United States would help to restrain America from entering the war. Furthermore, Ambassador Nomura doubted the efficacy of the aid which the United States intended to give to Russia.

If Japan did not make haste in arriving at a decision, the United States might lose interest in the "understanding", and Japan would then have to expand to the south, with a probable collision with the Netherlands East Indies and an eventual diplomatic break with Britain and Australia. As for Japan's allegiance to its Axis partners, Ambassador Nomura stated that adherence to the Tripartite Pact would in no way affect the preservation of peace in the Pacific. He urged that the Japanese governmental authorities persuade the United States of its true interest in the proposed "understanding".[144]

35. Tokyo Warns Its Diplomats of a Crisis.

On June 30, 1941, shortly after Germany had attacked Russia, Tokyo issued a general warning to all of its diplomatic representatives throughout the world that Japan had entered a critical period.[145] All intelligence reports were to be dispatched to the Foreign Office as soon as possible, and all documents referring to these reports were to be destroyed by fire.

Instructions were issued concerning the evacuation of Japanese personnel, the voiding of leases for rented property, the safe custody of Japanese government-owned property, and various other items relating to the discontinuance of Japanese diplomatic relations in certain areas. These instructions were not too significant in regard to the Hull-Nomura conversations, since the uneasiness expressed by Tokyo was merely a reflection of the general spirit of many nations not at war at this time. However, the instructions indicated that the Japanese government was preparing for any eventuality.

36. America's Attitude Toward the German–Russian War (July 1, 1941).

Ambassador Nomura reported Acting Secretary of State Sumner Welles' discussion of America's attitude toward the German-Soviet war. Remarking that America was equally opposed to a communistic or Nazi dictatorship, Mr. Welles declared that the present concern of the United States was the destruction of Hitlerism throughout the world, and for that reason aid to Russia had been ordered.[146]

President Roosevelt confirmed this statement on June 24, 1941 and said that since Russia had made no request for aid as yet, he did not know what would have to be sent. However, Russia had been exempted from the order of the Secretary of the Treasury on June 14, 1941 which had frozen all European funds in the United States, and, thus, Russia had four hundred million dollars available in the United States for the purchase of American materials. Furthermore, the United States had not invoked the neutrality act in the German-Russian war on the grounds that the act was not necessary for the preservation of American lives and the public peace. Aid to Russia under the Lend-Lease Act was being studied.

---

[144] II, 99.
[145] II, 100.
[146] II, 101.

Ambassador Nomura assured Tokyo that Japan was exercising a restraining influence on the entrance of the United States into war, but he believed that American public opinion was becoming more settled, and that decisive action only awaited the completion of preparations, which would be a matter of but a few months. Pointing out that many Americans believed in the inevitability of war, he indicated that all preparations were being made for a long struggle.[147]

Despite the views of Ambassador Nomura in the report described above, he informed his superiors, on July 2, 1941, that President Roosevelt had stressed, in a press conference on the preceding day, the hope that the United States could keep out of the war. Ambassador Nomura believed that this statement of President Roosevelt had been intended as an indirect reply to a speech of Prime Minister Konoye to allay any fears of Japan concerning a possible conflict between a Japanese-American "understanding" and the Tripartite Pact. Prime Minister Konoye had stated that the Tripartite Pact had been designed to keep both Japan and the United States out of the European war.[148] According to Ambassador Nomura, Postmaster General Frank C. Walker had conferred with President Roosevelt after the remarks of Prince Konoye, and President Roosevelt had decided to make an indirect reply to the Japanese Prime Minister.[149]

37. Special Committee Meeting (July 2, 1941).[150]

American and Japanese associates of Secretary Hull and Ambassador Nomura met for further discussion. Mr. Ballantine, Mr. Schmidt, Mr. Hamilton, Colonel Iwakuro, Mr. Wikawa and Mr. Matsudaira were present.

Mentioning the recent conciliatory interview Prime Minister Konoye had given to the American press, Mr. Wikawa stated that this had been in response to Secretary Hull's oral statement of June 21, 1941. For this reason, Prime Minister Konoye, emphasizing Japan's intention not to participate in or to assist any German program of world conquest, had stressed the absence of reasons for war between the United States and Japan. However, Mr. Ballantine pointed out that the interview had been granted to a Paramount Newsreel representative who had in turn given the information to a United Press correspondent. The interview was not too significant since the Prime Minister's remarks had not been published in Japan, and as reported in America, differed only slightly from previous comments of Japanese statesmen.[151]

In regard to the implication, in Secretary Hull's oral statement of June 21, 1941, of a division within the Japanese government, Mr. Iwakuro reported that secret information, acquired from State Department channels, indicated that the Hull-Nomura conversations had been closed, and that Japanese funds would be frozen in the near future. This information had resulted in unfortunate losses to the Japanese sinking fund allotted for the purchase of Japanese government bonds.

The Japanese representatives argued that once the "understanding" had been reached, Japan would be able to give evidence of her peaceful intentions, meanwhile, though recognizing the need for quick action, Japan was obliged to move cautiously. Much discussion then arose concerning the unanimity of the Japanese government concerning the proposed "understanding". The Japanese assured their American colleagues that with the exception of some small groups there was complete cooperation in Japan.

---

[147] *Ibid.*
[148] N.Y. *Times*, June 30, 1941, 7:2.
[149] II, 102.
[150] "Memorandum of a Conversation", July 2, 1941, by Max W. Schmidt, *S.D.*, II, 495–499.
[151] *Ibid.*, 495.

Mr. Schmidt reminded the Japanese diplomats that many of their statesmen had emphasized Japan's commitments under the Tripartite Pact. Consequently, the people of the United States believed that certain Japanese elements, supporting Germany, would oppose an "understanding" with the United States which would prevent Japan's aid to Chancellor Hitler, if the United States went to war against Germany. Mr. Wikawa replied that statements of Ambassador Nomura to Secretary Hull concerning Japanese intentions had the official support of the Japanese Army, Navy and Foreign Office, and Colonel Iwakuro confirmed Japanese unanimity in this respect. Mr. Ballantine indicated that it was not a question of the unanimity of the Japanese government concerning the proposal under discussion, but since there was some doubt as to the peaceful intentions of the Japanese, it was felt that Tokyo ought to present some concrete evidence as a proof of its good will.[152] The Americans asked for some concrete evidence that the Japanese government as a whole was anxious for peace instead of military conquest.[153]

The Japanese diplomats remarked that the Hull-Nomura conversations were kept very secret in Japan, owing to the opposition which might arise from other countries and certain Japanese elements. Furthermore, public statements of Japanese officials were often largely for home consumption. According to Mr. Hamilton, similar secrecy was in effect in the United States, and since President Roosevelt and Secretary Hull were able to "apply the brakes" in matters of policy, it seemed possible for the Japanese government also to adopt peaceful methods. Colonel Iwakuro stated that in view of Japan's Tripartite Pact obligations, it would be difficult to act in this fashion until the "understanding" had been reached.[154]

Commenting that delays in the current conversations were making both countries feel that the other was "insincere" and "playing with the other", Colonel Iwakuro declared that since their primary objective was to prevent hostilities between the United States and Japan, an agreement to avoid war should be reached first. All other problems could then be settled in the favorable atmosphere resulting from such an agreement.

In the opinion of Mr. Ballantine, however, the essential points at issue were first, Japan's attitude toward the European war, and second, Japan's desire for peace. Agreeing with Colonel Iwakuro that an understanding on fundamentals would facilitate the solution of other problems, Mr. Hamilton mentioned that Secretary Hull could not ignore the evidence from Japan and other sources which indicated that important Japanese elements did not desire peace.

Suggesting that mutual recognition of the right of self-defense would suffice for the exchange of letters proposed in the American draft of June 21, 1941, Colonel Iwakuro remarked that the United States' assistance to Russia was not pleasing to Japan. He expressed his own personal opinion that discussions on the China incident be dropped until the United States and Japan had reached an agreement for peace in the Pacific. Mr. Hamilton responded that peace in the Pacific involved many countries, and, in addition, there could be no peace if certain Japanese elements were to force an attack on the United States at some later stage of the European war.

The most important part of the whole conversation occurred when the Japanese urged that an "understanding" be reached immediately, with details left for the future, so as to eliminate the possibility of war between Japan and the United States. Mr. Hamilton then repeated his statement that if Japan followed peaceful courses, there would be no danger of war.[155]

---

[152]*Ibid.*, 496.
[153]*Ibid.*, 496–497.
[154]*Ibid.*, 497.
[155]*Ibid.*

38. Japan Decides to Move Southward and Act in Accordance with the Tripartite Pact.

That the Tripartite Pact was the basis of Japanese foreign policy was reemphasized in an Imperial conference report from Mr. Matsuoka to Japanese diplomats, which disclosed that pressure from various points in the south would be exerted to bring the Chungking regime in China to submission. Preparations for a southward advance by Japan were under way, and the policy already decided in regard to French Indo-China and Thailand was to be executed. Every effort was to be exerted to prevent the United States from entering the war, although, if the need should arise, Japan would act in accordance with the Tripartite Pact.[156]

Tokyo also announced to its representatives that the divesting of English and United States interests in China might be necessary, depending upon the results of Japanese negotiations with the English speaking people. If things came to the worst, Tokyo asked that all areas concerned cooperate in either destroying or seizing mining and other industrial equipment and ships of England and the United States.

39. Ambassador Nomura Urges Japan Not to Act in Accordance with the Tripartite Pact.

Ambassador Nomura, on July 3, 1941, informed Foreign Minister Matsuoka that relations between Japan and the United States would worsen if Japan collaborated with Germany against Russia. Because peace had to be maintained in the Far East and Japan's obligations to China had to be fulfilled, he urged Japan to stay out of the German-Russian war. Pointing out that a quick agreement to a Japanese-American "understanding" would make the question of self-defense applicable to both Japan and America, he commented that this would make legitimate a future Japanese stand against Russia.

Ambassador Nomura warned that if Japan moved its army southward at this time, there was absolutely no hope of an agreement with the United States. Knowing from various warnings received from the Foreign Office that a serious move was about to be made by his country, the Japanese Ambassador urged a speed decision as to the American "understanding", no matter what policy in regard to Russia was going to be followed.[157]

40. Ambassador Nomura Reassures Secretary Hull.

On July 4, 1941 Ambassador Nomura handed a note to Mr. Ballantine with the request that its contents be telephoned to Secretary Hull as soon as possible. This was done on July 5, 1941 by a member of the State Department. The text follows:

WASHINGTON, July 4, 1941.

MY DEAR MR. SECRETARY: I am glad to inform you that I am now authorized by the Foreign Minister to assure you that there is no divergence of views in the Government regarding its fundamental policy of adjusting Japanese-American relations on a fair basis.

Yours very sincerely, K. NOMURA.[159]

41. Interview with Ambassador Nomura.

(a) *State Department's Report.*[159]

On July 5, 1941, Mr. Hamilton and Mr. Ballantine called on Ambassador Nomura to deliver Secretary Hull's comments on Ambassador Nomura's letter of July 4, 1941. The State Depart-

---

[156]II, 103–104.

[157]II, 105–106.

[158]*S.D.,* II, 499.

[159]"Memorandum of a conversation", July 5, 1941, by Joseph W. Ballantine, *S.D.,* II, 499–502.

ment notified Ambassador Nomura that it had instructed Ambassador Grew in Tokyo to deliver to Prime Minister Konoye a message asking for assurances that reports of an imminent attack against Russia by Japan were without foundation.[160] Mention was also made of American efforts to maintain peace in the Pacific, and the statements of Ambassador Nomura and other Japanese leaders confirming Japan's support of this policy were cited.

Mr. Hamilton indicated that the telegram had been sent before Ambassador Nomura's letter of July 4, 1941 had been received. Though the letter contained assurances of friendliness on the part of Japan which were very pleasing to the United States, Mr. Hamilton remarked that answers of the Japanese government to the fundamental questions raised in Secretary Hull's oral statement of June 21, 1941 would be very helpful. The oral statement had not implied a divergence of views among the Japanese concerning the desirability of the proposed "understanding", but it had asked for evidence which would contradict the impression that certain elements of the Japanese government favored Hitler's world conquest rather than a course of peace.

Ambassador Nomura replied that a comparison of the original proposal and the American revision revealed important differences of viewpoints, which the Japanese government recognized. His letter of July 4, 1941 expressed the desire of his government to continue the conversations until the differences were eliminated. The China incident affected public opinion in Japan much more than in the United States, and, therefore, the Japanese government had to move very cautiously in this matter. However, the Japanese Ambassador promised to inform his superiors of the American viewpoint.

Mr. Hamilton then read to Ambassador Nomura a clipping from the *New York Times* relating to Japan's plans to acquire naval air bases in French Indo-China and Thailand, which would permit Japanese forces to threaten the Burma Road, Singapore and the Dutch East Indies. In view of this, he asked the Japanese Ambassador to explain the contradictory aspects of Japan's discussing a peace settlement for the Pacific while preparing for war. (See Part C—(g) *Japanese-French Relations,* which indicates that all of Japan's secret plans for the Far East were divulged to the State Department by United States Communication Intelligence).

The Japanese Ambassador replied that his country was forced to prepare for all possible eventualities since newspapers in the United States were full of plans for the encirclement of Japan, aid to China, Malaya and the Netherlands East Indies, visits of American squadrons to Australia, American aid to the Russian Far East, and the acquisition of air bases in Siberia. In addition, the possibility of a petroleum embargo by the United States against Japan made it necessary for Japan to make preparations for defense.

According to Mr. Hamilton, the United States was not preparing to acquire bases in Siberia, and he commented that there was a great difference between preparatory defense measures at home and seizing bases by force abroad. Ambassador Nomura declared that the Japanese government desired peace, and it had no intention at the moment to move either against Russia or southward. It was imperative, therefore, that the "understanding" be concluded as speedily as possible to avoid further aggravations resulting from action and counter-action by both Japan and America. Agreeing with these views, Mr. Hamilton commended Ambassador Nomura's statesmanlike remarks.

Mr. Hamilton then mentioned that associates of Ambassador Nomura had discussed the possibility of Japan's willingness to withdraw all their troops in China within two years. Replying that he was not conversant with details of this matter, the Japanese Ambassador men-

---

[160]"Statement handed by the American Ambassador in Japan (Grew) to Mr. Tomohiko Ushiba, Private Secretary of the Japanese Prime Minister (Prince Konoye)", on July 6, 1941, *S.D.*, II, 502–503.

tioned that the treaty with Mr. Wang Ching-wei would keep Japanese troops in China as long as the Anti-Comintern Pact was valid, which might be for two years but, perhaps, for much longer.

Throughout the whole conversation Mr. Hamilton emphasized that he spoke in the name of Secretary Hull, and at the end he informed Ambassador Nomura that the State Department expected a reply to the message sent to Prime Minister Konoye.

(b) *Ambassador Nomura's Report.*[161]

Unfortunately, two-thirds of Ambassador Nomura's report to Tokyo was not intercepted by American cryptanalytical agencies. The intercepted part referred only to the question of Japan's acquisition of bases in French Indo-China and Thailand, and outlined Ambassador Nomura's exposition of Japan's needs for self-defense. There was very little information of value in this message.[162]

42. Ambassador Nomura Analyzes President Roosevelt's Diplomatic Activities.

Ambassador Nomura submitted to Tokyo, on July 7, 1941, a long analysis of American public opinion in relation to President Roosevelt's diplomatic moves.[163] The Japanese Ambassador had learned that the United States was already using convoy systems, although Senator George, the Chairman of the Senate Foreign Relations Committee, had said that the Lend-Lease Act had been passed with the understanding that there would be no convoys, or that convoys would not be instituted without the consent of the Senate. Therefore, Senator George had attacked the government's use of convoys, and the attitude of his committee had stiffened toward the President. However, President Roosevelt had answered this opposition through Secretary Knox, who, speaking in Boston on June 30, 1941 had demanded that the United States Navy take action in the Atlantic immediately. According to Ambassador Nomura, President Roosevelt intended to use Secretary Stimson and Secretary Knox in imposing his definite decision on an indecisive Congress.

As a result of Secretary Knox's speech, a demand arose for a Senate investigation to determine whether or not convoys were being used, but Secretary Knox, in a press conference of July 2, 1941 denied their use. The Japanese Ambassador pointed out that they were already in operation. Moreover, Ambassador Nomura claimed that in the fall of 1940, President Roosevelt had instructed influential members of the Senate Foreign Relations Committee to use one of the incidents that were occurring between the United States and Japan as a pretext for war. President Roosevelt dropped the plan when members of the committee objected, and in the beginning of 1941, President Roosevelt entirely changed his attitude and earnestly desired an adjustment of United States-Japanese relations.[164]

According to this same report, President Roosevelt had first hoped, through aid to Britain, to ensure a British victory without entering the war, but Germany's victories in the Balkans and Crete had caused him to change his policy. At that time he had not yet formulated a new policy, and because of the problem of regulating relations with Japan he had postponed his fireside chat for two weeks.

In the view of the Japanese Ambassador, President Roosevelt's move to send aid to Russia had brought an unfavorable reaction from the America First Committee, which claimed ten million members. He also believed that President Roosevelt's calling Colonel Charles Lindbergh a "Copperhead" had been a great failure. Furthermore, twenty-six million Methodists,

---

[161]II, 107.
[162]*Ibid.*
[163]*II,* 108.
[164]*Ibid.*

Baptists, Presbyterians, Congregationalists and Disciples had passed resolutions opposed to war. In view of this disunity in public opinion and in Congress itself, President Roosevelt was undecided as to his future policy, but was determined to decide on some definite course of action.

Ambassador Nomura believed that Japan was America's foremost concern at this time. One way of solving President Roosevelt's dilemma would be to achieve a Japanese-American understanding, but even though President Roosevelt and Secretary Hull were desirous for peace in the Pacific, they doubted Japan's sincerity.

Ambassador Nomura warned his superior that if Japan expanded toward the south, the United States, despite the unpreparedness of the American army, would use the navy which was prepared for war with Japan. Thus, popular opinion would be unified, and America's dilemma would be solved, since its wish to fight on only one front could be realized in view of the German-Russian war, which would permit it to neglect the Atlantic.[165]

43. Mr. Matsuoka Replies to President Roosevelt.

On July 8, 1941 Mr. Matsuoka handed to Ambassador Grew, at the request of Prime Minister Konoye, a message for delivery to the President of the United States.[166] Declaring that Japan sincerely desired to prevent the European war from spreading to Greater East Asia and to maintain peace in the Pacific, it stated that so far Japan had not considered the possibility of joining the hostilities against Russia. A confidential copy of the Japanese oral statement, delivered to the Russian Ambassador in Tokyo on July 2, 1941, which indicated that Japan would preserve its neutrality with Russia, was attached to this message. The Japanese government also asked whether or not, as indicated by reports from a variety of sources, it was the intention of the President of the United States to intervene in the European war.[167]

During this interview, Ambassador Grew read to Mr. Matsuoka a statement from Secretary Hull, which refuted certain reports emanating from Tokyo concerning the uncertainty of America's foreign policy.[168] Several articles in Japanese newspapers had revealed Japan's fears that the United States and Great Britain would use Russia for military purposes against Japan. In addition, the Japanese press considered American aid to Russia as an unfriendly gesture against Japan.

According to Secretary Hull, the attitude of the United States in regard to the European war had been very clearly stated many times. Its sole aim was to protect the Western Hemisphere against German armies and, accordingly, aid was being given to Great Britain and to any other nation in opposition to those armies, e.g., Russia. All such aid was given in defense of America, and in no way did it threaten the security of nations not on the side of Chancellor Hitler.[169]

44. Ambassador Nomura Reports German–British Peace Negotiations.

While waiting for a reply from Tokyo in response to his telegrams asking for prompt action, Ambassador Nomura reported the existence in American financial circles of a great many rumors concerning American intervention for a German-British peace treaty.[170] According to one rumor,

---

[165]*Ibid.*

[166]"Statement handed by the Japanese Minister for Foreign Affairs (Matsuoka) to the American Ambassador in Japan (Grew)" on July 8, 1941, *S.D.*, II, 503–504.

[167]*Ibid.*

[168]"Memorandum by the Ambassador in Japan (Grew)", July 8, 1941, *S.D.*, II, 505.

[169]*Ibid.*

[170]II, 109–110.

an American-born German was working in the United States to bring about peace, and through the efforts of several prominent Americans he had been introduced to Secretary Hull with whom he had conferred concerning peace terms. However, neither President Roosevelt nor his associates would consider the project, though a number of cabinet members were in favor of it. Ambassador Nomura hastened to add that he could not vouch for the accuracy of this story,[171] but Mr. Matsuoka replied that he was very much interested in such reports, and asked for further details when available.[172]

45. Secretary Hull Refutes Ambassador Nomura's Report.

Complying with the request of the Japanese Foreign Office, on July 14, 1941 Ambassador Nomura supplied some interesting details of the secret activities of a German agent in America who was attempting to bring about peace between England and Germany.[173] According to Ambassador Nomura, a certain -----[a], accompanied by -----[a], had been introduced to the Secretary of State through the good offices of a relative of Secretary Hull, -----[a]. Ambassador Nomura stated that his tendencies were pro-Japanese.

The Japanese Ambassador reported that -----[a], an American of German extraction, who had lived in Berlin from 1920 to 1939 as representative of American financial interests, had become very intimate with Hitler, Goebbels, and Goering. Owing to his favorable position he had been able to protect the -----[a] properties in Germany, and had underwritten the Japan Electric Company through the New York organization of -----[a].

-----[a] had returned to the United States by way of Mexico, carrying with him an offer of a European peace plan made by Chancellor Hitler and Minister Goebbels, and bearing written documents from Nazi officials. Chancellor Hitler proposed to open peace negotiations with Britain at any time through the intercession of the United States. The integrity of the British Empire would be preserved; France, Belgium, and Holland were to continue in existence; Poland and Czechoslovakia were to be eliminated; Norway and Denmark were to be left out of the discussion.

Ambassador Nomura also reported that on February 15, 1941 a meeting had been held at the State Department with -----[a], Secretary Hull, the head of the European Division and other competent heads of departments, as well as two members of the Intelligence Section participating in the conversations. -----[a] had presented Chancellor Hitler's and Minister Goebbel's letter, and he had also requested that a telephone communication be established from the State Department to the Nazi authorities so that his official position in relation to Germany could be established. This had been done, and Minister Goebbels had substantiated his claims.

Four conversations were held between -----[a] and the State Department officials until April 11, 1941 when in the company of a State Department staff member he had gone by clipper to Berlin via Lisbon. After a conversation with Nazi authorities, he had returned to the United States, on May 27, 1941 under an assumed name to continue negotiations, in the course of which he had already talked with President Roosevelt. According to the Japanese Ambassador, -----[a] had been charged with negotiating the sale of German ships to the United States, as well as making peace proposals. In addition to -----[a], a secret German army representative was negotiating in Washington.

---

[a]DoD : All names withheld.
[171]*Ibid.*
[172]II, 111.
[173]II, 112–116.

The foregoing had caused a great disturbance in the State Department because of the differences of opinion among several members. Ambassador Nomura pointed to the fact that at the time the State Department representative, accompanying ——————[a], had conferred with Herr Hess, Marshal Goering, Minister Goebbels and the heads of the German army, Herr Hess had stressed the desire of the German leaders for peace. According to Ambassador Nomura's report, the United States and Great Britain had made a mistake in thinking that the massing of German troops on the Russian border was a form of deception and that no attack would be made. On the other hand, the Germans had believed that help to Russia from England and the United States was beyond possibility. Therefore, both governments had erred in their calculations.

Ambassador Nomura also emphasized that one of the reasons for the unsatisfactory progress of the American-Japanese negotiations was that Americans held the erroneous belief that there was a connection between the German peace movements and the Japanese negotiations.[174]

This extraordinary document elicited a very unusual response from Secretary of State Hull. In the files of United States Communication Intelligence, attached to the copy of the deciphered dispatch which contained this report of Ambassador Nomura, is a statement signed by Mr. Hull. It reads as follows:

> The entire subject matter in the communication of Ambassador Nomura to Tokyo No. 506 of July 14, 1941 beginning with "part 1 of 5" and including parts 2, 3 and 4, (through paragraph 7 of "part 4 of 5") in its entirety is wholly false and unsupported by a single fact or circumstance, other than that during the forepart of this year, ——————[a] secured an ordinary American passport to visit Germany and Italy allegedly on private business for a group of American persons in relation to a proposed purchase of German and Italian ships in North and South American ports, solely for the account of private American interests. The United States government in any event was not concerned in any way whatsoever.
>
> /s/ CORDELL HULL[175]

46. Ambassador Nomura Pleads for Speedier Action from Tokyo.

The first week of July, 1941 passed and still no reply came from Tokyo to Secretary Hull's oral statement of June 21, 1941, though Ambassador Nomura had sent several requests for speedy action. On July 8, 1941 Mr. Matsuoka inquired as to the meaning of the words "his associates" in a passage of the oral statement referring to the Japanese Ambassador and his associates.[176] Mr. Matsuoka also requested the texts of the letters which had been suggested for exchange in accordance with the revised American proposal of June 21, 1941.[177] These were sent by Ambassador Nomura.[178]

In view of these tantalizing requests, which indicated the interest of the Japanese Foreign Office in Secretary Hull's oral statement, Ambassador Nomura finally sent a very urgent plea for a definite decision, since the document had been in the hands of Mr. Matsuoka for two weeks. Remarking that American diplomats were very anxious to discover Japan's real intentions, Ambassador Nomura declared that the Americans, who were losing hope of ever seeing an improvement in Japanese-American relations, were beginning to doubt that the current

---

[a]DoD : All names withheld.

[174]II, 116.

[175]II, 112. Attached and signed by Mr. Hull.

[176]II, 117.

[177]II, 118.

[178]II, 119–120.

negotiations would ever amount to anything. Reliable information disclosed that Japanese delays were having an unfortunate effect in the United States, and this, coupled with the American belief that Japan would try to capitalize on the Russian-German war either by moving north against Russia or south against British and Dutch interests, jeopardized the whole Japanese-American situation. Both President Roosevelt and Secretary Hull, who had talked with the Japanese Ambassador seventeen times, according to Ambassador Nomura's own count, were very concerned. The United States Navy also considered the situation to be grave.

According to Ambassador Nomura, the Americans would not give in if Japan remained adamant. He believed that there was a great danger of the United States breaking off negotiations at the first opportunity rather than becoming less hostile. Indicating that the three main difficulties in the way of an "understanding" were first, the interpretation of the right of self-defense, second, the stationing of troops in China, and third, non-discrimination in commerce, Ambassador Nomura remarked that he was at his wit's end, but still did not want to break off negotiations. Expressing his willingness to present any other proposal which Mr. Matsuoka desired, the Japanese Ambassador urged that a decision be reached as quickly as possible on the proposals he had already submitted.[179]

47. Ambassador Nomura Requests Permission to Return Home (July 10, 1941).

On July 10, 1941 Foreign Minister Matsuoka directed Ambassador Nomura to send Minister-Counselor Wakasugi back to Tokyo so that certain information concerning the current negotiations could be supplied without dependence on telegrams.[180] Replying immediately to this directive, Ambassador Nomura requested that he be permitted to return to Japan to report the facts in person since his leaving would have no serious effect on the United States.

Pointing out that the United States had been eager to adjust Japanese-American relations immediately after the war had broken out between Russia and Germany he indicated that the United States was now very suspicious of Japan. A speedy conclusion of current negotiations would make possible a settlement of certain difficulties, but under present circumstances there would be no time for Tokyo to recall Mr. Wakasugi in order to obtain the facts of the situation, and then to reappoint him to continue the negotiations. Ambassador Nomura felt that the severance of diplomatic relations between Japan and the United States was much more imminent than the Japanese believed it to be. In view of these circumstances, Ambassador Nomura indicated that it would be useless for him to remain in the United States.[181]

On the same day, July 11, 1941, that Mr. Matsuoka delivered a severe rebuke to Ambassador Nomura concerning the diplomatic standing of his staff members in the minds of American representatives (See Part A—Section 48—*Mr. Matsuoka again Rebukes Ambassador Nomura*), Mr. Matsuoka refused to permit Ambassador Nomura to leave his position and return to Japan. Emphasizing his realization that there would be nothing better than to hear Ambassador Nomura report on the situation in person, the Foreign Minister declared that the critical nature of United States-Japanese relations made it increasingly necessary for Ambassador Nomura to remain where he was. Citing Emperor Hirohito's wishes concerning Ambassador Nomura's continuance at his post, Mr. Matsuoka pointed out that the return of the Japanese Ambassador at this time could not be permitted because of its effect on public opinion. Even if the achievement of an "understanding" seemed hopeless, it would be best for Ambassador Nomura to remain at his post to the last and to make the best of the situation.[182]

---

[179]II, 121–123.
[180]II, 124.
[181]II, 125.
[182]II, 126.

Three days later, on July 14, 1941, Ambassador Nomura again asked that he be allowed to give up his post in the United States.[183] Apologizing for any displeasure which he had caused Mr. Matsuoka because of his inexperience, he explained that his intention had been to remain and to do his utmost in the United States until the critical diplomatic situation had reached a possible solution. Expressing regret that his telegram had caused his country so much embarrassment, he promised to be especially cautious in the future, although he pointed out that his previous training had permitted him to exercise his own judgment to such an extent that he could not guarantee the absence of further difficulties. Ambassador Nomura expressed his views as follows:

> Therefore, no matter from what angle I regard the question, I cannot help but keenly feel that I should resign as soon as possible for the good of the country. In view of the political situation, I earnestly hope that you will not hesitate in transferring my duties to ----- person whom you have selected as being more in accordance with your desire. I fully realize that I am not the right man. I am, in fact, no more than a temporary stop-gap. As I have assured you previously, I have no intention whatsoever of bringing any degree of disaster to this position before my return to Japan. I most earnestly hope that you would consider this point carefully.[184]

Reiterating his opposition to the recalling of Mr. Wakasugi, he remarked that the point in question had been an "off the record" discussion of a private nature and was not important enough to require a personal report. Furthermore, Mr. Wakasugi had been sent to assist Ambassador Nomura in the performance of his duties, and wished to remain in Washington as long as Ambassador Nomura was stationed there. However, the Japanese Ambassador remarked that he would offer no further opposition, if Mr. Matsuoka insisted on Mr. Wakasugi's return to Japan.[185]

48. Mr. Matsuoka Again Rebukes Ambassador Nomura (July 11, 1941).

It will be recalled that Mr. Matsuoka had inquired of Ambassador Nomura concerning the meaning of the words "his associates" in a passage of the oral statement.[186] Ambassador Nomura responded that the term "associates" referred to all persons who had conferred at his orders with representatives of the United States; that is, Mr. Kaname Wakasugi, Mr. Katsuzo Okumura, Mr. Koto Matsudaira, Colonel Hideo Iwakuro, and Mr. Tadao Wikawa.[187] This explanation occasioned another severe rebuke to the Japanese Ambassador by Foreign Minister Matsuoka.

In a long dispatch on July 11, 1941, Mr. Matsuoka declared that the individuals named above were merely members of Ambassador Nomura's staff and were not his associates.[188] This condition would remain true until the Foreign Minister named one of them to a specific commission, and even Colonel Iwakuro, who had taken a prominent part in some of the special committee meetings, especially in military discussions, was not to be considered as an associate. Special warning was issued by the Foreign Minister concerning Mr. Tadao Wikawa, who was not connected with the Prime Minister or with any other member of the Japanese cabinet, and who was held in low esteem even by members of the Finance Ministry, to which he had been attached. Mr. Matsuoka directed Ambassador Nomura to correct immediately the misconception of United States authorities that the men mentioned above were his associates.

---

[183]II, 127.

[184]*Ibid.*

[185]*Ibid.*

[186]II, 117.

[187]II, 128.

[188]II, 129.

Mr. Matsuoka also objected to the implication contained in the oral statement that as long as there were questionable persons in the Prince Konoye cabinet, the understanding "could not be effective even if it were signed". According to Mr. Matsuoka, such a statement was a demand that the Japanese reorganize their Cabinet. For this reason Mr. Matsuoka declared that not only the government of Japan but its representatives had a perfect right to reject the oral statement, but in view of the delicate situation of the Japanese-American relations, as well as that of the rest of the world, he had decided to suffer in silence.

The Foreign Minister expressed the hope that Ambassador Nomura had insisted upon a full discussion of various points with the Americans to obtain detailed explanations since "the instrument has had only a very few, if any, comparable parallels in the history of the world".[189] Several points were then discussed by Mr. Matsuoka, who requested Ambassador Nomura to correct certain misconceptions of the Americans. First, both Prime Minister Konoye and Foreign Minister Matsuoka had been falsely quoted by the press concerning their remarks subsequent to the signing of the Tripartite Pact. Mr. Matsuoka had actually said that:

> Japan had every intention of being loyal to the terms of the Tripartite Pact, and should the United States go to war, forcing a clash between Japan and the United States, there would be, without a doubt, a horrible effect on all mankind.

Mr. Matsuoka claimed that if all the statements that he had made in Parliament and elsewhere were read carefully and calmly, it would be discovered that he had never exceeded the limits of the remarks expressed above. Complaining bitterly of many misquotations in the press, Mr. Matsuoka stated that he had adopted a policy of refusing to grant any interviews, except to persons whose characters were guaranteed by the United States Embassy, and for whose actions the United States Embassy agreed to be held responsible.

It is interesting to note that in this instance, as in the case of Mr. Matsuoka's complaints against the American and British Ambassadors to Tokyo for misquoting and mistranslating his remarks,[190] no specific instances of misquotations were given. It may be safe to assume, therefore, that Mr. Matsuoka objected to the interpretation placed upon his remarks by certain elements of the press. Although the press' interpretation of Mr. Matsuoka's attitude might have been faulty, the following passage in his secret dispatch speaks for itself:

> If the United States expects Japan to double cross her Axis partners, or even wishes Japan to assume a lukewarm attitude towards them on the basis of any of these public statements, the United States is being unreasonable, and is in for a disappointment. I am convinced that if the United States were in the same position as we, she would assume the same, or possibly an even stronger, attitude.[191]

Denying that there was a split between members of the Japanese cabinet, and calling all stories to this effect "lying reports", Mr. Matsuoka remarked that such rumors had been started from outside by those who had not been able to obtain cabinet appointments. Remarking that important matters had to be discussed thoroughly from all possible angles, Mr. Matsuoka indicated that this was being done in Tokyo at the moment.

Since rumors of dissension in Japan might have reached President Roosevelt and Secretary Hull, Mr. Matsuoka requested that Ambassador Nomura make every effort to correct such an erroneous opinion, for there was absolutely no difference of viewpoints between Prime Minister Konoye and himself concerning the necessity of improving Japanese-United States relations. Both were anxious to bring about an "understanding pact", as Mr. Matsuoka had made quite clear to Ambassador Nomura from the very beginning of his mission, and the War and Naval Ministers, as well as all the other ministers, were in complete accord in this matter. Ambassador

---

[189]*Ibid.*
[190]See Volume I, Section 62—*(England's Concern over Japanese Policies),* 166.
[191]II, 129.

Nomura was requested to explain the situation to President Roosevelt and Secretary Hull so that they would make no mistake.[192]

The tone of Mr. Matsuoka's reprimand was so indignant that Mr. Taro Terasaki, in a separate dispatch, advised Japanese representatives in Washington that Mr. Matsuoka's message had contained merely the Foreign Minister's immediate reactions to the oral statement. An expression of the official Japanese attitude concerning the American revision of the proposal would be sent to Washington in the very near future.[193]

49. Ambassador Nomura Replies to the Rebuke of the Foreign Minister (July 14, 1941).

A few days later, Ambassador Nomura replied to Mr. Matsuoka's reprimand. Agreeing with the Foreign Minister as to the importance of the oral statement of the United States, Ambassador Nomura did not believe that the Americans were trying to revise the Japanese cabinet, since their only aim was to discover the sincerity of the Japanese in improving mutual relations.[194]

The feeling of the Americans which had disturbed Mr. Matsuoka had arisen from a misunderstanding, because the American Embassy in Tokyo often sent home disturbing reports, and frequently prominent Japanese, who wished to thwart the Japanese-American negotiations, had also done damage. In addition, Germany and China had tried to end the negotiations, and Germany had originated a broadcast containing rumors of Mr. Matsuoka's resignation. On various occasions from the very beginning of his assignment, Ambassador Nomura had received Mr. Matsuoka's instructions concerning the desire of the Japanese for peace, but whatever the American representatives had been persuaded of Japan's good intentions, rumors from the financial circles of both nations had upset the situation.

Ambassador Nomura's disturbed state of mind concerning his failure to achieve his objectives in his post as Japanese Ambassador is demonstrated in the following passage:

I believed and never once doubted that it was at this stage the serious policy of the Imperial government to improve Japanese-American relations. But, since then, Oh, how often have I met with opposition! How often have I lost faith in my subordinates! But, in spite of that and enduring it all, to this day I have held to my post and while enduring every sort of bitterness I have stuck to my ideal; that is because I have had faith in what I conceived to be the primary policy of our Government. As I reflect upon the general atmosphere in this country when I took office, I can see how relations between our two countries were following an ever-roughening road. I thought that perhaps I could make our two countries each understand the position of the other; but, alas, I can see that that was only an airy story told in a dream![195]

In view of these unfavorable conditions and the evident dissatisfaction of some Japanese elements, Ambassador Nomura had become convinced that it would be hopeless to deal with the Secretary of State alone; thus, it had been decided to begin unofficial negotiations with certain other prominent Americans as well as with Secretary Hull. Seventeen private discussions had been held with Mr. Hull and several conferences with Postmaster General Frank C. Walker. Since Germany and China were also using secret agents, Ambassador Nomura was convinced that his method of undercover negotiations was the most productive.

As for the significance of the word "associates", according to Ambassador Nomura, the word simply meant cooperators, for example, Mr. Hamilton, Mr. Ballantine, and the Postmaster General were associates of Secretary Hull. The United States government did not believe that Colonel Iwakuro and Mr. Wikawa were authorized to represent the Japanese government, for it recognized that just as the Postmaster General and Secretary Hull understood the precise limits of their respective jurisdictions, so did Ambassador Nomura's subordinates.

---

[192] *Ibid.*
[193] II, 130.
[194] II, 131–138.
[195] II, 132.

The Japanese army and navy had been requested to send a competent man as assistant to the Japanese Ambassador, and Ambassador Nomura had supposed that Colonel Iwakuro was sent after consultation between the Foreign Office and military officials. Although Ambassador Nomura was grateful for the warning concerning Mr. Wikawa, after some difficulties at first, the man had been very useful as an interpreter in dealing with important American officials. Since Ambassador Nomura had used the word "associates" innocently, he had been very much perturbed to find he had been acting against Mr. Matsuoka's wishes.

The most important question, however, was whether or not Japan would adjust its relations with the United States at this critical moment, or give up all attempts to solve the difficulties. Warning that if this question were decided too quickly, a good opportunity for solving the problem would be lost forever, Ambassador Nomura then spoke of the necessity for ceasing all further bickering over unimportant details, and stressed his determination to exercise his own judgement until he was ordered back to Japan:

> I, therefore, do not wish to waste time at this critical moment bickering over the question of procedure. Besides, for compatriots to be arguing over details and to be casting suspicion on one another in the face of a serious crisis threatening the country would cause the enthusiasm and courage of those who are sincerely working in this matter to wilt, and would interfere with the progress of the negotiations. Since I feel this very keenly, I do not wish to go further into a discussion of the details.[196]

50. Interview with Ambassador Nomura (July 14, 1941).

(a) *State Department's Report.*[197]

Mr. Hamilton and Mr. Ballantine called on the Japanese Ambassador to express Secretary Hull's regrets at his inability, because of illness, to see Ambassador Nomura on the preceding day when he had called at Secretary Hull's hotel at White Sulphur Springs. The American representatives expressed their readiness to convey to Secretary Hull any new impressions which the Japanese Ambassador wished to communicate.

Ambassador Nomura said that he had informed Mr. Cecil W. Gray, Assistant to Secretary Hull, of his recently received instructions from Mr. Matsuoka to stress the unanimity of important Japanese leaders, such as the Prime Minister and the Minister of War, Navy, Home Affairs and Foreign Affairs, in their desire to improve relations with the United States.

Repeating his remarks, made on other occasions, that there was no question on this point, Mr. Hamilton pointed out that Secretary Hull in his oral statement of June 21, 1941 had cited evidence proving that important Japanese elements did not desire the policy of peace, which was the principal objective of the proposed "understanding". In view of this evidence, Secretary Hull desired to learn if Japan were willing to prevent these elements from crippling the effectiveness of a Japanese policy of peace.

Replying that Secretary Hull had previously mentioned this division in the Japanese government, Ambassador Nomura stated that though there might be rumors concerning a split in Japanese opinion, the Japanese government as a whole desired peace.[198]

(b) *Ambassador Nomura's Report.*[199]

Ambassador Nomura reported to Foreign Minister Matsuoka that he had sent his best wishes for a quick recovery to Secretary Hull who was recuperating at a summer resort away from Washington. On July 14, 1941 Mr. Hamilton had returned the visit of Ambassador Nomura to assure the Japanese Ambassador of Mr. Hull's gratitude for his kind thought. Ambassador

---

[196] II, 137.
[197] "Memorandum of a conversation", July 14, 1941, by Joseph W. Ballantine, *S.D.*, II, 505–506.
[198] *Ibid.*
[199] II, 139.

Nomura requested Mr. Hamilton to convey to Secretary Hull his assurances that all authorities in Japan, despite rumors to the contrary, were united in the hope that relations between Japan and the United States could be settled harmoniously.

Replying that Secretary Hull considered peace desirable between the United States and Japan, Mr. Hamilton hoped that Japan would not war against other countries. Ambassador Nomura then answered that the United States as well as Japan was obtaining military bases in other countries.[200]

51. Foreign Minister Matsuoka Condemns the Oral Statement and Attacks Ambassador Nomura (July 14, 1941).

On July 8, 1941 Foreign Minister Matsuoka had requested official confirmation of his belief that the oral statement presented by the United States on June 21, 1941 would not be included as an integral part of the proposal for an "understanding".[201]

Though he had received no reply from Ambassador Nomura as late as July 14, 1941 concerning his inquiry, Foreign Minister Matsuoka could no longer contain his indignation at the oral statement. Administering another severe rebuke to Ambassador Nomura, he called the oral statement a "detestable document",[202] whether or not it was intended to be included as part of the proposal for the "understanding".

Mr. Matsuoka objected to what he considered was an attempt by the United States to direct the affairs of Japan:

For one country to tell another totally independent power how its Government should be organized and criticize important elements in that Government and to suggest that this person or that person be eliminated, is unheard of. Under these circumstances, even if we would conclude this understanding, its result would be nil. I might say that it would be a mere phantasm. In the last paragraph just before the note there is something abominable written. They ask that we change the set-up of our Government and its attitude. Such a thing belongs to the realm of the fantastic. If my memory serves me rightly, during the summer of 1905, in connection with the Tangiers incident, the German Kaiser asked the French to banish Theophile Delcasse, but France did not listen, of course, and the incident was never settled harmoniously. A country can only tell its dependencies and protectorates such things as that. If you will carefully scrutinize this oral statement, you can well see that so far as the present government of Japan is concerned, it is enough to cause a rupture in the negotiations.[203]

Claiming that he had considered every angle of the present negotiations in the hopes of settling the current difficulties pleasantly and without harshness, Mr. Matsuoka indicated that the oral statement had disturbed him deeply.

Attacking Ambassador Nomura and some of his associates for maintaining views entirely at variance with the government of Japan, and insinuating that the Japanese Ambassador's opinions had been influenced by the United States, Mr. Matsuoka expressed himself as follows:

This Oral Statement: You, Sir, and your so-called fellow travellers, have an attitude which is entirely at variance with the attitude of our present Government and the horrible thing about it is that you have willingly allowed the United States to mold your opinions. Saddest of all, here in Japan you have a few adherents. For the representative of a country to directly oppose the Government he represents is almost unforgiveable and I know of no precedent for it in our history. For a representative of a given country to allow foreign leaders to influence him and for him, in turn, to try to influence his Government belongs not only to the realm of the preposterous, but also to that of base rudeness.[204]

---

[200] *Ibid.*
[201] II, 111.
[202] II, 140–143.
[203] II, 140.
[204] II, 141.

In explaining the delay in replying to the oral statement which had been in his hands for some time, Mr. Matsuoka claimed that he would have immediately expressed his resentment but for the fact that he wished to avoid offending the United States and had desired to bring the negotiations to a successful conclusion.

Reminding Ambassador Nomura that if Japan had presented a similar oral statement to the American government, the United States would have been very indignant, the Foreign Minister stated that it might be possible to adjust Japanese-American relations at some remote time in the future, but that "this sort of hideous document", standing like a shadow between the two nations, would be detrimental to mutual friendship.

Unless the United States rescinded the oral statement, Japan would not consider a plan for an "understanding", since it could not change its present cabinet. Mr. Matsuoka instructed Ambassador Nomura, therefore, to inform the American government that its oral statement was "extremely hateful to us", and without any delay to return the oral statement with the veto of the Japanese government and with the explanation that the long delay had occurred because of the wish of the Japanese not to hurt American feelings. Mr. Matsuoka then promised to send a revised proposal to Washington in a day or so.[205]

52. Foreign Minister Matsuoka Submits New Proposals (July 14, 1941).

Mr. Matsuoka finally sent to Ambassador Nomura a series of proposals, which had been discussed in Tokyo in secret conferences lasting for several days. Recognizing that many points of the American proposal differed from the suggestions of the Japanese, Mr. Matsuoka stated that they had finally decided upon a solution which was in keeping with the plans of the Japanese army.[206] He pointed out that they had decided to adopt several of the American clauses, despite their disagreement with them, but that some other clauses were not in conformity with the fundamental national policy of the Japanese and, therefore, were revised for reasons which he gave in detail.

In the clause outlining the attitude of America and Japan in regard to the European war, Mr. Matsuoka insisted on the retention of the principle that both nations would do their utmost to bring about international order by an early restoration of peace in Europe. He also suggested that in the phrase "assist in the bringing about of a settlement of the European war" there be inserted another phrase "at a fitting opportunity in the future" to make it easier for acceptance by the United States.

Analyzing the document, clause by clause and step by step, Mr. Matsuoka gave very detailed instructions to Ambassador Nomura. He insisted that the minutes of the negotiations should contain the repeated warnings of Japan that it did not approve the unfriendly actions of the United States against Germany.

As for the bringing about of peace between Japan and China, the Japanese claimed that it was hard to accept American provisions which drastically revised the gist of their original proposal. Indicating that the phrase "Chiang Regime" would be used instead of the title "Chungking Government" or the "Government of China", Japan wished merely to inform the United States that it earnestly desired to make peace with China, and that the intervention of the United States was requested. This did not mean that Japan wished an agreement with the United States concerning peace with China, since the China incident could not be decided by the intervention of any third country. Furthermore, the United States was to promise to stop assisting Generalissimo Chiang Kai-shek, if he would not listen to its request.

[205]II, 143.
[206]II, 144–152.

Concerning commerce between both countries, Japan accepted the American proposal but eliminated the American annex. As for economic activities of both countries in the "Pacific Area", Japan changed the latter phrase to "Southwestern Pacific", because that was where the need for cooperation was felt the most. In regard to the policy of both countries relating to the political stability of the Pacific area, Japan considered that the question of Philippine independence concerned the United States alone, though the independence of these islands and friendly treatment to Japanese residents should be guaranteed.[207]

An interesting sidelight on the reaction of certain Japanese diplomats to the comments of Mr. Matsuoka was found in a message from Mr. Terasaki, the Chief of the American Division of the Foreign Ministry at Tokyo, to Counselor Iguchi at Washington, in which he stated that both messages had been written by Foreign Minister Matsuoka himself.[208] Since the Foreign Minister had understood the American oral statement to mean that the United States was demanding a revision of the Japanese Cabinet, Mr. Terasaki suggested that Ambassador Nomura immediately send an explanation to offset this impression.[209]

53. Interview with Ambassador Nomura (July 15, 1941).

(a) *State Department's Report.*[210]

At the direction of the Secretary of State, Mr. Hamilton and Mr. Ballantine called on the Japanese Ambassador, on July 15, 1941, to discuss with him three points that had vital bearing on an amicable relationship between Japan and the United States. The first point concerned the oral statement given to Ambassador Nomura by Secretary Hull on June 21, 1941, and Mr. Hamilton expressed Mr. Hull's regrets that no reply had been made by the Japanese.

Ambassador Nomura responded that his letter of July 4, 1941 to Secretary Hull had been intended as an answer by his government to the American oral statement. Since the Japanese government was acting as a unit in spite of certain disagreements on policy, it felt that the United States should not question the attitude of individuals as had been done in Secretary Hull's proposal, since the suggested reconstruction of the Japanese cabinet amounted to an interference in Japan's internal affairs.

Immediately correcting what he believed to be a misinterpretation of the oral statement, Mr. Hamilton disclaimed any desire of the United States to interfere in the internal affairs of other countries. To clarify American aims, Mr. Hamilton said that the proposed understanding was based on a policy of peace. Because certain Japanese leaders obviously desired to support Nazi Germany in its movement for world conquest, it was necessary to know the attitude of the Japanese government as a whole.

Stating that his government was bound to an alliance with Germany and Italy, Ambassador Nomura replied that Japan, nevertheless, wished to pursue a course of peace. Declaring that his government had misunderstood the oral statement, the Japanese Ambassador admitted that his seventeen conferences with Secretary Hull had enabled him to understand fully the aims of the United States government. Mr. Hamilton then suggested that Ambassador Nomura explain these aims to his government to clarify all misunderstandings.

In connection with the second point, Mr. Hamilton asked about the recurrent rumors of Japan's plans to acquire naval and air bases in French Indo-China. Although without specific information from the Japanese government, Ambassador Nomura answered that Japan was

---

[207]II, 152.

[208]II, 153.

[209]*Ibid.*

[210]"Memorandum of a conversation", July 15, 1941, by Joseph W. Ballantine, *S.D.*, II, 506–509.

obliged to take precautionary measures against the encirclement being established by the alliance between China and Great Britain and by the increased aid of the United States to the Chungking government. Mentioning that if the United States were in Japan's place it would have acted earlier, the Japanese Ambassador pointed out that the military occupation of Iceland and the possibility of taking Dakar and the Azores were examples of American attempts to maintain their security. Mr. Hamilton reminded Ambassador Nomura that the overrunning of many countries by Germany provided sound reasons for these actions.

After discussing America's Good Neighbor Policy, which Ambassador Nomura admired and hoped that Japan would imitate, the conversation turned to the third and last point under discussion, Japan's obligations to the Axis under the Tripartite Pact. Expressing Japan's hopes that the United States would not enter the European conflict, Ambassador Nomura felt sure that there was nothing incompatible between the terms of the Tripartite Pact and the friendly relations of Japan and the United States. In the event of America's entering the war, Japan would have to use its own judgment whether the terms of Article III of the Tripartite Pact were applicable. The meeting then ended on the same note of cordiality that had been present throughout the entire conversation.

(b) *Ambassador Nomura's Report.*[211]

Ambassador Nomura reported that on the evening of July 15, 1941 Mr. Hamilton and Mr. Ballantine had called on him to inquire concerning the accuracy of information which indicated that Japan was planning to acquire naval and air bases in French Indo-China. (See Part C—(e) *Japanese-French Relations.*)

Ambassador Nomura replied that he knew nothing about these plans except what he had read in the newspapers, but in view of the assistance being given by both Britain and the United States to Chungking and the recent cooperation between the United States and Russia, Japan felt that it was being encircled. It was not surprising, therefore, that such rumors were current, especially since the United States had already occupied Iceland and was alleged to be seeking bases at Dakar and in the Azores. Ambassador Nomura promised, however, to present an official reply after he had an opportunity to consult his government.

The American representatives then asked whether or not, in addition to the Tripartite Pact, Japan had a special agreement with Germany and Italy whereby it would go to war against the United States in case the latter entered the European war. According to Ambassador Nomura, there was no such agreement, but in case the United States did enter the war, the duties specified in the third clause of the Tripartite Pact would come into effect. There was no need of asking Tokyo about these duties since all were acquainted with them. Japan was not able to tell at the moment whether everything the United States would do in the future could be considered self-defense, and for this reason, each movement would have to be considered individually. From the viewpoint of national defense, the United States was the safest of all countries, for there was little danger of invasion from Canada or Mexico. Pointing out that he had already discussed this situation with Secretary Hull, the Japanese Ambassador repeated his arguments about the much greater danger of invasion, as contrasted with the United States, which Japan was experiencing.[212]

---

[211] II, 154.
[212] *Ibid.*

54. Ambassador Grew Delivers an Oral Statement to the Japanese Foreign Office.

On July 16, 1941 the American Ambassador to Japan, Joseph C. Grew, handed an oral statement to the Japanese Vice Minister for Foreign Affairs, Chuichi Ohashi. This was a reply to the message sent to the President of the United States on July 7, 1941 by Prime Minister Fumimaro Konoye, who had asked if reports that the American government was planning to intervene in the European war were true.[213]

The oral statement declared that the policy of the United States was founded on the inalienable right of self-defense, and, benefiting from the experience of some fifteen countries in Europe which had been given categoric assurances by Germany that they would not be molested, the United States intended to employ any reasonable precaution necessary to ensure its present or future territorial integrity. Germany would be prevented from controlling the seas or obtaining any other strategic advantages which would directly threaten American security, for if the United States were to desist in any way from this basic policy, it would undoubtedly facilitate the aims of the aggressor nations to conquer the world by force.

55. Dissolution of the Japanese Cabinet (July 17, 1941).

On July 16, 1941 Mr. Matsuoka sent word to Washington that the Japanese Cabinet would have to resign. He ordered that the matter of the oral statement be attended to at once before the dissolution of the Cabinet took place.[214]

On the following day, July 17, 1941, Prime Minister Konoye and his whole Cabinet resigned. Emperor Hirohito accepted the resignations but asked Prime Minister Konoye to continue the administration of national affairs temporarily until he could select a successor.[215] However, the Japanese Emperor requested Prime Minister Konoye to form a new Cabinet, and though it was supposed that much totalitarian and military pressure had been at work to influence his selections, Prime Minister Konoye omitted Mr. Matsuoka.[216]

Admiral Teijiro Toyoda assumed the responsibilities of the Foreign Office on July 17, 1941, and Admiral Tsoroku Yamamoto replaced Mr. Ohashi as Vice Foreign Minister.

56. Mr. Wakasugi Confers with Mr. Hamilton (July 16, 1941).[217]

In the late afternoon of July 16, 1941, Mr. Wakasugi, the Japanese Minister, called to see Mr. Hamilton in regard to the conversation which had taken place between Ambassador Nomura, Mr. Hamilton and Mr. Ballantine on the preceding evening. Mr. Wakasugi stated that although both he and the Japanese Ambassador understood fully the terms of the agreement, his government had interpreted them as a mark of American interference in Japanese internal affairs. Because of the governmental crisis that had now arisen, the Ambassador deemed it advisable to return the oral statement which Secretary Hull had given him on June 21, 1941.

Since Secretary Hull had handed this document to Ambassador Nomura personnally, Mr. Hamilton expressed his disinclination to accept it without first receiving authorization directly from Mr. Hull. At this point, however, Mr. Hamilton took the opportunity of reiterating that the real purpose of the proposal was to establish peaceful relations between the two countries. Explaining further that the United States had no wish to interfere in the internal affairs

[213]"Oral Statement Handed by the American Ambassador in Japan (Grew) to the Japanese Vice Minister for Foreign Affairs (Ohashi)", July 16, 1941, *S.D.*, II, 509–510.

[214]II, 155.

[215]N.Y. *Times*, July 17, 1941; 1:5.

[216]N.Y. *Times*, July 19, 1941; 1:4.

[217]"Memorandum by the Chief of the Division of Far Eastern Affairs", Maxwell M. Hamilton, July 16, 1941, *S.D.*, II, 511–12.

of any government, Mr. Hamilton called for a copy of Secretary Hull's statement of July 16, 1937, and underlined the words, "We advocate abstinence by all nations ----- from interference in the internal affairs of other nations". Mr. Hamilton remarked that Secretary Hull's statement had summarized a fundamental principle which the United States had consistently adhered to in its dealings with all nations.

To Mr. Hamilton's suggestion that the Japanese Ambassador make a report embodying his own views of the oral statement, Mr. Wakasugi replied that this had already been done. Nevertheless, he requested the marked copy of Secretary Hull's statement for Ambassador Nomura. Stressing the urgency of the situation, Mr. Wakasugi also asked that Mr. Hamilton inform Secretary Hull as soon as possible. Mr. Hamilton agreed, but requested that the Japanese Ambassador not press the matter further until he had conferred with Mr. Hull.

57. Japanese Foreign Office Delivers Oral Statement to Ambassador Grew.

On July 17, 1941 Mr. Ohashi, the Japanese Vice Minister for Foreign Affairs, handed an oral statement to American Ambassador Grew, which acknowledged receipt of the American reply, dated July 16, 1941, to Prime Minister Konoye's letter of July 7, 1941.[218] Mr. Ohashi stated that the Japanese government did not intend to enter into a discussion concerning the points brought out in Ambassador Grew's letter, but it could not ignore the claims of the United States to invoke, without limitations, the right of self-defense. Neither could it concur with the indictment of Germany nor with the statement that those who urged the United States to desist from such a policy would be aiding aggressor nations.

58. Mr. Wakasugi Returns the American Oral Statement of June 21, 1941.

In accordance with the desire of the Japanese Ambassador to return the American oral statement of June 21, 1941, Mr. Wakasugi, the Japanese Minister, called on Mr. Hamilton on the afternoon of July 15, 1941.[219] Having now obtained permission to accept the document, Mr. Hamilton, reading a prepared statement in order to avoid any misunderstandings, received the oral statement in the name of Secretary Hull. He reminded Mr. Wakasugi that the oral statement was not, in itself, an official communication, but was simply a record of a statement voiced by Mr. Hull. Although both Ambassador Nomura and Mr. Wakasugi had professed to understand the true meaning of the document, though the Japanese government had not, Secretary Hull realized that retention of the statement might be a source of embarrassment.[220]

Emphasizing that the United States was concerned only with the policy of the Japanese government as a whole, Mr. Hamilton expressed the desire of his country to find in the attitude, utterances and acts of the Japanese government a sincere desire for peace. After expressing his appreciation for the attitude of the United States in regard to this matter, and assuring Mr. Hamilton that he understood fully American aims, Mr. Wakasugi returned the original copy of Secretary Hull's oral statement of June 21, 1941.

[218]"Oral Statement handed by the Japanese Vice Minister for Foreign Affairs (Ohashi) to the American Ambassador in Japan (Grew)", July 17, 1941, *S.D.*, II, 513.

[219]"Memorandum by the Chief of the Division of Far Eastern Affairs", July 17, 1941, *S.D.*, II, 513–514.

[220]"Statement by the Chief of the Division of Far Eastern Affairs (Hamilton) to the Japanese Minister (Wakasugi)", July 17, 1941, *S.D.*, II, 514.

59. Welles-Nomura Conversation (July 18, 1941).

(a) *Acting Secretary Welles' Report.* [221]

In the evening of July 18, 1941 Ambassador Nomura called on Mr. Sumner Welles to discuss Japan's isolation which had resulted from the closing of the trans-Siberian railroad. Under the Tripartite Pact, Germany could have rendered assistance to Japan as long as this communication line remained open, but the war with Russia had greatly altered this situation. However, with the cooperation of the United States Navy in the Pacific, the Japanese Ambassador felt certain that Japan would not be isolated.

When Mr. Welles questioned Ambassador Nomura regarding Japan's foreknowledge of the German attack upon Russia, he replied that neither Foreign Minister Matsuoka nor the Japanese government had been given any prior notification. The Acting Secretary of State then reminded Ambassador Nomura that without prior notice to Japan the German government had also entered into a non-aggression agreement with Russia shortly after Japan and Germany had signed an Anti-Communist Pact. This proved that a treaty with Chancellor Hitler was not worth the paper it was written on. According to Mr. Welles, the United States government would undertake negotiations only with a power that kept its obligations and regarded its words as sacred.

Ambassador Nomura then stated that he felt more sanguine with regard to the improvement of relations between the two countries under the new Japanese government, and had already asked for instructions in regard to the informal conversations with Secretary Hull. Both Mr. Welles and Ambassador Nomura expressed the common hope that no new developments would arise with the creation of a new Japanese Cabinet and that peace would be maintained in the Pacific.

(b) *Ambassador Nomura's Report.*

There is no report in the United States Communication Intelligence files concerning Ambassador Nomura's reactions to this conversation.

60. Mr. Wakasugi Explains the Nature of the Japanese-American Negotiations to Tokyo.

Believing that the Foreign Office in Tokyo had certain misconceptions concerning current Japanese-American negotiations, Mr. Wakasugi attempted to explain to his superiors in Japan the informal and unofficial character of the Hull-Nomura conversations. [222] Pointing out that the disturbance created in Tokyo by Ambassador Nomura's use of the word "associates", and the furor resulting from the American oral statement of June 21, 1941, gave evidence that Japanese authorities had received false impressions, Mr. Wakasugi asked that the new Foreign Minister be made aware that the negotiations in America were for the most part undercover operations without official sanction from either side. All the conversations were entirely "off the record" and were held away from the State Department, since it had been agreed that nothing official would be initiated until a common basis for an "understanding" could be reached. If no unanimity could be attained, the unofficial talks would be completely disregarded.

Mr. Wakasugi also reminded the Foreign Office that written memoranda did not constitute official negotiations, as was the impression in Tokyo. Admitting that the Japanese had used undercover methods in Washington, Mr. Wakasugi declared that though this was not a normal diplomatic procedure, it was the only course available under the circumstances.

---

[221] "Memorandum by the Acting Secretary of State", July 18, 1941, *S.D.*, II, 515–516.
[222] II, 156.

Summing up the situation in the light of actual events, Mr. Wakasugi agreed that no real advantage had accrued to the Japanese, and in view of the situation in China, Japanese representatives could not be very optimistic. Commenting that the Japanese representatives had done the best they could, even though the Foreign Office might be dissatisfied, Mr. Wakasugi remarked that it was now too late to retrace their steps; therefore, he requested further consideration.[223]

61. Ambassador Nomura Requests Instructions from the New Japanese Cabinet.

Ambassador Nomura informed Tokyo of his certainty that there had been no change in the fundamental Japanese policy of desiring to improve Japanese-American relations on a fair basis. However, he asked that his messages pertaining to the unofficial negotiations with Secretary Hull be studied so that instructions from the new cabinet might be sent to him.[224]

Remarking that he had studied carefully the instructions sent by the Foreign Office concerning the deletions, additions, and revisions which were to be made in the proposal for an "understanding", Ambassador Nomura pointed out that there were wide differences between the proposals of Japan and the United States. Furthermore, he expressed doubt that these new instructions (See Appendix II, No. 139) would help the negotiations.

Ambassador Nomura requested the Foreign Office to advise him of its views on two points: first, the attitudes of the two countries concerning the war in Europe, and second, the China incident. As for the first point, Ambassador Nomura claimed that President Roosevelt did not desire to announce at this time that Japan and the United States wished to mediate for peace in the European war. Reference in the proposal to this mediation would be deleted, therefore, and the phrase "encourage world peace" would be inserted. Ambassador Nomura believed that since a compromise had already been achieved, it would be disadvantageous to revive the question.

As to the rights of self-defense, the Japanese Ambassador believed that the United States desired to make the wording of this paragraph as elastic as possible so that it could be applied to any one of various possible developments in the European war. On the other hand, the Japanese could not permit such wide latitude in the interpretation of self-defense since a war could be begun in the name of self-defense. Ambassador Nomura suggested that it would be wise to compromise on some wording in the proposal which would prevent aggressive action, but which would permit self-defense. However, the interpretation of the United States was entirely unacceptable.

As for Part B of the proposal which pertained to the China incident, Ambassador Nomura reported that the Americans would not permit the deletion of the Annex on the grounds that if an agreement could not be reached concerning the contents of the Annex, there would be little use in discussing the actual proposal. Since the United States had been asked to advise China to negotiate peace, the Americans desired to be advised of the basis on which a peaceful settlement would be made.

Reporting that deletion of the Annex would mean the finish of the discussions, Ambassador Nomura advised that in future discussions of the Annex some troublesome questions would be forthcoming from the United States in regard to the stationing of anti-Communist troops and non-discrimination among Far Eastern business firms. He requested, therefore, that he be advised of the Foreign Office's views on these subjects. The Japanese Ambassador also warned that controversy was to be expected because of the Japanese deletion of the Annex relating to trade between the two countries. The granting of equal treatment in the Philippines to Japanese

---

[223]*Ibid.*
[224]II, 157.

residents, as well as to Filipinos, and the question of Japanese immigration to the United States were further difficulties foreseen by Ambassador Nomura.

Believing that both Americans and Japanese could find a way to agree on the interpretation of self-defense, Ambassador Nomura reported to his superiors that the garrisoning of Japanese troops in China to combat Communism would be very difficult for the Americans to accept. As for the occupation of French Indo-China, Ambassador Nomura reported that a peaceful penetration would not disturb American public opinion, but a resort to military force would bring the negotiations to an end.

Ambassador Nomura reported that Secretary Hull was expected back in Washington in the near future, and that he himself had accepted an invitation to visit Admiral Pratt's home in Maine.[225]

62. Ambassador Nomura Visits Rear Admiral Richard K. Turner.[226]

After first attempting to contact Admiral Stark and possibly Admiral Ingersoll, Ambassador Nomura called on Admiral Richard K. Turner, on July 20, 1941, to discuss with him certain points that needed to be clarified before any peaceful relationship between the United States and Japan could be based on a sound foundation. Insisting that he was not a trained diplomat and had accepted the post only at the insistence of high ranking naval and the more conservative groups of army officers, he nevertheless realized that the difficulties existing between the United States and Japan must be eliminated satisfactorily or a devastating naval war would ensue.

After numerous conferences with Mr. Hull, the Ambassador was convinced that a perfect concord was impossible, and that because of Japan's commitments to Germany, any agreement reached would have to be informal. He insisted, however, that the treaty with Germany would in no way restrain his country from acting according to its own convictions and for its own ultimate purposes.

Continuing then a discussion of the points which Japan considered essential for an agreement with the United States, Ambassador Nomura mentioned the right of either power to take the necessary steps to ensure self-defense as the basic principle for such a proposal. Using the export restrictions imposed on Japan as an example, the Ambassador pointed out that his country's economic position was now extremely unfavorable, and uninterrupted access to certain raw materials would be indispensable to its correction.

A second point causing friction between the two countries, according to Ambassador Nomura, was the increased support given to the Chungking regime by both the United States and Great Britain. The Japanese government attributed the continuation of the China incident to the constant supply of pilots and planes, and the assistance in the improvement of the Burma Road which America and Britain were continuing.

Since Japan considered the stationing of troops in Inner Mongolia for the suppression of the Chinese Communists in that region essential to the maintenance of its own security, the Japanese Ambassador included this as his third and last point.

Although anticipating an intensified American press campaign against Japan as the result of the action in French Indo-China, Ambassador Nomura informed Admiral Turner that within the next few days Japan would occupy French Indo-China purely as a precautionary measure. From his manner, it was evident that the Japanese Ambassador feared that the United States would make further military or economic moves as a result of this action. However, as a conciliatory

---

[225] *Ibid.*

[226] "The Director of the War Plans Division of the Navy Department (Rear Admiral Richard K. Turner) to the Chief of Naval Operations (Admiral Stark)", July 21, 1941, *S.D.*, II, 516–520.

measure, Ambassador Nomura suggested that were America to accept the conditions he had discussed, the Japanese would not take part in Atlantic warfare.

Promising to pass this information on to Admiral Stark, Admiral Turner, commenting briefly on the Japanese Ambassador's disclosure of Tokyo's plan to seize French Indo-China, explained that the security of America was largely dependent upon Great Britain, for, if that country were to collapse to the German military power, Nazism would be able to direct its ambitions toward the Western Hemisphere. The occupation of Indo-China by the Japanese would threaten the British position in Singapore and the Dutch position in the Netherlands East Indies, and it would also strike a severe blow at the integrity of the defense of the British Isles. From the military standpoint then, the United States was interested in sustaining the *status quo* in the southern portion of the Far East. Admiral Turner further indicated that though the Japanese actually had nothing to fear from the English, Americans or Dutch in these regions, if faced with German power, their problem would be great.

Since his government was collaborating with the Axis nations at this time, Ambassador Nomura felt bound to support their policies, and he ended the meeting with a request for permission to discuss these same matters with Admiral Stark in the near future.

63. Mr. Wakasugi Visits Acting Secretary of State Welles.

(a) *Acting Secretary Welles' Report.*[227]

At the request of Mr. Welles, and in the absence of the Japanese Ambassador from Washington, Mr. Wakasugi called for further discussion of the topics introduced in the informal conversations of Secretary Hull and Ambassador Nomura. After first assuring the Japanese Minister that he was authorized to express the views of Secretary Hull, Mr. Welles stated that the objective of these talks was the maintenance of peace in the Pacific by the abandonment of the policies of force or conquest by all nations in this area.

Recalling both Secretary Hull's and his own reiterated expositions of American basic policies, Mr. Welles insisted that the principles of his government would not permit it to aid in the encirclement which Japan feared. From various sources, however, (See Part C—(g) *Japanese-French Relations*) Mr. Welles had learned that Japan planned to occupy Indo-China in the near future as a precautionary and defensive step against this so-called threat to her security. Since such a move would be at variance with any agreement between the United States and Japan, the Acting Secretary of State felt free to ask frankly the intentions of Mr. Wakasugi's government.

It was realized that the installation of a new government in Japan had somewhat delayed the clarification of Japanese policies with regard to the Pacific, and the United States would be patient until Japanese public opinion would permit the carrying out of a new policy. The seizure of French Indo-China, however, would force all other nations to reconsider their positions.

In reply, Mr. Wakasugi stated that the Japanese Embassy had received no information concerning Japan's intention to seize Indo-China. (See Part C—(g) *Japanese-French Relations* for information which casts doubts on the accuracy of this statement.) With regard to the new Japanese government, he agreed with Mr. Welles' belief that since Foreign Minister Toyoda was in close accord with the attitude of Ambassador Nomura toward the United States, friendlier relations between the two countries should be achieved. Realizing from Mr. Welles' statements that the occupation of French Indo-China would seriously endanger such a goal, Mr. Wakasugi promised to convey this information to Ambassador Nomura immediately so that he could return to Washington to discuss the matter personally.

---

[227]"Memorandum by the Acting Secretary of State", July 21, 1941, *S.D.*, II, 520–522.

(b) *Ambassador Nomura's Report.*[228]

According to Ambassador Nomura's report of Mr. Wakasugi's visit on July 21, 1941, the Acting Secretary of State said that he had given careful study to recent world conditions, and, in the light of these developments, he wished to express the opinions reached by Secretary Hull and himself regarding the unofficial discussions which had been taking place between Ambassador Nomura and Secretary Hull. Though the objectives of the Japanese representatives were identical with those towards which Secretary Hull was striving, the United States had received definite information from various sources that Japan was planning to disturb the peaceful status of certain areas. Such actions would conflict with the views expressed by the Japanese Ambassador during all the conversations.

Quoting a statement of Ambassador Nomura in which he said that Britain, the United States and other nations were pressing Japan in an "encirclement", Mr. Welles indicated that such an expression was similar to the former complaints of Germany. Mr. Welles assured Mr. Wakasugi that Japan misunderstood the United States since the American government had no intention of encircling Japan, and was continuing the talks between Ambassador Nomura and Secretary Hull solely because of its desire to maintain peace. Mr. Welles informed Mr. Wakasugi that if Japan seized the southern portion of French Indo-China within the next few days, as his information indicated, such an act would definitely violate the spirit of the current Japanese-United States conversations which were being held to ensure peace in the Pacific. Mr. Welles then asked that he be advised of the Japanese viewpoint in this regard.

Mr. Wakasugi replied that he was aware that the present conversations were designed to improve Japanese-United States relations and that he was hopeful of their success. He asked if the "reliable source of information" mentioned by Mr. Welles referred to the United States Embassy in Japan. According to Ambassador Nomura, Mr. Welles avoided a clear answer but made a reply that the report was an accurate one. (See Part C—(g) *Japanese-French Relations* of this volume for the source of Mr. Welles' information.)

Mr. Wakasugi stated that he would report the matter to Ambassador Nomura, and in the meantime, requested permission to make an informal inquiry concerning the possible effect on the Japanese-United States conversations of Japan's planning to make a move into French Indo-China. Mr. Welles replied that such an act would truly violate the spirit of the discussions, and implied that further conversations would be in vain. However, Mr. Welles pointed out that the new Foreign Minister of Japan was a close friend of Ambassador Nomura, and moreover, since the new Cabinet had just taken over, it probably had not decided upon a definite policy as yet. The United States would await developments, therefore, before ending the discussions with the Japanese Ambassador.

Mr. Wakasugi promised to report immediately the details of this conversation to Ambassador Nomura, and then withdrew.[229]

64. Welles-Nomura Conversation (July 23, 1941).

(a) *Acting Secretary Welles' Report.*[230]

Two days after the conversation between Mr. Wakasugi and Mr. Welles had taken place, the Japanese Ambassador called on the Acting Secretary of State to discuss the prospective Japanese occupation of French Indo-China. Claiming to be not officially informed, Ambassador Nomura stated that he had learned from press reports that the Japanese government had con-

---

[228]II, 158.
[229]*Ibid.*
[230]"Memorandum by the Acting Secretary of State", July 23, 1941, *S.D.*, II, 522–526.

cluded an agreement with Vichy to send military forces to occupy certain portions of southern Indo-China. (See Appendix II, 819–821, 860)

Stressing the critical economic situation of Japan, especially with regard to such raw material as food supplies and fertilizer, Ambassador Nomura pointed out that deGaullist French agents and Chinese agitators were endangering the flow of goods from these territories to Japan. This was his government's main reason for taking action in that area. The second reason arose from the policies of certain foreign powers who seemed bent on destroying the military security of Japan.

Recognizing the hostile attitude of the press and the American public as a whole toward these recent developments, the Japanese Ambassador still hoped that the government itself would not "reach hasty conclusions", since any retaliatory measures, such as restricting oil exports to Japan, would only inflame Japanese public opinion. If given a little time to express its policies more clearly, Ambassador Nomura felt certain that the new Japanese Cabinet would reach a satisfactory agreement with the United States in spite of the opposition of "third powers".

Mr. Welles replied to Ambassador Nomura, as he had done to Mr. Wakasugi, that the policy the Japanese government was about to pursue was diametrically opposed to the one discussed in the informal conversations with Secretary Hull. He then took up the reasons which Ambassador Nomura had offered in explanation for the approaching action of his country, and refuted them one by one.

First, since any agreement reached with Vichy France must have resulted from pressure brought to bear on that government by Berlin, America could only regard such an agreement as Japan's offering assistance to Chancellor Hitler in his policy of world conquest. Secondly, with regard to Japan's need of raw materials, Mr. Wells was sure that the Japanese Ambassador realized that any satisfactory proposal reached between the two countries would have been predicated on equal economic opportunity and economic security for Japan, as well as other countries concerned in the Pacific. Therefore, the need for military precaution to prevent encirclement could not be regarded as a valid reason for Japan's aggressive steps. Furthermore, Mr. Welles felt certain that neither the governments of Great Britain, the Netherlands, nor even that of China constituted a menace to Japanese interests in the Pacific.

Passing over the activities of Chinese agitators and deGaullist sympathizers as not worthy of mention, Mr. Welles insisted that his government could see no reason for Japan's occupation of French Indo-China other than for purposes of an offensive in the South Seas area. If this were so, the following Japanese purposes which were detrimental to the United States could not be ignored: first, the Japanese government intended to pursue a course of force and conquest, and second, in occupying French Indo-China it was taking the last step before seizing additional territories in the South Seas.

In view of these intentions of Japan, further conversation between representatives of the two countries seemed to be baseless. However, the United States government was still willing to attempt the settlement of this question peacefully and would continue to show the utmost patience in its dealings with Japan. Ambassador Nomura agreed that such had been the stand of American representatives throughout these meetings.

Not attempting to place the blame on either country, the Japanese Ambassador felt, nevertheless, that the procrastination which had prevented these talks from reaching a successful conclusion was largely responsible for Japan's present action. Promising to report this discussion to Tokyo, the Japanese Ambassador parted from Mr. Welles with the intention of discussing the matter further with Secretary Hull, who was to return to Washington in the near future.

(b) *Ambassador Nomura's Report.*[231]

Ambassador Nomura informed Tokyo that he had called on Acting Secretary of State Welles, on the afternoon of July 23, 1941, to explain that Japan's occupation of French Indo-China was essential to its national security and economic safety. Furthermore, he explained that Japan was forced to act in face of embargoes which were being imposed by various countries. Since Japanese penetration of French Indo-China was being carried out peacefully, and with the full approval of the Vichy government, Ambassador Nomura hoped that the United States would not move hastily and would wait for further developments since an export embargo on oil for Japan would greatly disturb the Japanese people. According to Ambassador Nomura, the new Japanese Cabinet was anxious to bring the Japanese-United States conversations to a successful conclusion.

Mr. Welles replied that he could not reconcile the Japanese policy in French Indo-China with the basic principles of the plans under discussion by Secretary Hull and Ambassador Nomura. Since neither Great Britain nor the United States intended to attack French Indo-China, it was felt that Vichy had submitted as a result of Hitler's pressure, and that Japan intended to use French Indo-China as a base for further southward moves. Moreover, the United States was not making any hasty conclusions since its actions would simply reflect Japan's policies.

In answer to an inquiry from Ambassador Nomura, Acting Secretary Welles said that the Panama Canal had been indefinitely closed for repairs and no particular nation was suffering discriminatory action. Mr. Welles reported that Secretary Hull would return to duty very shortly and would discuss the situation with Ambassador Nomura.[232]

65. Tokyo Informs Ambassador Nomura that Japan Will Occupy Part of French Indo-China.

On July 23, 1941 Foreign Minister Toyoda informed Ambassaor Nomura that Japan had come to an agreement with the Vichy government concerning the joint defense of French Indo-China. Japanese occupation would take place in the southern part of French Indo-China on or about July 28 or 29, 1941.[233]

Ambassador Nomura was instructed to inform the United States that the territorial sovereignty of French Indo-China would be respected and there would be no interference in the domestic administration of French Indo-China. Furthermore, Japan was definitely interested in the Hull-Nomura discussions and was making this report to the United States about French Indo-China merely because it desired to reach an "understanding" with the United States.[234]

Foreign Minister Toyoda informed Ambassador Nomura that he had not yet decided on a definite foreign policy because of his having accepted his post only recently. He explained that the occupation of French Indo-China was unavoidable since it had been decided by the Japanese Cabinet before he assumed office, and was designed to be carried out peacefully for joint defense of French Indo-China. Though he intended to try to decrease friction between Japan and the English speaking powers, Admiral Toyoda warned that certain actions by the United States, such as freezing of assets, would create a very critical situation.[235]

---

[231]II, 159.

[232]*Ibid.*

[233]II, 160.

[234]*Ibid.*

[235]II, 161.

66. Details of the Secret Japanese-French Agreement.

Tokyo sent advance warning to Ambassador Nomura that a statement concerning French Indo-China would be issued at noon of July 26, 1941, Tokyo time (10:00 P.M. Washington time).[236] The statement would stress Japan's interest in the joint defense of French Indo-China and the friendly relations existing between France and Japan.[237]

The details of Japanese procedure in this instance were of great importance, for the knowledge of the contents of these secret reports to Ambassador Nomura gave American State Department officials an intimate understanding of the Far Eastern situation. (See Part C—Section (g) *Japanese-French Relations*.)

According to previous reports from Tokyo, Japanese Ambassador Kato had interviewed Foreign Minister Darlan in Vichy, and had presented to him Japanese demands concerning joint protection and military cooperation in French Indo-China. A reply was requested from the French by July 19, 1941. Ambassador Kato then interviewed Marshal Petain on July 15, 1941 and Admiral Darlan on July 16, 1941, and on both occasions he requested an immediate reply from Vichy.

On July 19, 1941, Foreign Minister Darlan replied to Ambassador Kato that Japan's demands would require consultation with Germany since France had an armistic agreement with the latter and was not in a position to make a decision alone. The Japanese considered this to be a pretext, and on July 20, 1941, Ambassador Kato returned to Admiral Darlan and demanded that all of the Japanese proposals be accepted immediately. Afterwards, the Japanese Ambassador conversed with another French official and discovered that France was inclined to accept the demands.

On the following day, July 21, 1941, Foreign Minister Darlan made an official reply:

(1) The French government cannot but submit to the demands of the Japanese government.

(2) The French government guarantees joint defense of French Indo-China on the basis of cooperation with the Japanese government; however, she will not participate in aggressive war.

(3) As soon as informed of the locales wherein Japanese troops will be stationed, France will evacuate them.

(4) The Japanese government will make public a declaration that she will respect the territorial integrity of Indo-China and French sovereignty over the Indo-Chinese Federation, and will make this statement at the earliest possible moment.[238]

According to the secret report from Tokyo, Admiral Darlan had used the phrase "cannot but submit to the demands of the Japanese government" to avoid criticism from the French both at home and abroad. The Vichy Foreign Minister also stipulated that Japan must not demand the retirement of French Indo-Chinese troops nor confiscate the material the French troops were using. If the Vichy government were to order French troops to be withdrawn from the areas in which they were stationed, unfortunate incidents would probably ensue because of the troops' displeasure with the order.

Ambassador Kato received the Vichy reply as an acceptance of all the Japanese demands. He handed Foreign Minister Darlan a prepared memorandum of acceptance and asked that the treaty be inscribed as an official document, whereupon he handed Admiral Darlan a proposal and a suggested text for a public statement. The French in turn offered several points, which were included in the correspondence, as follows:

(1) Support on the part of the Japanese government for supplementary defensive measures of the French Indo-China troops.

(2) Continued use of the existent military facilities by the French Indo-Chinese forces.

(3) A statement as early as possible from the Imperial government to the effect that the territorial integrity of French Indo-China and French sovereignty will be respected.

[236]II, 162–163.
[237]II, 164.
[238]II, 165.

(4) The term concerning the temporary evacuation of French Indo-Chinese troops shall be eliminated.[239]

The work on the correspondence was finished on July 22, and on July 23, 1941, in the presence of Rear Admiral Sumita and Governor General Jean Decoux, an agreement was signed at Hanoi. The Japanese army was scheduled to enter southern French Indo-China on July 28 and 29, 1941.[240]

67. Tokyo Assures the United States of Its Peaceful Intentions Despite the Occupation of French Indo-China.

Foreign Minister Toyoda continued to assure Ambassador Nomura that the occupation of French Indo-China was not intended as a blow to the current Japanese-American conversations. Stating that the recent occupation had been a matter of necessity for the maintenance of peace in the Pacific, and claiming that Japan's peaceful attitude was evident from its patience during the long drawn-out negotiations with French Indo-China, Foreign Minister Toyoda denied an American allegation that Japan had assured its Axis partners that the Japanese-American conversations would last only until Japan had completed its southward movement.

He denied also that Japan intended to wreck the conversations, for he insisted that the Japanese government had become united and was very anxious that the discussions be continued. He directed Ambassador Nomura to explain immediately to the United States Japan's real intentions in regard to French Indo-China.[241]

In another dispatch, Foreign Minister Toyoda expressed his hope that both the leaders of the United States and Japan would display a high degree of statesmanship in maintaining peace in the Pacific. However, the possibility that the United States would freeze Japanese funds or institute a general embargo on petroleum would have an adverse effect on many aspects of Japanese life, and would compel Japan to resort to retaliation. This would lead to a collapse of Japanese-American economic relations and would probably hasten the development of war. Instructions were issued to Ambassador Nomura, therefore, to confer with his financial adviser in requesting the United States to give favorable consideration to these economic factors.[242]

A message from the Japanese Financial Ministry to its representative in America ordered him to cooperate with Ambassador Nomura in expressing Japanese appreciation to American authorities for the exemption of Japan from the general freezing of assets which had been applied to Germany and Italy.[243] However, since rumors relating to the freezing of Japanese assets had arisen, Japan announced that it would be forced to take retaliatory measures, if necessary, by refusing to pay the principal and interest on debts in the United States, as well as by freezing all American property in Japan. The Financial Ministry's representative was instructed to urge American Treasury Department officials to give deep consideration to this matter so that through cooperation Japanese-United States relations would be prevented from becoming worse.[244]

---

[239]II, 166.
[240]II, *Ibid.*
[241]II, 167.
[242]II, 168.
[243]II, 169.
[244]II, *Ibid.*

68. Roosevelt-Nomura Conversations (July 24, 1941).

(a) *Acting Secretary Welles' Report.* [245]

At the request of the Japanese Ambassador a secret meeting with President Roosevelt was held with both Mr. Welles and Admiral Stark present to discuss the effect of Japan's plan to occupy French Indo-China. To explain more clearly his government's position, President Roosevelt referred to a conference held that morning with a home defense group under the leadership of Mayor La Guardia in which the vast quantity of oil exported to Japan was the main topic under discussion. Realizing that the restriction of oil supplies would have furnished the Japanese with an incentive to move down upon the Netherlands East Indies, the United States government had continued its export even during the past two years when America's home supply was fast diminishing. Notwithstanding the criticism that had been leveled against the administration for aiding a country that gave every indication of pursuing a policy of force and conquest, the shipments of oil had been continued. If Japan now attempted to seize oil supplies in the Netherlands East Indies, President Roosevelt stated that the Dutch aided by the British, would resist. America's policy would be one of assistance to Great Britain, thereby causing an extremely complicated and serious international situation.

Reiterating Mr. Welles' assertion that Japan had far more to gain by a peaceful agreement with the United States, President Roosevelt pointed out that not only would the Japanese obtain larger quantities of necessary supplies by this means than they could by force, but they would do so without the tremendous expenses of military occupation. Expressing his disbelief that Great Britain, the Netherlands Indies or China had designs on Japan, President Roosevelt felt forced to say that his government could only assume that Japan's purpose was one of offense rather than defense.

When the Japanese Ambassador expressed his own personal disagreement with this plan of his government, and with the understanding that the new Foreign Minister, Admiral Toyoda, was in agreement with Ambassador Nomura's views on many matters, President Roosevelt proposed a last-minute plan for stopping the aggression. If the Japanese government would withdraw its forces, President Roosevelt promised to obtain an agreement from Great Britain, the Netherlands and China to regard Indo-China as a neutralized country, thereby assuring Japan of the raw materials which she was seeking to secure. Furthermore, President Roosevelt would endeavor to procure a binding guarantee from the pertinent powers not to dislodge the Vichy French agents in that area.

Although promising to pass this proposal on to Tokyo, Ambassador Nomura was not overly optimistic for he indicated that such a step would be difficult because of the face-saving element involved.

Concluding his remarks with the opinion of the United States government that Japan's present policies were largely dominated by Germany, President Roosevelt reminded the Japanese Ambassador that Nazism constituted as grave a danger to the Far East as it did to Europe and the Western Hemisphere, since he believed that Chancellor Hitler was bound on world conquest. In view of this, America and Japan in cooperating with one another would be facing a common enemy. However, Ambassador Nomura denied President Roosevelt's allegation that Japan was under the influence of Germany and was not acting strictly in pursuit of her own policies.

---

[245] II, "Memorandum by the Acting Secretary of State", July 24, 1941, *S.D.*, II, 527–530.

(b) *Ambassador Nomura's Report.*[246]

Ambassador Nomura reported that because of the urgency of the current diplomatic situation he had asked the Chief of Naval Operations, Admiral Harold R. Stark, to request a personal conference with President Roosevelt. This secret meeting had taken place at 5:00 P.M., July 24, 1941, in the company of Acting Secretary Welles and Admiral Stark.

In conformity with the instructions from the Foreign Minister, Ambassador Nomura had explained that the occupation of French Indo-China had taken place because of economic considerations and in view of the necessity of stabilizing that area. Pointing to Japan's intentions to respect French Indo-China's territorial sovereignty, he repeated that the present Japanese Cabinet was eager for a Japanese-American "understanding" in order to maintain peace in the Pacific.

President Roosevelt replied that the American people had been insisting on an oil embargo against Japan, but he had opposed this in order to keep peace in the Pacific. In view of the present situation, however, President Roosevelt hinted that an embargo on oil was imminent. Mr. Roosevelt also remarked that if there were some method whereby French Indo-China could be evacuated, with the various countries concerned guaranteeing its neutrality so that all could have free access to raw materials in that territory, he would spare no effort to bring about an "understanding" since he was extremely sympathetic toward Japan's need of materials.[247]

On the following day, July 25, 1941, Ambassador Nomura sent a more complete report concerning the same meeting.[248] President Roosevelt had said that Chancellor Hitler's aim was subjugation of the world, and Ambassador Nomura reported that Mr. Roosevelt had made the same remark on a previous occasion (March 14, 1941) when his statement had been corroborated by Secretary Hull. According to President Roosevelt, when Chancellor Hitler had finished with Europe he would conquer Africa, and after that there would be no stopping him. Japan would eventually be fighting on the same side of the United States.

Quoting an old Japanese proverb which stated that "if a country likes to fight, it is already on the brink of being destroyed", Ambassador Nomura advised President Roosevelt that there had been no German pressure on Japan, and that his country had acted entirely on its own in occupying French Indo-China. Though President Roosevelt had apparently accepted this explanation, Ambassador Nomura warned his superiors that the American President and public were convinced that Japan, either in cooperation with Germany or independently, was awaiting an opportunity to move both southward and northward.[249]

Two days later, on July 27, 1941, Ambassador Nomura received instructions from his Foreign Minister to report his conversation of July 24, 1941 with President Roosevelt in even further detail.[250] Accordingly, Ambassador Nomura sent a long report giving some minutiae of this historic meeting. During the interview with President Roosevelt, Ambassador Nomura had held a memorandum prepared in Japanese, though he had conversed with Mr. Roosevelt in English, in which he had been carefully coached by Mr. Obata before the visit.

He had explained to President Roosevelt that the reasons for the occupation of French Indo-China by Japan were: first, to obtain foodstuffs which were necessary for the economic existence of Japan, and to avoid being crushed by the economic measures of other nations which

---

[246]II, 170.
[247]II, 171.
[248]II, 172.
[249]*Ibid.*
[250]II, 173.

would be imposed if Japan stood idly by; second, for reasons of Japanese national security, since Japan would be in danger if French Indo-China came under the influence of a third country; therefore, a joint defense was planned to stabilize peaceful relations; third, the occupation would take place peaceably, and since Japan would respect French Indo-China's territorial integrity and sovereignty, it would be desirable that the United States not take an extreme attitude.[251]

Ambassador Nomura expressed his regret that the United States doubted the sincerity of Japan, and emphasizing the Japanese government's desire to reach an "understanding" with the United States, he stated that the new Japanese Cabinet had twice issued instructions concerning this objective.

Admitting that the interpretation of the United States in regard to self-defense was a difficulty in the present discussions, Ambassador Nomura hoped that a compromise would be achieved and that a definite decision as to what constituted exercise of the right of self-defense could be decided after an "understanding" had been reached.

To confirm his opinion that all difficulties between the United States and Japan would eventually settle themselves, Ambassador Nomura remarked that the stationing of troops in China was not permanent and would be dealt with as part of an agreement with the Chinese government. Freedom of commerce would be achieved by a spontaneous settlement.[252]

According to Ambassador Nomura, President Roosevelt replied that demands for an oil embargo against Japan had been extensive but that he had toned them down because he wished to keep peace in the Pacific. Proclaiming his sympathy for Japan's needs for raw materials, President Roosevelt expressed his disapproval of the occupation of French Indo-China.

Stating that he had not conferred with the State Department on his next suggestion, President Roosevelt remarked that if Japan evacuated its troops from French Indo-China he would spare no efforts to have the various countries concerned guarantee the neutrality of French Indo-China and assure an equitable share of the raw materials in that area for all nations. Ambassador Nomura then discussed these points with President Roosevelt, who, after confirming them, turned to Acting Secretary Welles for comment, but the latter "maintaining a humble attitude" said nothing.[253] President Roosevelt at this point took out his cigarette case and offered it only to Ambassador Nomura.

Ambassador Nomura explained to his Foreign Minister that the evacuation of troops which President Roosevelt suggested was strange in one sense but not so strange in another sense, for it confirmed the American Good Neighbor policy in which military power was not used. Pointing out that the avoidance of military power and the principle of non-discriminatory freedom of trade were two points with which both President Roosevelt and Secretary of State Hull were much concerned, Ambassador Nomura commented on the success of such a policy in President Roosevelt's dealings with Latin American countries.

To President Roosevelt's accusation that the recent southern advance of Japan was a result of German pressure, Ambassador Nomura explained that Japan had acted solely on its own initiative. Seemingly, Mr. Roosevelt was not convinced by Ambassador Nomura's arguments.[254] Expressing his determination to improve Japanese-American relations, which according to President Roosevelt were deteriorating, Ambassador Nomura stated that although he had not yet been successful, he would not give up his intention to carry on to the end.

---

[251]II, 174.

[252]II, 175–176.

[253]II, 177.

[254]II, 178.

President Roosevelt declared that Hitler was determined to conquer the world and that after he had finished with Europe, he would conquer Africa and continue his attacks, not knowing when to stop. Thus, ten years from this time, Japan would fight on the same side with America against Germany. Ambassador Nomura had answered that those who take the sword would fall by the sword and that Japan was not going to use the sword.[255]

69. Mr. Wakasugi Confers with Mr. Hamilton (July 25, 1941).

Ambassador Nomura reported that he had sent Mr. Wakasugi to deliver to Mr. Hamilton a copy of the English text of a statement concerning the Japanese occupation of French Indo-China, which was to be published on July 26, 1941 by the Japanese government.[256] Mr. Wakasugi indicated that Japanese occupation would not affect the sovereignty and integrity of French Indo-China, nor would Japan meddle in the domestic politics of that country. Mr. Wakasugi also handed to Mr. Hamilton a note concerning the halting of traffic through the Panama Canal.

An unofficial discussion then arose concerning Japanese-United States relations, and both men expressed opinions on the possibility of counteracting the unfavorable trend of the current discussions. Remarking that Secretary Hull had worked very hard to maintain friendly relations with Japan in spite of much protest from the American people as well as from his Cabinet colleagues, Mr. Hamilton said that both President Roosevelt and Secretary Hull were convinced that Japan would profit not from the use of arms, but from a policy of peace. In any event, an expansion program of Japan similar to Chancellor Hitler's would make it impossible to continue the unofficial Japanese-United States discussions for peace.[257]

70. Ambassador Nomura's Relations with Admiral Stark, U.S.N.

Ambassador Nomura reported to Foreign Minister Toyoda, a former admiral of the Japanese Navy, that Admiral Stark, Chief of Naval Operations, had extended many courtesies to him ever since he had assumed his position as Japanese Ambassador in Washington. Ambassador Nomura believed that Admiral Pratt had spoken favorably concerning him to Admiral Stark. Both Ambassador Nomura and Admiral Stark agreed that peace was desirable, since the only result of a war between Japan and the United States would be mutual exhaustion.

In one of his conversations with Admiral Stark, Ambassador Nomura had commented on the excellent character and qualifications of some of the higher officials in the Navy Department. Ambassador Nomura requested that the following reply of Admiral Stark be relayed to Japanese Naval officials:

> To this, the Admiral replied that both the Assistant to the Chief of Naval Operations and the Director of War Plans were exceedingly able men. The same is true of the Chief of the Bureau of Aeronautics. As for the fleets, he continued, both Kimmel and King were recommended by him, and both are of the highest caliber. Although Hart had reached the age of retirement, he had been kept on inactive duty because of the critical times, he added.[258]

---

[255]*Ibid.*

[256]II, 179; "Memorandum by the Chief of the Division of Far Eastern Affairs (Hamilton)", July 25, 1941, *S.D.*, II, 265–266.

[257]*Ibid.*

[258]II, 180.

71. Japanese-American Conversation.

(a) *State Department Report.*[259]

On the day following Ambassador Nomura's conversation with President Roosevelt, Colonel Iwakuro and Mr. Wikawa invited Mr. Ballantine for lunch to clear up some of the details regarding the new rift in Japanese-American relations. Expressing his regret at recent developments, Colonel Iwakuro informed Mr. Ballantine that the question of Japanese occupation of bases in Indo-China had been raised before he had left for the United States. Though the basis for previous conversations had been to prevent this southward advance, the delay in reaching any understanding had caused officials in the Japanese government, though not its representatives in the United States, to doubt the sincerity of America's intentions. Pointing to Great Britain's recent embargo on rice exported from Burma to Japan and to the deGaullists activities, which threatened Japan's market in southern Indo-China, Colonel Iwakuro insisted that Japan was forced to make a precautionary move.

Although hoping to resume the informal meetings, Colonel Iwakuro assured Mr. Ballantine that they would not influence Japan to reverse its position in the Indo-China situation; nor, would they serve to prevent Japan from moving into Malaya and the Dutch East Indies, as it would be forced to do if further essential supplies were cut off, or if its assets were frozen by the United States. Colonel Iwakuro insisted that the American occupation of Iceland paralleled the Japanese occupation of French Indo-China.

Declining to modify in any way the attitude of the United States concerning Japanese aggression, Mr. Ballantine countered Colonel Iwakuro's charge concerning the American occupation of Iceland by stating that the country was independent, and that its Parliament possessed full constitutional authority to enter into agreements with foreign countries. To the suggestion that America had been influenced by the propaganda of powers interested in preventing the establishment of friendly relations between the United States and Japan, Mr. Ballantine replied that the United States had accumulated evidence that important elements in the Japanese government supported Chancellor Hitler's movement toward world conquest.

The meeting ended cordially, but with little actual optimism by either country's representatives concerning the value of future conversations.

(b) *Ambassador Nomura's Report.*

There is no record available concerning a Japanese report from Washington in regard to this conversation (DoD comment).

72. Ambassador Nomura Decides to Send Mr. Wakasugi and Colonel Iwakuro to Japan.

It will be recalled that Ambassador Nomura had objected strenuously to a previous request from Foreign Minister Matsuoka that Minister Wakasugi be sent back to Japan to report personally on certain Japanese-American affairs. Ambassador Nomura had stressed his desire to retain the services of his assistant, and had pointed out that the situation was so delicate that he needed the presence of Minister Waskasugi. It is evident, therefore, that only a very serious situation could have influenced Ambassador Nomura to request the return of both Minister Waskasugi and Colonel Iwakuro at this time. Although he desired to send a naval representative with the other two emissaries, lack of adequate personnel made such action impossible.[260]

---

[259]"Memorandum of a Conversation", July 25, 1941, by Joseph W. Ballantine, *S.D.,* II, 530–532.
[260]II, 181.

73. Attempts to Preserve Peace.

Ambassador Nomura reported to Tokyo that a prominent American Cabinet member was trying to preserve peace between the United States and Japan. This individual was not definitely identified in the text of the message. This Cabinet member told Ambassador Nomura that a secret Cabinet meeting had been held to discuss counter measures to Japan's southward move which it believed had been instigated by Germany to supplement its next attack in Europe.

According to this informant, the American Cabinet believed that continuing the Japanese-American discussions was useless, and it would not accept any excuses for the actions of the Japanese. Though the Cabinet member had been able to prevail on Secretary Hull and other Cabinet members up until this time to prevent the freezing of Japanese assets and the imposition of an oil export embargo, he now reported that both of these measures would soon be adopted, with the freezing of assets put into effect at an unexpectedly early date. However, this Cabinet member was trying to persuade American authorities to postpone these measures until he could discuss the matter with Secretary Hull who was expected to return to Washington in a few days.

In a side explanation to Foreign Minister Toyoda, Ambassador Nomura remarked that because his American friend was a new member of the Cabinet, he had been ignorant of the Japanese occupation of French Indo-China in the previous year. When he had learned of this matter on July 6, 1941, the Cabinet member asked Ambassador Nomura why Japan was making such an issue of its latest move. According to the Cabinet member, both he and Secretary Hull had been "put on the spot" because of recent developments in the Far East. He had recently held a long discussion with President Roosevelt in which Mr. Roosevelt expressed the opinion that some means could be found to make Japan reconsider her policy in the Pacific. Therefore, the Cabinet member would not discontinue his efforts to bring about a conciliation, and he hoped that Japan would respond favorably to his overtures.

According to Ambassador Nomura, Germany was still trying to bring about peace through the influence of the United States, though Japan was in no way involved in the plans proposed by Germany. The Cabinet member reported that though he and other Cabinet members opposed Germany's terms, they were favored by some of his colleagues who were against the Japanese-United States understanding.[261]

74. The United States Freezes Japanese Assets (July 25, 2941).

On July 25, 1941 the United States froze Japanese assets by an order similar to that by which assets of various European countries had been frozen on June 14, 1941. This measure brought all financial, import and export trade transactions in which Japanese interests were involved under the control of the United States, and imposed criminal penalties for violations of the order. Simultaneously, at the request of Generalissimo Chiang Kai-shek, President Roosevelt extended the freezing control to Chinese assets in the United States for the purpose of helping the Chinese government. Japanese banks in Los Angeles were inspected by examiners and all safes were sealed on the evening of July 25, 1941.[262]

The Japanese were much concerned lest the freezing of commercial assets include interference with the departure of Japanese ships from American ports. According to Ambassador Nomura, when Mr. Wakasugi had conferred with Mr. Hamilton of the State Department, he

[261]II, 182.

[262]II, 183.

had asked whether or not the American government intended to tie up or seize Japanese ships.[263] Mr. Hamilton had replied that the State Department had nothing to do with this, but when Mr. Wakasugi asked for an official declaration concerning the intention of the United States not to seize Japanese ships, Mr. Hamilton replied that he did not think it necessary for the American government to guarantee this point. Ambassador Nomura promised a further report to Tokyo whenever he received definite word regarding the seizure of Japanese ships.[264]

On July 27, 1941 Tokyo announced that in retaliation against Britain and the United States for freezing Japanese assets, Japanese restrictions on foreign business transactions would be put into effect on July 28, 1941. Similar action would be taken in Manchukuo and in China where all transactions involving Britain and America would be placed on a license basis.[265]

To Tokyo's request for information concerning the legal authority under which President Roosevelt had acted in freezing Japanese assets in the United States, Ambassador Nomura replied that the authority of the President was derived from the Espionage Act of July 15, 1917; a law authorizing the commandeering of ships; and the law stipulating the order of priority of commercial shipments for the sake of national defense.[266]

75. Ambassador Grew Visits Foreign Minister Toyoda (July 25, 1941).

(a) *Ambassador Grew's Report.*[266A]

Foreign Minister Toyoda informed Ambassador Grew that on the following day Japan would issue an official statement concerning its agreement with France to jointly defend French Indo-China, and for that reason he wished to inform the United States of Japan's reasons and intentions. He handed Ambassador Grew a copy of the Japanese statement, who, after he had read it, replied by citing some of the passages of a statement made to the press by Secretary Welles on the preceding day.

Denying that Japan was being encircled or acting to protect Indo-China, the American Ambassador expressed his pleasure in noting that the Japanese statement said, "Japan has no intention at all of making the southern part of Indo-China a base of armed advancement against adjoining areas". He said, however, that the United States had been so frequently disappointed by the promises of former Japanese Ministers that only facts and actions would be relied upon in the future.

Ambassador Grew then outlined the successive steps of Japan's southward advance, and indicated America's concern with the threats to Singapore and the Netherlands East Indies. Foreign Minister Toyoda again emphasized Japan's peaceful intentions and said that Japan had no territorial ambitions. He asked Ambassador Grew to convey this information to his government, and commented on the importance of avoiding measures which would provoke the Japanese people and disrupt Japanese-American relations.

(b) *Foreign Minister Toyoda's Report.*[267]

In his talk with Ambassador Grew on July 25, 1941, Foreign Minister Toyoda, pointing out that in the area of Burma, Singapore and French Indo-China, Japan was being encircled by

---

[263]II, 184; "Memorandum by the Chief of the Division of Far Eastern Affairs (Hamilton)", July 25, 1941, *S.D.*, II, 265–166.

[264]*Ibid.*

[265]II, 185

[266]II, 186.

[266A]"Memorandum by the Ambassador in Japan (Grew)", July 25, 1941, *S.D.*, II, 317–318; "Press Release issued by the Department of State on July 24, 1941", *S.D.*, II, 315–317; "The Japanese Minister for Foreign Affairs (Toyoda) to the American Ambassador in Japan (Grew)", *S.D.*, II, 318–319.

[267]II, 187.

hostile forces, compared Japan's occupation of French Indo-China as a measure of joint defense for that country to Britain's occupation of Syria.

Denying the accuracy of a statement made by Mr. Welles on July 24, 1941 at a press conference, which indicated that the occupation of northern French Indo-China by the Japanese was only a preliminary step toward a further southward advance, Foreign Minister Toyoda indicated that he had informed the American government of the action about to be taken by Japan because of his friendship with the American Ambassador.

According to Admiral Toyoda's report, Ambassador Grew had placed a great deal of importance on the point in the memorandum handed to him by the Foreign Minister, which indicated that Japan did not intend to use southern French Indo-China as a base for further advancement to adjacent territories. According to Ambassador Grew, the United States would be very happy to receive Japan's assurance that no further southward movement was intended.[268]

76. Ambassador Grew Visits Foreign Minister Toyoda (July 26, 1941).

(a) *Ambassador Grew's Report.*[269]

At the request of the Minister for Foreign Affairs, Admiral Toyoda, American Ambassador Grew called to discuss at length the strained situation which had arisen from the establishment of Japanese bases in southern Indo-China and the consequent freezing of Japanese assets in the United States. Since Ambassador Grew had received a report of Acting Secretary Welles' conversation with Ambassador Nomura, he conveyed the substance of it to the Foreign Minister. Profoundly concerned with the rupture of these Washington conferences, and particularly disturbed by Mr. Welles' remark regarding German pressure on the French government, Admiral Toyoda assured Mr. Grew that all French Indo-China negotiations had been carried on without any outside pressure. He also attempted to draw without success a comparison between the Japanese action and the measures taken by England in Syria.

Although Admiral Toyoda reiterated the view that the situation between the United States and Japan was based solely on an American misunderstanding of Japan's true purposes, Mr. Grew refuted this statement with the reply that the United States had learned from experience with other Japanese governments that little credence could be given to their pledges or assurances. Rather than have the meeting end in an atmosphere of defeatism, Ambassador Grew urged the Foreign Minister to exercise his influence in the prevention of further deterioration of relations between Japan and the United States.

(b) *Foreign Minister Toyoda's Report.*[270]

The Foreign Minister told Ambassador Nomura that Ambassador Grew had read to him the entire contents of a telegram which gave the details of a conversation on July 23, 1941 between Ambassador Nomura and Assistant Secretary of State Welles.

Foreign Minister Toyoda differed with Mr. Welles in his opinion that Japan's actions on French Indo-China had been a result of pressure from Germany. According to the Foreign Minister, Japan had acted only as a result of a friendly treaty between Japan and France for the purpose of jointly defending French Indo-China against the fate of Syria, though Mr. Welles believed that French Indo-China had been occupied to secure bases for further Japanese advances. According to Foreign Minister Toyoda, Japan had no object other than the maintenance of peace in the Pacific.

---

[268]*Ibid.*
[269]"Memorandum by the Ambassador in Japan (Grew)", July 26, 1941, *S.D.*, II, 532–534.
[270]II, 188.

Announcing his chagrin because Japanese-American relations had deteriorated so rapidly in less than two weeks after the formation of a new cabinet, Foreign Minister Toyoda blamed the situation on American misunderstanding of the real intentions of the Japanese government. Warning that further restrictions by the United States would provoke Japanese opinion, which was already resentful because of United States' aid to China, Foreign Minister Toyoda claimed that it would be difficult for the Japanese government to suppress the emotions of the Japanese people. To the Foreign Minister's inquiry concerning the accuracy of Mr. Welles' quotation of Secretary Hull's remarks that he "was unable to see that there was now any basis for continuing the talks which Admiral Nomura and Mr. Hull had been conducting", Ambassador Grew had made no definite reply on the grounds that he was not yet familiar with the recent order freezing Japanese assets.

Foreign Minister Toyoda instructed Ambassador Nomura and his subordinates to emphasize at every opportunity that Japan's action was one which could not have been avoided in the light of internal and external circumstances.[271]

77. Ambassador Grew Visits Foreign Minister Toyoda (July 27, 1941).

(a) *Ambassador Grew's Report.*[272]

Since the report of President Roosevelt's proposal to Ambassador Nomura had reached Mr. Grew after his meeting on July 26, 1941 with the Japanese Foreign Minister, on July 27, 1941 the American Ambassador called on Admiral Toyoda of his own initiative for an "off the record" conversation concerning these new developments. Emphasizing that he was acting without the official authority of his government and only because the matter warranted immediate action, Mr. Grew then began to discuss the substance of President Roosevelt's suggestion, only to learn that Ambassador Nomura had not yet informed the Japanese Foreign Office of its provisions.

When Admiral Toyoda had heard the terms of the proposed agreement, however, he stated that it had come too late, since public opinion in Japan was now aroused against the United States because of its freezing of Japanese assets. Nevertheless, he agreed to examine the President's proposal more carefully and to discuss it fully with other high officials.

Reminding the Foreign Minister that any reply to President Roosevelt's suggestion would have to be conveyed through the Japanese in Washington after the receipt of his report in Japan, Mr. Grew took this opportunity to express his own personal views. Referring to the full and free access to food supplies and raw materials permitted under this agreement, the American Ambassador stated that President Roosevelt's proposal adequately solved the problem of Japanese encirclement. When asked if this also applied to the Dutch East Indies as well as French Indo-China, Mr. Grew pointed out that the conversations in Washington had dealt with the question of equal opportunity and free movement of trade throughout the entire area of the Pacific.

Foreign Minister Toyoda again reiterated the resentment felt in Japan because of the freezing of Japanese assets by the United States. Though still speaking unofficially, Mr. Grew assured the Foreign Minister that the administration of this Executive Order was extremely flexible, and stated that he believed there would be no reluctance on the part of the American government to facilitate any Japanese efforts toward peace in the Pacific.

While recognizing the "face-saving" element that Japan must be concerned with, Mr. Grew urged Admiral Toyoda to act in conformity with the highest statesmanship, and to relieve the dangerous situation which had arisen.

---

[271]II, 189.

[272]"Memorandum by the Ambassador in Japan (Grew", July 27, 1941, *S.D.*, II, 534–537.

(b) *Foreign Minister Toyoda's Report.*

There is no dispatch available which gives the details of this meeting from the Japanese viewpoint (DoD comment).

78. Welles-Nomura Conversation (July 28, 1941).

(a) *Acting Secretary Welles' Report.*[273]

On the afternoon of July 28, 1941 the Japanese Ambassador called on the Acting Secretary of State to question him on certain American policies connected with the freezing order. When questioned regarding the status of Japanese vessels in American territorial waters, Mr. Welles stated that the Treasury Department, for the time being and under present conditions, would grant prompt clearance to any of these vessels in American ports, and that licenses would be freely issued to permit the purchase of food supplies for the crew and fuel for the ships.

Expressing his satisfaction with the attitude of the United States in this matter, Ambassador Nomura then spoke of his desire to see the present difficult situation passed over without further deterioration in the relations between the two countries. Reminding the Japanese Ambassador of the extreme patience demonstrated by the United States in its dealings with Japan, Mr. Welles rejected the Japanese representative's suggestion that some sort of a compromise be drafted.

Mr. Welles pointed out that the policy of America was the renunciation of force and conquest in the dealings between nations of the Pacific area, and the establishment of equal opportunity on non-discriminatory terms. Since President Roosevelt's proposal had assured Japan of the economic and commercial stability which it desired with regard to the United States, Great Britain, the Netherlands and China, there was no conceivable ground for any compromise solution. When Mr. Welles also expressed his surprise that the Japanese Ambassador had not immediately conveyed to Tokyo the complete terms of President Roosevelt's proposal, Ambassador Nomura replied that he had now done so.

In concluding the meeting, Mr. Welles informed the Japanese Ambassador that it seemed to him that Japan had now undertaken a policy completely different from that which had been under discussion with the United States, and hence any compromise would amount to an abandoning of American principles. When Ambassador Nomura requested that President Roosevelt see Colonel Iwakuro before the latter's departure for Japan, Mr. Welles, though not optimistic, promised to try to arrange an interview.

(b) *Ambassador Nomura's Report.*[274]

Ambassador Nomura reported to Tokyo that on July 28, 1941 he had conversed with Mr. Welles. Though peace had been maintained between the United States and Japan for ninety years, it was evident, Ambassador Nomura had declared, that unless some way out was found from the present policies being pursued by both Japan and the United States, relations would become increasingly critical.

Mr. Welles replied that the recent proposals of President Roosevelt were sound and that they were of considerable importance. In spite of this, Ambassador Grew had reported from Tokyo that Foreign Minister Toyoda had not yet been informed of them. Ambassador Nomura replied that only the gist of President Roosevelt's proposals had been reported at first, but a detailed report had been sent later.

Mr. Welles repeated the statement made by President Roosevelt that the United States would not interfere with the export of American materials to Japan, if Japan would avoid con-

---

[273]"Memorandum by the Acting Secretary of State", July 28, 1941, *S.D.,* II, 537–539.

[274]II, 190–191.

quest through the use of force. Furthermore, according to Mr. Welles, the safety of French Indo-China was not in danger.

79. Ambassador Nomura Warns Tokyo of the Dangers of War.

In the same report in which Ambassador Nomura discussed his latest conversation with Acting Secretary Welles, the Japanese Ambassador warned his Foreign Office that Japan was moving towards war in East Asia.

Ambassador Nomura expressed his sentiments as follows:

> If we look at the trend in a detached manner, we find that we are moving alone, heading toward the worst possible eventuality in East Asia, and may come up against Britain, the United States, the Netherlands East Indies, and China, and probably the U.S.S.R. as well.
>
> Our duty to restrain the United States in behalf of German ----- (two badly garbled lines) ----- the United States and Germany are avoiding armed conflict. In the meantime, and unconsciously, we are rushing towards a war against Great Britain and the United States; a war in which we we would have to stand alone against them.
>
> I beg of you to give careful considerations before you take any steps. It may be true that circumstances may arise which need immediate local attention from the military. Politically, however, I beseech you to take a broad view, consider all of the angles, before making a move. It is my undying hope that you proceed in behalf of the everlasting glory of our country.[275]

80. The United States Restricts Japanese Economic Activities.

On July 29, 1941 Ambassador Nomura was informed that in view of the great increase in the number of Japanese with diplomatic status living in New York, only the ranking Commercial Attaché and Financial Attaché would be placed on the diplomatic list. As for financial and commercial consuls and secretaries already on the diplomatic list, permission to increase their number or to replace them would not be given, in accordance with the policy begun in 1939. For this reason, Assistant Financial Attaché Yosimura would be permitted to reside in New York, but would not be placed on the diplomatic list.[276]

81. The Bombing of the Tutuila (July 30, 1941).

In the midst of the very delicate diplomatic situation created by the Japanese occupation of French Indo-China, an incident of dangerous potentialities occurred at Chungking, where, in an operation by twenty-six Japanese heavy bombers, one bomb struck near the *U.S.S. Tutuila* in an area very near to the United States Embassy. Acting Secretary of State Welles requested Ambassador Nomura to call upon him so that an official complaint could be registered.

(a) *Acting Secretary Welles' Report.*[277]

Mr. Welles stated that he had called in the Japanese Ambassador on the morning of July 30, 1941 to give him a copy of the report relating to the bombing of the American area in Chungking, and asked him for answers to the following questions:

1. Did this take place upon instruction by, or knowledge of, responsible authorities?
2. What responsibility, if any, would the Japanese government assume for it?
3. What precise measures in detail does the Japanese government intend to take toward effectively preventing a recurrence of any such action.

Mr. Welles reminded the Japanese Ambassador of the solemn pledge of the Japanese government at the time of the sinking of the *U.S.S. Panay* that such action would not be repeated.

---

[275]II, 190.

[276]II, 192.

[277]"The Acting Secretary of State to the Ambassador in Japan (Grew)", *S.D.*, I, 719–720.

Furthermore, similar pledges had been repeatedly disregarded. The Japanese Ambassador was requested to take the matter up immediately with his Minister for Foreign Affairs.

(b) *Ambassador Nomura's Report.*[278]

Ambassador Nomura reported that Acting Secretary Welles had requested him to call to receive the memorandum concerning the bombing of the *U.S.S. Tutuila.* Acting Secretary Welles, with an "extremely austere look",[279] and stating that he spoke in the name of President Roosevelt, had asked the following questions:

1. When the Panay incident happened the President got a guarantee that such a thing would not recur, so why did the present incident happen?

2. Under what sort of orders did the Japanese forces and responsible officials permit such a deed?

3. The American Embassy in Chungking and the gunboat are on the other side of the city, supposedly in a safe place, so how did this incident come about? Now, I want to get an immediate explanation from the Japanese government.

According to Ambassador Nomura's reply to Mr. Welles, the bombing had taken place accidently since the river at Chungking was very narrow and novice aviators were quite apt to make mistakes. In order to stop such untoward events, it would be necessary either to stop bombing Chungking or to move the American Embassy and the gunboat. Ambassador Nomura then asked permission to delay his official answer until he could report to his government.[280]

82. Ambassador Nomura Warns Tokyo of the Seriousness of the Tutuila Affair.

Ambassador Nomura pointed out that during his first conversation with President Roosevelt on the occasion of his formal introduction early in 1941, President Roosevelt had said that he and Secretary Hull had succeeded in restraining American popular opinion at the time of the *Panay* incident. However, another such incident would make it impossible to calm the storm.

Ambassador Nomura remarked that the latest incident had been most inopportune because popular demand for the freezing of Japanese funds was subsiding just when it happened. Ambassador Nomura did not attempt to disguise the disturbed feelings of American officials at this moment, as the following passage indicates:

Today I knew from the hard looks on their faces that they meant business and I could see that if we do not answer to suit them that they are going to take some drastic steps. . . .

Things being as they are, need I point out to you gentlemen that in my opinion it is necessary to take without one moment's hesitation some appeasement measures. Please wire me back at the earliest possible moment.[281]

83. Ambassador Nomura Suggests that Japan Discontinue the Bombing of Chungking.

In conformity with his views that some immediate action would have to be initiated to offset the bad impression created in America by the latest Japanese bombing in China, Ambassador Nomura suggested to his Foreign Minister that the best possible step would be to stop bombing Chungking for a time and to publish this decision without delay.[282]

Japanese authorities in Tokyo were as much concerned about the bombing of the *U.S.S. Tutuila* as was Ambassador Nomura himself. The Foreign Minister informed Ambassador Nomura that even before receiving official word from the American Embassy, he had sent

---

[278]II, 193–194.
[279]II, 193.
[280]*Ibid.*
[281]II, 195.
[282]II, 196.

Vice-Minister Yamamoto to express the deep regret of the Japanese government at this most unfortunate occurrence.[283] Furthermore, the Minister of the Navy sent an officer to call on the American Naval Attache to express the regret of the Japanese Navy for the damage done by Japanese Naval Air Forces.[284]

Ambassador Nomura was also informed that the Foreign Minister had requested Ambassador Grew to call on him to receive the expression of the regrets of the Japanese government at the same time that the American Ambassador presented the official text of the American complaint.[285] Foreign Minister Toyoda said that the incident was a mistake on the part of an aviator, but that no matter what the cause might be, it was much to be regretted since Japanese authorities had been exercising the greatest caution to prevent the recurrence of such incidents, and had recently issued strict orders concerning them. As a former military man, Foreign Minister Toyoda promised to see to it that Japanese military personnel would give absolute obedience to these instructions in the future.[286]

84. Tokyo Orders the Discontinuance of Bombing at Chungking.

Ambassador Nomura was requested to inform President Roosevelt immediately that, in view of the general state of relations between Japan and America, the bombing of Chungking would be suspended for a time. However, if this action were publicly announced in America, public opinion in Japan might be shocked. Pointing out that such a reaction might defeat the very purpose of the discontinuance of the bombing, Tokyo asked that the United States keep this decision confidential.[287]

Ambassador Nomura called on Acting Secretary Welles on the afternoon of July 31, 1941 to request that the apology of the Japanese government for the *Tutuila* incident be conveyed promptly to President Roosevelt. Furthermore, the Japanese government would suspend all bombing operations over the city area of Chungking, and the Japanese government was prepared to pay indemnities for any damage to American property which had occurred from this bombing, though in the opinion of Ambassador Nomura the damage had been accidental.[288]

After this, Ambassador Nomura was able to report to his government the announcement of the Acting Secretary of State that the United States had accepted Japan's apology in connection with the Tutuila incident and that the matter would henceforth be closed.[289]

85. Ambassador Nomura Reports British-German Peace Negotiations.

Ambassador Nomura reported to Tokyo, on July 28, 1941, that reports emanating from Turkey concerning British-German peace negotiations were not entirely without foundation. Furthermore, President Roosevelt and Acting Secretary Welles had intimated that Mayor LaGuardia of New York, former national head of civilian defense, had inadvertently divulged some information concerning this. Though Ambassador Nomura was not certain of the truth of these rumors, he pointed out that the German government had expanded its personnel in the United States and was successfully engaged in undercover work, especially among Americans of German extraction.[290]

---

[283]II, 197; *S.D.*, I, 720.
[284]*Ibid.*: *S.D.*, I, 722.
[285]II, 198.
[286]*Ibid.*
[287]II, 199.
[288]II, 200–201.
[289]II, 202.
[290]II, 203.

86. Welles-Nomura Conversation (July 31, 1941).

(a) *Acting Secretary Welles' Report.*[291]

Speaking in behalf of President Roosevelt, Secretary of State Sumner Welles informed the Japanese Ambassador that the United States had learned that Japan was now making the same economic and military demands on Thailand as it had on French Indo-China. While denouncing the act as totally without justification, President Roosevelt nevertheless offered to include Thailand in the proposal, which he had made with regard to French Indo-China, to guarantee Japan's trade and territorial integrity.

(b) *Ambassador Nomura's Report.*

There is no report available of Ambassador Nomura concerning this meeting (DoD comment).

87. Japan Explains to Germany Its Policy in the Hull-Nomura Conferences.

Foreign Minister Toyoda, on July 31, 1941, sent a very important message to Berlin in which he discussed the policy of Japan in its dealings with the United States and in its relations with its Axis partners. Pointing out that Ambassador Oshima in Berlin had been adivising the Japanese Foreign Office from time to time concerning what it ought to do to help Germany, which desired assistance in its war against Russia, (See Sections 137–141, 163) Foreign Minister Toyoda stated that after a conference with Japanese military authorities, he wished to enunciate the policies and views of the government, in accordance with which Ambassador Oshima was to act in the future. He reminded the Japanese Ambassador in Berlin that in a cabinet meeting on July 2, 1941 the broad outline of Japanese policy for the future had been drawn, and ever since that time the Japanese government had been devoting every effort to achieve the objectives of that policy.

Although the China incident had already lasted for four years and Japan had expended much strength in trying to end it, the dangers of the new situation which Japan had to face from the north and south made it necessary for it to prepare for an all-out war.[292] Despite the fact that Germany should understand the position of Japan very well since German diplomats in Tokyo had been made aware of it, Foreign Minister Toyoda feared that German authorities in Berlin were not fully informed. The reasons for the Japanese seizures of French Indo-China were expressed by Foreign Minister Toyoda as follows:

> Commercial and economic relations between Japan and third countries, led by England and the United States, are gradually becoming so horribly strained that we cannot endure it much longer. Consequently, our Empire, to save its very life, must take measures to secure the raw materials of the South Seas; our Empire must immediately take steps to break asunder this ever-strengthening chain of encirclement which is being woven under the guidance, and with the participation of England and the United States, acting like a cunning dragon seemingly asleep. That is why we decided to obtain military bases in French Indo-China and to have our troops occupy that territory.
>
> That step in itself, I dare say, gave England and the United States, not to mention Russia, quite a set-back in the Pacific that ought to help Germany, and now Japanese-American relations are more rapidly than ever treading the evil road. This shows what a blow it has been to the United States.[293]

According to Foreign Minister Toyoda, the Russian-German war had given Japan an excellent opportunity to settle the northern question, and already preparations had been made to take advantage of the situation. Caution would have to be exercised by Japan, however, so that the right moment for an attack would be well chosen, especially since, if the Russian-German war proceeded too swiftly, Japan would not have time to take any effective parallel action.

---

[291]"Memorandum by the Acting Secretary of State" July 31, 1941, by Sumner Welles, *S.D.*, II, 539–540.

[292]II, 204.

[293]II, 205.

Knowing that the Germans were dissatisfied because of Japanese negotiations with the United States, Foreign Minister Toyoda stated that Japan had desired to prevent the United States from getting into the European war, as well as to settle the Chinese incident. He claimed credit for keeping the United States out of the war as follows:

> Let him who will gainsay the fact that as a result we have indelibly impressed upon the United States the profoundness of the determination of the Empire of Japan and restrained her from plunging into the conflict against Germany.[294]

Remarking that the Japanese-American conversations had been started at a time which seemed opportune to Japan, Admiral Toyoda stated that complete trust between Japan and Germany was essential. Moreover, he reminded Ambassador Oshima that Germany had started the war with Russia to suit its own convenience when it was least desirable from the Japanese viewpoint, since Japan would now have to settle, not only the Chinese incident, but also to meet a new challenge from the north.[295]

Assuring Germany that Japan was making every effort to cooperate, Admiral Toyoda declared that the fundamental spirit of the Tripartite Pact consisted of allowing each partner a certain flexibility of action:

> What I mean to say is that each should understand that real cooperation does not necessarily mean complete symmetry of action. In other words, we should trust each other and while striving toward one general objective, each use our own discretion within the bounds of good judgment.
>
> Thus, all measures which our Empire shall take will be based upon a determination to bring about the success of the objectives of the Tripartite Pact. That this is a fact is proven by the promulgation of an Imperial rescript. We are ever working toward the realization of those objectives, and now during this dire emergency is certainly no time to engage in any light unpremeditated or over-speedy action.[296]

88. Tokyo Decides to Continue the Hull-Nomura Conversations.

On August 2, 1941 Foreign Minister Toyoda sent word that careful consideration was being given to the proposal of President Roosevelt that French Indo-China be neutralized in exchange for a guarantee of those essential raw materials which Japan needed. However, the Foreign Office warned that some time would elapse before the Japanese government would be able to express an opinion regarding the proposal because of the critical political situation at home and abroad, and also because of the great importance of the question.

Ambassador Nomura was requested to inform President Roosevelt of Japan's serious consideration of his proposal as indicated by its unusual action in trying to adjust Japanese-American relations.[297] Measures had been taken by Japan to avoid exciting Japanese public opinion, though, at the same time, American newspaper correspondents had been granted every facility. Furthermore, in order to avoid the recurrence of such unpleasant incidents as that of the *U.S.S. Tutuila*, Foreign Minister Toyoda advised the United States to free itself of legal theories and to cooperate with Japan by removing the gunboat to safe waters.[298] According to the Foreign Minister, disruption of Japanese-American negotiations would take place unless a higher degree of statesmanship were exercised by leaders of both America and Japan. He asked that the United States reciprocate Japan's action by avoiding fault-finding, and by maintaining an intelligent and constructive attitude. Ambassador Nomura was instructed to convey these sentiments to President Roosevelt so that Japanese-American diplomatic negotiations could continue in the future.[299]

---

[294]II, 206.
[295]*Ibid.*
[296]II, 207.
[297]II, 208.
[298]II, 209.
[299]II, 210.

89. Ambassador Nomura Consults an American Cabinet Member.[300]

Ambassador Nomura reported to Tokyo, on August 2, 1941, that in view of the fact that Japanese-American relations were growing worse constantly and that an embargo was currently being imposed on the export of oil, he had secretly interviewed a member of the American cabinet. During the course of the discussion, the Japanese Ambassador explained that the Japanese occupation of French Indo-China was necessary because of the general diplomatic situation and was not to be permanent. The integrity of adjacent countries, waters, and colonies was to be maintained, and negotiations were to be carried on to facilitate the supply of raw materials. However, the American Cabinet member had then asked whether or not Japan was preparing to occupy Siberia, which demonstrated, according to Ambassador Nomura, that he had paid little attention to the Japanese Ambassador's previous explanation.

The Cabinet member mentioned Secretary Hull's great disappointment at the latest action of Japan, since he had been intensely interested in adjusting Japanese-American relations. Both he and Secretary Hull were being ridiculed by their Cabinet colleagues as having been "easy men", and as having played into the hands of the Japanese.

The American Cabinet member was not identified in Ambassador Nomura's dispatch, however, he played a very active role in support of President Roosevelt's moves to avert a Japanese-American war. Ambassador Nomura reported that in this conversation of August 2, 1941 the Cabinet member stated that President Roosevelt did not want war.[301]

Ambassador Nomura summed up his opinions of the current diplomatic situation as follows:

Now this is the way I look at the matter: The United States is trying to restrain Japan, first of all, by waging an economic war, although the government authorities claim that they are merely taking counter-measures against Japan's policy. But, that the United States is at the same time making military preparations against the possible eventuality of a clash of arms is a fact with which you are already familiar. Furthermore, it seems that in order to attain her object, the United States is endeavoring to get Soviet Russia and China, to say nothing of Great Britain and the Dutch West Indies, to fall in line and cooperate with her. That the Russo-German war is lasting longer than expected has proved to be an advantage to the United States. However, the aforementioned cabinet member did not speak so optimistically as the President, in a newspaper interview yesterday, is reported to have alleged his confidant Hopkins to have spoken. The cabinet member believes firmly in the necessity of this war lasting for several years for the reason that due to destruction of her men and materials, and due to the shortage of oil, Germany would not be able to do anything on a great scale even after the fighting on the Eastern Front has come to an end, and that, since the United States will be able in the meantime to rapidly increase her production, the trend will be in favor of her.[302]

90. Ambassador Nomura Analyzes American Economic Restrictions Against Japan.

According to Ambassador Nomura, the recent embargo on oil shipments to Japan, established by the United States, was the first economic restriction of the United States since the freezing of funds. Pointing out that it was imposed not because of the bombing of the *Tutuila* but because of Japan's penetration to the south, Ambassador Nomura warned that American economic pressure would continue until it became clear that Japan was going to put an end to its policy of aggression. Meanwhile, it was reported that Japan intended to make new demands for military bases in Thailand, and that Japanese military forces were being increased. Furthermore, the sale of silk to the American public had been stopped, which would be a severe blow to Japan, although unemployment would also affect American silk workers.

---

[300]II, 211.
[301]*Ibid.*
[302]*Ibid.*

Ambassador Nomura reported that on August 2, 1941 the United States had issued a statement that Japanese aggression in French Indo-China constituted a threat to national security, and that the attitude of the United States toward France would be determined by the actions of Vichy in surrendering its territory to the Axis. In addition to this, Acting Secretary Welles, the British Ambassador, and the Ministers of Australia and South Africa had conferred on war measures and had discussed Dakar. According to the Japanese Ambassador, Mr. Harry Hopkins was in Moscow to ensure Russo-American cooperation in case of an attack in the north by Japan.[303]

Further details concerning American supervision of Japanese banks in Los Angeles as a result of the recent freezing directive were forwarded to Tokyo by Ambassador Nomura.[304] Tokyo announced that if America did not freeze the assets of Japanese diplomatic establishments, consulates and staff members in the United States and its other possessions, the Japanese government, in turn, would exempt American diplomatic establishments, consulates, and staff members in Japan, including Manchuria, Taiwan, and Chosen, from the regulations governing foreign transactions.[305]

91. Ambassador Nomura Requests the Assistance of Ambassador Kurusu.

On August 4, 1941 Ambassador Nomura reported that American newspapers, which were much concerned with Japanese-American relations, supported the strong position taken by the American government.[306] The Gallop Poll indicated that hostility toward Japan was running high, but newspaper editors believed that there was still some hope for a peaceful settlement.

Though Ambassador Nomura believed that the United States considered Japanese-American relations more important than its difficulties with Germany, he expected the situation to grow less critical gradually. Much would depend upon the course of the European war. Although Colonel Iwakuro and Mr. Wakasugi would report on the diplomatic situation to Foreign Minister Toyoda at Tokyo in the near future, Ambassador Nomura warned that the situation might change rapidly within a few days. Conscious of his tremendous responsibilities, Ambassador Nomura expressed himself as follows to Foreign Minister Toyoda:

Now I am in a responsible position. Though I could not offer any excuses, if I made a miscalculation now, there might be regrettable consequences. Furthermore, my astuteness is quite limited. Therefore, as soon as there is a means of transportation available, I would like for you to send me some such Foreign Office expert well versed in affairs at home and abroad as Ambassador Kurusu to work with me for awhile.

I know nothing at all about the Government's high policy which is shrouded in secrecy, so how can you expect me to take any action whatever when my hands are thus tied? Please think this over and send me a man immediately.[307]

92. Welles-Wakasugi Interview (August 4, 1941).

(a) *Acting Secretary Welles' Report.*[308]

Since Japanese Minister Wakasugi was leaving Washington to report personally to Prince Konoye and Foreign Minister Toyoda, he called on Acting Secretary of State Welles to ask for his analysis of the current state of relations between the United States and Japan. It was Mr.

---

[303]II, 212.

[304]II, 213–214.

[305]II, 215.

[306]II, 216.

[307]*Ibid.*

[308]"Memorandum by the Acting Secretary of State", August 4, 1941, by Acting Secretary (Sumner Welles), *S.D.*, II, 540–546.

Waskasugi's opinion that in order to bridge the gap between the two countries, Tokyo needed only a clear picture regarding the policies of the American government.

Agreeing fully with the Japanese Minister, Mr. Welles expressed the appreciation of Japan and the Japanese people that he had developed through his years of service as Secretary of the American Embassy in that country. Because of the friendly relations which had then existed between the two countries, Mr. Welles saw no good reason for their present state of decline. Mr. Wakasugi remarked that in the approximately thirty years he had spent in the United States, never before had such a dangerous crisis been reached.

Although Mr. Welles felt that the policies of his government had been clearly defined in various communications with Japan since 1939, as well as in letters exchanged between the Secretary of State and the Foreign Minister, and in the conversations with representatives of the Japanese government, nevertheless, he reiterated them at Mr. Wakasugi's request. As its fundamental premise, the United States maintained a policy of peace in the Pacific by the renunciation of all use of force and conquest against the autonomous peoples in that area, and by the establishment of equal opportunity and fair treatment for all powers interested in the Pacific. If Japan had adopted such a procedure, it would have enjoyed the opportunity of obtaining free access to raw materials and food supplies without endangering its national security by a military or naval engagement.

The national policies of the two countries had not converged during recent years, however, for Japan had steadily adopted an attitude of aggression toward the other peoples of the Far East. Mr. Welles remarked that this could be regarded only as the creation of a military overlordship of the Japanese Empire which was to be imposed on the countries in the South Pacific, and, perhaps, in time over other areas as well. In an attempt to explain his country's situation, Mr. Wakasugi stated that when Japan awoke from its long sleep of isolation, it found itself surrounded by imperialistic encroachment in all the South Pacific region, and in view of its need for land and trade, and because of its rapidly rising power as a great nation in the world, Japan was forced to take some aggressive steps.

Though recognizing Japan's need for interests outside its own natural boundaries, Mr. Welles asserted that the people of Japan would benefit more from peaceful and productive expansion resulting from greater commercial enterprises with other nations along the lines of equality and non-discrimination. Inevitably, the sole result of Japan's present militaristic course, according to Mr. Welles, would be economic prostration, and possibly social and financial collapse.

To Mr. Wakasugi's direct question on how far Japan could now expand without running the risk of war with the United States, Mr. Welles replied that no line could be drawn in regard to this matter, since the implementation of Japan's policy of conquest already had created a critical situation, which prejudiced the security of the United States. Repeating the terms of President Roosevelt's proposal of July 24, 1941, Mr. Welles insisted that the Japanese Minister could not deny that it gave security to Japan and to the other countries interested in the Far East.

Changing the subject, Mr. Wakasugi spoke of the solution of postwar problems, and expressed his belief that a new league of nations founded on the principles of the old League would prove neither practical nor successful. As he envisaged it, the solution lay in the creation of regional federations for Europe and Africa, the Western Hemisphere, the Far East, and finally for Russia. Disagreeing with Mr. Wakasugi's opinion, Mr. Welles stated that no economic difficulties could be solved unless a universal approach was adopted. Furthermore, he was particularly confident that no "new orders", inspired by either Germany or Japan, would bring matters to a peaceful conclusion.

(b) *Ambassador Nomura's Report.*[309]

Ambassador Nomura reported the gist of Mr. Wakasugi's conversation of August 4, 1941 with Acting Secretary Welles. Asking for a clear analysis of the attitude of the United States government so that he could report it to his government, Mr. Wakasugi had expressed his desire to learn what the United States wanted of Japan in connection with Japanese-American relations, and to exchange opinions concerning the world situation which would follow the end of the European war.

Mr. Welles replied that both he and Secretary Hull were desirous of maintaining and promoting friendly Japanese-American relations. The United States wished to continue the long mutual friendship of both nations, and it had no desire to wage aggression against Japan. Expressing his personal regard for Japan which he had held ever since his official position as Secretary to the American Embassy some twenty-five years ago, Mr. Welles stated that the only remaining hope in the very critical current situation was a dependency upon brilliant statesmanship, rather than upon force of arms. Mr. Wakasugi, agreeing with the analysis of Mr. Welles, indicated that Europeans and Americans would not, or could not, comprehend Japanese actions in the Far East because the Japanese program of national security collided with European territorial penetration and economic pressure.

Replying that he fully understood Japanese aspirations and objected only to the use of force in the achievement of these ambitions, Mr. Welles explained that President Roosevelt's proposal for the neutralization of French Indo-China was designed to satisfy Japan's two aims in occupying that territory: first, to counter the joint action of other nations against Japan; second, to obtain access to raw materials. Thus, if Japanese troops evacuated French Indo-China, and as a result Japan, the United States, Great Britain, the Netherlands, and China agreed to preserve French Indo-China's territorial integrity by establishing its neutrality, Japan's first aim would be achieved.

As for raw materials, the second objective of the Japanese, French Indo-China alone could hardly satisfy the demands of Japan. However, President Roosevelt would insist that all the nations in the Pacific would agree to accept Japan as an equal in sharing their stocks of materials. In reply to a question from Mr. Wakasugi, Mr. Welles gave assurance that the United States was prepared to conduct negotiations with Japan concerning Japanese demands, as well as to use its good offices to discuss Japan's needs with the other nations concerned.

Mr. Wakasugi then declared that the United States, under the policy of "Western Hemisphere Solidarity", controlled the Western Hemisphere for its own benefit, and was now beginning to particpate in Far Eastern affairs under the pretext of having special interests, though they dated back no farther than fifty or sixty years. To Mr. Wakasugi's query concerning the reasons for the United States' not limiting its influence to the Western Hemisphere and leaving the Orient to orientals, Mr. Welles replied that the policy of the United States was not based on its claims to special privileges in the Orient since it was prepared to give up these at any time. America was opposed, however, to the use of force since world peace and order could not be brought about if Japan were permitted to imitate Chancellor Hitler by converting various small countries into protectorates.

Although Mr. Wakasugi attempted to say that French Indo-China had been occupied peacefully with full agreement by the French government, Mr. Welles retorted that the Vichy government was not free and that its reception of the Japanese had been forced upon it. Mr. Wakasugi then stated that when two nations in dissimilar circumstances and with different

---

[309]II, 217–218.

policies insisted on their own interpretations, war could not be avoided. However, to prevent disaster, the actions of each country must be limited by some means, geographic or otherwise.

Mr. Wakasugi then asked what the United States demanded of Japan, and what the United States wanted for itself. According to Ambassador Nomura, Acting Secretary Welles avoided a clear reply to these questions, and said that reports had been received concerning Japan's intentions to move further south into Thailand. This action would make conditions worse than ever, for the United States believed that Japan would become better off financially and economically only if it followed a strictly peaceful policy.[310]

As for the postwar situation, Mr. Welles said that the basic principle of the future should be the equal accessibility to raw materials by all the countries of the world, and he urged the establishment, in one form or another, of a world-wide league to enforce order. According to Mr. Welles, talk of disarmament would almost certainly arise, but nothing would come of these talks unless raw materials were first made accessible.

Citing Mr. Stimson's policy at the time of the Manchurian incident, which held that the United States would not recognize any gains made by the use of force, Mr. Wakasugi indicated that American acquisitions in the Caribbean Sea had been the fruits of warfare. Mr. Welles replied that certain points of United States history were quite objectionable, but in modern times the United States had striven to correct these wrongs. Furthermore, if history were to repeat itself forever, progress could not be made in mankind since one had to change one's policies in accordance with the times.

At this point Ambassador Nomura informed Tokyo that he would omit some of the points discussed by Acting Secretary Welles and Mr. Wakasugi.

This ends *Part A* which described the delicate diplomatic situation confronting Secretary Hull and Ambassador Nomura in the early days of August 1941 when the invasion of French Indo-China by Japanese military forces seemed destined to end the Hull-Nomura conversations. However, just when there seemed to be no further hope of successfully continuing these discussions, the Japanese government sent a new proposal which Ambassador Nomura was instructed to present to Secretary Hull on August 6, 1941. This new presentation and the events consequent upon this renewed activity of the Japanese will be discussed in Chapter III, (Volume III) of this series.

---

[310]*Ibid.*

OUTLINE OF PART B[a]

Japanese Intelligence Reports in Diplomatic Messages.

(a) *Japanese Reports from the United States*

(b) *Japanese Reports from the Panama Canal*

(c) *Japanese Reports from Cuba*

(d) *Japanese Reports from the Philippine Islands*

(e) *Japanese Reports from the Hawaiian Islands*

PART B—JAPANESE INTELLIGENCE IN DIPLOMATIC MESSAGES

During the period from May 12 to August 6, 1941 the Japanese evinced great interest in the movement of American warships. The growing tension in diplomatic relations between the two countries was reflected in the naval intelligence reports transmitted by Japanese diplomats. Since these naval reports became increasingly significant as the year 1941 progressed, they will be discussed in a separate section *(Part B)* of each of the remaining volumes of this series. *Part C* will discuss Japanese diplomatic activities throughout the world.

93. Japanese Reports from the United States.

While the question of convoying American ships to England was still pending in Congress, Japan was expanding its intelligence network, especially in America. Fearing that a crisis might be reached before this organization could become well organized, Japan hurried to secure intelligence from its agents in the United States, Germany and Spain. Mr. Taro Terasaki, recently assigned as Chief of Japanese Intelligence and propaganda work in the United States, warned Tokyo that the United States government was tending toward entrance into the war. For this reason he emphasized, in a report to Tokyo on May 19, 1941, the importance of securing funds, establishing contacts with influential persons, and acquiring personnel for intelligence work. The Dies Committee and restrictive regulations regarding foreigners and Americans in foreign employ made the task difficult for the Japanese.[311]

On May 16, 1941 Tokyo, alarmed by a report that the United States had already stationed a fleet in the Indian Ocean, asked Japanese officials in Singapore to pay particular attention to the movements of American warships.[312] Japanese officials in San Francisco, Los Angeles, and Seattle were also directed, in the light of relations prevailing between Japan and the United States, to observe the movements of the American navy and to report on the number of ships pressed into service for the army and navy.[313] In accordance with these requests, it was reported to Tokyo that the *Saratoga*, the *Chester*, the *Louisville*, and the Twelfth Destroyer Squadron, with five other destroyers, had left San Diego on May 31, 1941.[314]

---

[a]See TABLE OF CONTENTS for a detailed listing of topics discussed in Part B.

[311]II, 219.
[312]II, 220.
[313]II, 221–223.
[314]II, 224.

94. Japanese Reports from the Panama Canal.

Tokyo addressed an inquiry regarding the movements of the aircraft carrier, *Lexington*, to Japanese officials in the Canal Zone,[315] and on June 6, 1941 a detailed intelligence report enumerating the number and types of vessels moving through the Canal was sent to Tokyo.[316]

Arrangements were made by the Japanese on June 17, 1941 to obtain copies of secret charts showing the locations of equipment, guns, and other military establishments in Panama. A Japanese agent, contacting Italian officials who were in possession of the charts, had obtained permission to have copies made, but was concerned, however, about the method by which the secret charts could be transported to Tokyo, since he believed that American surveillance would be vigilant.[317] Furthermore, because Tokyo suspected that some of the Japanese codes were being read, any telegram between Panama and Mexico regarding the transportation of the charts had to be in innocuous plain language.[318] Finally, because of the difficult situation created in Guatemala when Japanese diplomatic baggage had been opened by an aviation company affiliated with the United States,[319] Japan decided on June 27, 1941 to postpone temporarily the removal of the charts from Panama.[320]

Urged by Mr. Matsuoka to initiate appropriate action in protestation against the opening of the baggage of Japanese Minister Yoshiaki Miura by officials of the Pan American Airways, Ambassador Nomura thought it inadvisable to present the question as one of diplomatic prerogative. Instead, on June 20, 1941 he sent Mr. Sadao Iguchi to the office of the Chief of the Far Eastern Section to protest such treatment, and to request that the company be instructed as to the proper method of handling the luggage of Japanese diplomatic officials and couriers.[321] On July 2, 1941 Mr. Matsuoka instructed the Japanese minister in Mexico to file a written protest to the Guatemalan government in regard to this violation of diplomatic prerogative.[322]

On June 21, 1941 Mr. Minoru Izawa, declaring the present legation in Panama to be old and insecure, requested Tokyo's approval of a new mission.[323] Five days later, he wired that, owing to the international situation, the mission in Panama would probably be given up.[324] Meanwhile, Consul General Kiyoshi Yamagata, present at Panama on July 4, 1941 as a consultant to Mr. Izawa,[325] was ordered to cancel his trip to Colombia and to proceed immediately to Chile.[326] Secretary Usui was recalled to Buenos Aires from Panama as a result of Mr. Yamagata's assignment.[327]

Endeavoring to transmit to Tokyo any information which might shed light on Panama's future course of action, Mr. Izawa reported on August 4, 1941 that the President of Panama, according to a close relative, had stated in his last cabinet meeting that in the event of America's entering the war, he could see no course of action for his country other than its partici-

---

[315]II, 225.
[316]II, 226.
[317]II, 227.
[318]II, 228.
[319]II, 229–230.
[320]II, 231.
[321]II, 232.
[322]II, 233.
[323]II, 234.
[324]II, 235.
[325]II, 236.
[326]II, 237–239.
[327]II, 240–241.

pating in the war, in keeping with the terms of its agreement. Until that time, however, Panama would remain neutral.[328]

95. Japanese Reports from Cuba.

On August 2, 1941 two American battleships, four light cruisers, four destroyers, two Coast Guard cutters, and two heavy bombing planes were reported to have been in the naval harbor at Guantanamo between July 16–24, 1941.[329]

96. Japanese Reports from the Philippine Islands.

Japanese Consul Katsumi Nihro in the Philippines submitted many naval reports as to the movements of American men-of-war and cargo ships at Manila and Cavite. The transport *Washington*, previously at Manila on May 8, 1941, was reported on June 2, 1941 to have sailed to the port of Olongapo, where American troops were disembarked to guard Subic Bay. Eight destroyers and four submarines anchored at Manila had departed on June 2, 1941.[330] A list of the American ships in port at Manila on June 7, 1941 included eight destroyers, fourteen submarines, and two target towing ships. The transport *Henderson*, had sailed for an unknown destination on June 5, 1941 as had the *Rei* from Cavite.[331] Two supply ships listed in the Japanese reports were later found to be minelayers, and the arrival from the United States of two more vessels of the same class was noted.[332] Tokyo inquired on June 21, 1941 concerning the arrival at Manila of Major Conrow, and ten other American aviators who had departed on June 17, 1941 for Chungking.[333] Information that the United States Navy was interested in requisitioning until September, half of the American Consulate office space at Manila for espionage work, led Mr. Matsuoka, on July 1, 1941 to fear that this was the first step in establishing a special service for British-American-Chinese military liaison.[334] Besides keeping a close watch on naval personnel to verify this report, the Japanese kept under surveillance a number of persons who had entered the country as temporary tourists.[335] They also suspected that investigations regarding Japanese vessels, or Japanese persons in the Philippine Islands, were being carried out in mid-July, 1941 by British and American authorities, chiefly through the British Honorary Consul, Francisco Brown.[336]

Japanese curiosity was aroused by the fact that 1013 Chinese immigrants had entered the Philippines during June, a large increase over the monthly average of 250. The immigrants appeared to have been summoned by Chinese already residing in the Philippines, although they were not contract laborers, nor had they anything to do with military construction projects.[337]

Deeming it important to instigate a cultural propaganda program at Manila, Mr. Negishi, a Japanese agent was appointed in early July 1941, to engage in intelligence as well as cultural work.[338] Since requests for Japanese financial assistance had been made by three candidates

---

[328] II, 242.
[329] II, 243.
[330] II, 244.
[331] II, 245.
[332] II, 246.
[333] II, 247.
[334] II, 248.
[335] II, 249.
[336] II, 250.
[337] II, 251.
[338] II, 252–253.

for office in the Philippine assembly, Tokyo was asked on July 13, 1941 for 40,000 yen and permission to aid these candidates, if such support were found advisable after an investigation had been made of the men's chances of winning the election.[339]

The unloading of coast guns, ten gun platforms, and more than twenty light tanks from an American tender at Manila was reported on July 10, 1941, as was the arrival of the President Taft, transporting 800 to 1000 soldiers to the Philippines.[341] Reported from Manila was the arrival of the *President Harrison* and *President Coolidge* on July 31 and August 1, 1941 respectively.[342]

That the United States was making an effort to strengthen Philippine defenses was concluded by the Japanese from the fact that on July 25, 1941, 460 planes and approximately 1300 pilots were stationed there, with an army force of about 10,000 men. The Philippine army, with reserves, was estimated to be about 130,000 in all, and it was believed that in an emergency, an army of 100,000 Filipinos could be turned over to a United States commander.[343]

It was noted on August 2, 1941 that the color of American military and naval planes had not been changed and were not camouflaged, and that the number of planes flying above Manila had decreased considerably.[344] By August 4, 1941 all of the American warships at anchor, with the exception of several small destroyers near Corregidor, had sailed. From the crew of the *President Coolidge*, it was learned on August 4, 1941 that about 600 American soldiers had arrived in Manila.[345]

United States naval and military preparations at Cavite were under close surveillance by the Japanese. A report was made to Tokyo on July 15, 1941 that construction there would be delayed, since the master electric dynamo had been struck by lightning, and electricity had to be supplied by an auxiliary system.[346]

In regard to the financing of Japanese intelligence work in the Philippines, arrangements were being made to continue activities in case of the freezing of funds. It was decided, on July 25, 1941, to keep a large part of Japanese assets in cash, since it was possible to foresee the difficulty of securing secret funds if the situation should become serious. But with the freezing of Japanese assets on July 26, 1941, Consul Nihro wired that he could not hope to continue business as before.[347] Moreover, the Japanese Consul on August 2, 1941 asked for permission to control the allotment of secret funds at his own discretion.[348]

Following the freezing order occasioned by the French Indo-China affair, the reactions of the Filipinos were reported to Tokyo on July 27, 1941 by the Japanese Consul. Particular attention, he declared, had been paid to that part of President Roosevelt's speech of July 25, 1941, which said that retaliatory action against Japan would be taken within twenty-four hours. When the order freezing Japanese assets was announced, it had been predicted at Manila that this was only the first retaliatory step, and that an export embargo would be placed on shipments of oil and other war materials to Japan from the United States.

---

[339]II, 254.

[340]II, 255.

[341]II, 256–257.

[342]II, 258.

[343]II, 259–260.

[344]II, 261.

[345]II, 262.

[346]II, 263.

[347]II, 264–265.

[348]II, 266.

Tokyo was informed that the Filipinos had strongly censured the lack of resistance on the part of France, and claimed that the invasion of French Indo-China had resulted from pressure upon France by Japan. They were confused and disturbed by rumors that the Japanese had obtained military bases as a result of the Japanese-French agreement; that Japanese vessels regularly coming to the Philippines had been requisitioned or would cancel this service; that Japan was mobilizing at home on a gigantic scale, and that foreigners might no longer travel in Japan.[349]

97. Reports from the Hawaiian Islands.

The Japanese Consul in Honolulu reported that the *President Pierce* had sailed for the Philippines on June 12, 1941 with about 900 soldiers and 100 pilots aboard,[350] and that on June 14, 1941, a 5,000-ton light cruiser had entered Pearl Harbor for repairs.[351] On July 18, 1941 Tokyo learned that an English light cruiser was getting ready to undergo repairs at Cavite while four destroyers had departed from, and six submarines had entered Manila.[352] It is evident that not much information was sent in the dispatches from Honolulu to Tokyo during this period, but some very significant inquiries were made by Tokyo in September 1941. (See Volume III of this series)

---

[349] II, 267.
[350] II, 268.
[351] II, 269–270.
[352] II, 271.

OUTLINE OF PART C[a]

Japanese Diplomatic Acitivities Throughout the World.

(a) *Japanese-American Relations*

(b) *Japanese-Mexican Relations*

(c) *Japanese-South American Relations*

(d) *Japanese-British Relations*

(e) *Japanese-Axis Relations*

(f) *Japanese-Russian Relations*

(g) *Japanese-French Relations*

(h) *Japanese-Chungking Relations*

(i) *Japanese-Nanking Relations*

(j) *Japanese-Dutch Relations*

(k) *Japanese-Thaiese Relations*

PART C—JAPANESE DIPLOMATIC ACTIVITIES THROUGHOUT THE WORLD

(a) Japanese-American Relations

98. Ambassador Nomura Reports Anti-Convoy Feeling in America.

In a report to Tokyo on May 15, 1941 Ambassador Nomura declared that despite President Roosevelt's silence concerning convoys to England, opinion in American government circles was generally unfavorable to immediate convoying. He surmised that Mr. Roosevelt, who wished to avoid war with Germany in the Atlantic, hesitated to use convoys, and preferred to lend destroyers to Great Britain to do its own convoying.

Mr. Nomura also believed that Secretary Knox and the Navy Department were opposed to lending United States ships to Britain, since this would weaken the American navy. Furthermore, an article in the *New York Times*, May 15, 1941 had stated that if England were provided with 200 long range bombers, this "patrol" would serve to hold the activity of German submarines in check.[353]

99. Japanese Reports on World Reaction to President Roosevelt's Speech of May 27, 1941.

Reports concerning the trend of public opinion in the United States, China, and Portugal in regard to the future actions of the United States were sent to Tokyo. The Japanese were especially concerned with the impressions created by President Roosevelt's fireside chat of May 27, 1941.

(a) *United States.*

See *Part A*, Section 14 for the Japanese estimate of American public opinion in regard to this speech by President Roosevelt.

---

[a]See TABLE OF CONTENTS for a detailed listing of topics discussed in Part C.

[353]II, 272.

(b) *Italy*

The Japanese Minister at Rome reported that President Roosevelt's use of the term "un-limited national emergency", according to American correspondents, was not synonymous with full mobilization. In view of President Roosevelt's statement that the safety of the United States would be directly threatened should the Azores and Cape Verde Islands fall into the hands of Germany, many Italians said that this was a manifestation of American aspirations for the occupation of these islands.[354]

(c) *China.*

Since the President had omitted any reference to Japanese-American relations in his "fire-side chat" of May 27, 1941 inferences drawn by the Chinese from this omission were generally unfavorable to the United States, according to a Japanese report from Shanghai to Tokyo. The speech had especially disappointed Chungking because it gave the impression that China's political set up was an anti-Nazi defense line, whereas, in fact, Chungking wished to preserve the German-Chinese cultural association as an instrument through which to negotiate with Germany in case Germany were victorious. Describing the speech as a blow to the Chinese who had been expecting aid from the United States, the Japanese informant surmised that the Chinese Communists regarded the speech as conducive to the adjustment of relations between the Nationalist and Communist Parties. The Chinese newspaper, *Sinka Nippo* regarded the omission of reference to Japanese-American relations as indicative that the United States would stress the war in the Atlantic, paying little attention to developments in the Pacific.[355]

(d) *Portugal.*

Portugal was greatly shocked by President Roosevelt's reference to the Azores, according to the Japanese. A very important Portuguese official confidentially told the Japanese representative that many within his government were urging Premier Salazar to proclaim to the Portuguese and to the outside world Portugal's sovereignty over these islands. That pro-British and pro-American elements would be weakened, and that a strong anti-American sentiment would sweep through Portugal was predicted by the Brazilian Ambassador to Portugal. However, a condemnation of the speech, which was to have been published in a newspaper controlled by the government, was withheld because of the arrival of a special message from Secretary Hull which stated that the United States did not intend to occupy the Azores.[356]

A visit to Portugal by Captain James Roosevelt on June 14, 1941 was not given front page prominence, since, in the opinion of the Japanese, the Portuguese censorship authorities were anti-American. Captain Roosevelt was treated indifferently by the local government, and, according to the Japanese, there was no evidence that he had been dined by any of the Portuguese authorities.[357]

A proposal that a group of anti-Salazar Portuguese in Mozambique assist the Portuguese government to occupy Mozambique in the event that the United States and England should take over the Azores, led the government newspaper to beg that the people remain faithful, and to warn them against subversive activities. However, the Japanese Ambassador in Lisbon reported that Portugal did not appear to be in any great danger in regard to the safety of the Azores.[358]

---

[354] II, 273.

[355] II, 274.

[356] II, 275.

[357] II, 276.

[358] II, 277.

100. Japan Scrutinizes Passenger Lists.

A report from Honolulu informed Tokyo of a local broadcast on June 5, 1941, announcing that one or two Germans of dubious character had been taken aboard the *Tatsuta Maru*, which had sailed from San Francisco on June 2 and would reach Honolulu on June 10.[359] Since the *Tatsuta Maru* was to provide passage to Japan for Mr. Mehner Toklaus, a German citizen, who had recently resigned his teaching position at the University of Hawaii, an inquiry was made as to his status. According to Consul Nagao Kita, the German Ambassador in Tokyo, was cognizant of the man's resignation from the University and his trip to Japan.[360]

Another passenger, who had sailed from San Francisco to the Orient on a previous trip of the *Tatsuta Maru*, was Bishop Walsh, well known to both Mr. Matsuoka and Ambassador Nomura as continually working for Japanese-American diplomatic friendship.[361]

101. Japanese Speculations as to Entry of the United States into War.

The Japanese Ambassador to Berlin reported to Tokyo on June 7, 1941 that it was the opinion of Chancellor Hitler and Foreign Minister von Ribbentrop that the United States would hesitate to enter the war so long as the members of the Tripartite Pact maintained their firm attitude.[362]

On June 16, 1941 Ambassador Kato in Vichy also expressed the belief that the United States probably would not enter the war, since it appeared that it was already exerting its maximum efforts. Though America was preserving England, and the continuation of the war was probably due to the United States alone, according to Ambassador Kato, even if the United States did fight, all it could possibly do would be to prolong the war.[363]

Speculations of Cuban authorities as to the effect on the Western Hemisphere of the entry of both the United States and Spain into the war were reported to Tokyo from Havana. It was predicted that if Spain went to war, the United States would recognize the Communists rather than the Franco regime in Spain.[364]

Japanese intelligence sources in Rome divulged that on July 16, 1941 Mr. Harold Tittman, on the basis of information received from the United States Embassy in Japan, had reported to Papal authorities that the United States government believed in the increased likelihood of an agreement being reached soon between Japan and the United States. The report stated that the United States was also confident that when it entered the European war, Japan could be prevented from interfering by this agreement, which would include a settlement of the Japanese-Chinese incident with the understanding that American aid to China would be withdrawn, if the Chiang regime did not accept the conditions submitted. If all other efforts failed, as a last resort, the Vatican would be asked to mediate for peace with China.[365]

102. Incidents Disturbing Japanese-American Relations.

(a) *The Okada Incident.*

In view of the critical Japanese-American relations, the arising of incidents which were likely to affect public opinion now assumed increasing significance. On June 10, 1941, Ambas-

---

[359]II, 278.
[360]II, 279.
[361]II, 280.
[362]II, 281, 282.
[363]II, 283.
[364]II, 284.
[365]II, 285.

sador Nomura notified Tokyo that there were grounds for suspecting that the Okada incident had been used by the F.B.I. and the Dies Committee as a means of interfering with Japanese propaganda in the United States.[366]

Lt. Comdr. Okada, a Japanese naval officer stationed on the west coast of the United States, had been arrested and charged with speeding. The Japanese government felt that special consideration should be given their naval officers, and threatened, unless better treatment were forthcoming, to reciprocate in dealing with American naval officers in Japan. Mr. Sadao Iguchi, the Japanese Embassy Counselor in Washington, informed Mr. Hamilton, Chief of the Far Eastern Section of the American State Department, that he would like to receive an explanation of the Okada incident from the State Department, and requested that similar occurrences be prevented in the future.[367]

(b) *The Tachibana Incident.*

Secret reports to Tokyo revealed that in the case of Commander Tachibana, a Japanese naval officer who had been held by American authorities on charges of espionage, plans were being made to use dubious methods in his defense. Commander Tachibana's chauffeur was to be paid a subsidy of $25,000 and all court costs so that he would not give damaging testimony.[368]

Another west coast incident arose when a Japanese violated United States immigration laws by crossing the border into Mexico without a visa.[369]

(c) *Restrictions on Gasoline Exports to Japan.*

The *Azuma Maru* at Philadelphia was not allowed to load lubricating oil, and this caused Mr. Matsuoka to ask on June 21, 1941 that all facts and background of the case be transmitted to him. He warned that the Japanese government was watching the Tachibana affair, and also the restrictions placed on gasoline exports to Japan, so as to evaluate the sincerity of the United States toward Japan.[370] It was more than a mere coincidence, therefore, that on June 24, 1941 Commander Tachibana was released by American authorities to sail for Tokyo on the *Nitta Maru*.[371] A Japanese Foreign Office courier, Mr. Yamazaki, was aboard this same ship.[372]

(d) *Compromise of Japanese Codes.*

Another incident which had greatly disturbed Japan was the searching of the *Nichi Shin Maru* off the west coast by what were believed to be American customs officials on May 28, 1941. Since naval codes and secret documents had been confiscated during the search, the Japanese immediately filed with the local customs officials a protest demanding their return. The customs officials consented to return them at a later date after an investigation had been made.[373] Ironically enough the United States Communication Intelligence organization had completely broken this cryptographic system and was reading all messages enciphered therein. Thus, the public seizure of these codes was very ill-advised for it meant the almost immediate cancellation of this system by the Japanese.

---

[366]II, 286.
[367]II, 287–288.
[368]II, 289.
[369]II, 289.
[370]II, 291.
[371]II, 292.
[372]II, 293.
[373]II, 294–296.

(e) *American Missionaries in Korea.*

When a discussion arose as to the fate of some American missionaries, accused of distributing dangerous literature in Korea, Tokyo informed Ambassador Nomura on July 2, 1941 that the Governor General of Korea would cancel the prosecution of the missionaries, if the State Department would evacuate them.[378] Because he believed that the incident involving the missionaries in Korea was similar to the case in the United States of Lt. Comdr. Okada on whom sentence would be passed on July 21, 1941, Mr. Matsuoka again instructed Ambassador Nomura on July 8, 1941 to inform the State Department that Japan desired to have the accused missionaries evacuated.[379]

On July 9, 1941 Counselor Iguchi discussed the incident with Dr. Hooper of the Presbyterian Church, who argued that when the missionaries had translated the English text of their pamphlets into Korean, they had done so in such a manner as to prevent any misunderstanding on the part of Japan. For this reason, Ambassador Nomura suggested that in view of the settling of the Tachibana incident by the United States, and as a friendly gesture, it might be well to drop the matter since three of the missionary group were already returning to the United States. Furthermore, the missionaries had endeavored to cooperate with Japanese authorities by first submitting the pamphlets to the police.[380]

A reply of July 14, 1941 to this suggestion of Ambassador Nomura stated that as far as the authorities in Tokyo were concerned the matter would be settled as leniently as possible by returning to the United States thirteen of the thirty persons involved. Because of illness, a fourteenth member, Mr. Clark, was already scheduled to return to the United States. However, according to Mr. Matsuoka, there was no record of the missionaries having sent the translated material to the police station in spite of an agreement to do so. This violated the Japanese Army-Navy Criminal Law and the Law for the Provisional Control of Disturbing Literature,[381] but on July 17, 1941 Japan was willing to overlook this violation of its publication regulations, and to treat the question as being merely a matter of seditious literature.[382]

Since the interview with Dr. Hooper had revealed that the Presbyterian Church, as a matter of policy, would neither evacuate the missionaries nor issue orders for their evacuation, Ambassador Nomura suggested to Tokyo on July 19, 1941 that a conference be held with local church authorities and the matter settled there. Inasmuch as the pamphlets concerned were translated directly from English into Japanese in Tokyo, and then distributed, he did not see how there could be a problem in this connection. He suggested also that if no solution were reached at the local conference, the matter be dropped.[383]

103. Japan Fears American Seizure of Its Vessels.

In view of the critical diplomatic situation engendered by Japanese aggression in Asia, and since the United States was keeping a strict check on Japanese vessels,[384] Japanese shipping schedules were carefully supervised by Japanese diplomatic officials. Japanese officials in Washington were advised of the schedule of eight cargo Marus, which were to pass through the Panama Canal at the rate of one a day between July 16 and July 22, 1941.[385]

---

[378]II, 305–307.
[379]II, 308.
[380]II, 309–310.
[381]II, 311.
[382]II, 312–313.
[383]II, 314–315.
[384]II, 316.
[385]II, 317–319.

Ambassador Nomura believed that the State Department's plan for according to Japanese merchants, entering the Philippines as international traders, the same treatment which was accorded Filipinos arriving in Japan, was an attempt to get written promises from Japan because the Japanese-American Trade Agreement was no longer extant.[386] Calling on the American Chief of the Far Eastern Section in Washington on June 13, 1941, Consul Iguchi asked if it were necessary that Japan inform the United States government exactly what it intended to do in this matter. The section chief replied that it would be well for the Japanese to submit their plans to the State Department.[387]

More discord occurred on June 16, 1941, when the Japanese learned that the granting of permits for export of scrap iron from the United States would be discontinued.[388] In retaliation, and to lessen losses which might later be incurred by the stoppage of Japanese vessels to America, as well as to impress upon American authorities the need for reconsideration, they discussed rerouting Japanese vessels which were transporting essential products to America. Mr. Matsuoka informed his minister at Manila on June 18, 1941 that the shipment of materials to the United States was under discussion.[389]

In calling on the President of the Philippine Islands on July 2, 1941 to present a Japanese official, Mr. Koyama, the Japanese Minister expressed regret concerning the absconding of Japanese fishermen with fishing boats of Philippine registry, but seized the opportunity to point out that Philippine control over Japanese fishermen had been excessively severe. The Philippine President replied that he would like to have a special conference on the subject at a later date.[390]

On July 3, 1941, the Captain of the *Awajisan Maru*, informing Japanese authorities that he could not procure a permit for passage through the Panama Canal, asked for authorization to proceed to Japan by way of Cape Horn.[391] Tokyo was then informed that the exits to and from the Canal had been closed on July 5, 1941 while an investigation was being conducted.[392]

Other protests concerning the treatment of Japanese vessels in American ports were also being lodged with United States authorities. On July 11, 1941, the *Asuka Maru* at Boston had been boarded and searched by a party of approximately twenty Coast Guardsmen, and the ship's bottom had been inspected on the following day, the *Norfolk Maru* had been delayed a day at Baltimore because of an inspection of its bottom; and the *Yamatsuki Maru* had been delayed while waiting to pass through the Panama Canal.[393]

America was not the only nation imposing restrictions on foreign shipping, for the British Embassy in Washington announced that beginning with July 15, 1941, all materials going by way of England would require import permits. Ambassador Nomura reported that freight would be seized in case no permits were obtained.[394]

Following the closing of the Panama Canal to Japanese ships, the statement of General van Voorhis to the United States' Press was sent to Tokyo. General van Voorhis, in charge of the

---

[386]II, 320.
[387]II, 321.
[388]II, 322.
[389]II, 323.
[390]II, 324.
[391]II, 325–326.
[392]II, 327.
[393]II, 328.
[394]II, 329.

Canal Zone's defenses, had stated on July 21, 1941 that the delay in allowing ships to go through the canal was a temporary measure owing to the emptying of the locks for repairs, and that ships of many countries, as well as the Japanese, were going around Cape Horn or the Cape of Good Hope.[395]

The Japanese were much concerned during July, 1941 lest the seizure of their ships interfere with the speedy evacuation of their nationals from Panama and the Philippines.[396] Although assured by Acting Secretary Welles that permission to leave port would be granted, on July 30, 1941, the Japanese instructed the captain of the *Tatsuta Maru* to delay entry into San Francisco since American authorities had avoided making a definite commitment when Ambassador Nomura had called at the State Department. No guarantees had been made by American authorities with regard to the freight carried by the vessel, although a definite reply in this connection had been requested.[397]

In spite of the difficulties experienced by Japanese ships with schedules and cargo routing in American ports,[398] a request from New York for additional vessels was directed in early July 1941 to Japan. Mr. Matsuoka replied, however, that it would be impossible, because of the shortage of bottoms, to dispatch ships to the Atlantic Coast of North America, although there would be changes in ship movements to the Pacific Coast.[399]

The reason behind such a decision, as explained by Tokyo, was the fear that the United States would seize Japanese vessels, just as it had taken German and Italian ships. Although the Philippine Islands had granted permits for the exportation of military goods to Japan, it was hardly fitting that Japanese vessels should be used for the transportation of military goods between the Philippines and the United States. Thus, the decision was reached to take some of the Japanese vessels off the Philippine-United States route.[400]

Rumors that Japan was withdrawing her ships from the Pacific spread to Rome, where Ambassador Horikiri inquired of Tokyo on July 10, 1941 as to whether or not this order included all ships plying regularly between North and South America.[401] Foreign Minister Matsuoka reassured him that trips between Japan and the Philippines would continue, but that the operation of ships between the Philippine Islands and the east coast of North America would be discontinued. After August 1, 1941, all Japanese shipping on the east coast of North America was to be stopped, and Japanese ships on the east coast of South America were to operate around Cape Horn.[402] Only one sailing was to be maintained after September 1941 to the west coast of North America.[403]

To minimize the disturbance of public opinion created by the order affecting the disposition of its merchant ships, Japan declared that the reasons for the order were the shortage of ships in the seas near Japan and various circumstances which precluded loading on the eastern coast of the United States. Japanese diplomats were ordered to give widespread dissemination to this explanation of the new shipping order.

Ambassador Nomura was concerned with the pacifying of Japanese nationals in the United States who were cooperating with him fully, but who were cognizant also of the fact that Tokyo's

---

[395]II, 330.
[396]II, 331–332.
[397]II, 333.
[398]II, 334.
[399]II, 335.
[400]II, 336.
[401]II, 337.
[402]II, 338.
[403]II, 339.

official reasons were designed to serve as explanations only for Americans. In spite of orders issued by the Japanese navy, control by Japanese diplomats over Japanese nationals in the United States was becoming more difficult since confidence in the government of Japan was weakening.[404]

In view of the circumstances, Japanese representatives at Manila warned Tokyo on July 7, 1941 that unless a "show-down economic war" were resolved upon and prepared for, Japan might find herself in a predicament. It was feared that Philippine shippers would abandon the use of Japanese ships, thus making it impossible for Japan to take advantage of the privileges enjoyed by the Filipinos under the American export license system. It was also believed that the United States might prevent the exporting of goods which were then permitted to be shipped, or would resort to the freezing of assets.[405] Meanwhile, Japanese representatives were explaining that the stoppage of shipments from the Philippines to America had resulted from a shortage of ships and the reduction of exports to Japan, rather than from a sudden change in the diplomatic situation.[406]

Tokyo replied on July 7, 1941 that it was conscious of the difficulties created by its orders, but that measures for protecting its shipping against the United States had been decided long ago and must now be enforced. Shipping contracts for 22,000 tons of Filipino goods would have to be cancelled by government order owing to necessary changes in ship dispositions. However, since precedence for such cancellations existed in international law, the Japanese Foreign Minister pointed out that there was likely to be no great trouble over it.[407]

Ambassador Nomura was notified by the State Department on July 31, 1941 that Japanese ships carrying cargoes which were to be sent back without unloading would have until 2:00 p.m. Saturday, August 2, to enter an American port, and would then be given a reasonable time to depart. Japanese ships with cargoes destined for American ports were to change the manifests to indicate that the cargo was being shipped elsewhere. This would obviate compliance with a customs regulation requiring the unloading of goods manifested for American ports before a vessel could be given clearance.[408]

On August 2, 1941, Foreign Minister Toyoda issued instructions that the *Tatsuta Maru* stop at Honolulu, [409] while at the same time he inquired of his representative in San Francisco concerning a Domei dispatch which stated that a part of the cargo of the *Tatsuta Maru* had been seized for the owners.[410] Fearing that the cargo of the *Heian Maru* at Seattle would be attached by the owners, as in the case of the *Tatsuta Maru*, it was decided on August 2, 1941 after a conference to have the entire cargo unloaded at Vancouver.[411] It was learned however, that the *Heian Maru* had left Seattle hurriedly on August 4, 1941, for Japan, although nothing had been taken aboard but food and fuel for the ship.[412] A special inquiry was made by the Japanese concerning the arrival in American waters of the special duty ship, *Shiriyo*, scheduled to enter port on August 9, 1941.[413]

---

[404]II, 340–341.
[405]II, 342.
[406]II, 343.
[407]II, 344–345.
[408]II, 346.
[409]II, 347.
[410]II, 348.
[411]II, 349.
[412]II, 350.
[413]II, 351.

104. Japan Analyzes the Silver Shirts Movement.

Japanese plans to carry on sabotage in the United States included the use of Negroes and members of the Silver Shirts movement. In acquiring control of the Silver Shirts, Mr. Iwasaki, a Japanese agent in America, was to be sent to Japan for instructions, since indoctrination in Japanese plans "to establish justice in the United States" was thought to be a more suitable objective for their agents than mere pecuniary considerations.[414]

On June 28, 1941 Mr. Yoshio Muto submitted to Tokyo a report concerning the origin and principles of the Silver Shirts movement, but advised against Japan's having anything to do with it. He feared the Silver Shirts could hardly succeed in America since they were being investigated by the Dies Committee as a subversive activity and, thus, could not act openly. The organization had been dissolved in 1940, after six years of existence, but then an underground movement with similar objectives had sprung up. Its publications, heavily subsidized, were shipped from Indianapolis to points all over the country.

According to Mr. Muto, Chief Pelley of the Silver Shirts had asked Mr. Iwasaki on April 20, 1941, if the Japanese government would not help out with his plans, and he had also requested Jiro Koga, of the Japanese Society of Brethren Overseas, to contact the German Ambassador in Tokyo in case Japan would not grant this help. On several occasions Mr. Pelley had asked for a reply to this request for Japanese aid.

The Japanese reported that the Silver Shirts stressed the following principles in their published propaganda, some samples of which were later shipped to Tokyo: The Roosevelt administration was shot through with international Judaism and Communism, and was coming under the influence of British royalty, which was under the thumb of these elements; America should be defended from them, and America's foreign policy should save the human race from the enslaving grasp of the international Jews; as for the Orient and Europe, the United States should not interfere, but should look after its own interests.[415]

105. Japan Attempts to Employ American Negroes as Spies.

Since official reports were not too favorable towards their use of the Silver Shirts as subversive agents, Japanese intelligence agents turned their attention to American Negroes.[416] In a long Japanese report on the economic and social status of the Negro in the United States, it was pointed out that Negroes were not organized into a strong racial group, and instead of looking toward a social revolution, they were following the single principle of elevating themselves. The report stated that certain progressive organizations, such as the Negro Congress, the Negro Alliance and the National Association for the Advancement of Colored People were working toward the equalization of the Negro, with the largest Negro organizations financed by Jews. The Japanese expected great results from cooperating with these organizations since two Negro men, were being used to disseminate propaganda and to interview Negro leaders of great ability. Since some Negroes were being employed in navy arsenals and military establishments, considerable use could be made of them in gathering military intelligence.[417]

---

[414]II, 352.
[415]II, 353.
[416]II, 354.
[417]II, 355–357.

106. Rumors of a British-German Peace.

The possibility that Russia might be quickly shattered by the German army, and the consequent threat of a German invasion of England stimulated discussion of a British-German peace parley in July, 1941. Ambassador Nomura reported on July 8, 1941, that the United States was serving as a check or a brake on Germany, and that there were men in the State Department who favored peace in order to prevent the annihilation of the British Empire. The Secretary of Commerce, Jesse Jones, was of this opinion, Ambassador Nomura said; and Colonel Lindbergh and predicted that peace talks would bud in July and blossom in the autumn of 1941.[418]

Though assured by Foreign Minister von Ribbentrop that the peace rumors were but machinations of England and the United States, which were designed to drive a wedge between Germany and Japan, on July 10, 1941 the Japanese Foreign Minister hurriedly directed his Ambassador in Berlin to check German official opinion as to the interpretation of such activity.[419]

107. Japanese Reports on American Industrial Expansion.

To keep Tokyo informed as to the extent of the American expansion and acceleration of defense work, details concerning current contract amounts and items of production assigned to the automobile industry in the Chicago area were reported to Japan. Contracts of the United States armed forces with General Motors, Ford, Chrysler, and Packard corporations were enumerated as well as the type of machinery for which they had contracted.[420]

108. Japanese Interest in Russian-American Friendship.

On August 2, 1941, Mr. Morito Morishima, in New York, reported to Tokyo that Mr. Denny, an editorial writer for the Scripps-Howard Newspapers on diplomatic questions had said that since Germany and Russia were so deeply involved in the war, Russia was demanding not only complete material assistance, but also that joint British and American military activities be concentrated in Germany's rear and in Norway as well. This comment had been occasioned by Mr. Hopkins' mission to Russia, although officials in Washington explained that he had gone there to confer only on aid to the Soviets.

Mr. Morishima declared that it could not be predicted whether or not Mr. Hopkins and Commissar Stalin would be able to decide upon an agreement, but that it would seem clear that such was the object of his mission.[421] Furthermore, the State Department on August 4, 1941 announced that the validity of the American-Soviet Trade Agreement of August 6, 1937 had been extended to August 6, 1942.[422]

109. Japanese Security Precautions.

The problems of maintaining the security of their codes and of determining the reliability of the information relayed to Tokyo continued to be a matter of concern to the Japanese. On May 20, 1941 Ambassador Nomura began to identify the more reliable intelligence with "Joko", whereas "Jō otsu" was used to identify messages containing less reliable information.[423]

---

[418]II, 358.

[419]II, 359.

[420]II, 360.

[421]II, 361.

[422]II, 362.

[423]II, 363–364.

Because of the critical international situation, Japan had instructed Ambassador Nomura as early as May 1941, to separate all secret documents into a special class, and to burn all other documents, with the exception of a few that might be currently needed. Ambassador Nomura suggested, in addition, that all account books be burned, except those for the last three or four years, that all outstanding funds be collected, and that Japanese land on N Street in Washington be sold.[424] To effect these objectives, Ambassador Nomura asked on May 17, 1941 that an assistant be selected and sent to him immediately by the San Francisco Consul General.[425] On July 2, 1941 he requested permission to burn certain codes, some of which would be of no future use and others which were rarely used.[426]

In accordance with Tokyo's orders, Ambassador Nomura dispatched twenty-two boxes containing records and other materials on the *Norfolk Maru*, which sailed from Baltimore for Japan on July 12, 1941. In view of Japanese-American relations, it was suggested that entry into ports of call in South America be cancelled, if speed were necessary in returning these records to Yokohama.[427]

Tokyo also instructed Washington that in case of difficulty, use would be made of the intelligence dispatches sent out from Japan each night. However, to reach Tokyo from Washington, it would be necessary to have a wireless set in the Washington office, with an operator of exceptional ability, relaying dispatches via South America and the Jaluit Atoll. For this purpose Tokyo inquired on July 7, 1941 as to the feasibility of assembling a 100 or 200 watt transmitter under the guise of amateur apparatus, and of making trial communications of short transmissions. Such equipment would be advantageous in case extreme limitations or prohibitions were placed by the United States upon the use of radio in general.[428] However, on July 23, 1941 Ambassador Nomura, after concurring with Japanese naval experts, pointed to the inadvisability of installing the transmitter since it would be impossible to keep it concealed from American detectors. Furthermore, interference would make for inefficient transmissions.[429]

To assure the security of code machines and code books still in use, Tokyo planned to ship a special size safe to the United States. Since the matter of space in a Japanese telegraphic office and the place of landing the safe had to be considered, Ambassador Nomura suggested that the facilities in Washington be expanded, and that the safe be landed in Baltimore for delivery to Washington.[430]

Mr. Matsuoka stressed the extreme need of security in a dispatch of June 2, 1941 to all his diplomatic representatives throughout the world. Emphasizing the progress of the science of cryptography and cryptanalysis in various countries, he concluded that no absolute confidence could be placed in the secrecy of a code. He asked that the strictest attention be paid during the transfer and tenure of codes, and directed that code messages in a certain special system be sent only to Tokyo.[431] The sending of all other code messages was to be discontinued, thus alleviating the excessive load imposed on communication clerks because of the vigilance necessary for communication security. The duties of Japanese communication clerks were increasing.[433]

---

[424]II, 365.
[425]II, 366.
[426]II, 367.
[427]II, 368.
[428]II, 369.
[429]II, 370.
[430]II, 364, 371–372.
[431]II, 373.
[433]II, 375.

Following the receipt of this dispatch, Ambassador Nomura requested on July 3, 1941 that the clerical staff of his office be expanded because of the ever-increasing load of telegraphic communications, and since Mr. Watanabe, the telegraphic clerk, had been able to accomplish all the work only by his extreme diligence.[434]

In order to prepare for more critical developments, and because he had given up the probability of finding a separate building, on July 24, 1941 Ambassador Nomura again suggested an expansion of the Washington business office, since it had been necessary to change the reception rooms into document and night duty rooms. Additional office space would have to be made available to equip the telegraph room for an increase in personnel, and to make room for special safes. To effect these changes, Ambassador Nomura requested that $2,700 be appropriated.[435]

With the increase in the telegraphic load, not only was the Washington office short of clerks, but Mr. Morishima, in New York, was forced to request two members from other offices. On July 30, 1941 he asked Washington to send an aide from the Japanese Embassy.[436] In Washington, the Military and Naval attaches asked that they be permitted to move their offices to the Embassy, in view of the dangerous situation prevailing at that time. This request was submitted to Japan for approval.[437]

Since there was a possibility that their offices might be closed without warning, precautions for the safety of the Emperor's portraits in New York and Chicago were being taken by the Japanese. A student clerk, Mr. Hashizume, planned to take them on July 30, 1941 by train to San Francisco, where Minister Kaname Wakasugi would transport the pictures to Japan on the *Asama Maru*.[438]

PART C—JAPANESE DIPLOMATIC ACTIVITIES THROUGHOUT THE WORLD

(b) Japanese-Mexican Relations

110. Japan Establishes an Espionage Net in Mexico to Acquire Intelligence from the United States.

Minister Yoshiaki Miura was informed on June 2, 1941, that Japan had appropriated 100,000 yen to be used in Mexico City to collect intelligence concerning the United States. According to Mr. Matsuoka, Mexico City was the natural geographical center for an intelligence base, although Rio de Janeiro, Buenos Aires, and Santiago would also be useful. The Japanese Minister in Mexico was reminded that in cooperation with Japanese officials in Los Angeles, Houston, New Orleans, and New York, these funds were to be used principally for intelligence relating to the United States. If the United States entered the war, Japan would endeavor to use Japanese nationals to the best advantage in dividing the Rightist and Leftist labor organizations, and in promoting their anti-American revolutionary influence.[439]

---

[434]II, 376.
[435]II, 377–379.
[436]II, 380.
[437]II, 381.
[438]II, 382–383.
[439]II, 384.

In line with Japan's policy of bringing "fifth columnists" to Japan for instructions, Consul General Katsuya Sato, in Mexico, was preparing to send to Tokyo, Jose Llergo, an outstanding Mexican news reporter, whom he thought capable of greatly influencing the Mexican press.[440] Trips to Japan for two other men, underlings of Maximino Camacho, to facilitate their future use in propaganda, were also suggested by Minister Yoshiaki Miura. One of these, a Mr. Isaac Diaz, had been investigated by the Japanese Minister, but approval for the financing of his trip had not been granted by Tokyo.[441]

111. Japan Seeks Essential Military Supplies in Mexico.

On June 24, 1941 Minister Kiyoshi Yamagata in Mexico was attempting to negotiate for needed military materials, proposing payment by either the barter system or compensatory trade. However, he believed that there existed little likelihood of his succeeding by approaching Mexican authorities through the usual channels, inasmuch as additional pressure was being exerted by the United States, and because Mexican businessmen expected that sooner or later an embargo or export license system, affecting the export to Japan of mercury and other materials, would be initiated. Mr. Yamagata thought it advisable, therefore, to make purchases as quickly and as secretly as possible. Since he felt that political trends in the Caribbean and Central American countries should also be taken into consideration, Mr. Yamagata planned to visit Panama, Colombia and Peru.[442]

Experiencing difficulty in achieving satisfactory trade relations and in organizing intelligence activities, the Japanese Minister to Mexico, Yoshiaki Miura, had discussed with Mr. Yamagata the expansion of the Mexican office to meet wartime needs. Since Secretary Keizo Fujii, appointed as First Secretary of the Japanese Legation in Mexico, was finding it difficult to leave Spain because of lack of steamer accommodations, Minister Miura suggested the sending of a capable person in his place, who, in addition to taking general charge of the Mexican office, would have responsibility for either the trade or intelligence work. This would leave Secretary Sato free to look after other duties. Replacements were suggested for Mr. Kataoka and Mr. Samijima, who, although capable men, had been there too long to help in creating a new atmosphere in the office.[443] The suggestion that Mr. Sotomatsu Kato of Mexicali be sent to the Mexico City office was later thought to be inadvisable in view of current conditions,[444] and probably because of Mr. Kato's intelligence activities.[445]

112. Japanese Apprehension Concerning the Prospective Effects of the American-Mexican Negotiations.

Fearing that Japanese-Mexican trade would be seriously affected by negotiations under way between America and Mexico to exchange necessary war materials, Minister Miura, referring to an Associated Press release of a statement issued by the Mexican Foreign Office, thought that it would be best to discuss the matter openly with the Mexican Foreign Minister. He advised on June 27, 1941 that a detailed report would be forthcoming shortly.[446]

---

[440]II, 385.
[441]II, 386.
[442]II, 387–390.
[443]II, 391.
[444]II, 392.
[445]II, 393.
[446]II, 394.

Meanwhile, the safety of Japanese fishing ships in Mexican waters was a problem, although Minister Miura assured Tokyo on June 24, 1941 that it should merely watch cooly the course of events since for the time being there was nothing to worry about.[447]

On July 2, 1941, Minister Miura, disturbed by Associated Press reports from Washington to the effect that the pending American-Mexican treaty was designed to prevent the shipment of American materials anywhere outside the American countries, paid a visit to Foreign Minister Ezequiel Padilla. When asked if these reports were true, Mr. Padilla answered that Mexico was considering an agreement of this kind, but that the matter concerned only American powers, and had nothing to do with other countries.[448]

Minister Miura further inquired as to the possibility of Mexico's being prevented from selling her surplus materials to the Japanese. Admitting that the gist of the American proposal was that American goods were not to be shipped out of American states, Mr. Padilla said that Mexico was still considering the matter, but had as yet not decided. Minister Miura then pointed out that should such an agreement be concluded, the friendly relations which had existed between Mexico and Japan for a long time would be marred. Foreign Minister Padilla replied that the Mexican government was hesitating because disruption of the Japanese-Mexican relationship would be most regrettable, but that, since Mexico had to obtain machinery and other goods, it was necessary to sell Mexican goods to the United States. To say that Japan, instead of the United States, could sell the machinery to Mexico was quite beside the point.

Arguing that Japan was now in position to sell surpluses of heavy industrial goods, Minister Miura referred to a list offered by the Japanese Chief of the Commercial Section which Minister Yamagata had brought to Mexico. The Foreign Minister, however, avoided discussion of this by saying that these points were being studied by experts in various departments. Minister Miura assured the Foreign Minister that goods purchased by Japan would not be reshipped to Germany, and stated that it was the feeling of the Japanese government that the European war would end sooner than expected. Mr. Padilla, in closing the interview, said that he would consider the Japanese Minister's remarks in examining the treaty.[449]

113. Japan Establishes Espionage Routes from the United States to Mexico.

On June 28, 1941 Mr. Matsuoka, requesting Minister Miura to establish communication between Mexico and the United States at once in connection with the intelligence network to be organized, asked that regular reports concerning its progress be made.[450]

Mr. Kato, in Mexicali, reported on July 2, 1941 that if intelligence work were to be carried on, it was absolutely necessary that both new funds and personnel be supplied. Although there were many Japanese inhabitants in his vicinity, not one of them belonged to the intelligentsia. Minister Miura believed that in spite of the difficulty of conducting intelligence work in a border city having a population of only 15,000, the work there would be useful, provided that the intelligence nets in Los Angeles and vicinity were well organized, and especially if the withdrawal of Japanese officials from the United States should become necessary. For this reason, Minister Miura proposed to establish connections with Los Angeles and make necessary preparations.[451]

---

[447]II, 395.
[448]II, 396.
[449]II, 394, 396–398.
[450]II, 399.
[451]II, 393.

By July 4, 1941, impressed with the necessity of haste in view of the delicate Japanese-American situation, Minister Miura was attempting to establish an international route by which intelligence could be relayed from the United States to Tokyo. He planned to use Mexico City as headquarters for the collection of observations and opinions gathered from the espionage net in the United States. To effect quick passage into Mexico, he suggested that Japanese intelligence agents in the United States be reduced at once from their official status to that of civilians, thereby allowing them to make representations as individuals to the Mexican government.

Urging that before it became too late, Japanese agents in the border areas should secure passport visas and should begin to perform their intelligence duties, Minister Miura advocated the opening of offices in Laredo, El Paso, Nogales, and Mexicali to establish a route for the transmission of intelligence. On a trip to New Orleans and Houston, the Japanese Minister had discovered that the organizing of an intelligence net had been given not the slightest consideration. Mr. Yamagata's party, passing through Los Angeles, had discovered a similar situation. However, by July 4, 1941, these offices, under orders from Tokyo, had gradually brought their plans to a head.

Disclaiming responsibility for the organization of an espionage net in the United States, Minister Miura declared that this activity was definitely a function of Japanese diplomats in the United States. Believing that the establishment of the intelligence transmission route was separate from the creation of an espionage net, he argued that it was quite impossible for officials in Mexico City to bring the latter into being. To avert working at cross purposes, however, Minister Miura asked Tokyo for additional information.[452]

On July 22, after a conference with Messrs. Terasaki, Ito, and Kato, it was decided to abandon the idea of using Mexicali as an intelligence center. Mr. Miura argued that its location and its transportation and communication facilities were disadvantageous, and that its Japanese citizens were under the closest surveillance. Mexicali, he concluded, would not be suitable for any intelligence activity.[453]

To complete plans for the establishment of an espionage net, Consul Ito and Secretary Terasaki went to Mexico on an itinerary which included Mexico City, Panama, Port of Spain, and Rio de Janeiro.[454] After conferring with Secretary Terasaki and Consul Ito, Minister Miura, having had a change of mind, warned Tokyo that Mexico, as compared with Brazil, Argentina and Chile, should not be considered as a main base of intelligence, although a study of plans for intelligence routes and connections in Mexico should be continued. Aside from the fact that the general feeling in Mexico towards Japan was not pleasant, and that Mexico might be viewed as a dependency of the United States, difficulties in attempting to get information about internal conditions in the United States would occur. If Mexico went to war, it would be impossible, because of communications, to transfer or expand the Japanese intelligence organization.[455]

To support the establishment of the Japanese intelligence net, which was to have its headquarters in Mexico City, three routes to Mexico from the United States, via Laredo, Ciudad-Juarez and Mexicali, were being considered. A Chilean route from Manzanillo to Mexico, and

---

[452]II, 400–403.
[453]II, 404.
[454]II, 405–409.
[455]II, 410.

a Brazilian route by way of Vera Cruz were also to be formed. Japanese officials in the United States and Mexico were to work out the details of their own espionage nets so as to coordinate them, and they were to develop a plan for making contacts and exchanges on the border. The means for keeping in contact through telegraph, telephone, memoranda and word of mouth were to be decided upon at a later date. Mr. Matsuoka stressed the importance of preparing such routes against the coming of war, and warned that nothing should be done which would jeopardize their security.[456]

114. Japanese Plans to Operate a Secret Radio in Mexico.

Continuing their preparations for intelligence work in case the United States and Mexican offices were withdrawn, the Japanese planned to install a secret transmitter in Mexico City. If the apparatus were discovered by Mexico, Japanese officials were determined to plead diplomatic immunity. In view of the difficulty of procuring parts for the transmitter, the possibility of assembling the equipment in the United States was suggested.[457]

115. Japanese Concern with Mexico's Pro-American Attitude.

Summarizing the Mexican situation in a report to Tokyo on July 4, 1941, Minister Miura reiterated that in spite of his best efforts to foster anti-American and anti-war atmosphere in Mexico, he felt that it was impossible to achieve much along these lines. The success of Japanese plans would be determined by the political and foreign policy of Mexico, as directed by President Camacho and his Cabinet, and since these gentlemen were strongly pro-American, it was impossible to procure any information of value to Japan.

Pointing out that the first aim of the Japanese was to undermine the leadership which the United States held in regard to other nations of the hemisphere, Minister Miura felt that it was necessary to break up the so-called "Good Neighbor Policy", thereby destroying any possibility of future coordination among the American nations. For this reason, and following the suggestions of Military Attache Yoshiaki Nishi, he advised the supporting of a rebellion in Guatemala which would have to be quieted by United States' armed forces. This would violate the "Good Neighbor Policy" and would cause a cleavage between the countries on the American continent by upsetting the political balance as far south as Panama. Minister Miura advised that funds be appropriated to begin preparation, if his plan appeared feasible in the light of Japanese national policy.[458]

Commenting on the uselessness of attempting to sway official opinion in Mexico, Minister Miura stated that no other nation on the American continent was so influenced by the United States as was Mexico.[459] He found it difficult to judge whether or not Mexico would follow the United States into war, but, in any case, it was now impossible to carry on trans-Pacific commerce. Considering this fact, Minister Miura, as well as Japanese officials in San Francisco, were arranging for the secret return of the Emperor's portraits to Japan. One portrait was being returned in the custody of the captain of the *Ginyo Maru*, and another on the *Kamakura Maru*.[460] Mr. Matsuoka approved this plan, but warned that care should be taken in dealing with the captain of the vessel.[461]

---

[456]II, 411.

[457]II, 412.

[458]II, 413–414.

[459]II, 415.

[460]II, 416–418.

[461]II, 419–420.

116. Japan Considers the Evacuation of Its Nationals in the United States.

In the event that the Japanese-American relationship was severed, the Japanese Minister in Mexico was considering the evacuation of Japanese nationals from the United States. However, because of the manner in which the United States and Mexico had been treating Germans and Italians, Minister Miura felt that there was no possibility of Mexico's allowing Japanese residents from other countries to enter its borders.

The question of accommodating Japanese nationals from the United States was not an immediate one, since many Japanese in the United States would choose to remain there. If Mexico took an attitude completely in harmony with that of the United States, the repatriation of the Japanese in Mexico to Japan would be extremely difficult. In the light of this situation, preparations were made in Mexico City to call a meeting of fourteen or fifteen Japanese representatives from various parts of the country to discuss questions of mutual help, the maintenance of liaison between Mexico City and the districts, and the protection of enterprises and property of Japanese residents.[462]

Reporting on this meeting of July 19, 1941, Japanese officials listed several points which had been decided in relation to the best method of solving their problems in Mexico. They planned to establish an efficient system of liaison between the Mexico City office and other districts. The country would be divided into nine areas with a liaison officer in charge of each, and in this way, it would be possible to promote better feeling among the Mexicans toward the Japanese people, and to devise methods to be taken to protect Japanese firms, if indications began to point to the freezing of Japanese assets in Mexico.[463]

117. Japan Attempts to Exert Economic Pressure Against Mexico.

Minister Miura suggested to Foreign Minister Matsuoka, on July 10, 1941, that a Japanese Consulate be established at the port of Manzanillo. Although the port was relatively unimportant, both the United States and Great Britain had established consulates there. Not only was the American Consul bringing considerable pressure to bear on Mexican officials, but since Japan lacked a diplomatic office at this port, Americans were spying upon Japanese vessels to determine what goods were being shipped to Japan.[464] Apparently as a retaliatory measure against the strict control of Mexican exports to Japan, Mr. Matsuoka reported on July 10, 1941 that there was no Japanese export plan for the shipments of artificial silk to Mexico in July, because of the shortage of ships. Explaining that, owing to a government defense order, permits had to be obtained for the exportation of silk thread, he asked that Minister Miura send his opinion concerning the limiting of Japanese exports to Mexico.[465]

Three days later, Minister Miura wired that, although he had been unable to secure an interview with the Minister of Economics, he had cornered him at a social function and, as a result, had obtained an interview on July 12, 1941. In view of the prospective signing of the Mexican-American agreement, Minister Miura declared that should the major part of the present Japanese-Mexican trade come under the terms of the Mexican-American agreement, Japan and Mexico would be unable to continue their present close relations. He pointed out that Mexican mercury and other items were as essential to Japan as Japanese rayon was to Mexico. The Minister of Economics, however, avoided this discussion by saying that until

---

[462]II, 421.
[463]II, 422.
[464]II, 423.
[465]II, 424.

the pact had been agreed upon, he was in no position to talk about such a matter, but that in his own personal opinion, a Mexican law would be put into effect restricting the exporting of materials to nations other than those of the American continent. The Japanese Ambassador again argued without success, that his country was in a position to supply Mexico with a great deal of heavy industrial and chemical products.[466]

A rumor that the United States planned to establish a branch of the Treasury Department in Mexico City gave rise to Japanese fears that such a move was being undertaken to ensure that the provisions of the pending treaty were carried out.[467] Feeling that a definite position should be taken by Japan, at this time, in regard to the Mexican-American agreement on July 15, 1941, Minister Miura assembled Japanese businessmen, as well as his military and naval attaches, to discuss plans of procedure. It was decided that as a test of Mexico's intentions, Mexican officials should be asked to approve the exporting of goods already under contract to Japan. If Mexico refused to cooperate, the use of Japanese shipping would be denied to it, and a stoppage of rayon and other essential goods would ensue. Although two Japanese vessels loaded with rayon had arrived in Manzanillo and had already begun unloading, it was still possible to prevent the unloading of the *Heiyo Maru*, also laden with rayon, which was scheduled to arrive July 25, 1941.[468]

To an inquiry from Tokyo concerning the information that officials at Manzanillo would not give clearance to the *Akagi Maru*,[469] Minister Miura answered that, in spite of the pressure exerted by British and American Consuls, the ship had been able to sail, and that no such incident had occurred. The Japanese Minister, declaring that the facts had been misrepresented, asked that the source of the news be traced.[470] Three days later, Tokyo replied that the report had been wired from the American Metal Company of Manzanillo, a Mitsui subsidiary, by way of the company's New York branch.[471]

118. Japanese Reaction to American-Mexican Agreement (July 15, 1941).

The much feared agreement between the United States and Mexico was announced by official proclamation on July 15, 1941. In an interview with Mr. J. T. Bodet, the Mexican Foreign Minster, concerning this new development, Mr. Miura learned that the terms contained in the proclamation would be carried out without waiting for the completion of details. Mr. Bodet felt that the embargo law would be interpreted in its strictest sense and that even those articles previously contracted for would immediately come under the terms of the proclamation. In spite of the Japanese Minister's insistence that Japanese businessmen would suffer enormous losses, the Mexican Vice Minister was adamant in interpreting the Presidential proclamation as applicable both to goods previously and subsequently contracted for, and regardless of the nationality of the merchants handling them.[472] These statements were confirmed officially on July 19, 1941, when Minister Miura was asked to call on him.

The problem of keeping the cargo of the *Heiyo Maru* out of Mexico was a perplexing one, and Mr. Miura felt it necessary again to consult an assembly of Japanese nationals concerning this matter. Considering the difficulty of the ship's leaving Mexico while still loaded, and

---

[466]II, 425.
[467]II, 426.
[468]II, 427.
[469]II, 428.
[470]II, 429.
[471]II, 430.
[472]II, 431.

since it would be unable to transport its scheduled cargo from South America, Mr. Miura reported on the advisability of having the vessel peacefully unloaded. In view of the fact that Mexico had no other rayon supply, and that its need and the agitation of the few capitalists controlling raw materials would grow, the best solution appeared to be the authorization of no other shipments of rayon to Mexico.[473]

The proclamation of July 15, 1941, brought to an end the attempts of Japanese officials to work through Maximino Camacho, and thus, plans were laid to obtain materials through another agent. Armed with the assurance that the United States could not supply Mexico's need for rayon, one of Minister Miura's agents negotiated with the Mexican Economic Minister to trade 20,000 cases of rayon for 8,000 bottles of mercury. Various details of transportation and payment created difficulties, but were being discussed.[474]

Approving this move, Tokyo, on July 22, 1941, advised that until definite results could be obtained through their undercover operations, it would be necessary to negotiate officially for the exchange of goods already under contract. Japan's decision to stop the shipment in August of 7,000 boxes of rayon, was to be explained to the Mexican government by saying that Japan found it necessary to recognize only these contracts which assured Japan of the acquisition of needed goods. Because the amount of supplies which the United States could furnish Mexico would affect its activities to a large extent, Japan asked that all intelligence on this subject be forwarded.[475]

Japanese officials in Mexico were advised on July 23, 1941, that in view of Mexico's embargo of materials essential to Japan, the Japanese ministries had decided to prohibit the exporting not only of rayon, but of all other general merchandise to Mexico.[476]

Minister Miura, realizing that such a decision would react unfavorably upon opinion in South America, and that Japan could still obtain such items as petroleum products, pine tar, cotton and cotton "linters" declared that this trump card of complete prohibition of exports should be carefully played.[477] Submitting a report on artificial silk, mercury and other mineral products on the same day, he encouraged Japan to delay its embargo, since it was possible that the United States would not be able to supply the necessary amount of materials.[478] The Japanese government, regardless of loss or profit, was prepared to offer rayon at one-half the price of American rayon, if assurances were made that exports necessary to Japan would be sent in return. If this proposal were refused by the Mexican government, it was hoped that this information could be used at least to foster anti-American ideas by publicizing the fact that Mexicans could procure Japanese rayon at half the price at which they were now buying it from the United States.[479]

On July 30, 1941, Tokyo learned that it would be impossible to move a supply of Japanese lead left in Manzanillo. The Mexican Minister of Economics, queried by the Mitsui Company, said that the United States had asked that Japan not be allowed to export the lead, since it was necessary for defense, and that, therefore, he would have to refuse.[480]

---

[473]II, 432–433.
[474]II, 434.
[475]II, 435–436.
[476]II, 437.
[477]II, 438.
[478]II, 439–440.
[479]II, 441.
[480]II, 442.

With expenses mounting, and unable to cash salary checks in Mexico after the freezing of assets in America, Minister Miura suggested that his government find some way to make remittances. Informing Tokyo that he had but $12,000 on hand, he pointed out that expenses for June and July would leave him with a deficit of $600. Furthermore, he reminded his superiors that the Japanese army and navy, on January 24, 1941, had found a way to furnish their personnel with enough money for a whole year.[481]

119. Diplomatic Protection of Japanese Funds in Mexico.

The possibility of returning to Japan a 10,000,000 yen investment in a Mexican oil company had been discussed on July 14, 1941. Replying to Tokyo's suggestion that $350,000, said to be the capital of the Pacific Petroleum Company in Mexico, be credited to the Japanese Legation, so that it could not be seized, Minister Miura mentioned two objections: That if the money were turned back to Japan, all investment made so far would have in vain; and that not only would the status of the company be uncertain in case of an emergency, but it was impossible to predict whether, with only $300,000 left for research, it would be possible to discover an oil vein.[482]

With little hesitation, Foreign Minister Toyoda instructed that the $300,000 be turned over to the company at once, but that it be kept at the Legation to prevent the money from being frozen or seized. In the event that additional funds were needed, the matter would have to be given further consideration. When the United States froze Japanese funds on July 25, 1941, the Pacific Petroleum Company directed Mr. Okumura to turn their Mexican funds over to the Japanese Legation. Mr. Okumura informed the Japanese company that he would comply with these instructions, and that three of its employees were being sent home. Since the use of code telegrams had been prohibited since July 22, 1941, all telegrams pertaining to the business of the company were to be sent through the Japanese Legation.[483]

PART C—JAPANESE DIPLOMATIC ACTIVITIES THROUGHOUT THE WORLD

(c) Japanese-South American Relations.

120. Japan Acquires Intelligence Concerning the United States.

Much intelligence regarding the activities of the United States was sent from South America to Tokyo. From Rio de Janeiro it was alleged on June 4, 1941 that should the Suez-Near East situation develop unfavorably for Britain, America's Pacific policy would prevent Japan from attacking England in the Far East. Asserting that America's attitude toward Japan was becoming stronger and more "warlike", Ambassador Itaro Ishii pointed out that the United States was increasing the number of its bombers in the Pacific, was planning to ship essential military products to Generalissimo Chiang Kai-shek, and would soon direct an embargo against Japan. Since Germany would possibly bring pressure upon Spain and Portugal after the harvest season, it was rumored that the United States would prevent German seizure of the Atlantic islands of these two countries as well as of Dakar.[484]

---

[481]II, 443.
[482]II, 444–445.
[483]II, 446–448.
[484]II, 449.

The Japanese Ambassador in Brazil predicted that the American patrols, which had been proposed in place of the convoy system, would inevitably clash with German submarines or planes. Further illustrating the impossibility of the United States' staying out of war, Mr. Ishii declared that revisions to the Neutrality Act would undoubtedly be passed by Congress; that after American ships had been sunk, the United States government expected American public opinion to insist upon defense of its shipping; that such an expression as "the freedom of the seas" was but an excuse for maintaining control of the seas; and that the maintenance of American "non-belligerency" was but a stop-gap while preparations for war would be made until an incident occurred, or until American public opinion was swayed to the point where participation was possible.[485]

121. Alleged American Economic and Political Pressure in South America.

In an attempt to reassure South American countries which had instituted, or were about to institute, an export license system and other measures to limit exports to Japan, Tokyo advised its ambassadors to combat the belief that such products were being re-exported from Japan to Germany. They were to give assurance that Japan was importing but sixty per cent of her needs from Central and South America, and was in no position to re-export these products to any third country. Such restrictive measures were believed by the Japanese to be the result of machinations on the part of the United States.[486]

Meanwhile, an extensive shifting of the Japanese diplomatic staff took place in South America during July. Many of the changes involved the Naval and Military Attaches.[487] Japanese officials in South American countries were alarmed not only about the safety of their nationals, but also about their loyalty, as influenced by propaganda. A pamphlet, entitled *Americanism*, published by the Central Japanese Society in Los Angeles, was the subject of an inquiry from Mr. Ishii in Brazil. He was especially concerned with the comments made on these pamphlets by first-generation Japanese.[488]

(a) *Brazil.*

According to Mr. Ishii, Brazil, as one of the ABC powers of South America, was most vulnerable to the pressure applied to her by the United States. Commenting on the corruption which appeared to be in certain Brazilian circles, he advised that the United States was using large sums of money to infiltrate quite deeply, and, as a result, many Brazilians were saying that their President's power was wasting away. Mr. Ishii regretted that the Axis was not using counter-measures against American influence.[489]

In connection with the setting up of Japanese youth training centers in Brazil, Foreign Minister Toyoda warned that in order to forestall suspicion on the part of Brazilian authorities, it would be necessary to exercise caution. If the budget and actual operation of these centers were placed in the hands of Japanese diplomats in Brazil, it was feared that such activities might jeopardize their whole policy in that country. Rather than subsidize the Japanese training centers, Foreign Minister Toyoda felt that the functioning of such organizations should depend upon the instructor's personal merits.[490]

---

[485]II, 450.

[486]II, 451.

[487]II, 452, 460.

[488]II, 461.

[489]II, 462.

[490]II, 463.

Since caution was desirable in dealing with Brazil, Mr. Ishii had burned all secret papers of the Japanese Embassy in Rio de Janeiro which were dated up to 1934, and had taken precautions so that the other papers could be burned at any time. Arrangements were also made to transfer the Emperor's portrait back to Japan.[491]

(b) *Chile.*

A report to Tokyo from Santiago on June 2, 1941 announced that a member of the Chilean Military Commission had confidentially informed the German Ambassador that a request by the United States for the use of the Straits of Magellan had been refused in view of the Chilean peace policy.[492] However, members of the Chilean Congress revealed on June 6, 1941 that because the United States had begun to prevent the export of essential materials, Chile would do likewise.

Chile's Foreign Minister had predicted on June 6, 1941 that although there would hardly be a total embargo placed on exports to Japan, the license system would probably be instituted to reserve material needed by Chile. In addition, the re-exportation of war materials would probably be prohibited. Consul Ichiro Kawasaki, after secretly perusing a newly proposed Chilean bill, found that it dealt principally with re-exportation of materials and the export license system, and reported that there was strong support for its passage.[493]

Meanwhile, the terms of a Japanese-Chilean mineral contract with the "Cobaltera", an organization in Chile responsible for the handling of the entire annual output of ore for Japan, were being negotiated. Upon the conclusion of the contract, a loan of one million pesos was to be made to the company by the Japanese on the condition that it be used directly in the development of mines.[494]

According to Consul Kawasaki, the Communist Party and the pro-American wing of the Socialist Party had been creating dissension in Chile since the beginning of the German-Soviet conflict. The Chilean Communists had forgotten their age-old war against British and American capitalism, and were taking a strong anti-German stand. In accordance with this feeling, street demonstrations had been planned, but had been dispersed by the Chilean government's strict control. Moreover, anti-German moving pictures had been banned, and two influential newspapers were predicting the ultimate defeat of Russia.[495]

(c) *Argentina.*

In Argentina, a recent presidential decree had no unfavorable effect on Japanese trade, although the Japanese believed that the United States had tried to exert its influence.[496] Argentina, nevertheless, had placed no restrictions on Japanese shipping. Difficulty with Japanese telegraphic officials was now encountered in Argentina since the number of request messages between Japanese firms and their home offices was increasing. For this reason, Minister Shui Tomii asked that a designator be assigned for this particular type of message so as to assure priority for more urgent matters.[497]

---

[491] II, 464.
[492] II, 465.
[493] II, 466–468.
[494] II, 469.
[495] II, 470.
[496] II, 471.
[497] II, 472.

(d) *Ecuador—Peru.*

Reporting from Ecuador, Japanese Minister Iungo Yanai wired that the United States, taking advantage of the strained relationship between Peru and Ecuador, had established headquarters in Guayaquil, a commercial city in Ecuador, and was spreading fantastic stories "as were never heard of in heaven or earth". According to this source, the people of Ecuador, who entertained the most profound hatred for the Peruvians, expected to be attacked at any moment,[498] and were looking to Washington for assistance.[499] An interview of the Japanese Minister with the Foreign Minister of Ecuador on June 14, 1941, revealed that the border situation was becoming more and more "grave", and that Peru was preparing for war.[500]

By July 18, 1941, however, Tokyo learned that since Ecuador had agreed to apologize for an attack on the Peruvian consulate in Guayaquil, Peru had announced to the mediating powers, the United States, Brazil and Argentina, that she was in accord with their solution to the affair.[501] Tokyo was also informed that to maintain neutrality, Peru had issued, on June 27, 1941, a presidential decree prohibiting the entrance of submarines of belligerent powers into Peruvian waters and harbors.[502]

(e) *Colombia.*

In contrast with her relations with Peru, Colombia's relations with Ecuador were very friendly, and according to Japanese Minister Yanai, both flags were floating jointly everywhere, except on government buildings. For this reason Mr. Yanai, who had been assigned to serve in both Peru and Colombia, preferred to represent his country in Ecuador and Colombia, and had requested the permission of the Ecuadorian government to do so.[503] German activities in Colombia, he reported, were not succeeding, since powerful officials, such as the Colombian president, were beginning to favor England and the United States.[504]

(f) *Venezuela.*

A rumor, spread by the wives of influential men in Venezuela, to the effect that the United States had suggested that all Central and South American countries apply pressure on Japanese residents and had indicated methods whereby these Japanese would be forced to leave, was relayed to Tokyo. Mr. Goscoe Ohgimi, the Japanese Minister to Venezuela, said that every effort was being made to ascertain if the rumor had any basis.[505]

---

[498] II, 473.
[499] II, 474.
[500] II, 475.
[501] II, 476.
[502] II, 477.
[503] II, 475.
[504] II, 474.
[505] II, 478.

PART C—JAPANESE DIPLOMATIC ACTIVITIES THROUGHOUT THE WORLD

(d) Japanese–British Relations.

122. Japanese Security Precautions.

At the end of May 1941 Japan realized the need for greater security in its diplomatic code. At the same time that radical changes in the Japanese codes were effected in London, the special system used solely between Berlin and Tokyo was also to be revised.[506] Because of the continued inadequacy of Japanese courier service, new diplomatic codes had to be devised by Mr. Kawamoto at the London Embassy. They were then relayed to the Japanese Ambassador in Berlin who distributed the new systems to representatives of his government throughout Europe.[507] Copies of the regulations governing the use of this new system were forwarded to Japanese offices in America, Europe, and Japanese-controlled cities throughout China.[508]

In view of Great Britain's strict censorship of messages transmitted to and from Portugal, Japanese agents in Capetown were forced to send espionage reports concerning shipping movements through Tokyo, instead of through Portugal, to the Japanese Ambassador in Germany.[509]

123. Minor Incidents Disrupt Japanese-British Relations.

During the period from May to June 1941 British-Japanese relations were somewhat disturbed by several incidents of varying significance. On March 5, 1941 the Egyptian government had forbidden the use of any language but English and French in ordinary communications, and the use of code messages was entirely denied to the Japanese consulate in Alexandria. In May 1941 other restrictive measures were set in motion against the Japanese in Egypt,[510] and, according to Tokyo, Australia exhibited her faithfulness to England by growing more hostile in her dealings with Japan.

The Japanese saw the possibility of an ally in India, however, where the Punjab troops had refused to obey England, and where many favored Italy. Meanwhile the Sikhs and the Mohammedans were creating internal strife.[511]

The four year's detention of Mr. Davis, an English minister, who had been arrested in North China, caused a British protest to Tokyo on May 20, 1941. It was suggested that the Japanese find some grounds for releasing him.[512] In the meantime, the Japanese had been disturbed because the British consulate in Los Angeles had placed eleven seamen from the whaler *Tonan Maru* on a blacklist for unknown reasons.[513] When in June 1941 it was reported that England had discriminated against the Japanese in granting visas to travel throughout its Empire, Tokyo enacted retaliatory measures. All British applications for Japanese passports were thereafter referred to a special office before they were granted.[514]

On the other hand, though German claims to owning and operating factories in Shanghai and its vicinity were denied by the Japanese, demands made in June 1941 by the Sin Chang

---

[506] II, 479.
[507] II, 480.
[508] II, 481.
[509] II, 482.
[510] II, 483.
[511] II, 484.
[512] II, 485.
[513] II, 486.
[514] II, 487.

Company, a British firm, were readily granted.[515] On another occasion, when British firms in the Hunan Province were being discriminated against by the Japanese, Tokyo warned its representatives on June 10, 1941 that this type of treatment would not benefit Japan in view of the general political situation; and since such a misunderstanding would be extremely dangerous, it was requested that the discrimination be stopped immediately.[516]

However, such incidents as the flights over southern Thailand on May 10 and 22, 1941 by British planes, and the arresting and imprisonment of two British officers who had crossed the border, intensified the delicate situation between the two nations. From Bangkok, the capitol of Thailand, on June 12, 1941 came the report that large and systematic movements of the British along the borders constituted an imposing threat to Thailand.[517]

124. Japan Recalls Ambassador Shigemitsu from London.

In May 1941 the Japanese Ambassador in London was ordered home, ostensibly for conferences with the Japanese Foreign Minister. For the benefit of Sir Robert Craigie, the British Ambassador, and his government, this recall was explained as being merely a routine return to report on certain matters, but the Japanese Ambassador knew that he would never return to his post.[518] His efforts to restrain Japan from collaboration with the Axis had evidently displeased Mr. Matsuoka. Ambassador Mamoru Shigemitsu planned to go from Lisbon to New York,[519] and then to San Francisco where he was scheduled for passage aboard the *Yawata Maru* about the middle of July, 1941.[520] While in the United States he was to meet Ambassador Nomura in New York or Washington.[521]

125. Japanese Interest in British-German Peace Talk.

In June 1941 the Axis powers were convinced that the outcome of the European war was already decided. A Japanese report of the views of a British Foreign Office official stated that if the British government or one of its great statesmen such as Lloyd George were to present a peace proposal, the people would accept it. Winston Churchill's influence was believed to be declining, but Ernest Bevin did not intend to supplant him.[522] From United States sources it appeared that America was certain Japan would not enter the war, and for that reason was exhibiting little anxiety over the break-up of Japanese negotiations with the Dutch East Indies.[523]

Though rumors of a British-German peace were astir in the United States, German Foreign Minister Joachim von Ribbentrop assured Japanese Ambassador Oshima that the only reason such talk had been invented was to divorce Japan from the Tripartite Pact. On the other hand, Mr. Oshima himself believed that these rumors concerning England and Germany proved that London and Washington were cooperating on propaganda since they were anxious to weaken the Tripartite Pact and to sever relations between Berlin and Vichy. Furthermore, according to Ambassador Oshima, London was using the United States for its own aims in restraining Japan.[524]

---

[515] II, 488.
[516] II, 489.
[517] II, 490.
[518] II, 491.
[519] II, 492.
[520] II, 493.
[521] II, 493.
[522] II, 494.
[523] II, *Ibid.*
[524] II, 495.

126. Japanese Reports on British Shipping.

Tokyo was closely observing England's activities throughout the world, for during June 1941 many intelligence reports concerning British shipping movements were obtained. British shipping at this time was extremely heavy, and because of Italy's declaration of war, there was a tremendous increase of shipping via South Africa.

From Capetown on June 11, 1941 came detailed information concerning allied ships, unprotected by convoy escorts, which were transporting thousands of British troops to Egypt. French and Netherlands ships, commandeered by the British since the beginning of the war, also left the port of Durban on June 10, 1941 carrying 10,000 South African troops. Another ship carrying native Belgian Congo troops left Durban at approximately the same time.[525]

Aware of Japanese agents, Britain increased the secrecy surrounding these movements,[526] and access to any of the dock areas in Capetown and Durban was strictly forbidden.[527] Nevertheless, the Japanese attempted to discover the nationality, numbers and routes of the many ships in those harbors. The Japanese also learned that in clear weather shipping from North Eastern India put in at the Portuguese port of Laurenco Marques to escape Axis submarines.[528]

127. Japan Protests British Aid to China.

In spite of Japanese protests on June 4, 1941 against England's granting of aid to China, Foreign Minister Anthony Eden himself made it clear that England had little concern about offending the Tripartite powers. However, the Japanese Ambassador believed that Britain was giving greater consideration to the Japanese question.[529]

Nevertheless, two months later, on August 2, 1941 a report from Shanghai was evidence that Britain was still maintaining close collaboration with China, especially with the military authorities.[530]

128. Japan's Anxiety Concerning British-Russian Relations.

In early June 1941 the British Ambassador to Moscow, Sir Stafford Cripps, returned to England; and since relations between Germany and Russia were now at the breaking point, the Japanese felt that any Russo-British collaboration would endanger the interests of the Axis.[531] China was also interested in any agreement that the British might contract with Russia, since they hoped that it would also cover the Far Eastern situation and would provoke a British-Japanese collision.[532]

Tokyo was informed that on June 21, 1941, the day before war began between Germany and Russia, the British Ambassador in Rome had conferred with the Russian Ambassador. Speaking under instructions from London, the British Ambassador had stated that Britain was anxious to see the threat on the eastern border of Russian eliminated and the safety of the British colonies in the Pacific assured. He believed that one possible solution lay in effecting a compromise between China and Japan, based on the condition that Japan would withdraw from the Axis.

---

[525]II, 496–497.
[526]II, 482.
[527]II, 498.
[528]II, *Ibid.*
[529]II, 499.
[530]II, 500.
[531]II, 501.
[532]II, 502.

Since Russia did not feel that Japan would drop her affiliations with either Germany or Italy the Russian Ambassador replied that until Japan's attitude was more definite, his country did not wish to take any positive step regarding questions in the Far East. Furthermore, the Japanese-Chinese war was an important factor in preventing Japan from extending aid to the other Axis powers.[533]

129. Britain Inquires About Japanese Attitude Toward the German-Russian War.

Japan was interested in British reactions to the impending German-Russian situation, and England at the same time was anxious to know Japan's position. To British Ambassador Craigie's inquiries on July 4, 1941 regarding this matter, the Japanese Foreign Minister pointed out that the national policy of Japan was built on the Tripartite Pact. Nevertheless, the terms of this agreement in no way obligated Japan to declare war on Russia, nor had Germany requested the assistance of its allies.[534]

130. Japan Fears British Seizure of Its Ships (July 25, 1941).

With an eye toward the further establishment of its own military and economic independence, Japan greatly increased its shipping during the month of June. In accordance with this plan, the Japanese army desired to take over four ships which were anchored near Formosa, in spite of the fact that this action would violate customs regulations. The British were not expected to oppose this move.[535]

On July 4, 1941 Tokyo, anticipating difficulty with the British government in regard to nickel allotments which Japan was particularly anxious to acquire, instructed its Ambassador in London to approach Mr. Eden with the request that Japanese ships be allowed to proceed unmolested in the loading of another nickel allotment.[536] After July 25, 1941, however, when the freezing order had been put into effect, Japan, fearing that England and the United States would seize its ships, secretly instructed the captains of all ships at anchor to leave port immediately, and ships at sea were ordered to stand by.[537]

By the end of July 1941 Japan's anxiety concerning the possible detention of its ships had lessened, and the Foreign Minister permitted Japanese vessels to return to the foreign ports from which they had been recalled. With regard to the unloading of cargo, however, numerous difficulties still presented themselves; though it was hoped by Japan that after the cargo had been unloaded, payment could be applied to exports for the Japanese.[538]

131. Japan Protests British Reconnaissance in Far East.

Although keeping close check on British activities, Japan resented Britain's attempts to watch Japanese maneuvers. Tokyo protested, on July 24, 1941, that English aviators, flying over areas where Japanese forces had been operating, had openly reconnoitered troop and ship movements. In another instance, on July 16, 1941, a British warship had approached a Japanese submarine, and, after shooting three shells close to its bow, had sailed off in the direction of Hong-

---

[533]II, 503.
[534]II, 504.
[535]II, 505.
[536]II, 506.
[537]II, 507–508.
[538]II, 509.

kong. Reporting these occurrences to the British Consul General, the Japanese government warned that military action, for which Britain would be solely responsible, would be initiated if these happenings continued, since they not only interfered with the maneuvers of Japanese warships, but also constituted a mark of disrespect toward the Japanese government.[539]

132. Ambassador Craigie Unsuccessfully Urges Japan to Uphold Far Eastern Peace.

In attempting to adjust the estranged conditions existing with Japan, Ambassador Craigie had pointed out in June 1941 that of all the countries of the world, Japan alone was in an excellent position to maintain neutrality since Great Britain and Germany would fight a war to the finish, and the United States and Russia would eventually become involved in this struggle. Peace could be maintained in the Far East, however, and in order to prevent the war in Europe from spreading throughout the world, Japan must change her attitude of aggression.

England appreciated that the Japanese had a need for the rubber and tin which the Netherlands East Indies could provide, but it could not condone Japan's obtaining them by force. The Netherlands' officials, fearing the transshipment of these articles to Germany, had refused to send them to Japan, despite all the assurances from Tokyo that the material was for Japanese consumption.[540]

In the latter part of July 1941, Japan announced its intentions of stationing its troops in French Indo-China. The act was considered by the United States and England as a threat to the entire Southwest Pacific, despite Admiral Teijiro Toyoda's insistence that the mutual agreement between Japan and France for the joint defense of French Indo-China had been necessary because of alarming reports regarding the safety of that area, and in order to prevent any enveloping movement against Japan.

Emphatically denying that there had been any foundation for the alarming Japanese reports, the British Ambassador to Tokyo had declared on July 25, 1941 that Japan's action constituted a threat to English territorial rights and interests in Asia. While he thought that some compromise could be reached with Great Britain, he made it clear the the fulfillment of the Japanese plan would have serious consequences. Foreign Minister Toyoda declined to postpone the sending of troops to French Indo-China but assured England of Japan's peaceful purpose in this movement.[541]

133. Canada Terminates Existing Commercial Treaty With Japan.

After Japanese aggression in French Indo-China had forced the enactment of an order on July 25, 1941 freezing Japanese assets in Great Britain and the United States, the Canadian government felt that it was necessary to terminate the existing Canadian-Japanese commercial treaty.[542]

On July 26, 1941 Ambassador Yoshizawa called on the Prime Minister of Canada and once again insisted that Japan was entering French Indo-China only in order to forestall any anti-Japanese moves in the Pacific by other nations. While admitting that Great Britain might feel in imminent peril because of such a step, the Japanese Ambassador did not see any direct connection between the French Indo-China situation and the safety of Canada.

---

[539]II, 510–511.

[540]II, 512.

[541]II, 513.

[542]II, 514–515.

Ambassador Yoshizawa drew a parallel between Japanese occupation of French Indo-China and the seizure of Greenland and Iceland by the United States. To this comparison the Canadian Prime Minister replied that the United States would have faced a very grave danger if the Nazis had gained a foothold in that area, and, consequently, had been able to strike at the Western Hemisphere. The Japanese, however, had faced no such threat from the Allies in the Pacific.

Nevertheless, the Japanese representative referred to Anglo-American aid to Generalissimo Chiang Kai-shek as a thwarting of Japanese efforts to settle the Chinese question.[543] Furthermore, the deGaullists were actively opposing the Japanese in French Indo-China. With England and the United States establishing a joint blockade preparatory to applying unendurable economic pressure against them, the Japanese felt that there was little doubt of the unfriendly and dangerous attitude of other nations.[544]

PART C—JAPANESE DIPLOMATIC ACTIVITIES THROUGHOUT THE WORLD

(e) Japanese-Axis Relations.

134. Germany and Italy Explain the Hess Flight.

German and Italian officials took every opportunity to explain to Japanese representatives the reasons for Rudolph Hess' flight to Scotland. In Rome, Ambassador Hiroshi Oshima was received on May 13, 1941 by Foreign Minister Ciano, who represented the Hess incident as an inconsequential matter, and stressed that the whole affair would soon be forgotten even though British and American propagandists had attempted to emphasize it. At the same time, Foreign Minister Ciano stressed his belief that the Tripartite Pact was the most desirable foundation for Japanese diplomacy, and that German-Russian relations were deteriorating.[545]

On the next day, May 14, 1941, Ambassador Oshima talked with Foreign Minister von Ribbentrop who had come to Rome to discuss the Hess incident, among other things, with Premier Mussolini and Foreign Minister Ciano. At this meeting the German Foreign Minister explained to Ambassador Oshima that Herr Hess, while occupying a position of prominence in the Nazi party, had no knowledge of current political policy in Germany, and in addition was mentally and physically ill. The reason for his flight was an idealistic belief that an early peace could be attained by working upon the Fascist element of Great Britain to overthrow Prime Minister Churchill. His good intentions in this regard were not questioned by German authorities who stated that his mind was not normal.[546]

135. Japan Suspects a Move for British-German Peace.

Japanese diplomats were devoting much attention to the question of British-German peace. From another authoritative German source it was learned on May 14, 1941 that the German people were amazed and greatly affected by Hess' flight because of his important position in

---

[543]II, 516.
[544]II, *Ibid.*
[545]II, 517.
[546]II, 518.

the Reich and his great friendship with Chancellor Hitler. They found the event hard to explain because if he were mentally sick, as claimed, they could not understand why he had been given so much authority, and how it was possible for him to fly a plane to his exact destination in England.

There seemed to be no logical answer, according to this German source, except to say that Herr Hess was strongly pro-British and mentally sick. Since he did not always agree with Chancellor Hitler, particularly in regard to war against England, Herr Hess might have been anxious to leave Germany. It was also known that he possessed a great dislike for Foreign Minister von Ribbentrop.[547]

Ambassador Oshima was informed that the Hess flight had dealt a tremendous blow to the Nazi party, but he was reassured that Chancellor Hitler and Marshal Goering were still of one mind, and that because of the solidarity of the German government and its people the incident would not change German foreign policy.[548]

On May 16, 1941 Tokyo received a doubtful report from the Japanese Ambassador in Rome that Herr Hess had effected a meeting with Mr. Duff Cooper, who had then consulted with Prime Minister Winston Churchill. However, despite the intentions of Herr Hess and the belief of Chancellor Hitler that the war would be over in 1941, preparations for a long war appeared to be under way as Germany completed plans for attacking Russia. Ambassador Horikiri believed that the Hess flight could be regarded as part of Germany's grand scheme for a "peace offense" against the English.[549]

On May 18, 1941 Ambassador Oshima related other prevailing rumors regarding the Hess incident. He believed that a secret understanding might have existed between Chancellor Hitler and Herr Hess concerning a compromise between London and Berlin, especially in view of the delicate German and Russian relations and the growing possibility of the United States' entrance into the war.[550]

Another German authority divulged that Herr Hess had probably made the flight in good faith, but that since such an act constituted insubordination, he would be shot most assuredly.[551] Nevertheless, according to the Japanese Ambassador to Rome, on June 4, 1941, Italian official circles were of the opinion that Herr Hess must have been sent to England as a result of instructions from Marshal Goering.[552]

According to a report from Vienna on June 4, 1941, Herr Hess had informed Lord Hamilton in England that Chancellor Hitler still considered Russia and the Comintern to be the real enemies of the whole world. Accordingly, the Russian Ambassador to London had remarked that if Russia yielded to German demands concerning the Near East and cooperated with the Reich, the fate of the British Empire would be most gravely threatened. It was also reported that the British government and the King were seriously considering making peace with Germany.[553]

---

[547]II, 519.

[548]II, 520.

[549]II, 521.

[550]II, 522–523.

[551]II, 522.

[552]II, 524.

[552]II, 524.

[553]II, 525.

136. Ambassador Oshima Analyzes Germany's Plans.

Ambassador Oshima also informed his Foreign Minister of his own opinions on May 18, 1941. In view of Germany's many peace offers he believed that when the aims of *Mein Kampf* were realized, reconciliation between England and Germany could be attained since England's influence had been eliminated from the continent, and would eventually be destroyed in Africa. However, he also believed that because of Germany's current hold on the continent,

(a) Germany was no longer interested merely in removing England's political influence from the European continent;

(b) Germany must incorporate within the Axis Africa (including the Mediterranean area) and the Near East;

(c) Germany having developed to that point, will consolidate; then prepare for the great struggle of the future between Germany and the United States.[554]

Ambassador Oshima also thought that Germany was considering the taking over of the British fleet, since in bringing about reconciliation it would not be necessary for Germany voluntarily to take a backward step.

Germany expected Japan to restrain the United States in the Pacific, and to keep the American fleet out of the Atlantic. If the Japanese-American negotiations permitted the United States to send its warships into the Atlantic, Germany could still lighten its terms and achieve a peace. If the German-Russian war materialized, this would be another reason for Germany's offering peace to England. Ambassador Oshima believed, however, that England would not submit to these terms since they would amount to nothing less than unconditional surrender.[555]

A Japanese report of June 27, 1941 declared that Herr Hess had brought a peace offer to England, based on the premise that Chancellor Hitler's real objective was to crush Russia and stamp out Communism.[556]

137. Ambassador Oshima Rebukes Foreign Minister Matsuoka.

In answer to a query of May 15, 1941 from the Japanese Ambassador in Berlin concerning the basis for rumors of an approaching Japanese-American agreement, Mr. Matsuoka replied on May 17, 1941 that information in regard to the negotiations had not been sent to Germany because of the need for secrecy. In the United States, only the President, the Secretary of State, and one other Cabinet official were cognizant of the negotiations, and even the United States Ambassador in Japan had not been informed. Mr. Matsuoka reassured Ambassador Oshima that his silence in this affair did not imply a lack of trust in the Ambassador, and informed him that he would be advised of the entire matter when things had developed to a certain stage.[557]

Ambassador Oshima speedily dispatched several long messages to Mr. Matsuoka in which he discussed the bad effect a Japanese-American agreement might have on the Tripartite Pact. The Japanese Ambassador also expressed his wonder at Mr. Matsuoka's apparent disinterest in obtaining reports on the official attitudes of Italy and Germany to such an agreement.[558]

---

[554] II, 526–527.

[555] II, 527.

[556] II, 528.

[557] II, 529.

[558] II, 530–532.

138. Germany Attempts to Offset Japanese–American Negotiations.

In a long and important report of May 19, 1941 Ambassador Oshima informed Mr. Matsuoka that on May 3, 1941, Foreign Minister von Ribbentrop had learned of the Japanese-American negotiations from Ambassador Ott in Tokyo, and had immediately asked Ambassador Oshima to call on him. Ambassador Ott had reported the main points of the four articles of the agreement proposed to Japan by the United States on April 16, 1941, and Foreign Minister von Ribbentrop informed Ambassador Oshima of his inability to understand the motives of the Japanese government. The Japanese Ambassador insisted that Japan would do nothing inconsistent with the Tripartite Pact.[559]

On May 9, 1941 Ambassador Oshima was again called to the German Foreign Office where the Foreign Minister told him of Japan's provisional reply to the American proposal. Foreign Minister von Ribbentrop pointed out that the Japanese had originally proposed the negotiations; Japan had become deeply involved by this time; a certain group in Japan was influential enough to force Mr. Matsuoka into the negotiations; and, furthermore, the Japanese Foreign Minister had changed his mind about attacking Singapore.

The German Foreign Minister expressed his doubts as to the sincerity of President Roosevelt, and also commented on the possibility that Japan was seeking a loophole to escape its obligation to fight in accordance with the Tripartite Pact. These negotiations, which were weakening the Tripartite Pact, might also cause Japan to lose the opportunity of gaining supremacy in East Asia. As to Japan's course of action concerning the pending agreement, Foreign Minister von Ribbentrop favored the first of two German proposals that (a) Japan should reject the United States' proposal, or (b) Japan should consent to an agreement only on the condition that the United States would abandon its plan for convoy and patrol services, and would maintain absolute neutrality.[560]

Ambassador Oshima stated that his government would prefer the second proposal since this would make Britain fight Germany single-handedly and, thus, would hasten the end of the war. He also hoped that President Roosevelt might seize the opportunity to stop giving aid to Great Britain because this policy had proved to be ineffective. Ambassador Oshima realized that this was a remote possibility, but felt that in any event the second proposal would test President Roosevelt's sincerity in regard to aid to England, and at the same time it would convince certain Japanese of the impossibility of Japanese-American cooperation.

Herr von Ribbentrop disagreed with the Japanese Ambassador by pointing out that the negotiations gave the United States an opportunity to draw Japan away from Germany, and also might be used to silence American groups advocating peace since a Japanese-American understanding would give the United States a free hand in the Atlantic. However, the German Foreign Minister promised to send Ambassador Oshima's opinion, together with the two proposals, to Chancellor Hitler, who was living outside of Berlin at that time. As soon as Chancellor Hitler approved the plans, Germany would take up direct negotiations with Italy concerning the Japanese-American negotiations.[561]

139. Germany and Italy Disturbed by Japanese–American Negotiations.

Carrying out previous arrangements to visit Premier Mussolini, Ambassador Oshima left for Rome on May 10, 1941, the day after his interview with Foreign Minister von Ribbentrop.

---

[559]II, 531.
[560]*Ibid.*
[561]*Ibid.*

Two days later, the German Ambassador O. Furst von Bismarck, acting under instructions from his Foreign Minister, called on Ambassador Oshima to show him the German government's instructions to Ambassador Eugene Ott in Tokyo. Both Italy and Germany had concurred in the statement which outlined the second of the German proposals, the one which Foreign Minister von Ribbentrop had opposed. Chancellor Hitler had approved this second proposal, which had won the support of Ambassador Oshima.

Foreign Minister von Ribbentrop arrived by plane to confer with Premier Mussolini and Foreign Minister Ciano in Rome on May 13, 1941, and on the morning of May 14, 1941, he conferred with Ambassador Oshima. Expressing great dissatisfaction with Mr. Matsuoka's explanation as to why the Japanese-American negotiations had been started without awaiting Italian and German views, Foreign Minister von Ribbentrop stated that if Mr. Matsuoka had waited only a few hours longer before replying to the United States he would have received their opinions.

Ambassador Oshima declared that he did not know the facts of the situation, but thought that his Foreign Minister's action was due to the necessity of assuring absolute secrecy, and because the Emperor's approval had to be obtained. No disrespect had been intended for either Italy or Germany.

The German Foreign Minister was very disturbed because Foreign Minister Matsuoka had not mentioned the Japanese-American negotiations during his recent trip to Germany, despite the fact that they had a great bearing on the Tripartite Pact. Herr von Ribbentrop did not disguise his opinion that the negotiations had weakened the Pact, that President Roosevelt was not to be trusted, that Japanese negotiations with the United States should be abandoned, and that he did not approve of the German proposal which had received the support of Chancellor Hitler.

On the evening of this same day, Ambassador Oshima conferred with Foreign Minister Ciano who expressed views similar to those of the German Foreign Minister.[562]

140. Germany Alleges That Mr. Matsuoka Promised Japan's Aid in a War Against Russia.

When Ambassador Oshima returned to Berlin on May 17, 1941, he was requested to call on Vice Minister Weizsacker. Acting under instructions from Foreign Minister von Ribbentrop, the Vice Minister showed Ambassador Oshima a telegram from Ambassador Ott in Tokyo dealing with the Japanese reply to the United States' proposal, and Germany's instructions to Ambassador Ott concerning this reply. The German Vice Minister expressed his government's great concern with the outcome of this question, and stated that Germany was greatly interested in Foreign Minister Matsuoka's statement to Ambassador Ott that Japan would aid Germany in case of a German-Russian war.

When asked whether Mr. Matsuoka was fully acquainted with German-Russian relations, Ambassador Oshima replied that his Foreign Minister had had many opportunities to talk with Foreign Minister von Ribbentrop concerning these relations during his visit to Germany. As for the Japanese position in the event of a German-Russian war, all important questions of state had to be approved by the Emperor, and, consequently, any statement by Foreign Minister Matsuoka was merely an expression of his own personal views.[563]

In another report on May 19, 1941, Ambassador Oshima stressed Germany's dissatisfaction with regard to the proposed Japanese-American agreement. Germany was concerned over the

---

[562]*Ibid.*
[563]*Ibid.*

future of the Tripartite Pact, because its official circles felt that Japan's entrance into an agreement with the United States would be the same as giving approval to the violent anti-Axis actions of the United States. Although the agreement might prevent the entrance of the United States into the European war, it would indicate to the German people that Japan was evading its duty to enter the war. After the warm welcome awarded to Mr. Matsuoka on his recent visit, and the strengthening of ties among Axis nations, many Germans felt that they had been betrayed by the recent action of Japan.[564]

Ambassador Oshima recognized the fact that Japan needed a political and economic breathing spell which could be brought about by settling the China incident, but he pointed out that Germany and Italy were winning the European war and, therefore, it would be unwise for the sake of some immediate gains to lose the friendship of the Axis powers. Ambassador Oshima emphasized Foreign Minister Ribbentrop's belief that the agreement proposed by the United States was motivated only by its desire to separate Japan from the Axis. If Japan left the Axis, it would stand alone in international affairs during the critical period immediately following the war. If Japan abandoned its plan to expand southward and discontinued its threat to Singapore, Ambassador Oshima believed that Japan would be looked upon contemptuously not only by Britain and the United States, but by Germany and Italy as well.[565]

Furthermore, a Japanese-American agreement would mean that Japan was abandoning its claims to the establishment of a "New Order" in Greater East Asia, and the Japanese people would become confused as to the ultimate national goal. While very much opposed to any Japanese-American negotiations, Ambassador Oshima suggested that if Japan felt it necessary to enter into an agreement, the following points should be put into effect:

   (a) Japan was entering into an agreement with the United States to support the spirit of the Tripartite Pact and to make things easier for Germany and Italy in their war against England.
   (b) America was to change her policy with regard to the European war to one of strict neutrality at the same time that Japan clearly set forth the conditions of the Tripartite Pact under which it would be bound to enter the war.
   (c) Germany and Italy should not be permitted to think that certain Japanese groups, urging the maintenance of the status quo in the Far East as opposed to expansion of the militarists, had gained so much power that Japan had been forced to enter into an agreement with America.[566]

Ambassador Oshima also stressed the need for exchanging opinions with Germany and Italy so that they could be reassured of Japan's intention to adhere to the Tripartite Pact.[567]

141. Japan Stresses Its Allegiance to Axis.

On May 24, 1941 Mr. Matsuoka replied that he could understand the reasons for Ambassador Oshima's agitation over the negotiations, but reiterated that Japan would do nothing to contravene the spirit of the Tripartite Pact which was the cornerstone of Japan's national policy. According to Mr. Matsuoka, Foreign Minister von Ribbentrop and other German officials should have no anxiety or misunderstanding concerning Japanese acts.[568]

The Japanese Foreign Minister stressed that in view of the measures he had taken since he had returned to Japan, and because of the statements made by Ambassador Nomura to Secretary Hull, the United States was well aware of the Japanese determination to support the

---

[564]II, 532.
[565]*Ibid.*
[566]*Ibid.*
[567]II, 532–533.
[568]II, 534.

Tripartite Pact. Stating that he did not know what was in the back of President Roosevelt's mind, and remarking that no one else did either, Foreign Minister Matsuoka agreed in general with the assumption of Foreign Minister von Ribbentrop that London and Washington were attempting to separate the Axis powers by diplomacy.[569]

Commenting on the fact that Foreign Minister von Ribbentrop was disturbed because Japan had begun the negotiations with the United States before receiving any views from Germany, Mr. Matsuoka pointed out that he had delayed his answer almost four weeks from the date of the original proposal by the United States. On May 8, 1941 Tokyo had received a confidential report that the American Congress had approved the convoy policy, and that President Roosevelt was to approve it on May 14, 1941. Since Japan had been anxious to prevent the United States from approving convoys in order to eliminate the danger of American participation in the war, the Japanese counter proposal had been suddenly put forth on May 12, 1941.[570]

Mr. Matsuoka denied that he had acted in response to pressure from any Japanese group, and again insisted that his reason for not informing the Germans was to maintain security. The Japanese counter proposal had been successful because President Roosevelt had postponed his speech scheduled for May 14, 1941. Defending his position of withholding information, the Japanese Foreign Minister said he would continue to keep in touch with the Germans and Italians, but since Japan was a free country it was unnecessary to run to Germany and Italy for advice on every problem.[571]

In Moscow, Ambassador Yoshitsugu Tatekawa had learned in mid-May 1941 from the American Ambassador that conversations had started between Ambassador Grew and the Japanese Foreign Minister, possibly in regard to the question of the United States' aid to China. He had informed the American Ambassador, who had stressed the impossibility of a Japanese-American war, that if a war between America and Germany were provoked by the American fleet, Japan was obligated by the terms of the Tripartite treaty to fight against America.[572]

142. Foreign Minister Matsuoka Attempts to Prevent German-Russian War.

On May 27, 1941 Mr. Matsuoka denied that in a conversation with Ambassador Ott he had promised Japan's entrance into a German-Russian war. According to the Japanese Foreign Minister, he had indicated the impossibility of foretelling the attitude of Japan in such an event, though he had said that he could not visualize Japan's not striking at Russia, if Germany went to war.[573]

On the following day, May 28, 1941, Ambassador Oshima was ordered to deliver the following message to Foreign Minister von Ribbentrop:

> In view of the current international situation which so deeply involves my country, and of the internal situation within Japan, this minister sincerely hopes that the German Government, insofar as is possible, will avoid a military clash with the Soviet.[574]

Mr. Matsuoka continued trying to avert a Russian-German war until the outbreak of hostilities, and though he seemed to realize the futility of his efforts on June 20, 1941, he still hoped for a change in Germany's attitude.[575]

---

[569]II, 535.

[570]Ibid.

[571]II, Ibid.

[572]II, 536.

[573]II, 537.

[574]II, 538.

[575]II, 539–540.

143. Japan Informs Its Diplomats of the Japanese-American Negotiations.

On May 27, 1941 the Japanese Foreign Office informed its diplomats in Moscow, England, France, and Italy of the Japanese-American negotiations which were in progress in Washington. According to this message, Japan had entered negotiations with a view to maintaining the Tripartite Pact as the basis of its national policy, preventing the United States from convoying ships to England or from entering the war, and lastly, having the United States cease its aid to China. Important details of the proposed agreement were outlined, and a warning to keep the negotiations secret was issued.[576]

144. Japan Loses by Economic Collaboration with Germany.

Adherence to the Tripartite Pact in conjunction with its "New Order in East Asia" was beginning, as early as May 1941, to cause Japan no little concern over its already heavily burdened shipping. Conditions in Europe and South America had made the purchase and leasing of ship bottoms exceptionally difficult, and conversion of merchant vessels for military use had cut Japan's commercial shipping to sixty per cent of its former capacity. Accordingly, on May 12, 1941, Mr. Matsuoka informed Ambassador Oshima in Berlin of the great sacrifice Japan would be forced to make, if Germany were furnished additional aid.[577]

Not only in regard to shipping was Japan suffering losses for the sake of its alliance with Germany, but its all-important rubber markets in French Indo-China, the Netherlands East Indies and Thailand were cornered by German merchants, who operated without regard to price. By mid-May 1941, the situation had become so acute that some Japanese factories were shut down, thereby forcing a request to Ambassador Ott that Germany permit Japan to appropriate one half of the new consignment of rubber from French Indo-China which was scheduled to arrive soon in Japan for reshipment. This amount would be replaced as quickly as conditions permitted.[578]

Negotiations with Germany in regard to increasing Japan's tin allotment were also under way, but though experiencing a shortage, Japan agreed to purchase and refine one hundred and fifty tons of ore for consignment to Italy.[579] Since German newspapers were also manifesting a great interest in Japanese-Dutch trade negotiations, Japanese authorities feared that some jurisdictional dispute concerning Greater East Asia might occur.[580]

Not until June 20, 1941, after further bargaining, was the Japanese request answered by the Chief of the German Commerce Bureau in Berlin. According to a new proposition, Japan was to receive twenty-five hundred tons of rubber; there would be no further hindrance to its purchase of rubber from Indo-China and Thailand; and the amount left over, after shipments had been made to the United States and France, would be divided between Japan and Germany.[581]

---

[576]II, 541.
[577]II, 542.
[578]II, 543–544.
[579]II, 545.
[580]II, 546.
[581]II, 547–548.

145. Strengthening of Japanese-German Political Ties.

Despite its economic losses from collaboration with Germany in the Far East, Japan continued to cement diplomatic relations by doing favors for the Germans. In late May 1941, Tokyo directed its Minister in Mexico to receive $200,000 in American money from the German Minister for transfer to Berlin, via a Japanese ship to Tokyo.[582] But in turn a request was made by Tokyo, on June 9, 1941, that Major General Takuma Shimoyama be received at Berlin in the newly created position of Military Attache for Aviation.[583]

146. Japanese-Italian Collaboration.

Japanese-Italian solidarity was fostered through the Japanese Foreign Office and through the cultural activities of the Japanese International Cultural Advancement Society.[584] In order to awaken Italian interest in Japan, the Japanese Ambassador in Rome requested that an increased amount of Japanese publications be sent from Tokyo every twenty days.[585] In addition he discouraged any efforts toward furthering Japanese trade in Italy, and for this reason he advised that the head of a Japanese trade promotion office, who was disliked by his fellow Japanese in Rome, was considered unsuitable to fill the Commercial Attache post.[586]

According to a Japanese report, Germany had agreed that when the Axis had conquered Europe, Italy was to dominate the Mediterranean and Egypt.[587]

147. Japanese Estimate of German Strength (June 3, 1941).

On June 3, 1941 the Japanese Ambassador to Berlin reported that Hitler would conclude the war as soon as possible after a great battle which would take place in any of the following forms:

    (a) A direct attack and occupation of England proper;
    (b) A complete sweeping away of English power from the Eastern Mediterranean;
    (c) A war embracing Iraq;
    (d) North African battle taking place in Egypt and Suez;
    (e) The taking of Gibraltar;
    (f) A war in the territory surrounding Dakar;
    (g) Finally, a war against the Soviet.[588]

Germany's plans to pulverize the British Empire, and at the same time to defend German boundaries, impressed Ambassador Oshima and his economic and military attaches, who believed that Germany could also annihilate the Russian army within a short period.[589]

It was estimated, in this same report of June 3, 1941, that the German naval, air and army forces numbered from 10,000,000 to 12,000,000 men, 10,000 to 15,000 first class fighter planes, 20,000 second class fighters, 30,000 training and civilian aircraft, and monthly production amounting to 2,000 planes. Only 40,000 men had been killed in all battles since the beginning of the war. Aircraft and submarine production dominated the Axis industrial output, for the Germans had been very successful in their attacks on English shipping by these methods.[590]

---

[582]II, 549
[583]II, 550–551.
[584]II, 552.
[585]II, 553.
[586]II, 554.
[587]II, 555.
[588]II, 556.
[589]II, 557.
[590]II, 558.

A Japanese summary of German war reports from June 1 to June 15, 1941 announced the destruction of 177,400 tons of British shipping by aerial attack, and 128,800 tons by submarine.[591]

Though sincerely believing in the powerful "New Order" in Germany and its ability to wage war, Ambassador Oshima observed that the German people, in general, desired peace, despite Chancellor Hitler's ambition to bring England to annihilation.[592] Chancellor Hitler had informed Ambassador Oshima that Great Britain had invited Germany to join with her in clamping down on Italy in 1935, but suspecting that after the subjugation of Italy, Germany's downfall would follow, he had refused.[593]

148. Germany Protests Against Criticism by Japanese Press.

Although the Japanese press, according to Foreign Minister von Ribbentrop on June 4, 1941, was releasing articles in an attempt to divorce Japan and Germany, actually the Japanese Empire continued more and more solidly to support the Hitler program, since apparently it was much impressed by German success. Attempting to vindicate his government, Ambassador Oshima explained to Foreign Minister von Ribbentrop that though the rigid control exercised over the press in Germany did not exist in Japan, the Japanese thoroughly supported the Tripartite principles.[594]

149. Croatia Signs the Tripartite Pact.

Croatia was invited on June 5, 1941 to join the Tripartite powers. Dr. Ante Pavelic of Zagreb was to be Premier and Foreign Minister of this newly recognized government. Arrangements were made to have the agreement signed in the presence of Foreign Minister von Ribbentrop in Venice on June 14, 1941.[595]

150. Japan Assists an Axis-Supported Indian Revolutionary.

Japan was interested in the activities of Mr. Subhas Bose, a leader of a group of the Congress Party, who after deportation from India, had been living in Berlin.[596] Learning from the Italian Foreign Office, on June 4, 1941, that Mr. Bose was in Rome but had not as yet conferred with Premier Mussolini or Foreign Minister Ciano, Japan planned not to make a public commitment, since it felt that he might not be a capable revolutionary leader.[597] However, Japan offered to act as liaison between Mr. Bose and his party of a million supporters in the province of Bengal.[598]

151. Germany's Attitude Toward Portugal (June 1941).

Although in early June 1941 Spain was expected to join the Tripartite Pact, German authorities did not believe that Hitler would exert pressure on Portugal to make it follow suit.[599]

---

[591]II, 559.
[592]II, 560.
[593]II, 561.
[594]II, 562.
[595]II, 563.
[596]II, 564–565.
[597]*Ibid.*
[598]II, 565.
[599]II, 566.

152. Japan Congratulates Germany on the Fall of Crete.

Great accomplishments of Germany in World War II were the landing of troops on Crete early in May 1941, and the final annexation of the island in June 1941, after some unexpected resistance.[600] In referring to the Battle of Crete, Hitler told Ambassador Oshima that victory had been obtained entirely by new aerial tactics and that twelve thousand prisoners had been captured and eight battleships destroyed.[601]

On June 6, 1941 Ambassador Zenbei Horikiri in Rome called to congratulate Foreign Minister Ciano on the Axis conquest of Crete. Further moves against Alexandria and the Suez Canal were suggested by Ambassador Horikiri, who also expressed his belief that defeat of the British Isles would not be too difficult. In reply, Foreign Minister Ciano stated that Britain's home defenses, its fleet and air arms would make invasion somewhat costly. Furthermore, any move in North Africa would not be without a struggle.[602] As final resistance crumbled in Crete, however, the swiftly moving German Luftwaffe began to bomb Alexandria, Haifa and Cyprus.[603]

153. Vichy Begins to Collaborate with Germany.[604]

Tokyo was informed as early as May 10, 1941, that current discussions were facilitating German-French collaboration.[605] Negotiations between German authorities and Vice Premier Darlan were expected to culminate in new and better relations between these two governments. On May 14, 1941 Ambassador Kato at Vichy reviewed the Darlan-Hitler conference on May 12, 1941. According to a German Foreign Office staff member, the meeting of the two leaders had ensured German-French political and military cooperation. Collaboration would include Germany's use of sea and air bases in the French colonies in North Africa, supply lines in Syria and the French Navy. In return France was to be assured of the preservation of its Empire and colonies.[606] The authoritative German spokesman also predicted that Admiral Darlan, rather than Mr. Pierre Laval, would originate all further policies concerning Germany and France, since conversations between Admiral Darlan and Chancellor Hitler had been conducted at Berchtesgaden in a most amiable atmosphere.[607]

As proof of the friendly relations between the two governments, France obtained the release of 100,000 prisoners on May 19, 1941, as well as a reduction in the maintenance cost of Germany's army of occupation to 240,000,000 francs per day.[608] Ambassador Kato believed that the German-Vichy negotiations had been quite successful, and he remarked that Marshal Henri Petain's address of May 15, 1941 would influence French opinion in favor of Germany.

According to the Japanese Ambassador, relations between the United States and France took an unexpected turn for the worse after President Roosevelt, in a statement on May 15, 1941, had warned France against collaboration with Germany, and had then ordered guards to be placed aboard eleven French ships, including the *Normandie*, which were in American ports. Furthermore, Marshal Petain informed Ambassador Leahy that the assistance accorded France by the United States was not sufficient.[609]

---

[600]II, 567.

[601]II, 561.

[602]II, 568.

[603]II, 559.

[604]See Japanese-French Relations, Part C, Sections 198–199.

[605]II, 569.

[606]II, 570.

[607]II, 555.

[608]II, 571.

[609]*Ibid.*

The Japanese Ambassador at Rome stated on June 7, 1941 that France was expected to contract a peace treaty with Germany and Italy, and at the same time the questions of Croatia and Nice would be settled. Since French leaders were reported as ready to sign the Tripartite Pact, Japanese authorities believed that this would aid them in the Japanese-French Indo-China economic situation.[610]

154. Great Britain Opposes Vichy.

Meanwhile, the Japanese Ambassador in London, following his talk with the British Foreign Minister on or about June 6, 1941, had reported on British-French sentiment. Though recognizing that Mr. Pierre Laval, Admiral Darlan and Marshal Petain wished most ardently that Great Britain would follow Vichy and would assist in bringing about an early peace in Europe, Foreign Minister Anthony Eden announced that Great Britain was determined to finish the war, even though it had to act alone. He believed, however, that the biggest part of the French populace was not with Vichy in spirit.[611]

Three divisions of British troops, with some deGaullists and Abyssinians, invaded Syria in early June 1941, and according to Ambassador Kato's report of his conversation with General Huntziger, the French Minister of War, French defenses were exceptionally weak. However, the French Minister believed that the British advance could be temporarily halted.[612] Japanese sources from Turkey reported that despite French efforts to render assistance, Axis negotiations with Turkey for the transport of arms through Turkish territory had come to naught, and as a result, Syria would fall under the rule of British forces.[613]

155. Japanese Concern Over British Control of Iraq.

It was apparent to Japanese representatives that Axis interests in Iraq would be impeded by the new pro-British government, which had been established by Emir Abdul Illah to succeed the Cabinet of Premier Rashid Ali el Gailani, whose Iraqi Army, composed principally of doubtful Kirkuk-Mosul troops, had been crushed by the British.[614] Japanese agents in the Near and Middle East felt that unless Germany and Italy immediately counteracted the British influence, the whole Arabian movement of the Axis might be severely imperiled.

Ambassador Horikiri expressed his concern about Syria and Iraq to Foreign Minister Ciano on June 6, 1941.[615] This fear was well founded, for, on June 4, 1941, a definite rupture between Iraq and Italy had occurred, when Minister Muzahim Al-Pachachi, residing in Rome, had received orders to return home. To maintain Japanese harmony with Iraq, Japanese representatives in Rome were urged by their colleagues in Baghdad to finance the return of Minister Al-Pachachi.[616]

156. Turkey Signs Commercial Agreement with Germany.

Demands for support were made upon Turkey from all quarters as it attempted to preserve its neutrality. The Axis nations even considered the transfer of Syria to Turkey in exchange

---

[610]II, 572.
[611]II, 573.
[612]II, 574.
[613]II, 575.
[614]II, 576–577.
[615]II, 578–580, 563.
[616]II, 581.

for its support. However, as time passed, the Axis nations were encouraged by Turkey's attitude for the Japanese Ambassador to Berlin states, on May 22, 1941, that although Turkey had remained neutral, it was in fact becoming more closely allied with the Axis since it not only permitted Axis supplies to cross through Turkish territory, but was also expecting to be of assistance in an Axis move against India.[617]

On June 18, 1941 Turkey took an important step in staving off an attack from the west when German Ambassador Franz von Papen and Foreign Minister Shukru Saracoglu signed a Turkish-German Pact. Reporting the formulation of this pact to the Japanese Foreign Minister, Turkish Ambassador Tek, resident in Tokyo, was reassured by Mr. Matsuoka as to Chancellor Hitler's "high ideals" and also as to Turkey's good judgment in culminating such a treaty. Turkish diplomats took care to stipulate, however, that this treaty admitted no passage of troops through their neutral territory, though a comprehensive commercial pact would be contracted between Turkey and Germany.[618]

157. Japan Persuades Germany to Eliminate Pro-Chinese German Officials.

On July 3, 1941 Ambassador Oshima conferred with the German Ambassador to China, Henrich D. Stahmer, and requested that German officials in China, who were well known for their pro-Chinese and anti-Japanese attitudes, be replaced by Germans who were more deeply imbued with the spirit of National Socialism. The German Ambassador agreed to present the matter to Foreign Minister von Ribbentrop, and Ambassador Oshima's request for the names of anti-Japanese Germans was forwarded by Tokyo to all Japanese officials in China.[619]

158. German Merchants Seek Chinese Markets.

As time went on, Japanese officials became increasingly concerned with German policy in regard to its merchants in the Far East. Having learned from intelligence sources on July 9, 1941, that the German Economic Ministry had issued secret instructions to German merchants in Shanghai which would promote German control of trade, Mr. Matsuoka urged his representatives to impress upon Germany the need for a retraction of such orders, and to stress the necessity for fostering Japanese and German commercial equality. Should Germany not comply, Japan revealed that it would insist upon all of Japan's business being conducted through Japanese merchants. He urged that immediate action be taken to avert a serious break in relations.[620]

According to the Japanese, a group of German diplomatic officials was primarily concerned with its own immediate financial and commercial interests, and, therefore, Japanese restrictions on shipping, residence and transit in China had tended to create a consistently unfriendly attitude on the part of these men toward the Japanese Empire.[621] Another group of German officials, however, stressed the need for political concert between Germany, Japan and Manchukuo, but even this group, which had recognized the Nanking government and, thus, was able to negotiate with it, might also cause a delicate situation.[622]

---

[617]II, 567.
[618]II, 582.
[619]II, 583–584.
[620]II, 585.
[621]II, 586.
[622]*Ibid.*

On July 31, 1941 Tokyo urged Ambassador Oshima in Berlin to prevent situations leading to anti-Japanese and pro-Chungking conduct on the part of German merchants, such as the transfer of captured enemy shipping, and the violation of shipping rules.[623]

159. Japan Seeks a German-Nanking Commercial Agreement.

Looking forward to the establishment of a "New Order" in the Far East, Japan believed that a comprehensive agreement between Germany and China, with recognition of the leading positions of Japan and Germany, should be concluded at the end of the war. Since a large scale war in China was still under way, however, it seemed best that as individual questions came up, immediate friendly settlements should be made by an agreement between Japan, Germany and China. Several new clauses were to be added to the present German-Chinese treaty in order to grant special privileges to the signatories in the area in which they held leadership.[624]

Complaints from the German Consul General in Shanghai were received at Tokyo in July 1941 concerning the treatment being accorded to Germans in China. Impressed by these complaints, Japan recognized the necessity for according favorable treatment to Germans in China in order to improve German relationships with the new Nanking government.[625] A simple agreement, stipulating a most favored nation treatment for Germans in China, was suggested, but Japanese representatives in Nanking and Shanghai were directed to deal adroitly with the situation to ensure the special position of the new Chinese-Mongolian border as an area of joint Japanese-Chinese policy.[626]

160. Japan Reports a Lull in Japanese-American Negotiations.

On July 17, 1941 Mr. Matsuoka declared that his government had not been pressing the United States for an understanding, and that no concrete action had been taken for a month after the United States had submitted its supposedly final proposal in late June 1941. During this period of delay, whenever the German and Italian Ambassadors to Tokyo had sought some information as to the contents of the United States proposal, Mr. Matsuoka had stated merely that the provisions were slipshod and were not acceptable. However, he had not discontinued the negotiations abruptly because they affected both the domestic and foreign policy of Japan. Declaring that any treaty reached with the United States would have to be based on the Tripartite Pact, he stated that there was very little chance of reaching an agreement.[626a]

The German Ambassador to Tokyo informed Vice Minister Chuichi Ohashi on July 22, 1941 that Germany opposed the Japanese-American negotiations, and in view of the successes of Germany in the Russian war, Japan had better decide immediately on its course of future action. Remarking that Japan would occupy Southern French Indo-China in the next few days, and that this seizure would be merely a preparatory step for future activities, Vice Minister Ohashi pointed out that Germany's insistence on influencing Japan's national policy might possibly have an adverse effect on Axis relations.[626b]

161. Foreign Minister Matsuoka Resigns (July 18, 1941).

Japan's announcement of its neutrality in regard to the German-Russian war did not dispose of a critical internal situation at home. On July 16, 1941 Foreign Minister Matsuoka con-

---

[623]*Ibid.*
[624]II, 587.
[625]II, 588.
[626]II, 589.
[626a]II, 590.
[626b]II, 591.

128

fided in Ambassador Oshima that Japan's situation had looked so impossible when he had taken office that he had felt that nothing on earth could have saved it. However, it had always been his policy to attempt everything within his power to effect a solution. Nevertheless, Japan was now in a terrible predicament and Mr. Matsuoka was experiencing many tribulations.[626c] Some hint of what caused Mr. Matsuoka's anxiety was discerned on July 18, 1941 when, after a meeting of the Japanese Cabinet, Mr. Matsuoka was replaced by Admiral Teijiro Toyoda as Minister of Foreign Affairs.

Ambassador Horikiri in Rome pointed out that genuine sympathy was felt in Italy for Mr. Matsuoka, because he had succeeded in bringing about a union of the three Axis countries. Most Italians now believed that the status quo could not be maintained in the light of the Japanese change, but Japan emphasized that the shift in its Cabinet signified only the strengthening of popular unity, and would not impair its allegiance to the Tripartite Pact.[626d] According to Ambassador Horikiri, Japan's unshakable determination made a favorable impression upon authorities in Rome, who, nevertheless, continued to watch Japan's actions.[626e]

On July 24, 1941 in a message to Foreign Minister von Ribbentrop of Germany and on July 25, 1941 in a formal statement to Foreign Minister Ciano of Italy, Mr. Matsuoka reiterated Japan's intentions to remain true to its foreign policy, and expressed his appreciation for the kindness shown to him during his term of office.[626f]

162. Japan Retaliates Against the American Freezing Order.

The meeting of the Japanese Cabinet on July 27, 1941 decided upon retaliatory measures against the United States for freezing Japanese assets. Japan decided to draw up certain measures which would control foreign exchange and would entail all business activities of American citizens. However, if the United States were to act leniently in the future, Japanese authorities in Japan, Manchukuo, and China would be prepared to do likewise.[626g]

163. Ambassador Oshima Attempts to Change Japan's Policy.

Ambassador Oshima had continued his efforts to persuade Japanese authorities to support Germany in the war against Russia and to cease their negotiations with the United States. On July 17, 1941 he reported the displeasure of Foreign Minister von Ribbentrop and Chancellor Hitler with Japan's recent activities, and urged that Japan make the Tripartite Pact the foundation of its national policy.[626h]

Two weeks later, on July 31, 1941, he again disagreed with Tokyo's interpretation of Germany's motives in attacking Russia by pointing out that Germany was planning only a short war in Russia before attacking England. Ambassador Oshima anticipated the collapse of Commissar Stalin's government in the near future, and though admitting that America would enter the war, he minimized its ability to aid England.[626i]

[626c] II, 592.
[626d] II, 593–595.
[626e] II, 595.
[626f] II, 596–597.
[626g] II, 598.
[626h] II, 599.
[626i] II, 600.

PART C—JAPANESE DIPLOMATIC ACTIVITIES THROUGHOUT THE WORLD

(f) Japanese-Russian Relations.

164. Rumor of Russia Withdrawing Its Troops from German Borders (May 1941).

Immediately following the Hess incident, relations between Moscow and Berlin began to show definite signs of strain, and Japan's alliance with Germany and its Neutrality Pact with Russia placed it in a delicate position. Although Russia had been faithfully carrying out its economic agreements with Germany, it was noted in Berlin, as early as May 14, 1941, that Russia had withdrawn its troops from the German border, either in anticipation of war or with the purpose of avoiding it. Meanwhile, the German army continued its preparations, confident that it could easily conquer European Russia, if such were Chancellor Hitler's plan.[627]

165. Russia Restricts the Transportation of War Materials.

In the economic agreement of September 1939, Russia had invited Germany to transport goods through Russia, but in May 1941 a problem concerning war materials arose.[628] Russia began restricting the shipment of machine tools and other war machinery for making arms, bombs and planes, and though Japan's representatives commenced negotiations to have some of these restrictions relaxed, a negative response was expected.[629] Nor would Russia accept for transit goods assigned to countries with which it had not reached an agreement. To overcome this disadvantage, Tokyo ordered, in mid-May 1941 that freight which was to be shipped to Japan through either free or occupied territory was to be paid for in free German marks.[630]

Both Germany and Japan were disturbed because the worsening of German-Russian relations would eliminate the passage of import goods from Germany via Siberia.[631] Because of this the Japanese Ambassador in Berlin on June 18, 1941 forwarded to Tokyo the German suggestion that Japan add to the terms of the recently contracted Japan-Russian trade pact certain provisions which would make possible the transfer of goods through Russian territory to and from other countries, including unoccupied countries.[632]

On the other hand, Tokyo was informed on June 17, 1941 that courier service could be reopened between Manchukuo and Eruope, which indicated some relaxation of restrictions.[633]

166. Russia Seeks to Avoid War with Germany.

On May 15, 1941 Ambassador Tatekawa requested an explanation from Foreign Minister Molotov regarding the current rumors of war between Russia and Germany, and pointed out that, if such rumors were true, Japan would act only as mediator. Foreign Minister Molotov assured him that such talk was entirely without foundation and was designed only to discredit the Tripartite Pact. As a result of this interview, the Japanese Ambassador believed that Russia was attempting to avoid a clash with Germany, and that intensive Russian defense preparations along the western border were inconsequential in view of Russia's desire to avert war.[634]

---

[627]II, 601.
[628]II, 602.
[629]II, 603.
[630]II, 604–605.
[631]II, 606.
[632]II, 607.
[633]II, 608.
[634]II, 609.

According to a report of Ambassador Tatekawa on May 16, 1941 Germany had some 140 to 150 divisions concentrated on the western border with reinforcements close at hand, and Russia had but 116 divisions.[635] With this in mind, and considering the fact that Russian forces had long feared the German army, the Japanese Ambassador felt that there was no possibility of a clash because of Russian weakness.

Ambassador Tatekawa also pointed to the disadvantages of war for Germany, inasmuch as it was receiving the natural resources it needed from Russia. He believed that Germany could take the Ukraine, but that by fighting a defensive war Russia could nullify Germany's temporary gains. For all of these reasons, the Japanese Ambassador to Moscow stated that he did not see in the near future any chance of a major war developing between Germany and Russia.[636]

Vatican sources added strength to this belief in peace when they reported to Ambassador Horikiri that Russia had no alternative but to align itself with the Axis.[637]

Furthermore, though German intentions were not clear to Ambassador Oshima in Berlin, he felt that Russia would refrain from mobilization in the hopes of not giving Germany an excuse for an attack. However, he indicated his belief that Germany would defeat Russia in a short time, and that the United States and England would be of little assistance to Russia.[638]

167. European Observers Predict a German-Russian War.

Signs of a coming clash between Russia and Germany were perceived by some European observers, for on May 30, 1941 an eminent correspondent of the Catholic press confided to the Japanese Ambassador at Rome that German-Russian relations had reached "a pass of extreme tension", and another well-informed newspaperman predicted that hostilities with Russia would start about June 15, 1941. Many observers believed that Germany would delay an attack against England and would immediately enter into hostilities against Russia, which was then expected to seek conciliation.[639]

War rumors were also prevalent in the Balkans where northbound German troops and supply cars were noticed. It was reported on June 3, 1941 that certain diplomatic circles in Sofia would welcome an outbreak of war because such a conflict would lead to the overthrow of the Communist Party. It appeared that Russian influence had been completely swept out of Yugoslovia, although Serb and Croatian sympathy for the Slavs was still as strong as ever.[640]

168. Japanese-Russian Trade Agreement (June 9, 1941).

Both Japan and Russia were striving to attain an equitable solution in regard to fishing and trade agreements, and Ambassador Tatekawa in Moscow urged, on May 15, 1941 that Japan act not later than August, 1941 on the question of North Sakhalin, an island owned jointly by Russia and Japan.[641]

Foreign Minister Matsuoka replied, on May 28, 1941, that he intended to settle definitely the question of rights and interests in North Sakhalin within the coming year. He asked that Russia have confidence in him, since in conducting the commerce and fishery negotiations satisfactorily he expected to encounter some domestic opposition.

---

[635] II, 610.

[636] II, 611.

[637] II, 612.

[638] II, 613.

[639] II, 614.

[640] II, 615.

[641] II, 616.

Although Japan had decided to maintain its usual defenses in the North Seas, it issued special instructions, on May 28, 1941, to its subjects forbidding trespassing or any acts of a troublesome nature within Russian waters.[642] Some contention arose over the scheduled departure on June 15, 1941 of the *Kaiyo Maru* for Sakhalin Island, but Tokyo decided to send it, regardless of the attitude of Russia.[643]

On May 31, 1941 Ambassador Tatekawa presented the respects of his Foreign Minister to Mr. Molotov, who, having already expressed his desire for an immediate completion of negotiations, urged the Japanese Ambassador to expedite matters in Tokyo. Thereupon Ambassador Tatekawa pointed out to Mr. Matsuoka that although the conclusion of the Neutrality Pact with Russia had been generally accepted in Japan, an early settlement of the fisheries dispute would effectively silence the remaining opposition by demonstrating Russian sincerity in the negotiations.

It was evident that Moscow blamed Mr. Matsuoka for the delay, since on May 15, 1941 Mr. Molotov had drawn up and delivered the Russian statement regarding the fisheries question, and, as of June 1, 1941 no answer had been received from Tokyo.[644]

According to Mr. Molotov, only one problem impeded the final settlement which Ambassador Tatekawa hoped for within a week after June 1, 1941. This was the Russian demand that the differential between land and sea shipping expenses be made up for by payment in kind of Japanese commodities. The Japanese Ambassador on June 1, 1941 offered his opinion, in which Mr. Molotov concurred, that some formula for mutual agreement on the matter could be reached. Having submitted a revised proposal to the Russian, the Japanese Ambassador stated that the entire business would be concluded with a week.[645] After much discussion of details to be included in the document, the agreement was finally reached on June 9, 1941.[646]

169. Japanese-Russian Agreement as to Boundary Lines (June 10, 1941).

In an effort to protect Japanese-Russian relations and to support the recently signed neutrality pact, a conference had been opened at Chita on May 27, 1941 to discuss the Manchurian-Russian boarder delineation. Even though the Japanese army was of the opinion that the whole matter should be kept absolutely secret, Japanese diplomats decided to make a public statement concerning the agreement finally reached on June 10, 1941, since it was believed that such an announcement would further the already improved relations between the two countries.[647] Though the preliminary work had been finished, the actual demarcation of the line remained to be done. It was hoped that this could be accomplished by the end of the summer of 1941.[648]

On the same day that Japan and Russia concluded their agreement, a report, sent to Tokyo and Moscow from Hsinking, Manchoukuo, declared that twenty-seven armored trains were transporting 800 trucks between Chita and Manchuli. Japanese diplomats traveling through Russia always made detailed reports of the military activities they had observed en route.[649]

---

[642]II, 617.
[643]II, 618.
[644]II, 619.
[645]II, 620–621.
[646]II, 622–624.
[646]II, 622–624.
[647]II, 625–626.
[648]II, 627–628.
[649]II, 629.

It was pointed out that even for maneuvers, this was a large number of trucks, and in view of the international situation such activity deserved Japan's close attention.[650]

Russia agreed to Tokyo's request of June 16, 1941 that secrecy be observed regarding three diplomatic notes, which were to be known only to the Japanese Foreign Office and such officials as Russia approved.[651] Meanwhile, Japan was suspicious of Russia, and even on special occasions it insisted that Russian visitors be furnished with Japanese transportation.[652]

170. Russia Supplies Essential Materials to Germany.

From a commercial viewpoint, Russian-German relations in May and early June 1941 appeared unruffled for despite its overtaxed railroad facilities and recent loss of influence in the Balkans,[653] Russia continued to supply Germany with large quantities of materials even though, according to the Russian First Secretary at Rome no agreement regarding the joint exploitation of the Ukraine was in existence.[654] Furthermore, Tokyo was informed on June 5, 1941 that new contracts for raw materials between Russia and Italy were being considered, and that an Italian economic mission to Moscow was being organized.[655]

171. Germany's Demands on Russia.

On June 6, 1941 Japanese representatives in Sofia and Moscow reported that the following demands were to be made of Russia by Germany:

    (1) Return part of Bukovina to Rumania,
    (2) Reconsider the Russian-German border line in Galicia,
    (3) Allow Germany to enter the Ukraine, and
    (4) Permit her passage through the Caucasus.

The fact that Germany had not referred to Bessarabia in her demands was interpreted by Japanese spokesman as something of a compromise.[656] Mr. Izumi, a Japanese representative in Sofia, stated that the acceptance of these demands would shatter the Russian army's prestige, and he expected that the anti-Stalin wing would stage a coup d'etat. According to Mr. Izumi, it appeared that Russia was now forced to acquiesce or fight, and he believed that Russia was seriously menaced both from within and from without. Although there was still a possibility for peace, the German army was pressing Herr von Ribbentrop for a showdown, since it expected to defeat the Russian army in two or three weeks.[657] Some in diplomatic circles contended that Hitler was merely trying, at the risk of war, to bring Russia into the Tripartite Alliance.[658]

172. Japanese Diplomats Urge Russia to Accept German Demands.

Both Ambassador Tatekawa in Moscow on June 7, 1941 and Ambassador Horikiri in Rome on June 14, 1941 urged Mr. Matsuoka to intervene in bringing peace between Russia and Ger-

---

[650]II, 630.
[651]II, 631–632.
[652]II, 633.
[653]II, 610.
[654]II, 634.
[655]II, 635.
[656]II, 636.
[657]II, 637.
[658]II, 638.

many. The Foreign Minister was advised to press Russia to join the Axis, or to collaborate closely with anti-British and anti-American groups. Whatever the demands, Japan felt that Russia should accept in order to avoid war.[659]

Ambassador Tatekawa reported on June 7, 1941 that the German Ambassador in Moscow believed that Russia had acceded in the main to Germany's requests, and that there was no reason for an attack.[660] But on June 17, 1941 the Japanese consul at Ankara was informed by a member of the German Embassy that unless Russia conformed to Chancellor Hitler's demands within the next ten days, hostilities would begin.[661]

173. German Leaders Warn Japan of the Coming War.

On June 4, 1941 Ambassador Oshima reported the details of some important interviews he had just held with Foreign Minister von Ribbentrop and Chancellor Hitler in which both German leaders had agreed that in all probability Germany could not avoid war with Russia.[662] Though the war was not yet a certainty and the date had not yet been set, Herr von Ribbentrop advised Japan to make its preparations for the event as soon as possible. According to the German leader, the campaign would be successfully finished in three months.[663]

Although there were many rumors to the effect that negotiations were under way between Russia and Germany, Foreign Minister von Ribbentrop had dismissed them as being absolutely groundless. Moreover, he declared that Germany had completed all its preparations and that troop concentrations were massed along its eastern border where Russian troops had also been stationed.

Ambassador Oshima asked Herr von Ribbentrop whether or not war with Russia could be avoided since Germany's main objective was England. The German Foreign Minister replied that the attitude of the Soviet Union of late had become increasingly unfriendly toward Germany, and that there had even been an armed border clash between the two forces at the mouth of the Danube. According to the German Foreign Minister, it was evident that Russia was merely waiting for Germany to fail against England before declaring war itself.

Herr von Ribbentrop advised the Japanese Ambassador that the conquest of Russia at this time would give complete and undisputable control of the entire European continent to Germany, and would make it absolutely impossible for Great Britain and the United States to touch it. Moreover, such a conquest would split Russia to the great advantage of Japan.[664]

Ambassador Oshima advised Tokyo on June 6, 1941 to prevent the departure of Japanese citizens for Europe, via Siberia, because of the threatening situation, and a few days later the German Ambassador in Tokyo was ordered to keep Germans away from this route.[665]

174. Germany Denies Negotiating with Russia.

Despite the denials of Foreign Minister von Ribbentrop in his talks with Ambassador Oshima on June 3, 4, 1941 that Germany was negotiating with Russia, Tokyo, on June 14, 1941, ordered both Ambassador Horikiri in Rome and Ambassador Oshima in Berlin to inquire once again concerning this matter.[666]

---

[659]II, 639–640.
[660]II, 641.
[661]II, 642.
[662]II, 643–644.
[663]II, 646.
[664]*Ibid.*
[665]II, 647–648.
[666]II, 649–650.

Mr. Matsuoka's curiosity concerning a German-Russian rapprochement was again manifested on June 20, 1941, when he ordered Ambassador Oshima to discuss the gist of a reported conversation between the German Foreign Minister and the Russian Ambassador in Berlin.[667] Herr von Ribbentrop promptly denied that he had conversed with Ambassador Deganov, and reiterated that Germany had no intentions of negotiating with Russia.[668]

175. Prospects of an Anglo-Russian Oil Agreement.

Ambassador Cripps' mission to Moscow, according to a report to Tokyo from the Japanese Ambassador in London on June 13, 1941, had not materially improved Anglo-Russian relations though England had already become aware of the inevitability of the Russo-German conflict. The Japanese Ambassador in London believed that as a consequence, an Asiatic-European rapprochement, at least on Anglo-Russian oil, would evolve.[669]

176. Ambassador Tatekawa in Moscow Doubts the Possibility of a German-Russian War. (June 16, 1941).

Italian and German Ambassadors in Moscow conferred on June 15, 1941 concerning the evacuation of their diplomatic staffs and families, and though the Japanese diplomats were informed that no official word had been received from either Berlin or Rome, arrangements for the departure of female staff members were concluded. As to the causes for this move, Mr. Tatekawa was informed that all departures were for family reasons.[670] The Japanese Ambassador was inclined to believe that the Axis diplomats had received no official instructions for he could discover no signs of their burning their codes or taking any other final precautions.[671]

The Japanese Ambassador to Moscow was still convinced on June 16, 1941 that Russia, although encouraged by England and the United States, knew full well that it had to maintain a cooperative attitude toward Germany. Ambassador Tatekawa blamed British Ambassador Cripps for an unfounded rumor of war between Russia and Germany, which had been denied by Tass, the official Russian news agency.[672]

However, Tokyo announced on June 17, 1941 that British and Russian denials of the threatening German-Russian rupture were made to minimize the situation, and should be considered as mere propaganda. Significantly, the Japanese government expected the beginning of the Russian war to be followed by a British-Russian alliance, an American-Russian rapprochement, and, finally, the entrance of the United States into the war.[673]

177. Ambassador Oshima Warns of the Imminence of the Russian-German War.

According to Ambassador Oshima, preparations had already been completed for the German surprise attack, and the Rumanian army had been completely mobilized on June 13, 1941. Chancellor Hitler had returned to Berlin on June 14, 1941 while Generals Brauchitsch and Halder as well as other military leaders had already gone to the front line. In view of these facts, Ambassador Oshima urgently requested instructions as to Japan's policy towards the war.[674]

---

[667]II, 651.
[668]II, 652.
[669]II, 653.
[670]II, 654–655.
[671]II, 656.
[672]II, 657.
[673]II, 658.
[674]II, 659.

On June 18, 1941 Ambassador Oshima reported that the clearing of the weather in Germany and the fact that Russia was fully aware of Germany's intentions made the outbreak of war likely at any time. He emphasized the German army's assurance of annihilating the Russian army in four weeks, and urged that Japan should be well prepared for the ending of the war in the near future.[675]

178. Japanese-Russian Financial Relations Remain Stable.

Japan continued to carry on normal financial relations with Russia, and, on June 20, 1941 after America's freezing of German and Italian capital, it made preparations to transfer American money remittances directly from Tokyo to Moscow, rather than through Berlin.[676]

179. Japan Denies Its Friendly Relations with Russia Have Inconvenienced Germany.

Herr von Ribbentrop intimated on June 21, 1941 that Japan was responsible for Russia's ability to move its Far Eastern forces to European Russia, whereupon Ambassador Oshima pointed out to the German Foreign Minister that it was only natural for Russia to concentrate its troops in its most vital possessions, and that Japanese-Russian relations had nothing to do with this move.[677]

180. Germany Attacks Russia (June 22, 1941).

Germany attacked Russia at 4 A.M., Moscow time, on June 22, 1941, just one hour before the German Ambassador to Moscow presented to Mr. Molotov a note he had received from Berlin on the previous evening.

Not all members of the German Foreign Staff whole-heartedly supported the attack, for the German Ambassador to Moscow, meeting with Ambassador Tatekawa, expressed his distinct disapproval. He had known since April 17, 1941 that Germany was going to attack Russia, and he believed that there was no reason for it to do so since Russia had not been deliberately obstructing Germany's military action. He concluded that powerful military leaders must have been guiding Chancellor Hitler.[678]

After the outbreak of hostilities, the German Consul General met with Ambassador Ota at Vladivostok on the afternoon of June 22, 1941 and he explained that since the Comintern had been engaging for many months in activities within Poland, Czechoslovakia, Yugoslavia, and Hungary, as well as other countries coming under the jurisdiction of the Third Reich, and had also refused to withdraw its troops from the border (See Japanese-Russian Relations, Section 164), Russia had actually precipitated the final breach in German-Russian relations.

The Axis representative continued by saying that the war had been started by Germany, and that he saw no reason why Japan, for the present, should not maintain neutrality. The German diplomat's request that German nationals be cared for in Japan and in Manchuria was granted, but when Mr. Ota offered to safeguard the documents of the departing diplomat, he learned that all German codes and important documents had been burned the night before.[679]

---

[675]II, 660.

[676]II, 661.

[677]II, 662.

[678]II, 663.

[679]II, 665.

Reports on the first day's fighting divulged that Russian troops along the border had not been completely mobilized. Five hundred Russian planes were reported shot down or destroyed on the ground, and a Russian air raid on Tilsit did little damage. Twenty-five Roumanian divisions under Marshal Antonescu and fifteen divisions under Marshal Karl Gustaf Mannerheim were assisting the Germans. According to Ambassador Oshima, the success of the day's fighting contributed to the Axis' great confidence in the ultimate outcome of the conflict.[680]

Although it was accepted that Germany would destroy the Ukraine and Caucasus, Ambassador Ota, talking with the U.S. Consul General in Vladivostok, learned that not all observers were agreed that Germany would pierce the heart of Russia.[681] Stating that he was convinced that President Roosevelt would announce America's participation in the war and the extension of military assistance to Russia, the American representative expressed the hope that Japan, which was in a unique position, would move with caution.[682]

181. Japan Assures Germany of Its Support of the Axis.

On that same eventful day, June 22, 1941, Ambassador Ott called at the Japanese Foreign Office in Tokyo to show the text of the German note which had been delivered to Russia, and to announce that Hitler planned to "use every might and means to march against the U.S.S.R." In response to an inquiry from Mr. Matsuoka, the German Ambassador admitted that there was no declaration of war against Russia in the note. Two days later June 24, 1941, it had been decided that no move in regard to the German-Russian war would be taken without full consultation with the German government. Japan again reiterated its desire to act entirely in accordance with the Tripartite Pact and stated that in regard to Poland, it would not quibble over details.[683]

It had been agreed that German officials in Moscow would be taken to Iran, and German interests would be placed in charge of the Bulgarian Minister. At Vladivostok, the German Consul General had severed all connections with the outside world on June 25, 1941, and arrangements were being made for him to embark on the Kasai Maru.[684]

Tokyo was informed on June 22, 1941 that Germany, simultaneously with its military attack on Russia, planned to establish a pro-German regime in Moscow, and also to set up separate governments in the Ukraine, White Russia, and the Baltic shore nations. Lithuania and Latvia would coalesce and Finland would be annexed to Estonia.[685]

182. Japan Investigates a German-British Rapprochement.

As battles raged on the Russian front in June, 1941 it was believed by some observers that the Russian army would retire to the Ural region to carry on a long war; the Germans, therefore, would seek an early termination of the war, and then would turn to the solution of the British question. There were rumors also that the future objective of the war would be changed and that a peace proposal would be submitted to Britain early in July, 1941.[686] In the light of the foregoing, some concern was felt by Tokyo concerning an unverified report that Foreign

---

[680] II, 666–667.
[681] II, 668.
[682] II, *Ibid.*
[683] II, 663–669.
[684] II, 670.
[685] II, 671.
[686] II, 672, 673.

Minister von Ribbentrop had submitted an anti-Comintern proposal to the British Ambassador in Ankara.[687]

But Ambassador Oshima reported Chancellor Hitler's statement of June 22, 1941, which declared that since Anglo-Russian cooperation had become very evident, a large German force would be sent to the eastern front. Following this statement, German papers emphasized that the Russian campaign was a prelude to the British campaign, and that the two campaigns were indivisible.[688]

183. Japan Gauges World Reaction to the Russo-German Conflict.

Japanese diplomats throughout the world were reporting the attitudes in regard to the Russo-German war of the countries to which they had been assigned. Close attention was paid to the views of England and the United States by all Japanese representatives. Japanese estimates of the public opinion in various countries of the world now follows:

(a) *Great Britain.*

According to a Japanese report, Prime Minister Churchill's speech of June 22, 1941, in which he promised aid to Russia, was the occasion for the return of Ambassador Cripps to Moscow and the journey of General Sir Archibald Wavell to confer with Russian military forces.

Conferring with the Russian Ambassador in London, Foreign Minister Anthony Eden was reported to have urged Russia to wage a protracted war, for, according to the Japanese interpretation of Great Britain's attitude, unless the war was long-drawn out, Russia would be forced to fight without British assistance.[689] Ambassador Oshima observed that Great Britain, convinced by past failures, which it had experienced "by interfering at the outset of the last several wars", was merely extending verbal encouragement in the belief that it would be dangerous to ally itself with Russia too soon.[690]

(b) *United States.*

Japan also believed that the United States was following a policy of watchful waiting, and that in the event of a German victory it would not fulfill its promise to aid Russia. It seemed obvious to Japan, on July 4, 1941, that since Mr. Steinhardt, the American Ambassador who appeared to be anti-Russian, had not yet met with the British military mission in Moscow, and since only low-ranking officers were currently located at the American Embassy, no three-power military conference was likely to be under way at this time.[691]

Ambassador Tatekawa in Moscow was convinced that Ambassador Steinhardt was hopefully awaiting Russia's downfall since the latter had asked the Japanese Ambassador to question Foreign Minister Molotov concerning the methods of evacuating foreign diplomatic officials from Moscow. Having been asked to defer this question lest he should insult the Russian government, Mr. Steinhardt removed all his diplomatic personnel to distant villas.[692]

In the light of the growing Russian-American solidarity, the Japanese Ambassador in Rome suggested on August 5, 1941 that Japan act immediately to settle its Russian border question. Fearing the task of facing the combined Russian and American forces, he thought it timely for

---

[687]II, 674.
[688]*Ibid.*
[689]II, 675.
[690]II, 676–677.
[691]II, 678.
[692]II, *Ibid.*

Japan to use its occupation of French Indo-China merely as a threat against England and the United States, and at the same time to prepare quickly to attack northward.[693]

(c) *Spain.*

From Spain came General Franco's request that Spanish volunteers be allowed to assist Germany in its crusade against Communism. Although little military value could be seen in such an alliance, Axis leaders were aware of its importance as material for propaganda in South America.[694]

(d) *Sweden.*

Internal dissension obscured Swedish foreign policy, but German sources believed that the anti-Russian faction in Sweden was gradually winning more strength than the anti-German group.[695]

(e) *Finland.*

Ambassador Oshima was informed that Finland's declaration of neutrality was intended to camouflage a lack of preparedness, and that finally, when sufficiently armed, it would launch an attack on its former enemy, Russia.[696] Finnish defenses had been improved during the preceding year, and the eastern border was observed to be firmly guarded. Although no emergency mobilization had been ordered, it was reported that 10,000 men had been called to arms on June 15, 1941. Women's relief detachments had been formed, antiaircraft posts manned, and members of the Young Men's Associations had joined the German forces.[697] On June 26, 1941 Finland entered the war.

(f) *Manchukuo.*

Repercussions of the Russo-German conflict were watched with special care within Japanese-controlled Manchukuo because of its difficult border problems and internal differences. Immediately after the outbreak of hostilities on Russia's western front, Russian troops along the eastern Manchurian border were observed engaging in athletics. However, Japanese observers, not misled by this pretense, perceived efficient Russian defense preparations going on in the background.[698]

On June 24, 1941 Russia seemed to be refraining from any provocation within Manchukuo, but Japan believed that Russian espionage agents were working with an already established underground organization. The populace seemed to be calm, but some Japanese sympathizers advocated an immediate thrust at Russia. A few White Russians also manifested a desire to rid eastern Asia of Soviet Russian influence. On the other hand, some Japanese were known to be apprehensive lest Manchukuo become involved in the conflict, though the natives expressed no opinion.[699]

The possibility that the Chinese Communist army might move to Outer Mongolia on the pretext that China must defend both Russia and Outer Mongolia was considered by Japan. On June 25, 1941 the Russian army was increasing its supply of armor and armament and mobilizing on the Manchurian border for any emergency.[700]

---

[693]II, 679–681.

[694]II, 676.

[695]II, *Ibid.*

[696]II, 677.

[697]II, 682.

[698]II, 683.

[699]*Ibid.*

[700]II, 684.

In an effort to prevent the U.S.S.R. from suspecting Japan's hostile attitude, the Japanese Kwantung army maintained an appearance of reserve. Officially, Manchukuo adhered to a policy of friendliness, although many young officers of the Kwantung army favored an offensive to settle the Russian question once and for all. Meanwhile, negotiations were being carried on between the Manchukuo Bureau of General Affairs and Japan regarding the supply of materials in case of a Japanese-Russian war.[701]

On June 30, 1941 Japanese agents at Hsinking disclosed that the Russian army had intensified its scouting along the Russian-Manchukuoan border, for pursuit planes, replacing bombers, were concentrated in the first lines. This move was believed to indicate that temporary defense preparations had been replaced by permanent fortifications, and that Russia was in readiness for immediate action.[702]

Continual cruising by Russian planes over the Manchukuoan border evoked the disapproval of Japanese authorities, who in early July, 1941 complained to the Russian Consul General in Harbin, whereupon reciprocal charges against the Japanese were received.[703] The Kwantung army had become quite active in northern Manchuria but Japan believed that a tremendous number of troops would be required to occupy the region east of Lake Baikal, and this would occasion many difficulties in governing the region. In addition, should a Japanese invasion be successful, communications would become a major problem.[704]

Tokyo was informed on July 1, 1941 that in Manchuria the working classes were concerning themselves principally with crop conditions, but they feared a Russian attack on Japan. Japanese agents further discerned that Russian nationals in Manchuria, especially young men subject to military service, were apprehensive about the prospective war. In addition some Jews in Manchukuo who appeared to be anti-German, feared that Japan's entry into the war would affect them commercially.[705]

In view of the fact that espionage activities of other nations might flourish within Manchukuo, on July 4, 1941 Japanese authorities prepared to restrict the entrance, passage, and residence therein of members of any other nations, especially the United States and England. To carry out this policy, Kwantung authorities were urged to participate in a passport control conference.[706]

It was suggested, on July 4, 1941 that Japanese Foreign Office officials, who from long experience had become well acquainted with Russian affairs, should be assigned to positions in Manchukuo to maintain liaison with the Japanese intelligence organizations in Harbin, Hilar, Botanko, Taoan, and Hei-ho.[707]

On July 10–11, 1941 newly assigned Japanese consuls conferred about world conditions as affected by the German-Russian war, the ability of the Soviet Union to resist Germany, and violences perpetrated by the Comintern against Manchukuo. Russian strategy and the general trend of the Manchukuoan population were also discussed, and opinions were exchanged on matter of espionage and counter-espionage. Staff Officer Kotani, reporting on the relative quality of Russian forces, stated that both officers and men were of fairly high caliber, particularly in the air and tank forces. He revealed that they exhibited considerable tactical knowledge and ability, and were quite patriotic.

[701]II, 685.
[702]II, 686.
[703]II, 687.
[704]II, 688.
[705]II, 689.
[706]II, 690.
[707]II, 691.

In the event of a war between Russia and Japan, Japan expected that Russia would:

a. Promote riots and strikes in factories;
b. Incite disorganization in the Manchukuoan army;
c. Promote disunity through anti-Japanese and communistic elements;
d. Instigate activities among the banditry;
e. Engage in destruction and gunfire;
f. Spread disease germs;
g. Throw credit into chaos.[708]

Another important point under discussion was the increasing weakness of Japanese leadership among the people of Manchukuo, for which a Japanese spokesman blamed the non-materialization of various plans and conflicting economic policies.[709]

(g) *China.*

From Shanghai came the announcement that both Soviet and White Russians had enthusiastically united for the defense of their homeland.[710] At the outbreak of German-Russian hostilities, the Nanking government under Japanese direction, voiced its opinion that emphasis should now be placed on peace for China, since it was evident that the Chungking government could no longer depend on aid from Russia.[711] On July 1, 1941 Chinese authorities were reported as speculating concerning the attitude of the Chungking government toward the Chinese Communist Party. It was believed that a comprehensive settlement of the Japanese-Chinese incident resulting from a victory for Germany would eliminate all future anxieties of Japan.

With respect to Russian strength, the Chinese officials discussed whether or not Commissar Stalin would realize, before his complete annihilation, the inevitability of Russia's defeat and would consider a compromise. They pointed out that this would agree with Germany's position, since it was believed that Hitler had no intention of annihilating Russia. In view of the possibility of an early conclusion of the German-Russian war, they felt that it was unwise for Japan and China to rupture existing relations with Russia.[712]

Though there were some Chungking authorities who seemed to advocate the coalition of Chungking with Great Britain and the United States, Japanese agents reported that a great majority were of the opinion that no definite steps should be taken until a favorable situation had been reached in world affairs. With this policy in mind, Chungking authorities guided public opinion by restricting all newspapers from favoring too much either Germany or Russia.[713]

Various foreign representatives were extremely active in Chungking on July 1, 1941, especially the Russian Ambassador who proposed a Chungking-Russian alliance. In reply, China's Foreign Minister stated that no objection to concluding the alliance existed, but inasmuch as Great Britain and America desired to cooperate with Russia in the European war, it was important that China await future developments. In addition, China was aware of the possibility that Russia would collapse in the near future, thus putting an end to all future aid; therefore, it was felt, in accord with the existing sentiment, that these factors should be taken into consideration, if a treaty were to be made between Chungking and Moscow.[714]

---

[708]II, 692.

[709]*Ibid.*

[710]II, 693.

[711]II, 694.

[712]II, 695.

[713]II, 696.

[714]*Ibid.*

It was noted by the Japanese that since the commencement of Russo-German hostility, Generalissimo Chiang Kai-shek had softened his demands on the Chinese Communist army, and had been taking the attitude that it would be sufficient if the army merely refrained from revolt against Chungking. In further dealings with the Communist organization, he apparently had promised to consider General Chou En-Lai's demand for remunerations covering the months of May and June 1941, a demand based on the fact that General Chou En-Lai's army had strictly observed orders from Chungking and had participated in open warfare against Japan.[715] On August 4, 1941 Japanese intelligence agents were ordered by Tokyo to discover whether or not Russians in Shanghai were transshipping East Indian rubber to Vladivostok, and were purchasing petroleum from American and British firms for delivery to Vladivostok.[716]

(h) Turkey.

By signing a non-aggression pact with Germany on June 25, 1941 Turkey sought further to guarantee its neutrality in the German-Russian war, which it had announced on June 23, 1941. It was generally believed at this time that after defeating Russia, Germany would move southward from the Caucasus through Iraq and Syria to attack Egypt.[717] On the other hand, Turkey's increasing of her border troops to five divisions indicated to another observer that it intended to avoid war at all cost. It had also sealed the future of Syria by prohibiting the passage of French arms.[718]

On July 12, 1941, however, Japan believed that Turkey, despite its neutral policy at the outbreak of German-Russo hostilities, had begun to manifest through the press its long harbored resentment against Russia.[719] Two weeks later, on July 29, 1941, the Japanese Ambassador in Ankara reported that after occupying the Caucasus, Germany, disregarding its recent pact, would march through Turkey to attack Iraq. War would break out in the Near East by autumn, as Japan saw it, for Turkey had no alternative but to refuse both belligerents or decide to which she would yield. In either case the unavoidable result would be war. The Japanese Ambassador in Ankara was much impressed with German might, and predicted that Germany would soon crush the Turks.[720]

(i) Hungary.

Hungary declared war on June 27, 1941 and now most of the countries of Europe were embroiled in the war.[721] According to Ambassador Oshima, this tremendous spreading of the war was contrary to the wishes of Germany since Chancellor Hitler's motive was not to destroy world culture, but to save it from Bolshevism.[722] Stressing the necessity of Japan's redoubling its efforts in promoting an Axis victory, Ambassador Oshima pointed out that his country had undertaken such an obligation in signing the anti-Comintern pact.[723]

(j) India.

Since Japan was cognizant of the role that India might play in the overthrow of English influence in the Far East, it supported the activities of certain Indian revolutionaries. Fearing

---

[715]*Ibid.*
[716]II, 697.
[717]II, 698–699.
[718]II, 575.
[719]II, 700.
[720]II, 701–702.
[721]II, 703–704.
[722]II, 703–705.
[723]II, 703.

that America would endeavor to stimulate liberalism in India, and that Great Britain would attempt to compromise with the Indian Congress, one of these leaders in Berlin, presumably Mr. Bose, sent a message to his colleagues in India via the Japanese diplomatic communication system. It requested some indication of Indian reaction to the Russo-German war, and urged that any compromise between Great Britain and the Indian Congress be sabotaged.

According to the opinion of this leader, India's only hope for independence lay in an Axis victory. Believing that Germany's victory over Russia was just a matter of weeks, he predicted that Chancellor Hitler would make some pronouncement immediately about India's independence, and suggested that this pronouncement be followed by a revolution. Arrangements were to be made immediately in order to take over rule of India at the proper time, and reliable agents, unknown to the British, were to be sent to work in certain localities. India should approve the current Japanese policy in the Far East, including Indo-China, since it conformed to the objective of Indian nationalists.[724]

184. Japan Is Warned of Soviet Strength.

Although first reports from the Russian front pointed to an early German victory, some keen analysts credited Russia with a reserve power suspected by few foreign governments. Despite the fact that many besides Foreign Minister von Ribbentrop and Ambassador Oshima urged Mr. Matsuoka to declare war against Russia, others, including the First Secretary of the Japanese Embassy in Hsinking, formerly attached to the Japanese Embassy in Moscow, advised that Russia, possessing rich resources in territory, manpower, and material, and after twenty-four years of communistic education, completely unified behind Stalin, should not be underestimated.

The former Moscow staff member also pointed to the fact that within the next few months a severe Russian winter would hamper a German advance. Russia's powerful defense line along the Manchukuo border also served as a sign of reserve strength.[725]

185. Russia Seeks Japan's Support of the Neutrality Pact.

From the beginning of hostilities, Russia's Ambassador to Tokyo attempted to cement Russo-Japanese relations, and tried to determine Japan's feelings with regard to its neutrality agreement with Russia. On June 23, 1941 Ambassador Smetanin called on Foreign Minister Matsuoka to determine whether or not Japan intended to honor the Neutrality Pact. Foreign Minister Matsuoka replied that the Neutrality Pact with Russia had no relation to the Tripartite Pact, and that the Japanese government was still undetermined regarding its attitude on the present turn of events. However, in discussing Japan's foreign policy with Stalin at a time when he had not anticipated a Russo-German war, Foreign Minister Matsuoka had stated that Japan would not collaborate with Britain and America.

Declaring that if he had suspected the coming of war between Germany and Russia, he would not have hesitated to have undertaken the role of mediator, Mr. Matsuoka asked Ambassador Smetanin why Japan was not given such an opportunity. The Russian representative replied that since the terms of the Russo-German agreement had been carried out wholeheartedly by Russia, Germany could find no cause for complaint, and, therefore, it had attacked suddenly without forewarning or a declaration of war.

---

[724]II, 706.
[725]II, 707.

To Mr. Matsuoka's inquiry concerning the connection between the unexpected return of Ambassador Cripps to England and Prime Minister Churchill's promise to aid to Russia, Ambassador Smetanin answered that many ambassadors returned home for rest after an extended term of service. The Japanese Foreign Minister again stressed that Japan had thrown in its lot with Germany and Italy, but that since he had always worked for the improvement of relations between Russia and Japan, he felt that an outbreak of hostilities between the two countries would be most unfortunate. Ambassador Smetanin replied that both he and the British Ambassador had also been working directly for the improvement of Russo-Japanese relations, and that he hoped Mr. Matsuoka's government would take an objective view of the situation.[726]

From Vichy came word that the Russian Ambassador resident there had also sought, on June 25, 1941 to determine the Japanese attitude toward the German-Russian war. The Japanese Ambassador replied that, having received no instructions from Tokyo, he could not very well express an official opinion, but he knew that Japan would consider all conditions very carefully in the light of the Tripartite and Neutrality Pacts. Emphasizing the fact that Russia had been strictly observing the Russo-German treaty when Germany attacked suddenly, without provocation, the Russian Ambassador expressed the wish that Japan and Russia would maintain friendly relations.[727]

In Tokyo on June 24, 1941 Foreign Minister Matsuoka told the Italian Ambassador, who had called on him, that as yet no policy had been determined with regard to Japan's entrance into the war. He again stressed the fact that neither the Tripartite Pact nor the Neutrality Pact had a direct bearing on each other, and that the Tripartite Pact was still a pivot for Japanese foreign relations.[728]

Although Japan had made no decision as to its action, Japanese Consul Ota in Vladivostok divulged, on June 26, 1941, that preparations had been made to burn his codes, machines, and special telegrams if an emergency occurred.[729]

According to a Japanese report of June 27, 1941 Foreign Minister Molotov, who believed that Japan had possessed previous knowledge of the German attack, was reminded by Ambassador Tatekawa that Mr. Matsuoka had denied the widespread war rumors during the latter part of May, and that the Japanese government, even if it had received some unofficial warning, was not aware of Germany's decision to attack until a few days before hostilities began. As proof he related that two Japanese officials had left Tokyo for Germany on June 20, 1941 and two others had been dispatched to Iran on June 21, 1941; therefore, it was even conceivable that Japan had no advance information at all regarding the German plan.

Mr. Molotov commented that since there was nothing in the Tripartite Pact regarding Soviet Russia, Japan was not obligated to oppose Russia. Since the two governments were neighbors, he hoped that the recently improved relations between them could be maintained in the future. Expressing a similar desire that nothing should be done to upset their friendly relations, Ambassador Tatekawa indicated that Japan expected Russia to refrain henceforth from agitating the laboring classes, and he suggested that the issuance of entrance visas to Russia be expedited. Mr. Molotov denied emphatically the existence of a pre-war British-Russian alliance, but admitted that arrangements were made for such a treaty after the outbreak of war.[730]

---

[726]II, 708.

[727]II, 709.
[728]II, 710.
[729]II, 711.
[730]II, 712.

186. Ambassador Tatekawa Urges Support of Neutrality Pact.

Ambassador Tatekawa, expressing his views on June 27, 1941 with regard to Japan's imminent decision, stated that he realized the difficulty of the situation for the Foreign Office since Japan was divided in opinion. Despite the fact that some gesture of support for the Tripartite Pact should be made, he believed that since Japan in all probability would not be capable of offering Germany complete military cooperation, it would be well to maintain the status quo and to exert every effort to conclude the China affair. Though Ambassador Tatekawa was aware of the current German victories, he stated that there were no guarantees against some radical change in the war situation.[731]

187. Germany Seeks Active Support for the Tripartite Pact.

As the Russian war progressed, German authorities pressed for Japan's aid, but Foreign Minister Matsuoka reminded Ambassador Oshima in Berlin that at the time of his visit to Germany, Herr von Ribbentrop had said nothing about seeking Japan's help. Since Herr von Ribbentrop seemed to be puzzled because Japan was not making necessary preparations to take part in the war, Mr. Matsuoka explained to Ambassador Ott, on June 27, 1941, that he had assumed that Germany was not anxious to have Japan join in the war against Russia.[732]

188. Japanese Ambassadors in Rome and Berlin Urge Support of Germany.

The Japanese Ambassador in Rome declared, on June 30, 1941, that if the present Cabinet adopted an anti-Russian policy, the world would receive the impression that Japan was an opportunistic country. Therefore, he urged the adoption of some intermediate step to precede any military action against Russia.[733]

The Japanese Ambassador in Rome also urged Japan to assist in irradicating the power of Russia, the great root of all evil, and pointed out that Japan, for its own self-interest, needed to prevent other powers from using Asiatic Russia as a base for anti-Axis assistance. He believed that a clear statement of policy would strengthen the morale of Japan's people at home, and would contribute to an adjustment of military relations with the Axis. This would make it easier for other nations to understand Japan's position.[734]

Ambassador Oshima continued to favor Japan's entrance into the war on the side of the Axis. Pointing out on June 28, 1941, that Japan's indecision, as reflected in the many conferences being held in Tokyo and reported in the European press, affected the honor and integrity of his country, the pro-Axis Ambassador urged Foreign Minister Matsuoka to disregard further arguments and to come to an immediate decision.[735] The Japanese Ambassador to Turkey also supported the views of his colleagues in Berlin and in Rome that Japan should take advantage of the splendid opportunity to settle its problems with Russia rather than desist because of American and English pressure.[736]

Foreign Minister Matsuoka responded, on June 28, 1941, to Ambassador Oshima's repeated requests for instructions concerning Japan's attitude towards the war by advising him to be patient until a final decision was reached. Promising to send instructions in a few days, he

[731]II, 713.
[732]II, 714.
[733]II, 715.
[734]II, 716.
[735]II, 717.
[736]II, 718.

indicated that there was no unanimity in government opinion.[737] After this, Ambassador Oshima apparently felt that there was no other alternative but to wait for instructions, but he was hopeful that the Japanese government would persuade its people to join the anti-Russian war.[738]

189. Japan Decides Against Intervention in German-Russian War.

On July 2, 1941 the Japanese Diet in the presence of the Emperor reached its decision, and Foreign Minister Matsuoka informed Foreign Minister von Ribbentrop that, although Japan would not fail to act in accordance with the spirit of the Tripartite Pact, it was imperative that it not relax its efforts in the south at this time; thus, it would be contrary to Japan's best interests to break off relations with Russia. However, as a vital contribution to the common cause of the Axis, Japan would secure bases in French Indo-China to strengthen its pressure upon Great Britain and the United States.[739] Japan's policy was summed up by Foreign Minister Matsuoka as follows:

   1. Imperial Japan shall adhere to the policy of contributing to the world peace by establishing the Great East Asia Sphere of Coprosperity, regardless of how the world situation may change.

   2. The Imperial Government shall continue its endeavor to dispose of the China incident, and shall take measures with a view to advancing southward in order to establish firmly a basis for her self-existence and self-protection.[740]

Mr. Matsuoka had conveyed the Cabinet's decision to Ambassador Smetanin on July 1, 1941. At that time both agreed to issue written statements to the effect that friendly Japanese-Russian relations must be preserved at all costs. Stating that the Japanese government wished to extend its good offices to both Germany and Russia, Mr. Matsuoka expressed his wish that in the light of the complexity of the situation and Japan's difficult position, Russia would exercise due caution.[741]

Foreign Minister Matsuoka also sent an oral statement to Foreign Minister Molotov in which he expressed Japan's hope for a speedy termination of hostilities between Germany and Russia, or at least that they not be extended to the Far East where Japan had many vital interests.[742]

That Germany was displeased with Japan's decision can not be doubted for Herr von Ribbentrop, aware of the division of opinion in the Japanese government, had sent an urgent message to Tokyo, through Ambassador Oshima, which had arrived too late to change the course of events.[743] This displeasure was reflected in the actions of Ambassador Oshima, a strong supporter of the Axis, who on the following day, July 3, 1941, requested that he be called back to Tokyo because of illness.[744] It was also evident that disagreement with the final decision existed in the Japanese Foreign Office itself.[745]

Foreign Minister Matsuoka sympathized with Ambassador Oshima in regard to his physical condition, but, on July 5, 1941, he insisted that the Japanese Ambassador to Germany should sacrifice personal desire for the good of his country by remaining in Berlin. Assuring his

---

[737]II, 719.

[738]II, 720.

[739]II, 721-727.

[740]II, 727.

[741]II, 728-729.

[742]II, 723-724.

[743]II, 721-722.

[744]II, 730.

[745]II, 731.

representative in Germany that the German, Italian, and Russian Ambassadors had received oral statements in explanation of Japan's position, Mr. Matsuoka felt confident that Foreign Minister von Ribbentrop would fully understand.[746]

190. Germany Is Displeased with Japan's Non-Intervention.

In a message of July 12, 1941 which appeared to be directed to Foreign Minister von Ribbentrop, Mr. Matsuoka reiterated Japan's reasons for its decision.[747] Explaining that since Japan was not a dictatorship, and at present it was disunited in its feeling toward the Russo-German crisis, and since some of the Japanese people still entertained a sentimental feeling for Great Britain and the United States, he pointed out that Japan could not under any circumstances support Germany in its drive against Russia.

Mr. Matsuoka said that although Germany's current victories were inspiring, there were some differences of opinion between the Germans and the Japanese regarding the possibility of the United States entering the war. Though Germany minimized the possibility of United States' intervention, and would continue to do so,[748] Japan, not reassured, expressed the desire that the Axis take some common measure to prevent such a possibility.[749]

Despite the agreement of July 2, 1941, all was not smooth sailing between Japan and Russia for on July 12, 1941 Ambassador Smetanin again visited Mr. Matsuoka to relate that the British and American Ambassadors had informed him of a statement, supposedly issued by the Japanese Foreign Minister, that the neutrality agreement with Russia had become an impotent instrument, and that Japan did not feel obligated to adhere to its terms.[750] Mr. Matsuoka explained that he felt neither the Neutrality Pact nor the Tripartite Pact were applicable to the present war, though Japan's foreign policy was based on the Tripartite Pact. Neither Germany nor Italy had invoked the Tripartite Pact to demand Japan's entrance into the war, and Mr. Matsuoka predicted that such a demand would not be forthcoming. Japan would determine its policy independently and without regard for either treaty.

Mr. Matsuoka then asked about reports concerning the transferring of Kamchatka from Russia to the United States, and the infusion of British military officers and other personnel into Siberia. He stated that such reports tended to excite Japanese public opinion.[751]

191. Japanese Reports on Progress of Russo-German War.

Reports from Japanese Foreign Office representatives in the field kept Mr. Matsuoka informed of the progress of the war:

(a) *Report from Moscow.*
Ambassador Tatekawa, reporting on wartime conditions in Moscow, revealed that since the beginning of hostilities he had noted long food lines. Strict military control was being exercised over all dwellings and dormitories, and though crowds listened to air defense instructions in every open space, little enthusiasm for the war was being shown.[752]

---

[746]II, 732.
[747]II, 733–735.
[748]II, 736.
[749]II, 735.
[750]II, 737–738.
[751]*Ibid.*
[752]II, 739.

On June 23, 1941 the staff of the German Embassy in Moscow had been ordered to vacate the former Polish and Austrian Legations which it had been occupying. Staff members were to be cared for at dwellings belonging to the Embassy, but all telephone connections and contact with the outside were severed. Since the Italian Embassy had no communication from its home government, Mr. Tatekawa could not predict when its staff members would leave for Italy.[753]

According to the Japanese Ambassador, Russian air defense maneuvers were carried out with considerable effectiveness, and all citizens seemed to maintain an attitude of calm. On June 24, 1941 he noted a decrease of the use of cabs in the city, and diminishing food lines because of the abundance of food.[754] A Russian communique, which was sent to Tokyo, announced that Russian counter offensives on the Western border appeared to be successful since on the first two days of the war 50,000 prisoners had been taken, and 300 tanks destroyed.[755]

Several weeks later on July 15, 1941, Japanese representatives in Moscow believed that Germany would succeed in entering the Russian capital from several directions, if it won battles at Polotsk and Vitebsk which appeared to be the key to the whole war. They pointed out, however, that Russian strategy featured a defense strip 40 kilometers in depth, which was capable of holding for a long time, and unless the Germans succeeded in breaking through the last defense bases within two weeks, considerable time would be required to reassemble attacking forces.

Since it was believed that about one-third of the cream of Russian air and mechanized forces had been lost in the first day's battles, the Japanese in Moscow reported that the complete defeat of Russia was only a matter of time. An acute shortage of food and daily necessities already was being felt in Moscow, and, if the war continued, a strict ration card system was to go into effect.[756]

(b) *Report from Vladivostok.*

The Japanese Consul General in Vladivostok, reported the situation on June 23, 1941 as being calm as on previous days with coastal defense areas under rigid military control.[757] On June 25, 1941 a detailed report of conditions in Vladivostok since the outbreak of hostilities was transmitted to Tokyo. The mobilization of Russian troops had been observed, and Mr. Ota reported that apparently no change had occurred in the citizens' attitude toward Japan.

The Russian fleet, although inactive for several days, had been noted departing for maneuvers, leaving one light cruiser, a mine layer, a submarine tender, four destroyers and ten to twenty submarines in the harbor, all apparently undergoing repairs.[758] Fleet and air exercises which appeared to be designed for defense against Japan were greatly handicapped by the number of ships under repair in the harbor.[759]

A few days later, on July 3, 1941, Russian naval authorities seemed to be intensifying their security program and to be preparing to meet any eventuality.[760] Shipment of arms and food stuffs from Vladivostok had been reduced considerably by July 8, 1941 and rigid control limited the visible food supply. Tokyo was also informed that official Russian newspapers continued to express the need for taking precautions in regard to the Japanese.[761]

---

[753]II, 740–741.
[754]II, 741.
[755]II, 742.
[756]II, 743.
[757]II, 744.
[758]II, 745.
[759]II, 746.
[760]*Ibid.*
[761]747.

(c) *Report from Berlin.*

Ambassador Oshima in Berlin kept Japan fully informed of the war's progress from an Axis viewpoint. On the morning of June 24, 1941 Foreign Minister von Ribbentrop divulged to Ambassador Oshima that up to the night of June 23, 1941 over 2000 Russian airplanes had been destroyed in the air and on the ground, thus annihilating Russia's first line of defense and giving Germany mastery of the air.

Raids conducted by the Russian air force were inconsequential, according to Herr von Ribbentrop, since German casualties amounted only to twenty dead with no damage to military objectives. It was believed that more than half of the Russian air force had been destroyed on the ground, and since the Russians had proved more unskilled in the matter of handling machinery and piloting planes than had been expected, Germany was confident that it would be as successful in this war as it had been in Poland.[762]

According to Ambassador Oshima, by June 29, 1941, the German army, under the command of Chancellor Hitler who had proceeded to General Headquarters in East Prussia on June 23, 1941 had completely absorbed the enemy on land as well as in the air. Herr von Ribbentrop, who was to follow Chancellor Hitler to the front, reported the satisfactory performance of Rumanian troops in these advances.[763] He also stated that the Russian navy in the Baltic Sea had been quite inactive and, although the sea passage from Germany to Helsinki was recognized as dangerous, this difficulty would not impede German progress. In concluding his report, Ambassador Oshima pointed out that German successes had exceeded all expectations.[764]

The German Foreign Minister informed Ambassador Oshima on June 24, 1941 that Germany, before finishing its preparations in Finland, had begun the war suddenly to surprise Russia. For this reason, Finland was disguising its intentions to collaborate with German troops by pretending to be neutral.[765]

Ambassador Oshima was kept well informed concerning German progress along the eastern front by Foreign Minister von Ribbentrop who revealed on July 3, 1941 that Hungarian forces were quickly following the Russian army which had fallen back, and that the Russian armored forces along the Southern front had been completely surrounded. In the central and northern fronts the Russian troops, caught within the second pincer movement, had been divided, and after a bitter battle on the Finnish front, German forces had smashed into the Petsamo area. German air forces continued to show much activity, but few Russian planes were noted over German territory.[766]

The Chief of the German Trade Bureau, Emil Wiehl, in conference with Japanese Minister Sikao Matsashima on July 3, 1941, reported that in the invasion of Russian territory, the antipathy of the Russian people towards Commissar Stalin had been noted, and in the light of this fact, Germany expected to see an early overthrow of the Stalin regime.[767]

On July 8, 1941 Herr von Ribbentrop again informed Ambassador Oshima of Germany's success, but indicated that, if it were agreeable to Ambassador Oshima, he would stop his special progress reports since the press and radio were releasing the news.[768] Nevertheless, detailed reports of the progress of hostilities continued to flow into Tokyo.

---

[762]II, 748.
[763]II, 749.
[764]*Ibid.*
[765]II, 677.
[766]II, 750.
[767]II, 751.
[768]II, 752.

On July 14, 1941 Ambassador Oshima accepted the invitation of Herr von Ribbentrop to observe front line activities, where he expected to meet Chancellor Hitler. After visiting General Headquarters and inspecting the battlefields, he returned to Berlin on July 19, 1941.[769]

Meanwhile, in addition to the military offensive, the German propaganda office was known to be sending anti-Russian broadcasts into Russian territory.[770] These attempts to propagandize the Russian people were met in turn by Russian interference with Tokyo-Berlin and Washington-Berlin telegraphic and telephonic communications, which had been unintelligible on a number of occasions since July 4, 1941. However, photo-transmission was not impeded.[771]

On August 1, 1941 Ambassador Oshima revealed that according to a "reliable German source," Russian casualties had reached 2,500,000. Marshal Timoshenko's central forces and General Voreshilou's northern forces had suffered serious losses, and Marshal Budenny's troops in the south were gradually becoming victims of German encircling tactics. In the north a striking force was reported to have reached Leningrad on July 30, 1941; however, in accordance with German practice, public announcement was not to be made until the city had definitely fallen. Furthermore, about 10,000 Russian planes had already been destroyed, and it was believed that only one-third of the Russian air forces remained in action. Because of Germany's policy of not announcing war developments, Russia, Britain and the United States had become flooded with various reports of German set backs, which the anti-Axis nations were apparently using for political gains in such areas as Turkey.[772]

(d) *Report from Hsinking, Manchuria.*

Some Japanese observers believed that the Russian forces possessed tremendous air, tank and man power and pointed out that Germany was fortunate in not having delayed its attack, since such hesitancy would have given the Soviet Union time to complete a gigantic arms program.[773]

Discussing Germany's reasons for its sudden onslaught against Russia, Secretary Yoshitami in Hsinking indicated that Germany had 162 divisions on the east front which it could not use elsewhere, and, therefore, it had attacked Russia to win the Ukraine's iron, coal, and grain and Caucasian petroleum. Since Germany did not want to crush England, it felt that a defeat of Russia would help it to achieve an understanding with both England and America. Many British had ties with Germany, e.g., the Duke of Windsor who had been exiled to America by Prime Minister Churchill because of his pro-German feeling.[774]

According to Secretary Yoshitami, the fact that Russian forces remained at their post without retreating was a welcome discovery since German strategists placed much importance on annihilating the enemy in the field of operations, and Germany's real objective was the crushing of the Russian army to remove all anxiety in the future.[775]

Germany hoped that its attack on Russia would lessen war sentiment in the United States. Furthermore, Herr Hess' flight to England had been designed to obtain British colloboration in a struggle against Communism. Even if Germany failed to gain British support for its campaign against Russia, it would obtain enough materials to wage a long drawn out war against England.[776]

---

[769]II, 753–754.

[770]II, 755.

[771]II, 756.

[772]II, 757.

[773]II, 672.

[774]*Ibid.*

[775]II, 757.

[776]758.

(e) *Report from Ankara, Turkey.*

On July 31, 1941 Foreign Minister Sorocoglu of Turkey informed a Japanese diplomat that the collapse of Russia would occur in another month or a month and a half. The German Ambassador in Ankara was also informed that Turkish army circles agreed with this observation.[777]

(f) *Report from Stockholm, Sweden.*

According to a pro-German Swedish reporter, who on August 2, 1941 had completed a survey of the front lines in the Baranovitshi area, no matter how much strength Russia could muster, Germany's ultimate success was already established. However, the Russian air force was still very powerful and the Russian reserve strength was undiminished for conspicous resistance was being offered around Leningrad. According to this reporter, German officers realized fully that the reserve power of the Red army was great, and that new types of American tanks and planes had been put into action in the region of the Volga and in Siberia.[778]

All was not smooth traveling for the German army since unexpected obstacles rendered it impossible to establish liaison between units. Despite Ambassador Oshima's report that the general public in Russia, particularly the farmers, seemed to welcome the arrival of German forces, and that no actual guerilla warfare was being conducted,[779] the Swedish reporter declared:

> Since entering old Russia, Germany's greatest ordeals have been the result of guerilla tactics used by the Soviet soldiers and the civilian inhabitants. There is a thickly wooded area in the Pripet swamps. There are still many, many remaining troops taking refuge in it. A German force endeavored to rout them; but knowing nothing of the area, failed completely. These people have become wild men—savages. When they are on the verge of starvation, in order to seek food they emerge upon the neighboring villages. They know that the only safety for the hopeless is to hope for no safety and with a courage born of desperation they set upon the sentries and tear them to pieces. Such of these as have been taken prisoners are mostly without overcoats. They are all hatless and barefooted, and few of them indeed have any underwear; but they know not the meaning of answering a command. The word obedience is not in their vocabulary and the Germans would be better off without them because whenever they try to handle them, they get their hands burned.[780]

The Germans were discovering that captured Russians were not opposed to the war and did not intend to revolt against the authority of Commissar Stalin. The lack of anti-Stalin feeling in the Ukraine surprised the Germans, who continued to maintain that they would win the war, but who were uneasy about maintaining postwar peace, since they were conscious that the seizure of Moscow would not terminate the guerilla warfare. Comparing the German-Russian war to that of Japan with China, and to Napoleon's disastrous campaign in Spain, the reporter said that no one knew what would happen after it ended.[781]

192. Japan Assists in Exchange of Embassy Officials by Belligerent Powers.

Although some Japanese in Germany were preparing to return home, it was expected that difficulty would be met in regard to passage aboard American shipping lines. On June 22, 1941 Ambassador Oshima had requested Tokyo to negotiate so that returning Japanese would be allowed aboard American ships.

---

[777]II, 759.

[778]II, 760–761.

[779]II, 757.

[780]II, 760.

[781]II, 761.

During July 1941 consultation was carried on with regard to the disposition of the Japanese Naval Mission stranded in Berlin and passage for seventy others through South America.[782] The Japanese Minister resident in Iran requested that a Japanese ship be sent to the Persian Gulf in order to evacuate Japanese residents in that country.[783]

Shortly after the outbreak of the German-Russian war, plans were undertaken for the reciprocal exchange of German and Russian diplomatic personnel in Turkey. Apparently, the Russian Ambassador was receiving courteous protection in Berlin and the Bulgarian Embassy was taking proper care of German interests in Moscow.[784]

Japan intervened on June 28, 1941 to suggest that diplomats of belligerent countries, who were stranded in Moscow, be exchanged in accordance with international practice.[785] On July 1, 1941 the Russian Embassy in Tokyo requested that Japan assist in the return of 160 members of the families of its staff who planned to sail for Russia on July 6 and July 16, 1941.[786]

As the Russian forces continued to fall back before the German onslaught, the evacuation of Moscow seemed to be inevitable and the Japanese Embassy's officials made preparations to accompany the Russian government in its retreat. A large number of Japanese representatives were in a position to leave permanently, and it was decided to transfer them to other European countries rather than have them return to Japan.[787]

Japan's responsibility for protecting Italian interests in Russia, as well as in several other nations at war with Italy, was recognized with reservations by Moscow, but it appeared that the Italian diplomats had evacuated with the German Embassy's staff.[788] The Italian Embassy in Moscow was quickly put under guard, and by July 6, 1941 Japan had taken over the protection of Italy's property there.[789] The Chinese Embassy in Berlin was to be commandeered by Japanese authorities, since the entire Chinese diplomatic staff had departed for Switzerland on July 10, 1941.[790]

193. Germany Demands Withdrawal of Polish Diplomats from Tokyo.

New developments in German-Japanese relations centered around Germany's request on July 4, 1941 that the Polish Embassy's staff be withdrawn from Japan. Ambassador Oshima concurred that this was a reasonable demand in light of the facts that Germany and Soviet Russia were at war, and that Germany had consented to Japan's retention of the staff of the Dutch Ministry.[791] But on July 10, 1941 in the midst of arranging for the withdrawal of the Polish diplomats, Mr. Matsuoka hesitated and decided to postpone the evacuation.[792]

In regard to turning over to Germany the lands and buildings belonging to the Polish and Czech diplomatic establishments, the Japanese Foreign Minister stated on July 15, 1941 that Japan had no objections, but it would be difficult to obtain an appropriation for liquidating

---

[782]II, 762, 763.

[783]II, 763.

[784]II, 764.

[785]II, 765.

[786]II, 766.

[787]II, 767–769.

[788]II, 768–769.

[789]II, 770–771.

[790]II, 772.

[791]II, 773.

[792]II, 774.

the liabilities on them. Mr. Matsuoka also stated that Japan would not be in a position, no matter what the future course of events, to make such a philanthropic contribution in regard to the occupied diplomatic establishments of Belgium and France.[793]

194. Japanese–German Trade Continues Through Russia.

In adopting a comprehensive policy concerning commerce between Japan and Germany, Japan decided that though all new business deals would be postponed, those already under contract would not be cancelled, and payments for deals already arranged were to be kept in the Yokohama Specie Bank.[794]

Although the Axis nations believed that actual fighting in the German-Russian war would not last very long, officials both in Berlin and Tokyo realized that it would be some time before transportation facilities returned to normal. Japan was very anxious to ensure the safe transmission through Russia of materials purchased in Germany.[795]

Since Japanese firms were anxious to obtain 27,000 tons of freight which had accumulated in Germany, investigators were ordered on July 1, 1941 to divide the goods into priority classifications to expedite delivery of this material within the next six months.[796]

Another difficulty arose over the ownership of Japanese goods en route to Europe through Russia. Although Russia contended that it had proof of German ownership of these goods, Japanese authorities thought it possible to demonstrate that the material had not yet passed out of Japanese possession. With regard to some of the freight, however, it was feared that the certificate required by the Russians for unimpeded passage would not be available.[797]

Despite Germany's activity along the eastern battlefront, trade between Tokyo and Berlin continued. Plans were made, however, on July 15, 1941, to defer the conclusion of a contract regarding the supplying of heavy machinery to Japan until assurance that it would be shipped could be obtained. Negotiations with regard to these and other special items were to be carried on, however, so that the contract could be signed quickly, if necessary.[798]

Japan decided to make payment only after the supplies were delivered, since there was a danger of Germany's cancelling the contracts. In view of its increasing needs, Japan was disturbed by its fear that supplies from Germany would soon be greatly reduced.[799]

According to Mr. Matsuoka, Japan had planned to spend, in a five-year period, the sum of 250,000,000 yen on German machinery, patents and drawings, and also intended to exchange technicians with Germany. However, further reductions in Japanese exports made difficult the problem of repaying to Germany the credit of 100,000,000 yen. Though many questions necessarily awaited settlement of the German-Russian situation, Japan suggested that a basic agreement be reached as a necessary prelude to economic mutual assistance.[800]

Japanese trade with Italy continued all during the difficult relations between the Axis powers and Russia, but on one occasion Italy refused a Japanese request for permission to ship supplies from Switzerland to Japan, via America.[801]

---

[793] II, 775.
[794] II, 777.
[795] II, 776.
[796] II, 778.
[797] II, 779.
[798] II, 780.
[799] II, 781.
[800] II, 782.
[801] II, 783.

195. Admiral Teijiro Toyoda Becomes Foreign Minister (July 18, 1941).

Upon taking office, the new Foreign Minister, Teijiro Toyoda, expressed his desire to clarify Japan's position, and in order to accomplish this, he asked Ambassador Tatekawa, on July 19, 1941, to remain at his post and cooperate with the new faction.[802] Ambassador Tatekawa replied that although he had felt far from equal to his task in Moscow, he had stayed because of his belief in Mr. Matsuoka's policy of directing Russia into the Tripartite alliance, or at least, of keeping Russia from joining Great Britain and the United States. Since, he now expected Japan to formulate an entirely new policy with regard to Russia, it would not be easy for him to carry out plans which violated previous Japanese promises; therefore, he requested his recall to Japan.[803]

196. Japan Hesitates to Provoke Russia.

Two days later, on July 22, 1941, Ambassador Tatekawa reported that since conditions had grown more threatening in the Far East, all Japanese code machines and instruction books in Moscow were to be either burned or destroyed.[804]

Despite Ambassador Tatekawa's request for a recall, Japan was making special efforts to prevent any activity which would tend to provoke Russia. Several incidents regarding transportation of supplies and departure of cargo vessels from Shanghai to Vladivostok were treated cautiously,[805] and suggestions, on August 5, 1941, that the trans-Siberian railroad be captured in order to faciliate communications between Japan and Germany failed to win Japanese approval.[806]

PART C—JAPANESE DIPLOMATIC ACTIVITIES THROUGHOUT THE WORLD

(g) Japanese–French Relations.

197. France Protests Against Japanese Aggression.

After the signing of the armistice with Germany in 1940, France was without strength to fight against ill treatment at the hands of Axis powers, though it made many ineffective protests. On June 10, 1941, French Ambassador Arsene Henry called on Foreign Minister Matsuoka to protest against the mistreatment of French missionaries by the Japanese after the occupation of Weichow, an island off the coast of South China. Rumors were also circulating, he said, that two white men, who had been missing since 1940, had met with foul play at the hands of the Japanese. Furthermore, he complained that one exiled Chinese minister and six nuns were under strict Japanese surveillance, and all religious activities had been banned. Since the French Ambassador then requested that the Chinese minister and the nuns be permitted to leave the island, Mr. Matsuoka ordered Japanese officials in Canton to make a careful investigation.[807]

The French Ambassador had also protested against the handing over of documents to the Japanese because this might be disadvantageous to French rights and interests in the unoccupied

---

[802]II, 784.
[803]II, 785.
[804]II, 786.
[805]II, 787.
[806]II, 788.
[807]II, 789.

areas of China. However, by way of reply, the Chief of the Japanese East Asia Bureau, on June 18, 1941, advised a French Commerical attaché that the attitude of the French authorities was creating an unfavorable impression among the Japanese.[808]

As early as June 7, 1941 Japanese diplomats had been informed that the Japanese army in Indo-China had decided to seize and requisition property destined for China, but that France's fears as to an infringement upon its sovereignty would be alleviated by a Franco-Japanese agreement.[809]

198. France Begins Collaboration With Germany (June, 1941).

During the five-month interval from the dismissal of Vice Premier Pierre Laval by Marshal Philippe Petain in December 1940 to the time of the Berchtesgaden conferences of May 1941, there had been no friendly political relations between France and Germany. However, Ambassador Sotomatsu Kato, in an important report, informed Tokyo on June 11, 1941 that because of the success of Germany in the Balkans, the Vichy government had decided that its only remaining alternative was cooperation with Germany. Declarations of such cooperation had come in rapid succession from Marshal Petain and Vice Premier Darlan on the heels of the Berchtesgaden conferences, and the Vichy government had begun to propagandize in favor of Franco-German collaboration, while steadily putting it in practice. On the other hand, Mr. Kato pointed out that no clear pattern of German-French collaboration had yet manifested itself.[810]

Though a large part of France would continue to be occupied by German soldiers, there would be a large number of Anglo-American sympathizers who would act in unison with General de Gaulle. Furthermore, the conclusion of a separate peace either by France or Germany was a problem that could not be settled at this time, since the return by Germany of occupied territory to France was hardly conceivable during war. In view of conditions which would result from America's inevitable participation in the war, Germany was considering the protection of French possessions, which might be used as bases by enemy countries.

As far as the continent of Europe was concerned, according to Ambassador Kato, France could see that a German victory was inevitable. Germany, as the leading power after the war, would abolish meaningless boundary lines while respecting the autonomy and independence of the various peoples of Europe. It would, however, expect all to work together for the common welfare and interest.

France-German collaboration was necessary, Ambassador Kato further indicated, since Germany recognized that the establishment of this new order in Europe would be very difficult without France's cooperation.[811] But on June 12, 1941, Foreign Minister Matsuoka informed Ambassador Kato that though he was anxious for a German-French agreement to bring peace to Europe, he had no plan to act as mediator between France and Germany.[812]

199. Japan Requests German Aid in Acquiring Indo-Chinese Bases.

Deeming it advisable to secure the support of her Axis partners, Japan, on July 16, 1941 advised Germany of its desire for airplane bases in French Indo-China, as well as for free access

---

[808]II, 790.
[809]II, 791.
[810]II, 792.
[811]*Ibid.*
[812]II, 793.

for its warships to the ports of that area. Foreign Minister Joachim von Ribbentrop was asked to persuade the Vichy government to agree secretly to these proposals, and to urge French Indo-China officials to acquiesce without misgivings concerning Japan's intentions so that the expansion and strengthening of Japanese forces could begin. Foreign Minister Matsuoka added, "It goes without saying that our Empire has no intention of invading French Indo-China".[813]

If German intercession did not succeed, the Japanese government was determined to employ whatever measures were necessary.[814] On June 17, 1941, a list of the French Indo-Chinese airports and harbors to be used by Japan, selected in order of their importance by Japan and French Indo-China, was sent to Berlin.[815]

200. Japan Requests Germany to Withdraw from French Indo–Chinese Negotiations.

It soon became apparent that the Japanese Foreign Minister had misgivings concerning Germany's ability to persuade Vichy to accept Japan's proposal, since he requested Herr von Ribbentrop not to attempt negotiations unless success were absolutely assured. He feared that if a publicity leak divulged that the Japanese were persuading Germany to exert pressure on Vichy, all further Japanese plans would be thwarted.[816] This warning was further emphasized on June 22, 1941 by Foreign Minister Matsuoka who added that if occupation could not be achieved by diplomacy, his government was determined to obtain its objective by force.[817]

Japan had also decided during June 1941 to take charge of the rubber exports of French Indo-China, of which 8,875 tons were awaiting shipment. The acquiring of the rubber supply was to depend, however, on future negotiations with the French government.[818]

Japanese authorities concluded, by July 4, 1941, that Foreign Minister von Ribbentrop would not succeed in his attempts to have the Vichy government acceed to Japanese demands, and for this reason, requested him to refrain from speaking of the matter. Japan would undertake its own negotiations with Vichy, and if its request were refused, it would fight. After hostilities began, however, verbal assistance might be requested from Germany.[819]

201. Japan Presses France to Recognize the Nanking Government.

That France might be more favorably inclined toward Japan in future negotiations, the Japanese Ambassador to Germany, on June 28, 1941, advised Tokyo not to press the issue of French recognition of the Wang regime. Despite Japanese Ambassador Hiroshi Oshima's advice that this matter be dropped, Tokyo insisted that France be pressed to recognize its puppet government in China.[820] However, France did not recognize the People's Government in China at this time, nor did it during 1941.

---

[813]II, 794, 795.
[814]II, 794.
[815]II, 796.
[816]II, 797.
[817]II, 798, 799.
[818]II, 800.
[819]II, 801, 802.
[820]II, 803, 804.

202. Japan Desires a Joint Defense Treaty for French Indo-China.

Foreign Minister Matsuoka informed his representative in Vichy, on July 8, 1941, that an agreement should be negotiated between the two countries for the joint defense of French Indo-China, and since he desired the basic negotiations to take place at Vichy, he urged the Japanese Ambassador to France to act with great assurance and firmness.[821] Meanwhile, every effort was being made by Japan to win the good will of the French Indo-Chinese people. As a measure to increase Japanese influence in that area, Mr. Matsuoka decided to comply with a request that Japanese airplanes be sold to French authorities to increase air service between Japan and Thailand.[822]

203. French Resistance to Japanese Economic Control.

On July 11, 1941 the Japanese Ambassador in Vichy was informed that ratification of the economic treaty between Japan and French Indo-China had taken place. Just before its adoption Japan had decided to dispatch an investigating committee to French Indo-China to look after Japanese rights and interests as enumerated in Article 5 of the protocol. When informed of this plan, the French had protested that such a survey would have to be referred to the economic conference called for in Article 7 of the protocol, and that an investigating committee could not be allowed until it had been approved by the conference.

Foreign Minister Matsuoka explained that because this difficulty had arisen just before the ratification of the treaty, Japan had refrained from taking any issue with the French in this matter. However, Japan would refuse to recognize France's position, since it was absolutely necessary that it make a survey of the natural resources of French Indo-China to permit planning for their development.

Mr. Matsuoka feared that the French were trying to prevent Japan's economic advance, and regretted that French Indo-China appeared to have no intention of cooperating with Japan. The French were expected to accede to Japan's request in this matter just as Japan had planned it.[823] The chairman of the investigating committee was to be given the status of an envoy, and several others from headquarters were to reside in French Indo-China to keep in touch with French authorities. Other experts, also, were to be sent from Japan from time to time, to make investigations in regard to mining, agricultural and forestry industries, and marine products.[824]

204. Axis Cooperation in French Indo-China Trade.

On July 11, 1941, in a report from Vichy, it was learned that since the Germans had agreed to the Japanese schedule for shipping rubber and other strategic materials, the Japanese Ambassador at Vichy had asked a French agent to arrange at once for the shipping of these supplies. The French agent professed to know of no understanding between Germany and France concerning French Indo-Chinese rubber destined for France, and asked that an inquiry be made.[825] Tokyo assured its Ambassador in Vichy that the Germans had agreed to its proposals, and urged prompt action on the part of the French.[826]

---

[821] II, 805.
[822] II, 806.
[823] II, 807.
[824] *Ibid.*
[825] II, 808.
[826] II, 809, 810.

205. Japan Delivers an Ultimatum to France (July 12, 1941).

On July 12, 1941 after an early warning to Japanese representatives in Vichy to keep the legation force in readiness for important messages, Tokyo sent the terms of an ultimatum to France.[827] Japan declared that because of new international conditions, both the acquisition of military bases and the Japanese occupation of French Indo-China were necessary for the establishment of Japan's "Far Eastern Sphere of Co-Prosperity". Since America and England had been constricting Japan by encirclement, Japan's southern expansion was vital to its existence and self defense. The occupation would be without bloodshed, according to Mr. Matsuoka, if the French cooperated. A speedy completion of negotiations was necessary so that the United States and Great Britain would have no time to interfere.[828]

Japan realized that France would find this military request strange, but the occupation was necessary because of current conditions.[829] France was to be assured that Japan had no designs of infringement upon French Indo-China, although Japanese authorities knew that French factions not desiring to cooperate with Japan were plotting with the British and Americans. Professing to be deeply concerned over the threat of encirclement of Japan by various foreign powers, Mr. Matsuoka warned French authorities that an unfavorable situation would result should French Indo-China secede from France and come under the control of another foreign power. Therefore, to safeguard French Indo-China from invasion by a third power, as in the case of Syria, France was obliged to cooperate with Japan. Furthermore, since France intended to guarantee the safety of French Indo-China, it would have to join hands, militarily, with Japan. Mr. Matsuoka pointed out that it was clear in the light of recent events that defeated France was not in a position to defend its colonies in every part of the world. Thus, the only way for France to save French Indo-China was to place absolute confidence in Japan, and to accept its proposals without reservation.[830]

206. Terms of Japanese Ultimatum to France.

Giving France eight days to consider the ultimatum, Tokyo demanded that it accept by July 20, 1941 the following terms relating to the joint defense of French Indo-China:

(a) (Japan's) Dispatching to southern French Indo-China the required number of troops, several ships and the required number of air detachments.

(b) To permit the use and our establishment of the facilities at the following places:

Air bases	SIEMU–REABU:
8 places:	BUNOPEN:
	TURAN:
	N–YATORAN:
	BIENHOA:
	SAIGON:
	SOKUTORAN: and
	KONBON–TOHATUSIYU.
Naval bases	SAIGON: and
2 places	KAMURANH

Note: With the exception of Saigon and Bienhoa, these place names in French Indo-China are in Kana spelling.

---

[827]II, 811.
[828]II, 812.
[829]II, 813.
[830]II, 814.

(c) To recognize the right of the expeditionary force to conduct maneuvers, to reside, and to freely move about and to provide special facilities for these purposes. (This includes a cancellation of all matters in the NISHIHARA–MARUTAN Agreement placing a limitation upon the right of residence and freedom of movement of the expeditionary force.)

(d) To take all suitable measures in order to prevent a collision between the French Indo-China forces and the Japanese forces at the points of landing or thereabouts which will be specified in a special telegram.

(e) Recognition of the principal conditions relative to the movement of the expeditionary forces. (The landing forces are the same as those mentioned in (b) . . .

(f) As regards details of the expeditionary force, they should be decided at a conference to be held at the military headquarters in French Indo-China (the SUMIDA Organization) with the French Indo-China authorities after the French authorities have approved of our proposal. However, in case these details have not been agreed upon by the time the landing forces have arrived at the points of landing, they should be decided after the landing has been accomplished.

(g) To issue currency for the use of the expeditionary force.[831]

In addition to these terms, French Indo-Chinese authorities were to guarantee partial support to the Japanese Army of Occupation.[832] In a letter, which was to be presented to the Vichy government by the Japanese Ambassador, Mr. Matsuoka further stipulated, on July 12, 1941, that the French government, to avoid collision between Japanese and French forces, should withdraw French Indo-China garrisons and air forces from points at which Japanese forces would be disembarking. In case the French government complied with these proposals, the agreement in regard to joint defense was to take the form of a protocol, whereas details concerning the Japanese expeditionary forces, which would be decided by the military authorities of the two countries, would be incorporated in a treaty.[833]

207. Japan Attempts to Justify its Ultimatum.

For the information of Mr. Andre Roban, the French plenipotentiary to French Indo-China, a message from Mr. Matsuoka, also on July 12, 1941, summarized Japanese demands concerning French Indo-China. Mr. Roban was informed that Japanese requests for military bases were made unavoidably in the defense of the rights of Japan's position in the Far East. Since he was well aware of the war situation, and particularly of conditions in the Far East, the French plenipotentiary was asked to offer Japan's expressions of friendship to his government and to urge the acceptance of Japan's proposals. Foreign Minister Matsuoka declared that he knew full well the previous efforts of Mr. Roban to maintain Franco-Japanese friendship, but requested that he go to even greater trouble in this most serious problem.[834]

208. Japan Points to Secret American and British Agreements.

In further justification of the ultimatum, the Japanese government, again on July 12, 1941, issued summaries reviewing the political, military, and economic threats to Japan's position in the Far East. Tokyo argued not only that the de Gaulle faction in French Indo-China was working against Japan, but that England, Canada, Australia, the Netherlands Indies, and the United States had entered into an agreement for the joint defense of the Pacific, and had brought about the participation of Chiang Kai-Shek in their united front.

---

[831] II, 815.
[832] II, 816.
[833] II, 817.
[834] II, 818.

According to Mr. Matsuoka, a secret British-French agreement of January 1941 provided for British control of certain fast French ships whenever they entered Japanese waters, of if war broke out between France and Japan. Furthermore, on March 19, 1941, England and China had signed a military agreement, covering aid to the Chinese and a joint defense of Burma.[835] Construction of the Burma railroad was planned, and in addition, the United States had entered into an agreement with China for the joint use of Chinese air fields after the arrival of its military fliers. Furthermore, on the basis of the British-American-Chinese agreement, preparations were afoot in Singapore to establish an allied general staff. Mr. Matsuoka stated that a British-Chinese military alliance would be concluded between July 10 and July 20, 1941, and would become effective at the same time that Japan moved to the south.

England was expected to bring about military, political, and economic pressure, and particularly the last, by freezing Thaiese funds in London.[836] Consequently, Japan felt that it must expand economically, since England and the United States had already started an embargo against Japan of petroleum and other essential goods. British scrap iron, nickel, hemp bags, jute, manganese, rubber, tin and bauxite were also being embargoed, and through pressure brought to bear by America and England, the supply of rice, rubber, tin, and other goods reaching Japan from Thailand and French Indo-China was decreasing. Thus, since Britain, the United States, China, and the Netherlands were daily making stronger military preparations, and the possibility of encirclement was becoming greater, it had become necessary for Japan to take the initiative.[837]

209. Tokyo Issues Propaganda in Explanation of Its Action in French Indo-China.

For the information of its representatives in the Far East, Tokyo, on July 17, 1941, outlined several reasons for the establishment of Japanese military bases and the stationing of troops in French Indo-China. Japanese diplomats were directed to explain, on the pretext of presenting their own personal opinions, that Japan had no intention of using bases in the southern part of French Indo-China as jumping-off places for further military penetration. Tokyo further argued that the territorial integrity of French Indo-China had to be guaranteed to protect Japan's interests, and that the occupation had to be effected to avoid possible clashes with the Netherlands East Indies and in the Malaya area.[838]

Japan also claimed that the procurement of needed materials in French Indo-China and Thailand was a matter of life or death, and that its position was being endangered by the anti-Japanese attitude of both Britain and the United States, which were urging the de Gaulle faction and the Chinese in the southern part of French Indo-China to oppose Japan. Added to this were the reports of a Sino-British alliance, and the activities of the United States air forces in China. Therefore, Japan claimed that for reasons of self-defense, it could no longer delay its movement into French Indo-China.[839]

---

[835]II, 819, 820.

[836]II, 820.

[837]II, 821.

[838]II, 822.

[839]II, 823.

210. French Foreknowledge of Japanese Plans.

As to the disposition of France toward an occupation of French Indo-China, Ambassador Kato reported concerning a talk he had with Vice Premier Darlan on July 1, 1941, from which he had received a strong impression that the Vice Premier "had never dreamed of anything like this." Later, however, in a conference between Japanese and French military officials, just a few days before the presentation of the Japanese ultimatum, the French representatives had asked questions which indicated that they had learned of Japan's plans, although the Japanese representatives had professed to know nothing concerning the matter.[840]

211. The Hankow Incident (July 12, 1941).

Simultaneously with the sending of its ultimatum to Vichy, Japan was forced to turn its attention to Hankow, China, where a clash, considered by the Japanese Naval authorities to have grave international complications, occurred in the French concession on July 12, 1941. A fight between seven or eight Japanese civilians attached to the naval base and French guards of the Hankow concession had resulted in the death of a Japanese chauffeur and the wounding of another. With the permission of Tokyo, Japanese Naval authorities in Hankow had immediately requested from the French the right to partial police control over the French concession, the right of Japanese troops to patrol this area, the transit of armed militia in case of necessity, the official approval of these demands by the French control board, and an apology from its chairman. However, the taking over of the whole French concession at Hankow was to be postponed, until further orders were issued by Tokyo.[841]

Tokyo learned further details of the Hankow incident on July 15, 1941. Five Japanese chauffeurs, attached to the Naval base, had gone to a Chinese restaurant in the French concession, and had later talked with some Chinese Geisha girls on the street. While they were thus engaged, a French concession policeman came on the scene, and an altercation began. When Mr. Shimisu, the Japanese Navy chauffeur, attempted to flee, he had been wounded by police gunfire and stabbed with bayonets. After the first policeman fired, other policemen with rifles had arrived, and all shot at the Japanese Navy automobile in which the Japanese, including Mr. Shimizu, were attempting to flee. Bayonets were also used, and although one of the policemen had received a bayonet wound, it was clear, said Japanese representatives, that the French had stabbed each other, since none of the Japanese was armed and they had been released by the police on the afternoon of July 12, 1941. According to the Japanese account, the shooting of unarmed men revealed a murderous intent, and the firing on a Navy automobile was an insult to the Japanese Navy.[842]

212. Japanese Policy Towards French Concessions In China.

By July 18, 1941 it was evident that the Hankow incident was to become a test case of Japanese policy towards all French concessions in China. The Japanese Consul in Shanghai, asserting that action taken in regard to this incident would affect Japanese policy towards the French concession in Shanghai, declared that "taking general control of police power" would be no different from taking control of the administrative power in the concession. Although it might be possible to exercise a separate police power in a concession where the Japanese Army also operated, this would not be a comprehensive control of police power.

---

[840]II, 824.
[841]II, 825, 826.
[842]II, 827.

Before Tokyo decided on its action in Hankow, he urged that it should determine carefully its general policy in regard to the French concessions in Tientsin, Canton and Shanghai. Emphasizing the importance of this decision from the standpoint of England and the United States, he pointed out that Japan might be accused of abusing a weaker country, if caution were not observed.[843] However, Tokyo would finally consider it necessary to bring the concession under Japanese control, without actually taking it over.[844]

213. Japanese Preliminary Demands in Hankow.

In order to prevent a recurrence of the Hankow disorder, Tokyo directed on July 21, 1941 that all Japanese military personnel as well as Japanese civilians be forbidden to enter the French concession. The text of the Japanese demands were:

1. Demotion and dismissal of the Annam policeman.
2. The employment by the French concession authorities as police (including patrolmen) of such Japanese or Chinese as are designated by us.
3. Abolition of all weapons carried by French concession patrolmen, except bayonets.
4. Permission for Japanese army patrols to make the rounds of the French concession.
5. Permission for Japanese armored units to cross the French concession in case the need should occur.
6. An apology from the authorities concerned in this incident.
7. Indemnity for the injured of Y 63,875.
8. Compensation for the damaged car, Y 8,175.
9. Punishment for the offenders and those concerned in the incident.[845]

On July 22, 1941 Tokyo informed its representatives that the French concessions would not be taken over, nor would the exercise of full police power be suggested since this also touched upon the very nature of the concessions.[846] Three days later, on July 25, 1941, the French Counselor in Tokyo, calling on Vice Minister Kumaichi Yamamoto, requested that a peaceful settlement be reached.[847]

214. Japan's Final Terms in the Hankow Incident.

The Japanese representatives in Hankow reported to Tokyo, on July 31, 1941, what seemed to be the final details of the settlement. These included: the dismissal and immediate repatriation of all Annan policemen; an apology by the Superintendent of Police; a 40,000 yen indemnity; the employment of Chinese policemen, designated by Japan, in place of the 65 Annan policemen dismissed; the arms of the French concession police were to be limited to bayonets; two qualified Chinese, designated by Japan, were to be employed as police superintendents; and one reliable French speaking Japanese or Chinese was to be a liaison officer between Japanese and French authorities. In addition Japanese military and naval patrols and gendarmes were to have access to the concession as well as Japanese troops, who would be allowed to cross the concession at will.[848]

---

[843]II, 828.
[844]II, 829.
[845]II, 830.
[846]II, 831.
[847]II, 832.
[848]II, 833.

215. Japan Plans to Use French Indo-China as a Base for Attacks on Singapore and the East Indies.

The Hankow incident was the least of France's difficulties at this time, for Japan was preparing other moves against French interests. On July 14, 1941 the Japanese Ambassador in Vichy was informed that preparations were being completed for the Japanese army to move against French Indo-China on or about July 20, 1941.[849] This was a reflection of an important statement of Japanese objectives and military plans in the Far East, which was announced also on July 14, 1941 by Japanese military officials in Canton. It explained that a recent mobilization order had expressed the irrevocable resolution of Japan to put an end to Anglo-American interference, with Axis assistance, if possible, but alone if necessary.

Because these military officials did not wish to arouse the feelings of the Japanese populace, and desired to face a new war with a calm and cool attitude, formalities such as dining and saying farewell to the troops had been omitted. The Japanese plans were expressed as follows:

The immediate object of our occupation of French Indo-China will be to achieve our purposes there. Secondly, its purpose is, when the international situation is suitable, to launch therefrom a rapid attack. This venture we will carry out in spite of any difficulties which may arise. We will endeavor to the last to occupy French Indo-China peacefully but, if resistance is offered, we will crush it by force, occupy the country and set up martial law. After the occupation of French Indo-China, next on our schedule is the sending of an ultimatum to the Netherlands Indies. In the seizing of Singapore the Navy will play the principal part. As for the Army, in seizing Singapore it will need only one division and in seizing the Netherlands Indies, only two. In the main, through the activities of our air arm (in your city, the Spratly Islands, Parao, Thaiese Singora, Portuguese Timor and French Indo-China) and our submarine fleet (in the South Seas Mandate Islands, Hainan Island, and French Indo-China) we will once and for all crush Anglo-American military power and their ability to assist in any schemes against us.

The troops soon to occupy French Indo-China will be reorganized as the 25th Army Corps (one Army Corps consists of four divisions) and also the 30th Army Corps, consisting of the South China forces, which will be assigned to special duty with airplanes, tanks, and howitzers. General IIDA (the IIDA Army mentioned in preceding telegrams has been changed to the Nishimura detachment) will be placed in command and general military headquarters will be set up in Saigon. All preparations have been made. The ship fees have been paid and the expedition will soon proceed from here.[850]

Berlin was advised on July 15, 1941 that Japanese-French negotiations had begun, and Foreign Minister Matsuoka made the following significant statement:

This marks the first step in our southward advance; at the same time, it signified a very grave life and death step in our relations with England and America. We have thrown in our lot with Germany and Italy in harmony with the Tripartite Pact and intend to cooperate with them.[851]

216. Japan Sets the Date for the Occupation of French Indo-China.

On July 16, 1941 Japan informed its representatives in Hanoi and Saigon of the impending invasion of the Southern portion of French Indo-China. Even though the French government and French Indo-Chinese authorities might oppose this move, Japan was determined to carry it through. All Japanese nationals were to be evacuated by July 23, 1941, and the Imperial portraits were to be placed in the custody of the Provincial Office at Takao. For security, all telegraphic codes with the exception of those absolutely essential were to be burned, and other telegraphic and secret materials were likewise to be destroyed.[852]

On July 16, 1941 Japanese military authorities in Canton informed Tokyo that the troops slated to occupy French Indo-China were scheduled to leave Canton on July 17, 1941, and to arrive at Saigon two weeks later, after stopping over at Hainan Island.[853]

---

[849]II, 834.

[850]II, 835.

[851]II, 836.

[852]II, 837.

[853]II, 838.

217. Japan Requests Germany and Italy to Recommend to France Acceptance of Japan's Proposals.

Though Japan understood that Vichy was looking to Germany for support in refusing or lessening Japanese demands, Foreign Vice-Minister Chuichi Ohashi invited the German and Italian ambassadors in Tokyo to call separately on July 15, 1941, and asked that their governments recommend to France acceptance of Japan's ultimatum. Both ambassadors replied that the request would be communicated to their respective governments at once.[854]

218. New Japanese Cabinet Continues Japan's Policy towards French Indo-China.

When the Japanese Cabinet resigned on July 17, 1941, the Foreign Office thought it necessary, on July 19, to inform the Vichy government that Japan's policy towards French Indo-China would in no way be affected. This was mentioned to counteract any erroneous belief which might arise concerning Japan's intention of changing her attitude or demands.[855]

Informed on July 19, 1941 that Japanese military preparations were complete, and that regardless of the French answer, the Army of Occupation would move forward on July 24, 1941, (previously set for July 17, 1941),[856] Ambassador Kato directed the French government to warn French Indo-Chinese authorities to avert a clash of armed forces.[857] Ambassador Kato had been instructed that in case the French accepted the ultimatum, he should make them accede to all Japanese demands; but if they rejected it, he was to inform the French that Japan had no alternative but to occupy southern French Indo-China. The Japanese Ambassador in Vichy had also been instructed to tell French authorities that their reply would have to reach Japan not later than July 23, 1941.[858]

219. Japan Informs Germany of Its Irrevocable Decision to Occupy French Indo-China.

After being informed by Ambassador Kato that the French government, ostensibly in consideration of the Berlin-Vichy armistice, had found it necessary to confer with the Germans on this matter, Vice Minister Chuichi Ohashi advised Ambassador Eugene Ott of Germany that whether the Japanese ultimatum were accepted or refused, military action would be taken. This might jeopardize the status of French Indo-China, as well as Tokyo-Vichy and Berlin-Vichy relations. Ambassador Ott indicated that the Russian war might prevent Germany from exerting pressure on Vichy, but promised to deliver Tokyo's message to Berlin immediately.[859]

220. Japan Demands a French Agreement by July 22, 1941.

Ambassador Kato reported to Tokyo that in conferring with Vice Premier Darlan on July 19, 1941, he had presented a demand that France accede to the proposal by 6:00 P.M. on Tuesday, July 22. The Vice Premier answered that a reply would probably be given on the next day, July 21, 1941, after a conference with Marshal Petain.[860]

---

[854]II, 839.

[855]II, 840.

[856]II, 838, 841.

[857]II, 841.

[858]II, 842.

[859]II, 843.

[860]II, 844, 845.

221. Ambassador Kato Learns Unofficial Details of Anticipated Agreement.

Ambassador Kato, following his talk with Vice Premier Darlan, conferred with Mr. Lenoir Messien, Council President, who informed him, unofficially, that a final decision had been reached as follows:

(a) France recognizes Japan's demands.

(b) Japan shall first of all make a public statement concerning the maintenance of the territorial integrity of French Indo-China.

(c) The French forces will cooperate with the Japanese only in resisting the infringement of third powers and will cooperate in no aggressive schemes whatever.[861]

President Messien said that an official reply would be forthcoming on the matter, either on July 20 or July 21, 1941. The Council President added that France could not expect its army to cooperate with Japan unless some sort of assurance by means of a public message, such as the one contained in Prince Konoye's message to Marshal Petain, were published. France was cooperating with the Japanese simply for defense, and would not engage in military aggression.[862]

The Japanese Ambassador, in view of an anticipated demand of French authorities for assurance, in the form of a protocol, that the French Indo-Chinese army would not have to participate in plans of an offensive nature, asked that he be advised immediately of Japan's decision on this matter.[863]

222. Tokyo and Vichy Discuss Details of the Agreement.

Tokyo agreed to accept the protocol desired by the French, but realizing that his ForeignOffice would wish to have the final text in both French and Japanese, the Japanese Ambassador in Vichy suggested that only the French language be used since speed was the prime requisite. If both languages were used, the French authorities would be able to delay a great many days in examining the Japanese text.[864]

The tentative protocol as drafted by the French on July 21, 1941 stated that the exceptional facilities accorded the Japanese could not, under any circumstances, have the character of a military occupation, and that the Japanese should confine themselves strictly to the needs of the military operations. Although they were to be subject to French military authorities, Japanese expeditionary forces would be accorded freedom of passage between the point of disembarking and the zone of operations, and their military activities would be limited to the territories located north of the Red River. In the zone of operations, the French administrative and military authorities were to remain at their posts and in possession of all their powers. The armed Japanese forces were not to exceed two-thirds of the effectives actually mobilized in Tonking, which meant they were not to exceed 25,000 men.[865] The details of the actual landing points, number of troops, and places to station them would be decided upon as soon as the French officially recognized Japan's demands.[866]

In answer to the questions raised by Ambassador Kato, the Japanese Foreign Office replied that the following decisions had been made: the title of the protocol dealing with joint defenses

---

[861]II, 846.
[862]*Ibid.*
[863]II, 847.
[864]II, 848.
[865]II, 849.
[866]II, 850.

would be changed to read "Regarding Territorial Integrity and Joint Defenses of French Indo-China", and an article would be added to the original draft, stating that "The Japanese government declares that it will respect the territorial integrity of Indo-China, and the sovereignty of France over the Indo-China Federation". Although Japan had no objection to the statement in the French reply of acceptance that the French Indo-Chinese army would not cooperate in any plans of aggression, such a demand was not to be incorporated into the formal document. If the French were to insist, Japan preferred to have a secret exchange of notes in regard to the matter, or a statement by the French only. As a last resort, it was suggested that this clause be added as a qualifying explanation to Article I of the protocol.

Directing that in the protocol no time limit be set on the occupation despite the wishes of the French for such a restriction, Tokyo explained that it would be possible to change the protocol at any time by mutual agreement between the two countries. However, if France insisted, Japan would agree to a five-year time limit.[867]

223. France Accepts Japan's Ultimatum (July 21, 1941).

The text of the French acceptance of the Japanese ultimatum was delivered to Ambassador Kato on July 21, 1941 by Vice Premier Darlan,[868] who explained that France had no alternative but to accept the Japanese demands. There would be those, he pointed out, who would protest against the paradox of France's resisting the British in Syria on one hand and welcoming Japanese troops in French Indo-China on the other hand.

Vice Premier Darlan asked that Japan publish the statement assuring the sovereignty of French Indo-China, which had been set forth in a supplement to the French reply to the Japanese demands. The Vice Premier also requested that his country be assured by Japan that French Indo-Chinese forces would not be removed from their posts, that demands would not be made on the various facilities being used by the French forces, and that war and merchant vessels would not be ordered from their present berths.[869]

224. Ambassador Kato Explains France's Acceptance.

The Japanese Ambassador to Vichy declared on the following day, July 22, 1941, that the reason why the French had so readily accepted Japan's proposal was that they saw how resolute Japan's determination was, and how swift its action. In short, France had no alternative but to yield. Although territorial integrity of Indo-China had been granted, Japan had decided on a military occupation, according to Ambassador Kato, under the guise of a joint agreement with France.

Pointing out that the France-Japanese relationship was very delicate, the Japanese Ambassador warned Tokyo that, if France were forced to participate in whatever military operations Japan should undertake, the French people and officials would become so incensed that a permanent estrangement might result. Furthermore, Vice Premier Darlan had advised that if the withdrawal of French troops were demanded, or if private property were confiscated, the wrath of the French in southern French Indo-China would be "terrible".[870]

---

[867]II, 851.
[868]II, 852.
[869]II, 853, 854.
[870]II, 855.

225. Tokyo Agrees to Accept the French Protocol.

On July 22, 1941, Tokyo, apparently not yet aware of Vichy's formal acceptance, had instructed Ambassador Kato that if the French government's reply did not differ from the statement made by Council President Messien, he was to inform French officials that Japan would comply with their wishes.[871] Unfortunately, some of the dispatches relating to these negotiations were not intercepted by United States Communication Intelligence agencies, and so some of the points discussed cannot be clarified.

Ambassador Kato was also instructed to proceed with negotiations on the basis of the French draft, but after the draft had been put into its final shape, Tokyo would compose a Japanese version of the text.[872] Tokyo received word from Ambassador Kato as to the official French confirmation of the agreement later on in the day of July 22, 1941.[873]

226. France Begins Pro-Japanese Propaganda.

To an inquiry concerning the treatment of the Japanese-French agreement in the French press, the Japanese Ambassador reported, on July 24, 1941, that in all probability, newspaper editors had "waxed fanciful" because no official statement had been made by the Vichy government. Vice Minister Roshier had stated in a private interview with a Japanese representative that insofar as France was concerned, it was necessary to prepare public opinion to counteract recent propaganda of England and the United States. He had stressed the necessity of publicly expressing France's "willing cooperation" with Japan in the Far East.[874]

227. Japan Launches a World-Wide Propaganda Campaign.

Japan prepared to launch a world-wide propaganda campaign simultaneously with its occupation of French Indo-China. Instructions for the dissemination of propaganda concerning the occupation of French Indo-China were very detailed. The main objective was to induce the French Indo-Chinese to give whole-hearted cooperation to the Japanese during any emergency that might arise. At the same time the Japanese hoped to have the people of the South Seas place more reliance on Japan, and since they could not carry out their plans for propaganda in Burma, Malaya, India, Netherlands East Indies and Australia, they felt it best to develop their interests in French Indo-China and Thailand. Particular attention was to be paid to the Netherlands East Indies for the sake of the oil therein, and to Australia so that its movement for independence would be encouraged.[875]

Planning to issue a statement discussing the defense of greater East Asia, the emancipation of oppressed people, the destruction of the British and United States policy of the "almighty dollar", and the promotion of anti-Communism, the Japanese intented to encourage the Wang regime on one hand and to apply pressure on the Chungking government on the other. Meanwhile, they expected the Chinese and the South Sea natives to develop loyalty to Japan. To offset British, American, Chinese and Dutch propaganda, the Japanese propagandists were not to give the impression that further military penetrations were to be made southwards nor that military ties with Thailand were being sought.

---

[871] II, 856.

[872] II, 857.

[873] II, 858.

[874] II, 859.

[875] II, 860.

As for propaganda work in the United States, the Japanese were to emphasize that United States' policies could not lead to world peace. Furthermore, the Japanese planned to conduct a racial campaign in the countries of Central and South America to separate them from North America. In the Soviet Union, the Japanese were to intimate that the United States was interested only in the South Pacific.[876]

228. Japan Refuses to Set a Time Limit on the Occupation of French Indo-China.

On July 22, 1941 the French Vice Premier reiterated that France was participating in the agreement with Japan only with the view of safeguarding Indo-Chinese territory, and that it understood that the presence of the Japanese forces was temporary, and would cease when the foreseen danger had been removed.[877] In answer to this statement, Tokyo informed Mr. Kato that he was never to use the term "temporary" in connection with the protocol, since Japan did not wish to make any promises whatever. Instead, Ambassador Kato was to state that "The presence of Japanese forces in waters of the union will terminate when the danger is removed."[878]

229. Japan and France Sign a Joint Defense Agreement for French Indo-China.

On July 23, 1941, an agreement for joint defense of French Indo-China was signed by Japan and France. All that remained to be done was the drawing up of the protocol which was to be published later.[879]

Ambassador Kato, on July 24, 1941, submitted a French suggestion to Tokyo that a clause concerning damages resulting from the occupation of the Japanese Army be written into the protocol or into a diplomatic note. Advising that it would be well to leave this matter to the Army of Occupation, Mr. Kato replied that France shared the responsibility for defending the colony, and that to write the matter into a formal diplomatic document would not be proper.[880]

The Japanese Ambassador informed Foreign Minister Toyoda that France was ready to accept the second Japanese draft of the protocol, with the exception of two minor changes. Tokyo approved these changes, but in regard to the retention of Japanese troops, it directed elimination of the phrase "this shall be only temporary".[881] During the next two days, minor considerations were being cleared up. It was decided that in the French text the name of France should be placed first, whereas in the Japanese text, Japan's name should come first.[882]

The Japanese Privy Council was scheduled to meet in full session on July 28, 1941, and immediately following its approval of the protocol, Vichy was to be notified by telegraph. As soon as Ambassador Kato received this official notification, he was to have the protocol signed and the texts exchanged. The hour, date, and manner of signing was to be sent immediately to Tokyo so that the whole text of the protocol could be published at that time.[883]

---

[876]*Ibid.*
[877]II, 861.
[878]II, 862.
[879]II, 863, 864.
[880]II, 865.
[881]II, 866, 867.
[882]II, 868, 869.
[883]II, 870.

230. Japan Thanks Germany for Its Assistance.

The signing of the joint Japanese-French treaty was announced on July 24, 1941 to Ambassador Oshima, who was asked to inform the German government that Japan and France had succeeded in coming to an agreement. While thanking German officials for their cooperation, Ambassador Oshima was to inform them confidentially of the contents of the Japanese government's statement which would be issued at noon, July 26, 1941.[884] A similar announcement which outlined Japan's motives for its actions and gave some details of the negotiations was sent to the Nanking government in China.[885]

231. British Press Attacks the Japanese Occupation.

From London came the report that English newspapers were interpreting the securing of military bases in French Indo-China as the first step by Japan in a further movement against Singapore and the Netherlands East Indies. For this reason, it was suggested that an official statement be issued by Tokyo to the effect that the Japanese-French Indo-China agreement had been originated to preserve the peace of East Asia, and that no aggression was intended.[886]

232. Japan Reorganizes Its Representation in French Indo-China.

After the signing of the treaty with France, Foreign Minister Toyoda immediately concerned himself with plans to establish a powerful diplomatic organization in French Indo-China, which would involve disbanding the Japanese headquarters in Hanoi. Declaring that such a plan had no object other than to place all diplomatic activities under one head, he asked that France be notified that a special ambassador would be sent to French Indo-China, and that members of the Japanese Army, Navy, and Foreign Office would be assigned to work with him. All negotiations between the Army of Occupation and Indo-Chinese authorities were to be carried on through the new Japanese Ambassador.[887]

233. Japanese Leaders Congratulate French Authorities.

Following the conclusion of negotiations, congratulatory messages were sent to Marshal Petain and Vice Premier Darlan. Prime Minister Konoye, in commending Marshal Petain on France's courageous decision, expressed his firm belief that this act would serve to cement friendly relations between the two countries, and Foreign Minister Toyoda conveyed his sincere appreciation to Vice Premier Darlan for making possible the signing of this pact.[888]

---

[884] II, 871.
[885] II, 872.
[886] II, 873.
[887] II, 874.
[888] II, 875, 876.

PART C—JAPANESE DIPLOMATIC ACTIVITIES THROUGHOUT THE WORLD

(h) Japanese–Chungking Relations.

234. Conflicting Rumors of a Japanese–Chinese Peace.

Japanese diplomats in Rome reported on May 20, 1941 that Generalissimo Chiang Kai-shek's proposal to send a personal diplomatic envoy to the Vatican had been refused because the Vatican could cooperate only in policies of peace between China and Japan.[889] Several days later Tokyo was notified that because of distrust of Japan's behavior, Chungking authorities would not talk of peace unless they received a guarantee from the United States.[890]

According to Tokyo's own estimate of the Chinese situation, Japanese plans to establish a "New Order" in East Asia were being impeded by British-American aid to China and by an encirclement by England, the United States and the Netherlands. Many Japanese felt, however, that England was wavering due to its defeats and the Japanese threat to the south, and it was the belief of some that Japanese successes were discouraging the Chinese.[891]

Ambassador Biddle in England was quoted in a Japanese report as saying to a friend that Ambassador Winant would soon arrive in Washington to discuss the Chinese problem, and that Lord Hankey planned to make an unofficial trip to persuade the United States to bring an end to Chinese difficulties. Mr. Biddle remarked that it was an opportune time for such a project. However, many Japanese authorities believed that China, having been spurred on by British-American aid and by the hope that the United States would fight Japan, was abandoning any schemes of capitulation, and was planning to fight on to the bitter end.[892]

As for opinion in the United States, Japanese officials reported on May 26, 1941 that Senators Wheeler, George, and Nye of the Senate Foreign Relations Committee had asked the President to suspend aid to China, but that Mr. Roosevelt had avoided comment.[893]

235. American and British Aid to China.

In spite of rumors of a Japanese-Chinese peace, Chinese-American collaboration in air and truck transportation of military supplies through Russia was reported on May 27, 1941, following Captain James Roosevelt's visit to Generalissimo Chiang Kai-shek.[894] Five hundred American trucks were to be furnished for the transportation of military supplies.[895] Further evidence that the United States was continuing her aid to China was supplied by Japanese intelligence agents who reported on May 29, 1941 that a part of the $50,000,000 American loan to China would be used to purchase 800 airplanes from the United States. Noting that American pilots and mechanics would be sent to handle the planes, the Japanese also were aware that a Boeing plane, one of the two types contracted for, could leave a base in China, raid Tokyo for two hours, and then return to China.[896]

---

[889] II, 877.
[890] II, 878.
[891] II, 879–880.
[892] II, 881, 877.
[893] II, 882.
[894] II, 883.
[895] II, 884.
[896] II, 885.

Though the United States would send men to improve the Burma Road in order to increase the flow of goods to China, they would not take part in the war. Furthermore, because the outbreak of the Russo-German war had stopped the supply of materials from Russia, Tokyo was informed on July 10, 1941 that the activities of the pacifists in Chungking were already gaining ground. However, American representative, Mr. Owen Latimore, had been sent to China to counteract talk of an early peace,[897] and high officials in Chungking were elated over this indication of unified British-American-Russian aid to China.[898] But a report from Hongkong on July 16, 1941 concerning a recent conference of American, British, Chinese and Russian representatives assured Tokyo that there was no possibility of a military alliance of these four nations since the lack of aid given to China demonstrated that the other three powers were more concerned with their difficulties than with China's plight.[899]

However, by the end of July 1941, the British and American program for aiding the stricken peoples of China had progressed so well that plans were made with the Chungking government for the defense of Yunnan by a British mechanized force and American air units. The reorganization of the tin mines, the reopening of the Temmen highway, and the development of the traffic facilities of Keinan would help to guarantee the economic security of this area.[900]

According to a report on August 4, 1941 from Chungking sources, the Financial Reconstruction Program in China, entirely separate from the Industrial Commercial Bureau, was controlled by British and American experts. The Japanese were informed that Madame Chiang Kai-shek, with Mr. Kung Hsiang-Hsi, a member of the Central Executive Bureau of Kiangsu Province, handled all diplomatic affairs.[901]

To expedite transportation between Calcutta and Chungking, British, American and Chinese forces were planning to build a military road through Darjeeling, Tibet and Seita. In connection with the construction of this road, Tokyo was informed on August 5, 1941 that engineering materials were being assembled and prepared in the United States. Fourteen or fifteen American aviators and bomber technicians with twenty more to follow, were already en route to Chungking with a cargo consisting of military material and large caliber guns which had left San Francisco on July 15, 1941.[902]

236. Japan Fears Chungking-Chinese Communist Collaboration.

Japan feared the great potential power of China, and, therefore, was greatly concerned with the growing collaboration between the Kuomintang and Communist Parties. A Japanese report of May 24, 1941 discussed prospective negotiations for a Chinese Communist-Kuomintang rapprochement.[903] In a report to Tokyo on June 4, 1941 discussing a meeting of Japanese intelligence agents, it was stated that the solution of outstanding questions between Japan and Russia as well as the movements of the Chinese and the Manchukuoan Communist Parties would be discussed at the next conference.[904]

---

[897]II, 886.
[898]II, 887.
[899]II, 888–889.
[900]II, 890.
[901]II, 891.
[902]II, 892.
[903]II, 893.
[904]II, 894.

237. Japan Safeguards its Codes and Secret Documents.

During the months of May–July 1941, Japan maintained strict security in regard to its codes. On May 27, 1941 Foreign Minister Matsuoka, warning the Japanese representative at Singapore that a secret abbreviation code was being sent there, asked him to ascertain if there were any possibility of it being inspected by non-Japanese.[905] The Japanese Foreign Minister also emphasized that in order to insure the secrecy of their diplomatic telegraphic systems, code messages were to be avoided when the enemy was aware of the contents of the dispatch.[906]

Reports from Manchuria in early June 1941 not only showed that the Japanese were exercising care in the transmission of coded dispatches,[907] but also revealed their concern over the opening of their mail.[908]

On July 5, 1941 Japanese representatives in Hongkong revealed that their secret documents and telegraphic material had been placed in care of the Consul at Hankow with instructions to burn them should the necessity arise,[909] and on July 14, 1941 the Imperial portraits from Hongkong reached the Japanese Consul in Canton.[910] Such action was taken in preparation for an emergency, for with the German-Soviet war in progress, Japan recognized that it had a rare opportunity to strengthen its position in the south.[911]

238. Japan Negotiates for Critical Products in China.

It was reported from Shanghai on June 5, 1941 that Japanese negotiations with foreign oil firms were to be renewed, probably along the same lines as those begun in November 1940 between the China branch of the Japanese Board of Planning, the field service of the Japanese War Department, and the Standard Oil Company, but never completed because of Tokyo's objections. Under that agreement, 50,000 drums of 86 octane gasoline were to be delivered to Shanghai on the condition that they be moved to the interior.[912]

A report from Tientsin on July 16, 1941 dealt with the difficulty of obtaining powdered milk for babies in North China. Negotiations with the Ministry of Commerce and Industry were to be undertaken for the immediate shipment of this vital commodity.[913] Since Tokyo had also been unable to import opium and certain ingredients for medicines from foreign countries, it requested on July 16, 1941 that Manchukuoan officials turn back to the Japanese government for home use the opium and narcotics seized in North China.[914]

Because of the lack of gasoline as a result of America's and Britain's freezing order, transportation within Tainan became increasingly difficult. Since cotton deliveries were imminent, and the demands of the Shantung automobile association were great, Japanese representatives suggested that gasoline stocks of the local Asia, Standard and Texas companies be used.[915] On August 5, 1941 purchases of gasoline from the stores of the three foreign oil companies was permitted by the Japanese, but only under strict supervision.[916]

---

[905]II, 895.
[906]II, 896.
[907]II, 897.
[908]II, 898.
[909]II, 899.
[910]II, 900–901.
[911]II, 901.
[912]II, 902.
[913]II, 903.
[914]II, 904.
[915]II, 905.
[916]II, 906.

239. Japan Curtails Chungking's Supplies.

The drastic methods taken by the Japanese to cut off China's supplies caused both British and French officials to protest, on June 10, 1941, the confiscation of nearly $890,000 in Chinese money found by the Japanese military authorities in the French Concession, Shanghai.[917] During economic negotiations held between the representatives of China, Manchukuo, Japan and Germany, the latter also expressed its disapproval of the Japanese embargo of goods belonging to Chinese and German firms in Hankow which had been slated for shipment to Shanghai. Tokyo replied on June 23, 1941 that since the question of transporting such goods involved consultation with the military authorities, the problem could not be handled through ordinary channels.[918]

According to a Japanese intelligence report, Mr. Mi Chi Fang, a Chungking representative in Shanghai, received a warning on July 6, 1941 that Tokyo was expected to declare war and to confiscate all Chinese assets in Shanghai; therefore, all Chinese firms and merchants in Shanghai were ordered to transfer their commercial interests to foreign names.[919]

Japan realized, according to a report on July 17, 1941, that if Chungking could be completely cut off from its foreign allies, Chiang Kai-shek's army could hold out no longer than ten months and the China incident would be at an end.[920] Therefore, all aid from America and Britain was watched carefully. On July 28, 1941 an order was issued by the North China army that Japanese forces at other points should place all factories and warehouses belonging to the British and Americans under close observation. In order not to provoke either of these countries, no action that could be construed as coercion was to be taken nor was the supervision to be so close as to arouse suspicion.[921]

240. Chinese Reaction to German–Russian War.

The Japanese noted that on June 23, 1941 the Chinese Communist Party sent a message to Chungking expressing its friendly attitude toward Soviet Russia. The closing of German and Italian Embassies as well as Consulates, and the expulsion of Axis nationals from China were demanded, and in turn, full cooperation with Chungking for the successful conclusion of the war was promised. On the other hand, the pro-German faction leader, Mr. Chu Chia Hua, urged the Chinese government to confer with both German and Italian authorities before announcing a definite stand with regard to the Russian question.[922]

Other intelligence reports emanating from China on June 27, 1941 disclosed that Mr. Chiang Po-Ching, governor of the Chekian province, was endeavoring to maintain effective relations with Germany, and that, following this policy, the showing of Charlie Chaplin's motion picture, "The Dictator", had been prohibited in Chungking. Since Mr. Chiang Po-Ching believed that the German military efforts in Russia had been 70% preparation and 30% propaganda, with the reverse being true of Russia, he predicted that Germany would bring the Russian war to a speedy conclusion.

---

[917]II, 907.
[918]II, 908.
[919]II, 909.
[920]II, 910.
[921]II, 911.
[922]II, 503. (Japanese–British Relations)

According to Mr. Chiang Po-Ching, Mr. T. V. Soong and Madame Chiang Kai-shek had been advocating the necessity of opposing Japan through Anglo-Russian and United States-Russian collaboration. Though Russia had suspended aid to China, Mr. Chinag Po-Ching believed that there was some hope of getting supplies from Australia for the next two or three years. He also pointed out that the Chinese Communists, who had always opposed Anglo-American imperialism, were now finding it necessary to reverse their position and to depend on America and Britain.[923]

241. Japanese Report of Divergent Views of Chungking and Chinese Communists.

Because the attitude of the Chungking government toward the Japanese-Soviet neutrality pact affected Kuomintang-Communist relations and Generalissimo Chiang Kai-shek's position in regard to peace with Japan, these reactions were carefully observed by the Japanese in the latter part of June 1941.[924]

Investigating the relations between the Nationalist Party and the Communist Party in China, Ambassador Gauss, according to a Japanese report of June 16, 1941 had learned from the Russian Ambassador that since the conclusion of the Japanese-Soviet agreement and the agreement of the United States to assist in the stabilizing of Chinese currency, intensified suppression of Chinese Communists had been noticed. Russia's decision to cut off war materials to China had caused internal dissension, and the refusal of the Nationalist Party to grant military funds to the 18th Army and the rejection of an allegedly sincere peace offer by the Communist Party widened the breach between the two factions. The Russian Ambassador remarked that although the Chinese Communist Party had long endeavored to avoid civil strife, the imprisonment of its leaders and ruthless suppression by the intransigent Chungking faction would encourage the Chinese Communists to defend the democratic political rights of the people.[925]

According to a report from Hongkong on June 28, 1941, Chungking had found that its efforts to get the Chinese Communists to comply with orders were facilitated not only by the lining up of Britain, the United States, and Soviet Russia behind Chungking, but also by the gradual growth of the opinion that a peace was not yet possible between Britain and Germany. The Chinese Communists were reported, however, as believing that little prospect of improvement existed for Russia's relation with the United States and Britain, and that Russia, by taking advantage of the weakening of all belligerent powers, would eventually win the war.

They felt that Chungking was unwise in not defining her attitude toward Germany and Italy since Chungking could not depend on future assistance from the United States, and China's position was growing more precarious with the decrease of aid from Russia, and because of the United States' efforts to appease Japan. Furthermore, friction between Chungking and the Communist Party would not cease owing to the increasing activity of pro-German and pro-Japanese factions within the country.

Since Japan would devote its entire effort to settling the China incident, the Communists believed that China must realize that Japan would bring stronger military and political pressure to bear. Japan would demand, in accordance with the Tripartite Pact, concessions in the Far East from Soviet Russia, and for this it would also endeavor to secure the consent of the United States and Great Britain.[926]

---

[923]II, 912.

[924]II, 913.

[925]II, 914.

[926]II, 915.

242. Japan Decides Not to Occupy Macao.

Possibly because its attention was focused elsewhere, on June 25, 1941 Japan abandoned its plan to occupy Macao, since Tokyo realized that no benefit could be derived from the occupation.[927] Nevertheless, on June 28, 1941 army and naval officials, as well as the local government, were warned to maintain strict surveillance of the smuggling practices being carried on at Macao to aid Generalissimo Chiang Kai-shek.[928]

243. Japan Suspects an American-British-Chinese Military Alliance.

Reports alleging the existence of an American-British-Chinese military alliance flowed into Japan on June 24–27, 1941. They announced that provisions had been received in Honkong for the use of American aviation volunteers who were to establish air bases in interior China, ostensibly as an aid to Generalissimo Chiang Kai-shek but in reality in preparation for war with Japan.[929] A general staff composed of British, Chinese, and American officers was being established for the defense of Yunan, Kweichow, Kwangsi, Burma, Malay, and the Thaiese border; the new aviation bases were to be used jointly by the three powers.[930]

Some Chinese elements were following a devious path in foreign policy for on June 16, 1941 it was reported that the American-British-Chinese alliance advocated by Mr. Kuo Tai-Chi, the former Chinese Ambassador to Britain, had been set aside by Chungking in favor of parallel diplomatic policies toward Germany, Soviet Russia, and Great Britain.[931]

At some time between July 15 and July 20, 1941, Boeing B17's and eighteen heavy bombers supplied by the United States were expected to reach Rangoon, and to leave there about the middle of August for the interior of China.[932] Further information gleaned by the Japanese pointed to the erection of many American air bases in the southwestern provinces of China, and stated that approximately 200 American planes had been furnished for guarding Burma Road traffic and establishing an air service linking Rangoon, Singapore, and the Philippines. In preparation for war on Japan, 120 Chinese pilots had been sent to Chungking to establish air bases in interior China.[933]

Peking, where First Chief Secretary Smythe of the American Embassy had been replaced by Commercial Attache Butrick on June 23, 1941, was kept under close observation by the Japanese. They were interested in learning whether the visit which Ambassador Gauss and Mr. Butrick had recently made to Chungking meant that the American representatives would reside there permanently.[934]

244. China Joins Anti-Axis Propaganda Association.

The Japanese had learned on June 4, 1941 that Mr. James Roosevelt had proposed to Generalissimo Chiang Kai-shek the establishment of an international league for free governments of Europe in order to counteract the effects of Axis propaganda in South America, South and Western Asia and Africa.[935] Japanese agents in China commented on July 24, 1941 that as a

---

[927]II, 916–917.
[928]II, 918.
[929]II, 919–920.
[930]II, 921.
[931]II, 922.
[932]II, 923.
[933]II, 924.
[934]II, 925.
[935]II, 926.

result of this plan, Generalissimo Chiang Kai-shek was sending a number of graduates of foreign schools to the United States to engage in propaganda and intelligence work. In accordance with the policy formulated by the United States and China, this cooperative propaganda association was to work out ways and means of dealing with all phases of the Far Eastern situation and to exchange intelligence between the United States and China.[936]

245. Japanese Espionage in China.

Evidence of the success of the Japanese espionage organization in China was found in a dispatch of June 2, 1941 which listed the amount of yen assigned for their special agents. Because Shanghai was the chief source of Japanese intelligence in China, this appropriation was particularly high.[937] On the other hand, the capture of Rojibi, a special activities agent in Macao, about June 23, 1941 disclosed to the Chungking government that its messages were being intercepted and turned over to the Japanese.[938]

In order to educate young Chinese men who would cooperate with the Japanese in their South Seas activities, Tokyo was asked on June 16, 1941 to subsidize a Shanghai institution known as the Self-Strength School. Although apparently devoted solely to business and commerce, the school actually trained specially-selected Chinese students to act as Japanese spies in peacetime and as fifth columnists in the event of war.[939]

Further information regarding the selection and training of Japanese special secret agents was revealed on July 16, 1941,[940] for after the unfortunate incident at the French Concession,[941] Japanese diplomats desired to choose students of foreign languages, who were of a diplomatic type, rather than members of the Japanese military.[942]

As a result of confidential contacts with Chinese connected with the Japanese office in Canton, by July 21, 1941 eight Chinese had been selected for this work.[943]

246. Japan Learns of a Chungking-Chinese Communist Agreement.

Tokyo was informed on July 7, 1941 that since both the Chinese Nationalists and Communists agreed that national interests superseded all other considerations and that unity was their only hope, they were apparently ready to reach an agreement. Having received instructions from the Third International on June 19, 1941 and again on July 2, 1941, the Chinese Communists in Enan agreed to cooperate with the Sinkiang province and Outer Mongolia in forming a revolutionary committee. When the necessity arose, the Central Revolutionary Military Committee of the Chinese Communists was to be dissolved in favor of a joint Nationalist-Communist organization, and within a month the Communist army was to be newly equipped. Furthermore, to eliminate the outstanding difficulty in the way of collaboration between the Nationalists and the Communists, a large part of the Communist army in Central China was to be withdrawn.[944]

---

[936]II, 927.
[937]II, 928.
[938]II, 929.
[939]II, 930–933.
[940]II, 934.
[941]See Japanese-French Relations.
[942]II, 934.
[943]II, 935.
[944]II, 936.

About July 14, 1941 the Third International began organizing a Far Eastern Council for revolutionary offense to assist the Chungking regime. Absorbing men and women from Mongolia, Ningsia, Chinghai, and Tibet, this council was to instruct and organize them into armies. Under the command of Russian army officers, the military section of this group was to be arranged into twelve shock columns, consisting of sixty thousand men, of which one column would be a chemical detachment of 6,000 men. Getting behind the lines of the Japanese forces in four provinces in both northern and northeastern China, these units were to engage in partisan warfare, burning materials belonging to the Japanese army. Other troops cooperating with the Outer Mongolian Russian army were to create disturbances in the rear of the enemy forces. Since the Soviet Ambassador, Mr. Pahi Jushukin, had promised Chungking that such troops would not take an active part in the territories under its jurisdiction, the support of Generalissimo Chiang Kai-shek was obtained.[945]

Detachments of the Chinese Communist army under Liu Po-Chao were transferred to Suihoku around August 2, 1941 in compliance with an order issued by the Russian army and with Chungking's tacit consent. In the future the Chinese Communist army was apparently to cooperate with the Russian army, and it was expected that arms and munitions would be supplied from Outer Mongolia. By the end of August 1941 approximately 4,500 men would be attending to the transportation of this material.[946]

It was revealed on August 4, 1941 that the Japanese were greatly concerned over the activities of the Chinese Communists among the workers in the Kailan coal mines, for if the operation of these mines were halted for any reason, it would seriously impair Japanese moves.[947]

247. President Roosevelt Appoints a Political Adviser to Generalissimo Chiang Kai-shek.

In addition to sending American technical advisers to China to give military assistance, according to a Japanese report of July 8, 1941 President Roosevelt had also appointed Mr. Latimore to act as adviser to the Chungking government. Though China was gratified that the United States was taking an active interest in its affairs, it was rumored that Chinese authorities were displeased because Mr. Latimore lacked experience in political matters and had little knowledge and understanding of China's affairs.[948] Immediately after Mr. Latimore's arrival in Hongkong on July 15, 1941 a newspaper article, probably inspired by the Chungking government, had made it clear that Mr. Latimore should not interfere with Chungking's policy regarding the strengthening of the international popular front by dealing with the Communists.[949]

Tokyo learned on August 2, 1941 that upon his arrival at Chungking, and after exchanging opinions with Ambassador Gauss and Mr. Fox, Mr. Latimore had emphasized that for the strengthening of China it would be necessary to reorganize part of the Chinese government.[950]

---

[945] II, 937.
[946] II, 938.
[947] II, 939.
[948] II, 940.
[949] II, 941.
[950] II, 942.

248. Japanese Use of Newspapers in China.

The Japanese employed newspapers as a cover for other activities. With regard to securing visas which were currently pending for Tokyo staff members, Foreign Minister Matsuoka suggested that the application for Mr. Harold Fujii be made as a press correspondent since Mr. Iwatete's status as an "extra" secretary in Singapore had already aroused suspicion, and having another official attached to the Domei news service would be less conspicuous.[951]

Anxious to gain the confidence of the newspaper men, Japanese officials occasionally imparted to them information of confidential nature that was not intended for publication, but which would acquaint them with the general state of affairs throughout the Empire. At times, however, this confidence was abused, and information was sent out without permission, causing Tokyo great concern.[952] Close supervision of the press was constant, for a "disrespectful article" reflecting China's attitude toward Japan and appearing in the China Weekly Review on June 21, 1941 was reported to Tokyo.[953]

Preparations were begun on July 16, 1941 for a newspaper conference to be held in Canton, which representatives of both Japanese and Chinese papers would attend. They had been invited in order to increase cooperation among the Japanese agencies guiding public opinion so that the establishment of a co-prosperity sphere in East Asia might be facilitated. With the Chief of the Japanese Publicity Department acting as chairman, the meeting was to be addressed by the head of the Nanking government.[954]

To start a Chinese language newspaper in Saigon which would have an editorial policy favorable to Japan, Tokyo was attempting to locate, in the early part of August 1941, Chinese who were capable of publishing and manning the staff of the proposed paper.[955]

249. Japan Deals with its Chinese Allies.

From Peking on July 14, 1941 came the disclosure that the Shansi army, supplied with funds, arms, and ammunition by their former enemy, Japan, was to sign a peace treaty in the city of Yangue in the Shansi province after arranging an armistice with Tokyo. Simultaneously, the Shansi army was to announce its separation from Chungking, its opposition to Communism and its cooperation in the establishment of a new order in the Far East. In return, Japan was to arrange credit for the currency published in the Shansi province and to aid in the reestablishment of business. Because of the effect it might have on Chungking, Japan decided to report the official results of this conference with the Shansi army as a failure.[956]

To carry out its own national policy and to cope with the world situation, according to a statement from Tokyo, the Japanese government underwent a change on July 16, 1941 and established a new Cabinet. Tokyo insisted, however, that neither its foreign policy nor its attitude toward Nanking, the seat of occupied China, had changed in any way. Increased power and progress was pledged to China by the Japanese Cabinet in return for cooperation in the realization of stability in the Far East.[957]

---

[951]II, 943.
[952]II, 944.
[953]II, 945.
[954]II, 946–947.
[955]II, 948.
[956]II, 949–950.
[957]II, 951.

250. Generalissimo Chiang Kai-shek Reorganizes His Armies.

For the purpose of effecting unity under the joint commands of Chen Cheng and Pai Chunghsi, and at the same time to coordinate the activities of miscellaneous forces in preparation for a future attack on Thailand and French Indo-China, Generalissimo Chiang Kai-shek reorganized his armies and appointed some new leaders in July 1941.[958] At some time between July 7 and July 20, 1941 special duty troops and other foot soldiers were to move into Burma under secret orders and to form a second line of defense, and Chungking planned to move an army from southern Konan into that area.

Since Great Britain felt that the Chinese army should be responsible for the defense of certain areas, and since the responsibility involved both military and economic questions, studies were being made with the military attache from the British Embassy so as to reach an agreement.[959]

251. Effect of the United States' Freezing Order on China.

On July 26, 1941 Japanese officials conferred in Shanghai to discuss the freezing order of the United States. While certain retaliatory measures, such as the confiscation of property, were taken against America, no effective financial counter moves had been adopted by the Japanese in Shanghai beyond the prohibition of exports.[960] However, a plan to strengthen the method of adjusting exports from China to third countries was considered, and in order to gain greater control over the removal of materials, it was agreed that regulations published by Japanese financial officials were to apply to China. Further studies were to be made concerning other means for the exploitation of China, and the results were to be submitted to the controlling Japanese authorities.[961]

The order freezing Japanese assets also froze Chinese funds at China's own request. From Shanghai, on July 28, 1941, came the report that the order freezing Chinese credits in the United States made it impossible for American banks in China to guarantee payments in American currency in New York.[962]

Tokyo was not keeping its representatives in China informed of details regarding the freezing of Chinese funds since on August 2, 1941 Peking requested further information.[963] Japanese representatives in Shanghai reported on August 4, 1941 that Mr. Fox, connected with the American Commission for Collections and believed responsible for the original freezing order of the United States, had suggested the revision of the freezing of both Japanese and Chinese assets in order to reconstruct Chungking's financial position. Furthermore, Mr. Henchman, the manager of the Shanghai-Hongkong Bank was willing to give Mr. Fox every support in this matter.[964] The Japanese knew that Mr. Fox had carried out extensive investigation into Chinese financial affairs, and had been urging Chungking to institute some fundamental economic reforms.[965]

---

[958]II, 952.

[959]II, 953.

[960]II, 954–955.

[961]II, 954.

[962]II, 956.

[963]II, 957.

[964]II, 955.

[965]II, 958.

After August 5, 1941 American and British business firms in Tsingtao had to secure the approval of an adviser appointed by the Japanese authorities for their operations, and unconditional compliance with various orders was demanded. No transfer of the ownership of factories or materials could be made without official approval. Furthermore, the raising of funds and the distribution of profits were also to be in the hands of the Japanese.[966]

252. Japanese Restrictions on Shipping and Travel.

In July 1941 many changes were made with regard to foreign shipping in Japanese waters. No foreign ships were permitted to drop anchor at any port on the Inland Sea, in northern Kyushu, and along the northern coast of the Yamagachi Prefecture with the exception of Kobe, Osaka, and Hakodate, and all but Japanese vessels were held up at the harbor entrance of these three ports. Extreme care was also observed in allowing foreigners to embark on any ship.[967]

Because of the difficult diplomatic situation during August 1941 owing to the Russo-German war, the strained relations between Japan and England and the United States, and the change in the Japanese Cabinet, restrictions had been placed upon the travel of foreigners throughout Japan, Manchukuo and China. Visas were granted, particularly to military men, only after a complicated procedure.[968]

253. Japan Makes Plans to Conquer Siberia.

In August 1941 the Japanese army established the administrative policy that was to be applied to the conquered areas of Siberia. Under a group of administrators, executive sections including general affairs, peace preservation, transportation, communications, economics and public affairs were to be provided for, and investigations to protect Japanese interests were to be carried on by several independent bureaus.[969]

PART C—JAPANESE DIPLOMATIC ACTIVITIES THROUGHOUT THE WORLD

(i) Japanese–Nanking Relations.

254. Germans in Nanking Request An Explanation of Japanese–American Negotiations.

On May 24, 1941 the German Consul General in Nanking called on a Japanese representative and requested an explanation of the rumors that Japan was seeking the aid of the United States in making peace with Chungking. Mr. Nakamura emphatically denied that Japan had any intention of risking the friendship of the Axis by cooperation with the United States. The German diplomat also pointed out that German merchants were worse off under Japanese jurisdiction than they had been under the authority of Chungking.[970]

---

[966]II, 959.
[967]II, 960.
[968]II, 961–962.
[969]II, 963.
[970]II, 964.

255. Japan Is Disturbed by German-Russian-Chungking Communications Agreement.

The establishment of communications between Chungking and Germany through Moscow on June 1, 1941 caused Tokyo great concern.[971] When Ambassador Hiroshi Oshima in Berlin, investigated the situation, he found that a daily plane service had been established and an agreement had been made between the postal authorities of Germany and Soviet Russia regarding the handling and cost of mail between Berlin and Chungking. He reported that no apparent political significance was attached to the matter.[972]

256. Japan Prepares a Reception for Mr. Wang Chin Wei.

During June 1941 Tokyo hastened elaborate preparations for the visit of Mr. Wang Chin Wei, the chief of the Nanking government, and his entourage to Japan. Tokyo ordered that Mr. Wang Chin Wei was to be accorded all the honors of a visiting sovereign at least during his brief reception in the Imperial Court.[973] Special plans regarding his audience with the Emperor and arrangements for the meeting of his representatives with the Japanese ministers were outlined.[974] Japanese and Chinese newspapers were given careful instructions and, on June 9, 1941, Tokyo issued to its representatives in Nanking the official report concerning the visit which was to appear in the evening papers of June 14, 1941. Mr. Wang went from Nanking to Tokyo via Shanghai,[975] and the Shanghai Mainichi, commenting upon his former trip to Tokyo, divulged a fact which had been kept secret heretofore by Tokyo.[976]

Because Mr. Wang was apprehensive for the safety of his life,[977] particularly after a member of the Nanking government, who had formerly been associated with Generalissimo Chiang Kai-shek, had been captured by Chungking agents,[978] a heavy guard of police officers was detailed to escort the party as far as the suburbs of Shanghai.[979] Special railroad arrangements in Japan were also made for the official party.[980]

As a result of the visit, Japan decided to grant official recognition to the Nanking government on July 1, 1941 and to extend it a loan at the same time. However, since it was felt that the German-Russian war might delay recognition, the loan was announced on June 28, 1941,[981] about the time the publicity ban concerning Mr. Wang's movements was lifted after his return to China.[982]

257. Germany Recognizes Nanking.

Before Mr. Wang's arrival at the Emperor's court, assurances of Germany's support had been received by Japan. On June 10, 1941, at the request of Mr. Matsuoka, Foreign Minister

---

[971] II, 965.
[972] II, 966.
[973] II, 967.
[974] II, 968.
[975] II, 969–971.
[976] II, 972.
[977] II, 973.
[978] II, 974.
[979] II, 975.
[980] II, 976.
[981] II, 977.
[982] II, 978.

von Ribbentrop reiterated Berlin's willingness to recognize the Nanking government at any time.[983] Since it was Ambassador Oshima's opinion that this attitude would not change,[984] he suggested that Japan either formally request the recognition of the Wang regime or else convey to the German government the reasons why it was not sought at this time.[985]

On June 27, 1941 Ambassador Oshima revealed that Berlin's recognition of the Nanking government would be in the form of a commercial treaty giving German firms full rights in China.[986] Since Tokyo wished that no news of the German and Italian recognition reach the newspapers before it received official confirmation, it prohibited, on June 28, 1941, any discussion of the question for the time being.[987]

After relations with Chungking had been severed by Germany, its recognition of the Nanking government was made public. Immediately, the Chinese Ambassador to Germany, Mr. Chin Kai, sent a note severely criticizing Berlin for siding with the Japanese, but Germany returned the note as unacceptable. Ambassador Oshima informed Tokyo that by July 10, 1941 the members of the Chinese Embassy and Consulate would leave Germany.[988]

Since there were German citizens residing within the Chungking sphere of influence in China, Germany, expressing its concern, requested the assistance of Japan in safeguarding its nationals in that area.[989]

258. Italy Recognizes the Nanking Government.

Italy was as ready to extend recognition to Nanking as Germany had been. Foreign Minister Ciano informed Ambassador Horikiri, on June 26, 1941, that since the Italian Ambassador to China had lived there three years without presenting his credentials to Chungking, the formal recognition of the Nanking government presented no difficulties from a political point of view. However, Italy would consult with Germany before making its formal reply.[990]

On June 30, 1941 Italian diplomats in other countries were instructed to recommend that other signatories to the Tripartite Pact recognize the Japanese-controlled portion of China. At the suggestion of Italy, the Spanish government was expected to adopt a similar attitude regarding Nanking.[991] Croatia announced through the Italian government that it was recognizing the Nanking regime on July 1, 1941,[992] and a few days later arrangements were made to have Croatia recognize another Japanese puppet state in China, Manchukuo.[993]

259. Chungking Severs Relations with Germany and Italy.

After the announcements of the recognition of Nanking by Germany and Italy on July 1, 1941, Chungking, on July 3, 1941, severed diplomatic relations with both Axis powers and evacuated its staff from both countries immediately.[994]

---

[983]II, 979–980.
[984]II, 981.
[985]II, 982.
[986]II, 983–984.
[987]II, 985.
[988]II, 986.
[989]II, *Ibid*.
[990]II, 987.
[991]II, 988.
[992]II, 989.
[993]II, 990.
[994]II, 991–992.

The Italian Ambassador in Shanghai was scheduled to proceed to Nanking on July 1, 1941,[995] and, on July 4, 1941, preparations were underway for the evacuation of Acting Ambassador Adolfo Allesandrini and Italian officials from Chungking.[996] Meanwhile, on July 2, 1941, Wang expressed his appreciation to Japan for the influence it had exerted in behalf of his government.[997]

260. Japan Requests France to Recognize the Nanking Government.

Calling on Admiral Darlan on July 1, 1941, the Japanese Ambassador to Vichy pointed to the growing influence of the Nanking government in China, and in view of the recognition of Nanking by Germany and Italy and the prospective recognition by other European countries, requested that France also recognize it.[998]

Though France was bound by the terms of the German peace treaty, Admiral Darlan explained that France did not necessarily have to act in the same manner as the Axis powers, and until a revised treaty was drawn up giving France an opportunity to cooperate in the new European situation, it was actually in no position to do so. In pointing out the effect of the proposed Japanese aggression against French Indo-China, the Vichy official stated that as long as Generalissimo Chiang Kai-shek controlled the domain bordering on Indo-China, France's position was precarious. If, however, Russia's aid to Chungking were to vanish, thereby weakening Generalissimo Chiang Kai-shek's forces, or if German-French collaboration improved, France could consolidate her policies with those of Germany and Italy.[999]

As a result of his talk with Admiral Darlan, Ambassador Kato informed Tokyo that it would be wise not to press the French too much on the matter of recognition,[1000] but on July 4, 1941 the Foreign Office ordered him to renew his efforts.[1001]

The Japanese Ambassador in Vichy responded promptly in an effort to explain to Foreign Minister Matsuoka his reluctance to exert pressure on France. Pointing out that Japan was seeking bases in French Indo-China on the grounds that the French could not defend it, Ambassador Kato remarked that French recognition of Mr. Wang's government might imply that there was no danger to French Indo-China from other countries. Furthermore, if French-Japanese negotiations broke down over the question of bases, it would be disadvantageous to Japan, if, in reciprocation, the Nanking government had recognized Vichy.[1002]

Ambassador Oshima in Berlin also advised Tokyo not to press for French recognition of Nanking.[1003] Nevertheless, Ambassador Kato again approached Vice-Premier Darlan on July 14, 1941 in regard to recognition for Nanking, only to receive the vague answer that the problem would be given careful consideration.[1004]

Japan and French Indo-China entered into a joint defense agreement on July 23, 1941 and in view of this move, on July 31, 1941 the Japanese felt that the French would not be making

---

[995] II, 988.
[996] II, 993
[997] II, 994.
[998] II, 995.
[999] II, *Ibid.*
[1000] II, *Ibid.*
[1001] II, 996.
[1002] II, 997.
[1003] II, 998.
[1004] II, 999.

too great a concession by going a step further and recognizing the Nanking government. The report that Chungking was sending an influential ambassador, Mr. Wei Tao-Ming, to France increased Japan's desire to have the French take a pro-Japanese stand at this time.[1005]

261. Axis-Dominated Countries Recognize Nanking.

On July 8, 1941 Japan requested Germany's assistance in having both Denmark and Finland recognize Nanking and, at the same time, Manchuria.[1006] On July 12, 1941 Mr. E. Freiherr Weiszaecker, Chief of the Political Section of the German Foreign Office, explained that Herr von Ribbentrop's approval would have to be obtained before any action could be taken,[1007] but a few days later Germany ordered its ministers in Finland and Denmark to submit the request for recognition to those governments. Japan also submitted the request to the ministers of Finland and Denmark, and the Nanking government arranged the details of the recognition.[1008] A short time later, on July 23, 1941, it was reported that Finland had recognized Manchukuo and that recognition of the Nanking government was soon to follow.[1009] Denmark was to recognize Nanking in mid-August, 1941.

Because of Thailand's neutral position in regard to the war in Europe, Tokyo, on July 4, 1941, expressed doubt that it could force Thaiese recognition of Nanking. However, Prime Minister Pibul was to be asked to consider the matter.[1010] It was announced on July 29, 1941 that Thailand would recognize Manchukuo on August 1, 1941.[1011]

262. Japan Removes Anti-Axis Chinese Diplomats.

Japan and Germany collaborated in choosing diplomatic representatives who were pro-Axis in sentiment. On June 28, 1941 Mr. Matsuoka announced that Tokyo would assist Nanking in replacing diplomats from Chungking in the countries that had recognized the Nanking government, with the exception of those persons who could be persuaded to swear allegiance to Nanking and to sever connections with Generalissimo Chiang Kai-shek.[1012] However, the Japanese were forced to tolerate some of the Chinese diplomats since satisfactory substitutes were difficult to obtain.[1013]

In an attempt to strengthen its position in China, in early July, 1941, Japan requested Germany to eliminate from its consulates, and diplomatic establishments in China, those German officials who were stubbornly anti-Japanese.[1014]

263. Japan Attempts to Win Over Chinese Diplomats from Chungking.

During June and July, 1941 much attention was paid to winning over Mr. Chin Kai, the Chinese Ambassador to Berlin, to Japanese views through some connections with the Manchu-

---

[1005]II, 1000.
[1006]II, 1001.
[1007]II, 1002.
[1008]II, 1003.
[1009]II, 1004–1006.
[1010]II, 1007.
[1011]II, 1008.
[1012]II, 1009–1011.
[1013]II, 1012.
[1014]II, 1013.

kuoan Minister in Berlin.[1015] Regardless of any declaration of loyalty that Mr. Chin Kai might make to the Nanking regime, however, the Japanese Ambassador in Berlin, who was to take over matters connected with the management of the Chinese Embassy in Berlin, requested on June 30, 1941 that the Chinese diplomat not be allowed to serve in Germany.[1016] In view of his past connection with the Chungking government, the Japanese Ambassador in Rome suggested on July 1, 1941, that Mr. Chin Kai be sent to Nanking to show his willingness to serve the "New Order" in East Asia.[1017] However, a few days later, Ambassador Oshima stated that although Mr. Chin Kai was possibly useful, he was not considered a suitable person to represent Mr. Wang's government.[1018]

Furthermore, on July 10, 1941 the Japanese Ambassador in Berlin reported that Mr. Chin Kai and his staff had left for Switzerland to arrange their return to China, and he asked that they be kept under close observation.[1019] To add to Tokyo's difficulties, on July 11, 1941 the Japanese Ambassador in Italy reported that the Chinese Ambassador in Italy was also identified as a strong Chiang admirer and vigorously opposed to Japan.[1020]

Nevertheless, on July 14, 1941 Tokyo was revealed as still attempting to persuade Ambassador Chin Kai to accept the Wang regime.[1021] On July 24, 1941 Mr. Fujii, a telegraphic secretary in Spain, called on Mr. Chin Kai to speak to him in the name of the Japanese Ambassador in Madrid. Because of the strained Japanese-Chinese relation, the former Chinese Ambassador would not grant an interview, but Tokyo intended to approach him again in Hongkong.[1022]

264. Nanking Requests Return of Ambassador Honda.

To stabilize its position, and to consolidate its gains, the Nanking government in the latter part of July 1941 was exerting every means to induce Ambassador Kumataro Honda to return from Tokyo. Japanese representatives in China suspected that certain officials in Chungking were envious of Mr. Wang's position, and that with the encouragement of Ambassador Honda they could easily be persuaded to align themselves with Nanking. They pointed out, however, that if such an important official as Ambassador Honda stayed away from Nanking, the officials in Chungking would lose interest.[1023]

265. Japan Controls Nanking's Relations with Germany and Italy.

In return for the continued cooperation which Germany had given Japan in obtaining the recognition of Nanking, Berlin, on July 3, 1941, requested assurance, before making a proposal for a German-Nanking Trade Agreement, that Germans in Nanking would be accorded the same privileges as the Japanese.[1024] However, the Japanese announced that they were to be consulted first, instead of the Nanking government, in all questions concerning foreign interests.[1025]

[1015]II, 1009–1011.
[1016]II, 1014.
[1017]II, 1015.
[1018]II, 1016.
[1019]II, 1017.
[1020]II, 1018.
[1021]II, 1019.
[1022]II, 1020.
[1023]II, 1021.
[1024]II, 984.
[1025]II, 1022.

Both Germany and Italy were informed that trade negotiations would be handled by the North China Political Council which was controlled by Japanese advisers.[1026] In view of this, while Japanese authorities were completing negotiations with the Nanking government, Mr. Shiniokuro Hidaka, the Japanese Minister to Nanking, advised Mr. Wang to keep in close contact with Japan when discussing matters concerning both Germany and Italy.[1027]

266. Reorganization of the Nanking Government.

At a directors' meeting of the Far Eastern Reconstruction Bureau on July 12, 1941, it was decided that the balance of the customers' revenue in Canton should be transferred to the Nanking government, after deducting the deficit created prior to the establishment of the new regime, and some other expenses. If, however, the revenue allotted to Nanking were so insufficient that deficits would occur in the appropriations necessary for the execution of its anti-Communist policy, then the money accumulated as a share of the Foreign Loan Collateral Fund in Shanghai would also be given to Nanking.[1028]

Commercial Attache Yoshio Nakamura and Ambassador Honda cooperated in planning for the reorganization of the Nanking government to bring about a closer relationship with Japan. In order to accomplish this matter, however, the full cooperation of the Japanese army, through the So forces, would have to be obtained. Nevertheless, it was felt, on July 23, 1941, that the reorganization of the Nanking government, with the full approval and cooperation of Mr. Wang, would be successfully achieved by August 10, 1941.[1029]

267. Formal Installation of Mr. Wang.

During the last days of July 1941, the formal installation of Mr. Wang, as head of the Nanking government, was scheduled to take place. To emphasize the consolidation of Japanese holdings in China, trips to Manchuria and Kwantung during the latter part of July and the first ten days in August, 1941 were planned for Mr. Wang.[1030] On August 2, 1941, Mr. Wang went to Canton, where he was greeted by the military commander and by the highest ranking Japanese and Chinese military and governmental officials, as well as the German and Italian Consuls General. At a session of the Far Eastern Newspaper Conference on August 4, 1941, he was slated to receive congratulatory notes from Prime Minister Konoye and Foreign Minister Matsuoka.[1031]

PART C—JAPANESE DIPLOMATIC ACTIVITIES THROUGHOUT THE WORLD

(j) Japanese-Netherlands East Indies Relations.

268. Japan Attempts Political and Economic Domination of the Netherlands East Indies.

According to a Japanese resume of Japanese-Dutch trade negotiations, in November, 1939 Tokyo had proposed the commencing of trade negotiations with the Dutch East Indies, and the

---

[1026]II, 1023–1024.
[1027]II, 1025.
[1028]II, 1026–1027.
[1029]II, 1028–1029.
[1030]II, 1030–1032.
[1031]II, 1033–1034.

Dutch government had agreed in principle. However, with the spread of the European war to Holland in May 1940, and the resulting mobilization of the economic resources of the East Indies, plans for these conferences were laid aside.

Though Japanese leaders were striving to create a "New Order" in the Far East, Japan had become increasingly dependent upon the natural resources of the Dutch East Indies just when the European war began to absorb them. Japan requested a guarantee from Dutch leaders that certain strategic materials would be made available, and Tokyo declared that the Dutch had promised to continue economic relations with Japan, no matter what happened in Europe, since cooperation with Japan would aid Dutch interests and would provide stability in the Far East.[1032]

The Japanese continued to exert pressure throughout 1940 and 1941, and two missions came from Tokyo, ostensibly for economic discussions, but in reality seeking political domination. However, according to reliable information received on May 21, 1941, the Japanese learned that the Dutch had decided against their trade proposals and would demand the return of the Japanese representatives to their home country.[1033]

On the same day Foreign Minister Matsuoka announced that the Dutch, at the suggestion of the British, were about to impose a general embargo on rubber and tin exports from the East Indies to Japan as British Malaya had already done. Out of deference to the Japanese delegates and trade representatives in Batavia, Mr. Hoogstraten[1034] was withholding the publication of this embargo procedure until Japanese representatives had time to withdraw from the Netherlands East Indies.[1035]

In view of these reports, on May 22, 1941 the Japanese Vice Minister questioned Mr. Pabst, the Netherlands Minister to Tokyo, concerning the influence of the United States and Great Britain in restricting Dutch exports to Japan. He also made it clear that under existing circumstances Japan felt it wise to recall its representative, Mr. Yoshizawa, and possibly plan further retaliatory measures. Realizing that the Dutch attitude was based on the assumption that these vital materials were being reshipped to Germany, the Japanese Vice Minister attempted to avoid discussing this problem by stating that rubber and tin imported from the Netherlands East Indies were to be used in the rapidly expanding Japanese arms production. Anxious to keep Japanese-Dutch relations on a friendly basis in spite of the disagreement in policy, Mr. Pabst stated that some understanding would be reached if Japan would reveal the figures concerning the actual demand for the supply of these raw materials.[1036]

269. Dutch Opposition to a Japanese Order.

An obstacle to Japanese-Dutch economic cooperation had already arisen in the early part of May 1941 when an order from Foreign Minister Matsuoka directed all foreign firms in Japan to make entries in their accounts in the Japanese language. This would facilitate checking by Tokyo in the event that Japan's credits abroad were frozen.[1037] Since Japanese organizations, as well as other foreign firms in the East Indies, were permitted to keep their books in either the English or Malayan language, Dutch officials pointed out that if, in retaliation, the Dutch

---

[1032]II, 1035.

[1033]II, 1036.

[1034]Spelled Hofstraaten in nearly all translated dispatches in the files of U.S. Communication Intelligence.

[1035]II, 1037, 1038.

[1036]II, 1039.

[1037]II, 1040.

government required Japanese commercial and industrial enterprises to make their entries in Dutch, the inconvenience would be tremendous and great losses would undoubtedly be incurred. In order to work out some agreement, therefore, a conference was called by commercial representatives of the two countries. Japanese officials in Batavia urged Mr. Matsuoka to do nothing which would force Dutch officials to retaliate by demanding that all Japanese firms in the East Indies make entries in the Dutch language.[1038]

270. Japan Makes New Proposals to the Dutch.

Learning in the latter part of May 1941 that British and Dutch commercial attaches in Tokyo were making surveys of Japanese rubber needs, the Chief of the Japanese Trade Bureau called the Netherlands delegate to his office on May 30, 1941 and showed him statistics which had been prepared concerning Japanese consumption of raw rubber, shipments to Manchukuo and China, and the probable amount of imports. Explaining to the Dutch official that even by economizing on its needs Japan would experience a rubber shortage, since it needed 30,000 tons, the Tokyo representative asked that Mr. Yoshizawa's request for 20,000 tons of rubber be honored by the Netherlands. The Netherlands' commercial attache assured the Japanese government that the matter would be taken up with his minister in Batavia.[1039]

Foreign Minister Matsuoka was certain on May 28, 1941, despite secret reports to the contrary,[1040] that the government of the Netherlands East Indies was not considering breaking off negotiations entirely, for the Dutch officials had promised to give careful consideration to some revised Japanese proposals presented on May 14, 1941.[1041] Details of the Japanese proposals were uncovered by American cryptanalysts on June 12, 1941.[1042] As many permits for entry into the East Indies as could possibly be granted, at least 1,600 a year, were desired for Japanese employees. Furthermore, in order to permit Japanese penetration into obscure and inconvenient places, a fixed number of Japanese doctors were to be allowed to practice throughout this area.

While assuring the government at Batavia that it had no desire to impair Dutch national defense or the economic stability of local inhabitants, Japan demanded permission to establish and expand independent as well as joint enterprises throughout the East Indies. Furthermore, Japan asked that it be granted petroleum rights in certain areas. To ensure the establishment of adequate communications between the two countries, a direct airline was to be set up at the first opportunity. A modern cable line between Japan and the East Indies was to be constructed under Japanese supervision, and existing wireless communications were to be improved.

In the event that world circumstances made it imperative that Japan increase its shipping tonnage, certain coastal ports were to be opened immediately in order to facilitate the unloading of special goods. Referring to the quota set on East Indies' exports, Japan emphasized its need for rubber, tin, bauxite, copra and palm oil. In regards to Dutch acceptance of Japanese imports, a minimum of approximately 80% of the Netherlands East Indies products exported to Japan was to be established.[1043]

[1038]II, 1041.
[1039]II, 1042.
[1040]II, 1043.
[1041]II, 1044.
[1042]Hubertus J. van Mook—*The Netherlands Indies and Japan*, W. W. Norton and Co., N.Y., 1944, pp. 99–106 for complete English text.
[1043]II, 1045.

271. Dutch Indignation at Japanese Newspaper Attacks.

On June 1, 1941 at a critical moment in the current negotiations, Japanese representatives in Batavia requested Tokyo to restrain the Japanese press from attacking the government and people of the Dutch East Indies, since Mr. Hoogstraten, chief of the commercial section of the Netherlands Indies government, had already officially denounced recent stories appearing in Japanese newspapers. Unless the newspaper attacks were retracted, the Japanese Minister in Batavia believed that Japan would be unable to obtain the concessions it desired from the Dutch.[1044]

272. Japanese Propaganda in the Netherlands Indies.

In an attempt to influence public opinion in the Netherlands Indies, Tokyo had allotted large sums of money for propaganda. Though there was some doubt as to the wisdom of its subsidizing a Japanese language newspaper in the East Indies, on June 2, 1941, Tokyo was considering the project, for it had already established many official and semi-official organizations in Taiwan to aid Japan's advance in the South Seas, and these were apparently quite successful.[1045]

The Japanese Minister in Batavia reported on June 22, 1941 that the regular European language periodicals which Tokyo sent on for distribution in the East Indies were widely read, if of cultural value, but that anything smacking of Axis propaganda was immediately rejected by the Dutch. With regard to the future distribution of propaganda material, Mr. Ishizawa reported that his agency intended in the future to concentrate its activities in a given local area.[1046]

Negotiations were under way by July 17, 1941 to have Japan subsidize the *East India Daily* and the Chinese *Suratan.*[1047]

273. The Netherlands Reject the Japanese Proposals (June 6, 1941).

On June 6, 1941 the Netherlands government delivered its reply to the Japanese proposals of May 14, 1941. Though noting with satisfaction the modifications which Japan's representatives had made as a reult of discussions on various points at issue, and expressing its appreciation for the endeavors of the Tokyo delegation to adapt its propositions to the emergencies of the world situation, and at the same time to make them compatible with Netherlands East Indies' policies, the Dutch pointed out that the views of the Japanese government were still basically and radically at variance with their principles.[1048]

(a) *No Special Privileges for Japanese.*

In emphasizing the supposed inadequate development of natural resources in the Netherlands Indies, the Dutch declared that the Japanese had mistakenly assumed that interdependence existed between the two countries. Special privileges for Japanese interests in the Netherlands would militate against the fundamental economic policy of the Netherlands gov-

---

[1044]II, 1046.
[1045]II, 1047.
[1046]II, 1048.
[1047]II, 1049.
[1048]II, 1050.

ernment which stressed nondiscrimination against friendly foreign powers. Since they were capable of developing their own economic life and resources, the peoples of the Netherlands archipelago had little desire to weaken their own economy by the too liberal admittance of foreign interests. In view of certain conditions it was absolutely necessary to open up the resources and the reserve labor market of this area to the subjects of the Dutch kingdom. Therefore, the relations between the Netherlands and foreign countries for the duration of the war must necessarily be affected by subjection of trade to certain unavoidable restrictions in order to promote the war effort, not only of the Netherlands East Indies, but also of the Dutch kingdom and its allies. Consequently, the Japanese government should understand that labor permits could be granted to foreigners only if the vacancies could not be filled by Netherlands' subjects.

While an expeditious handling of such applications for labor permits was assured, the admission of Japanese nationals could not be guaranteed according to the quota asked in the Japanese memorandum. According to the Dutch, not only would this constitute an inadmissable discrimination against other foreign countries, but it would also impair the interests of their own workers. Favorable consideration was promised for Japan's request that Japanese doctors be permitted to care for Japanese residents, but their medical practice could not be extended to others than Japanese living in the East Indies.[1049]

(b) *Restriction of Certain Enterprises to Dutch.*

If the establishment of any enterprises by foreigners constituted a fitting contribution to the economic development of the country, no objection would be made by the Netherlands' government. However, it was necessary to reserve the more important branches of industry, including the exploration and exploitation of mineral oil products, fisheries, mining, and other commercial businesses, for Dutch subjects. Industrial education of the rural masses was already one of the main problems of the Netherlands' government without further complications arising from the competition of powerful foreign firms.[1050]

(c) *No Need for Cables.*

Referring to the Japanese proposals for the improvement of traffic connections between the Netherlands East Indies and Japan by air lines to Bangkok, Saigon, and other places, the Netherlands' government expressed a willingness to cooperate, though pointing out that future development of air transportation was uncertain. As to improvement of radio communications, the Netherlands could see no reason for the duplication of their already established telegraphic system by expensive submarine cables.[1051]

(d) *No Expansion of Coastal Navigation.*

In regard to coastal navigation around the Netherlands East Indies, the Dutch made it clear that although special privileges had already been granted to certain vessels, including Japanese ships, it was the general policy to prevent any foreign ships from carrying on such activity. However, for the maintenance of Dutch enterprises, coastal shipping privileges would be granted within certain limitations.[1052]

[1049] II, *Ibid.*

[1050] II, *Ibid.*

[1051] II, *Ibid.*

[1052] II, *Ibid.*

(e) *Dutch Restrictions on Imports Into the Indies and Exports to Japan.*

Since the great market of the Netherlands East Indies was dependent upon trade with many countries, it was necessary that the Dutch themselves made adjustments with regard to the import and export situation. Furthermore, in order to prevent their exports from providing the enemy with materials of strategic value, the Netherlands must impose certain restrictions. Consequently, no definite quota for any of their commodities for an extended period of time could be guaranteed to a foreign country. Nevertheless, the Japanese government was assured that abrupt changes in the Netherlands Indies commercial policy would be avoided.

Though unsettled circumstances made it almost impossible to establish any trade commitments during the next twelve months, the Netherlands' government was prepared to issue permits for the exportation of goods during the next six months. As long as the prices and terms of delivery could meet competition from other countries, Japan would be allowed to send imports to the East Indies.[1053]

On the basis of the so-called Hoogstraten-Ishizawa and the van Mook-Kotani agreements, Netherlands officials believed that the position of the Japanese importers had been satisfactorily settled. Appreciating the difficulty of the Japanese government in adjusting its internal economic policy on the basis of uncertain trade importations, the Netherlands' government expressly stated its export regulations for the year 1941.[1054]

(f) *Netherlands Proposals.*

The Netherlands made several proposals to the Japanese. Because a shortage of sugar was known to exist not only in the Japanese Empire but also in adjacent regions, Tokyo was to import Javanese sugar at the rate of 150,000 tons a year for the remaining months of 1941. The amount of ebony imported into Japan from the Netherlands East Indies, as well as the shipment of coffee, was to be established at a definite rate for the same period of time. Various schedules were established for the exportation of other essential raw materials.[1055]

274. Japanese Negotiators Recommend Acceptance of Dutch Proposals.

At the same time that the Netherlands' reply to the Japanese proposals was sent to Tokyo, the Japanese Consul in Batavia, on June 7, 1941, suggested the acceptance of the Dutch proposals since they were the best that Japan could hope to get, though the Dutch had not agreed to Japanese demands concerning oil, rubber, and bauxite.[1056]

At a conference between Mr. Hubertus van Mook, Director of Economic Affairs in the Netherlands East Indies, and Tokyo's representatives on June 10, 1941, the Japanese Minister discovered that the intentions of the Dutch officials were considerably more liberal and elastic than the document of the Netherlands' reply had indicated.[1057] However, on June 12, 1941, Tokyo informed its diplomats throughout the world that the Dutch had definitely rejected Japan's proposals, and had refused to export all the raw materials desired by the Japanese. Furthermore, they threatened to cut off all exports, if Japan reshipped them to Germany.[1058]

[1053] II, *Ibid.*
[1054] II, *Ibid.*
[1055] II, 1051.
[1056] II, 1052, 1053.
[1057] II, 1054.
[1058] II, 1055.

275. Japanese Security Precautions for Diplomatic Codes.

Japan began early in June 1941 to safeguard its state secrets in regard to the Netherlands Indies by adopting new security precautions. When the Japanese Consul in Soerabaya returned a safe to Japan, it was examined by Dutch officials; and as a result, the Japanese Consul in Batavia asserted on June 7, 1941 that there was little prospect of sending secret documents to Japan without inspection by the Netherlands' government.[1059]

To ensure safe communications with the home office, the Japanese Minister in Batavia suggested that reports be exchanged verbally as much as possible, rather than by telegrams. To avoid difficulties with Dutch officials, he was particularly insistent that official couriers coming into the Netherlands Indies be members of the Foreign Office.[1060] To expedite the special handling of messages for military attaches, on June 28, 1941, Tokyo ordered that a caption word including A or M as its second and fifth letters be used as a designator.[1061]

On July 10, 1941, Foreign Minister Matsuoka notified Batavia that a courier, Mr. Zoku Nomoto, who was carrying with him secret documents and cipher machines for both Batavia and Singapore, would have to be passed through the customs. Mr. Ishizawa had already informed Tokyo that baggage could be passed through without examination, provided official seals were attached.[1062]

On August 4, 1941, Tokyo sent out a circular covering the destruction of obsolete codes and the care of the current ones.[1063] During this month, the existing code was also to be replaced by a new and more secret system.[1064]

276. Japan Discriminates Against Dutch Firms.

Meanwhile, in Tokyo, agreements with Dutch business interests were reached as of June 5, 1941, and negotiations were begun with the leaders of the Japan-South Seas General Merchandise Export Guild. In order to insure the Guild's participation and concurrence in Japanese trade negotiations, it was stipulated that its branches in Japan should not be assessed by the Finance Ministry, as were the Dutch firms. The Japanese anticipated that this would dissatisfy Dutch business establishments in Japan, though other Japanese export guilds would probably join the agreement because of the new conditions.[1065]

On previous occasions Japanese guilds had refused to admit Dutch firms, but in late June 1941, as a result of Tokyo's intercession, the Dutch received better treatment from the guilds.[1066]

277. Japanese Business Methods in the East Indies.

Tokyo was informed on June 9, 1941 that branches of the Mitsui, Mitsubishi, Nomura, Iwai, and Kasho companies in Batavia had made competitive offers for June loadings of rubber, and immediate counteraction was suggested.[1067]

[1059] II, 1056.
[1060] II, 1057.
[1061] II, 1058.
[1062] II, 1059.
[1063] II, 1060.
[1064] II, 1061.
[1065] II, 1062.
[1066] II, 1063.
[1067] II, 1064.

Three members of a large Japanese banking and investment corporation had gone to the Netherlands East Indies to establish a joint stock company dealing with rubber plantations in Borneo and Soerabaya. Directing the Japanese Minister to obtain another month's stay in the East Indies for these gentlemen, Tokyo, on June 12, 1941, expressed the hope that they would accomplish their objective. By such close supervision of Japanese business interests was Japan striving to control the East Indies' rubber market.[1068]

278. Japan Foresees the Discontinuance of Negotiations.

Tokyo stated on June 14, 1941 that it was becoming impossible for the two countries to successfully carry on further negotiations, since the reply of the Dutch East Indies' authorities reserved the right to alter at will the export volume of those materials which the Japanese regarded as indispensable. Japan asserted that no international agreement could be made on the basis of such an attitude.

Although the Dutch claimed that the object of its foreign policy was based on furthering the progress and prosperity of its own peoples, Japan felt that the Netherlands East Indies could accomplish much more by firmly establishing commercial cooperation with Japan, and in this way contributing to the peace of the Far East. Claiming to be the economical benefactor of the Dutch East Indies, Japan insisted that merely out of consideration for the unity of purpose existing between the two countries, it had contributed generously to the development of these islands.[1069]

279. Japan Plans to Publicize the Discontinuance of Its Negotiations.

Batavian authorities revealed to the Japanese Minister on June 14, 1941 that Tokyo was planning to publish the results of the negotiations between the two countries without first informing the various Dutch authorities that a diplomatic rupture was inevitable. The Japanese Minister at Batavia warned his Foreign Office that the result of such unilateral action would be detrimental to future agreements.[1070] Tokyo replied on June 14, 1941 that since the negotiations had failed, publicity in regard to the matter was solely a responsibility of Tokyo and was no concern of the Dutch.

The Japanese also pointed out that during the meetings of November 1940, when a compromise had been reached regarding the purchase of petroleum, joint communiques issued by Dutch petroleum interests had advised the public of the quantities involved. Furthermore, Tokyo stated that the Netherlands Indies, according to authoritative intelligence, had kept the United States and Great Britain constantly informed regarding every detail during the discussions.

In addition the Japanese were indignant because the Netherlands East Indies had sent to its ministry in Tokyo both the Japanese proposal of May 14, 1941, and the Netherlands' reply of June 6, 1941 in plain text.[1071] This was very irritating to the Japanese because their code clerks in Batavia had spent ten hours in enciphering the message which the Dutch had already transmitted in plain text.[1072] In view of the dangers to their cryptographic systems from this procedure, Tokyo thereafter permitted its representatives to send foreign text messages in a simpler code system or even in plain text.[1073]

[1068]II, 1065.
[1069]II, 1035.
[1070]II, 1066.
[1071]II, 1067.
[1072]II, 1068.
[1073]II, 1069.

280. Japanese Minister in Batavia Protests Against Tokyo's Procedure.

Japanese Minister Daihyo in Batavia warned Tokyo on June 16, 1941 that if the Japanese were to publish the results of the conferences with the Dutch government, extreme care must be taken in wording the report lest a bad impression be created, particularly since they were breaking off negotiations with the Dutch. The Foreign Office in Tokyo should not give the impression that Japanese public opinion, contrary to the policies of the Japanese government, was in any way controlling its actions, since this would impair the dignity of Japan.

Because there were at least 7,000 Japanese living in the Netherlands East Indies, Minister Daihyo desired to continue normal relations, at least with the Dutch government. At the same time, however, he pointed out that to declare openly that Consul General Ishizawa was to continue the negotiations after the negotiations had failed would be a black mark against Japanese prestige. Therefore, until more natural circumstances permitted, Minister Daihyo suggested that no revelation of the Japanese desire for further talks with the Dutch be made. While the needs of Japan demanded that the petroleum question be settled immediately, it could not be considered separately, since it was but one part of the trade negotiations.[1074]

281. Tokyo Accedes to Minister Daihyo's Request.

Tokyo replied promptly to Minister Daihyo's protest on June 16, 1941, and requested him to assure the Dutch East Indies that any further negotiations would not be an attempt to save the Japanese Cabinet from embarrassment. By discontinuing the talks and recalling its representatives, Tokyo was endeavoring to prevent the rise of circumstances which might infuriate the Japanese people and turn them against the Dutch East Indies. In addition, the Japanese government wished to avoid giving the world the impression that normal relations with the Dutch East Indies had been disrupted, and that the two countries were not at swords' points. Therefore, Japanese Consul General Ishizawa was to indicate in any public announcements that discussions would be continued from time to time with the Dutch.[1075]

282. The Netherlands East Indies and Japan Issue a Joint Communique (June 17, 1941).

On June 17, 1941, after a conference between Mr. Yoshizawa, Mr. Ishizawa, Mr. van Mook and Mr. Hoogstraten which did not change the answer of the Netherlands in any way, a joint communique was issued as follows:

> Both the Netherland and the Japanese delegations greatly regret that the economic negotiations, which has been conducted between them, has unfortunately come to no satisfactory result. It is needless, however, to add that the discontinuation of the present negotiation will lead to no change in the normal relations between the Netherlands Indies and Japan.[1076]

Although no agreement had been drawn up between the two governments as a result of their extended conferences, Foreign Minister Matsuoka expressed the opinion on June 18, 1941 that the Japanese would be able to obtain through ordinary business deals the types of goods that the Dutch considered unimportant. However, as a political gesture to warn the Dutch that Japan needed vital raw materials, the Japanese representative, Mr. Yoshizawa, urged the Governor General of the Indies to reconsider his stand. Nothing came of this, and the Japanese negotiators were ordered to withdraw.[1077]

[1074]II, 1070.
[1075]II, 1071.
[1076]Hubertus J. van Mook—*op. cit.*, p. 122.
[1077]II, 1072.

283. Japan's Urgent Need for Petroleum and Tin.

In view of the Japanese need for petroleum, on June 18, 1941 the Chief of the Japanese Fuel Bureau requested his petroleum representative, Mr. Ito, to remain in Batavia even after other delegates had returned home. Since the international situation was extremely delicate, he directed Mr. Ito to obtain fulfillment of oil contracts which had already been made by the Dutch.

Mr. Matsuoka promised that Japan would not make any direct demands for future oil purchases or for the development of oil fields in the East Indies.[1078] But on June 21, 1941, the Japanese Consul General was instructed by Tokyo to protest immediately to the Dutch authorities against the concentration of Dutch oil products and transportation in British hands.[1079]

To take advantage of any possible diplomatic change after the breakdown of negotiations in June 1941, the Japanese desired to keep their commercial representatives in Batavia so as to be able to renew negotiations for oil rights with the Dutch. Problems other than oil rights, according to the Chief of the Japanese Fuel Bureau, were to be given secondary considerations for the time being.[1080]

A difference of opinion arose on June 19, 1941 between two Japanese representatives in Batavia. Mr. Hatanaka felt that because the negotiations had been discontinued, the acquisition of raw materials could be handled by the local branch of Mitsui, and Mr. Ito could return to Tokyo, leaving Mr. Hatanaka to carry on alone. On the other hand, Mr. Ito believed that the Dutch were just about to accept the Japanese separate proposal and wished, therefore, to remain until the affair could be finished.[1081] But on June 22, 1941, Mr. Ito reported that he was returning to Tokyo since he could do nothing more concerning the petroleum question.[1082]

By virtue of the rupture of the negotiations, Mr. van Mook, the Director of Economic Affairs in the East Indies, had explained that the negotiators had no authority to enter discussions pertaining to other matters of trade. Thus, questions regarding the shipment of fuel would come as usual under the jurisdiction of the Bureau of Mines and would be discussed by competent industrialists. However, Mr. van Mook pointed out that at present the Bureau had been divested of the authority to deal with such matters because of the political aspects involved. Regardless of whatever point of view the Japanese might take concerning future acquisition of rights and interests, Mr. van Mook insisted that present agreements were impossible.[1083]

The withdrawal of Saito, a Japanese fuel negotiator, a few weeks later attested to the belief of Japanese authorities that the decision was irrevocable.[1084] Nevertheless, some time later on July 30, 1941, the Chief of the Netherlands East Indies Trade Bureau assured the Japanese Minister that his government had no intention of abrogating the existing oil agreement; nor did he believe that the Dutch oil company would refuse to sell the product. Regarding this latter point, the Japanese official stated that the company was delaying the loading of oil for which payment had already been made. Assuring the Japanese Minister that the company was undoubtedly discussing the provisions which called for payment in dollars, the Dutch official stated that Mr. van Mook and representatives of the oil company were to confer on the following day. Although company officials would be heard before any decision were made, it was hoped that an agreement, satisfactory to all parties, would be concluded.[1085]

[1078]II, 1073.

[1079]II, 1074.

[1080]II, 1075.

[1081]II, 1076, 1077.

[1082]II, 1078.

[1083]II, 1079.

[1084]II, 1080.

[1085]II, 1081.

As a result of Mr. Ito's report,[1086] the Chief of the Fuel Section, expressing his appreciation for their difficult experiences, directed both Mr. Ito and Mr. Hatanaka to return home.[1087] A report from Minister Daihyo, which stressed the futility of keeping Japanese oil negotiators in Batavia in the face of the Dutch refusal to deal with them, probably had much to do with their return.[1088]

The Japanese were concerned about other vital materials as well as oil. Though the Mitsubishi Company had previously obtained a year's contract to export 3,000 tons of tin from the Netherlands East Indies, the Dutch had reduced that amount to a mere 2,300 tons. However, even after the negotiations had been broken off, the Japanese were hopeful that the Dutch might change their uncompromising attitude concerning tin and manganese.[1089]

284. The Netherlands Indies Reduces Shipping to Japan.

Mr. Ishizawa reported on June 21, 1941 that the Dutch were cutting down on all shipping to Japan in an attempt to apply a wartime embargo act. Instructions had been issued by the Finance Minister to limit material sent to Japan to 20,000 tons per month. According to the Japanese, this reduction of shipping was connected with Netherlands national defense and had been ordered by Dutch shipping authorities in New York, and therefore, it was hard to discover the reasons for it.[1090] In order to conceal Japanese purchases in the East Indies, on June 21, 1941 Mr. Ishizawa suggested that all telegrams regarding such matters be sent secretly to him in Batavia.[1091]

285. Japan Suspects American Support of Netherlands Indies.

Because Holland was one of the nations joined against the Axis, and because its own fundamental policies were closely akin to those of England and the United States, the Netherlands East Indies was greatly affected by the position of the United States in regard to the Japanese "New Order" in Asia. As early as June 22, 1941, according to the Japanese Ambassador in Rome, an intelligence report, sent to the Vatican by the Apostolic Delegate to Batavia, had indicated that the United States, at first, had brought pressure to bear upon the Netherlands East Indies in a scheme to obtain an excellent bargaining position, so as to force Japan into neutrality, if the United States went to war.

Later, however, the United States, with Great Britain, had made the Netherlands East Indies part of a defensive line that included the Philippines, China and Thailand, and thus, by cooperative encirclement, had attempted to force Japan to accept its material aid. Because of this action, according to Ambassador Horikiri's version of the report, the Netherlanders became still more certain that Japan would attack their territory.[1092]

Military cooperation between America, Great Britain, and the Netherlands government was announced by a Japanese report of July 17, 1941, which also indicated that an American air base was being built in Papua, New Guinea.[1093] The Japanese Minister to Batavia reported a

---

[1086] II, 1078.
[1087] II, 1082.
[1088] II, 1083.
[1089] II, 1084.
[1090] II, 1085.
[1091] II, 1086.
[1092] II, 1087.
[1093] II, 1088.

week later, on July 26, 1941, that if the United States should carry out a general embargo, the Dutch people were convinced that Japan would extend its southward march to include Singapore and the Netherlands East Indies. On the other hand, although there was to be a blackout for three days of an area centering on Batavia and Baitenzorugu in preparation for any future air raid, the people of Batavia, as a whole, showed little concern over a possible breach of diplomatic relations with Japan.[1094]

286. Reaction of Netherlands Indies to German-Russian War.

After war began between Germany and Soviet Russia, the Japanese Consul in Batavia stated in an interview with Mr. Hoogstraten on June 23, 1941 that now the Dutch could cease being anxious over the re-exportation to Germany of material purchased in the Indies, and that they could ship supplies to Japan in an unlimited amount. Still uncertain of the Japanese position, however, the Dutch were not willing to make agreements on the hypothesis that Japan would not aid its German partner. On the other hand the Japanese feared that the Netherlanders would lend their full support to Russia, because they were fighting Germany.

According to the Japanese Minister in Batavia, the Dutch believed that the conflict between Germany and Russia would serve to dissipate Nazi strength, while the fighting power of the British, aided by the United States, would increase. In answer to the Japanese Consul's statement that Europe would then come under the control of Commissar Stalin instead of Hitler, Mr. Hoogstraten asserted that Russia had no great ambition in western Europe. Furthermore, with the destruction of Hitlerism and the cooperation of Great Britain, his mother country, Holland, could be restored.[1095]

When the Japanese Consul was questioned by Mr. Hoogstraten regarding Japan's attitude toward the Russo-German conflict, he replied that the Tripartite Pact with Germany stipulated that the relations between the respective treaty powers and Soviet Russia were in no way to be affected by the alliance; therefore, the present hostilities would have no immediate effect upon Japan. In spite of the reassurance which the Japanese gave Dutch officials regarding their neutrality in the European war, the Japanese Minister still feared that the Netherlands East Indies would become more anti-Japanese and that exports to Japan would be reduced to permit large-scale shipments to Soviet Russia. He suggested that Japan formulate and maintain a definite policy with regard to this situation.[1096]

Since there was always the possibility of Japan's attacking Russia, Mr. Ishizawa made inquiries to sound out the effect of such a move upon the Netherlands East Indies. In his report to Tokyo on July 15, 1941 he announced that if Japan did not commit any direct hostile acts against the Netherlands Indies, there was little chance of war between the two countries, although further regulation of exports to Japan would be inevitable if a Japanese-Russian war broke out. Mr. Ishizawa pointed to the friendly attitude of the Netherlanders toward Italian residents, in spite of Italy's alliance with Germany, as proof that the Japanese would be treated in the same way.[1097]

[1094]II, 1089.

[1095]II, 1090.

[1096]II, *Ibid.*

[1097]II, 1091.

287. After Effects of Discontinuance of Japanese-Dutch Negotiations.

Ten days after the publication of the joint communique which announced the discontinuance of the Japanese-Dutch economic negotiations, the Japanese Minister in Batavia, on June 26, 1941 reported to Tokyo that the atmosphere had become more favorable to Japan and that Japanese residents in the East Indies were not much perturbed.[1098] However, the Japanese-Dutch Society was to be closed in late July 1941,[1099] and about July 15, 1941 the Mitsubishi Company ordered its officials in Batavia to evacuate their families.[1100]

As a result of this prospective exodus, the Japanese Minister inquired whether the order of the Mitsubishi Company stemmed from the Japanese Foreign Office or was issued independently. In addition, the Mitsubishi representative informed his home office that general conditions were calm in the East Indies, and for this reason Japanese families did not desire to return to Japan. He also pointed out that the sending of evacuation orders in plain language, as had been done in this instance, would disturb the Dutch government, would not make it change its decision, and would only damage Japanese interests by lessening production.[1101]

288. Netherlands Indies Resent Japanese Intelligence Activities.

When the second Japanese economic mission had come to the Netherlands East Indies, Colonels Maeda and Oga, and Lt. Col. Ishii of the Japanese army had accompanied it. The Netherlands army had been very disturbed by their arrival, but the Dutch refrained from refusing them admittance to avoid affronting Japan. However, after Minister Yoshizawa departed with his associates, on June 27, 1941 Mr. Hoogstraten pointed out that the officers had been more engrossed in inspecting all parts of the Netherlands Indies than in taking part in the negotiations, and he requested Mr. Ishizawa to arrange for their departure on a ship leaving for Japan on July 3, 1941.[1102]

Tokyo inquired, on July 3, 1941, whether the refusal of the Netherlands Indies to permit a certain Japanese naval officer to return was based on the undesirability of the officer or on a general policy of not accepting Japanese language officers.[1103] The refusal of the Dutch to permit the return of a Japanese Vice Consul was because of his previous activities among the radical elements of the native population.[1104]

Whether the visit of the Japanese army officers had been valuable in securing vital information regarding military strength in the East Indies cannot be definitely ascertained, but it was known that the activities of Japanese spies in that area were attaining some measure of success. According to one spy report on July 18, 1941, details of airfields south of Batavia, west of Serang and on the western tip of Java were known.[1105]

Cooperation between the Netherlands East Indies, Australia, England and the United States was noted in a Japanese message from Batavia on July 18, 1941. United States naval officers stationed in a certain section of Soerabaya and Java, as well as British and Australian army officers in Bandon and Batavia, were conducting military training at this time. It was suspected that at other points on the island, allied officers acted as instructors or liaison officers.[1106]

[1098]II, 1092.
[1099]II, 1093.
[1100]II, 1094.
[1101]II, 1095.
[1102]II, 1096.
[1103]II, 1097.
[1104]II, 1098.
[1105]II, 1099.
[1106]II, 1100.

In order to direct the military efforts of the Dutch Indies, Sir Robert Brooke-Popham, the British Commander in Chief of the Far East forces, and a United States Naval aviation officer, Normer, as well as one officer each from the Australian army and navy, arrived in that vicinity some time before July 23, 1941.[1107]

289. The Netherlands East Indies Reduces Exports to Japan.

Though business conditions appeared to be normal,[1108] cancellation or postponement of exports which had already been agreed to by the Dutch drew protests from Tokyo. Listing palm oil, kapok, tannin, scrap iron, rubber and kopra among the products affected by the reduction of exports to Japan, Japanese representatives in Batavia insisted in mid-July 1941 that the Dutch had failed to carry out their contracts since in the case of all vital products, almost half the quantity ordered had been stopped.[1109]

The Dutch authorities promised to reconsider their decision in view of these previous commitments.[1110] Hoping to receive as much as possible, Tokyo directed on July 18, 1941 that all articles already contracted for were to be exported immediately, aboard the Nichiran Maru and the Chirubuto Maru which had been assigned to the Netherlands East Indies.[1111]

290. Dutch Reprisals Against Japanese Communications.

Around July 26, 1941 Tokyo was informed that the Netherlands East Indies threatened to carry out reprisals if Tokyo decreed that only English or Japanese could be spoken in telephone conversations to the East Indies. The Netherlands government in turn would forbid the use of the Japanese language over its international telephone wires. The Dutch put the order prohibiting the use of the Japanese language into effect on July 29, 1941, and Tokyo hastened to negotiate with Batavia immediately in an attempt to have it retracted.[1112]

291. Japan Allays Dutch Fears Concerning a Japanese-British War.

According to a statement made on July 26, 1941 by Mr. Utuheren of the Dutch Immigration Office, the occupation of southern French Indo-China by Japan had damaged Japanese relations with England and the United States, and if war broke out between the Japanese and the English, there was little doubt that the Netherlands East Indies would fight on the side of England. The Japanese Minister replied that the United States and England had been increasing their assistance to China, and that the Chinese, in turn, were hindering Japan from procuring necessary French Indo-Chinese goods. Though asserting that if Japan had not acted immediately, British economic and military influence would have dominated French Indo-China, the Japanese Minister expressed the opinion that the possibility of war between Japan and England was remote.

Certain Netherlands Indies' officials were also convinced that Great Britain and Japan would not war over the French Indo-China issue, but they considered the concentration of Japanese

---

[1107]II, 1101.
[1108]II, 1102.
[1109]II, 1103.
[1110]II, 1104.
[1111]II, 1105.
[1112]II, 1106, 1107.

forces in the southern part of French Indo-China to be a potential threat toward the Netherlands Indies. A meeting of important officials at the Governor's mansion made it apparent that the Netherlands Indies was giving deep consideration to its official attitude regarding the Japanese occupation of French Indo-China.[1113]

292. Japan Releases a Confiscated Cargo.

In an attempt to checkmate any movement of war materials to the Chungking government, in the early part of July 1941 the Japanese in Shanghai had held up and investigated a ship with a cargo of machinery purchased by the Dutch. This occasioned a protest from the Netherlands East Indies and Great Britain. Stressing the importance of the matter, Mr. Hoogstraten, the Dutch Commerce Bureau Chief, had then requested that the machinery be handed over immediately to the Netherlanders.[1114]

According to the Japanese, the exportation had been illegal, since no permit had been obtained from the proper military authorities,[1115] and in addition, the vessel had acted contrary to the orders of the Japanese water police. Furthermore, a bank connected with this transaction was in alliance with the Chungking regime. However, since Japan had no wish to incur the hostility of such an important trading country as the Netherlands East Indies, and because Japanese enterprises in the area were too valuable to be endangered by retaliation for one shipment of goods, Tokyo decided against confiscating this machinery.[1116]

On July 25, 1941 the Netherlands Indies' director, Mr. van Mook was informed that the machinery had been released and he expressed his appreciation to Japanese authorities.[1117] A promise of increased trade had previously been made by the Netherlands Indies' authorities who agreed not to transfer the machinery in question to Chungking.[1118]

293. The Netherlands Indies Freezes Japanese Funds.

The Netherlands Indies learned on July 26, 1941 that the United States and Great Britain had suspended monetary and economic intercourse with Japan. After much hurried activity, the Netherlands Indies was able to issue measures, on July 28, 1941, which suspended the monetary agreement and all monetary transactions with Japan, applied the Export Licensing Law to all exports to the Japanese Empire, Manchuria, occupied China, and Indo-China, and subjected all banks to a system of permits affecting monetary or credit transactions with Japanese subjects.[1119]

294. Economic Cooperation of the Netherlands Indies With England and the United States.

The Japanese Minister in Batavia reported to Tokyo on July 28, 1941 that despite some laxness in enforcing economic sanctions, the Netherlands East Indies was cooperating with England and the United States in economic warfare against Japan. Furthermore, Mr. van Mook

---

[1113]II, 1108.
[1114]II, 1109.
[1115]II, 1110.
[1116]II, 1111.
[1117]II, 1112.
[1118]II, 1110.
[1119]Hubertus J. van Mook—*op. cit.*, pp. 126–127.

asserted that if the Japanese continued their aggression, the Indies might conclude a military alliance with the United States and England. Nevertheless, the Japanese Minister believed that the Netherlands Indies was anxious to avert an attack by Japan.[1120]

Since the betterment of Japanese-Dutch relations was a matter of extreme urgency, Mr. Hoogstraten and Mr. Ishizawa met on July 30, 1941 to seek a solution of the problem. To explain Japan's southward sweep into French Indo-China, Mr. Ishizawa stated that its purpose was to cooperate with the government of France in facilitating the defense of that territory. However, Mr. Hoogstraten assumed that Japan's antagonism toward his country was increasing because Japan had established military bases there.

In spite of Japanese protests that no ulterior motives were involved, the Netherlands East Indies viewed Japanese army, naval, and air bases in the southern part of French Indo-China as a threat to her territorial integrity. At this point Mr. Ishizawa reminded Mr. Hoogstraten that the Dutch had boasted of the firm establishment of an American-British-Chinese-Dutch joint front, and in view of the strong defense which the Dutch had attained by these alliances, Japan could not understand their fear of Axis strength.

In spite of the Japanese Minister's remarks, Mr. Hoogstraten insisted that curtailments of military supplies to Japan were necessary for the defense of the Netherlands Indies. Mr. Ishizawa then advised Mr. Hoogstraten that Japan would find other means of obtaining these essential materials.[1121]

After his conversation with Mr. Hoogstraten on July 30, 1941, the Japanese Minister in Batavia declared emphatically that as long as Japanese forces remained in French Indo-China, the Netherlands Indies would treat Japan as an enemy. In order to combat the punitive trade embargoes imposed by the Dutch, he suggested certain Japanese counter-measures. Although the freezing order regarding Japan's assets had thus far been strictly enforced, the Japanese Minister felt that since the Netherlanders were also being greatly inconvenienced by it, negotiations between Mr. Imagawa of the Specie Bank, and officials of the Administrative Bureau and the Java Bank might produce a favorable solution. In the meantime, however, trade between the two countries was becoming more restricted, and Mr. Ishizawa felt that decisive measures should be initiated against the Netherlands East Indies.[1122]

295. Japan Retaliates by Freezing Netherlands Assets.

In retaliation for the economic measures which the Dutch had taken against the Japanese, Tokyo froze Netherlands assets throughout the Japanese Empire. On July 30, 1941, Mr. Hoogstraten and the Japanese Minister at Batavia discussed various points connected with the freezing orders of both countries. The Dutch official claimed that the Japanese should permit the exportation of not only goods which had been paid for, but also goods under contract, since their title had been transferred to the Netherlands East Indies. If, as a result of the freezing order, the Dutch merchants lost the entire stock of goods purchased from Japan, Mr. Hoogstraten warned that the Netherlands East Indies would use the frozen Japanese funds as collateral for the twelve million guilders involved.[1123]

Replying that Japan did not intend to prevent shipment of goods which had been already purchased, the Japanese Minister stated that his country was at present experimenting with the first export embargo it had ever imposed. Furthermore, he insisted that the Netherlands' government had no justification for taking any retaliatory measures against Japan.

[1120]II, 1113.
[1121]II, 1114.
[1122]II, 1115.
[1123]II, 1116.

Mr. Hoogstraten assured Mr. Ishizawa that if Dutch merchants were permitted to ship their goods from Japan, not only would certain Japanese funds be released, but sugar and similar products would also be shipped from the Netherlands Indies to Japan. However, because the Japanese occupation of the southern part of French Indo-China constituted a direct threat to the Indies, a comparatively strict limitation would still be observed on the exportation of petroleum and other war materials in which the Japanese Minister was particularly interested. Regarding the abrogation of the petroleum agreement, Mr. Hoogstraten stated that his government had no intention of permitting the oil companies to export the undelivered portion of the oil under contract.[1124]

Since the Japanese Minister in Batavia felt that the Netherlands East Indies would still continue to tighten restrictions on exported commodities to Japan, he again suggested on August 1, 1941 that strict counter-measures be taken. Knowing that an embargo against food supplies, such as salt-fish from French Indo-China, would give rise to a serious problem for the Netherlands Indies, the Japanese planned to prevent this and other essential items from reaching the East Indies.[1125]

Further discussion by the Japanese Minister with Mr. Hoogstraten finally won some concessions, according to a report to Tokyo on August 2, 1941, for the Netherlands Indies granted permission for one shipment of rubber, tin, and ilmonite.[1126] Nevertheless, during the first few days of August 1941, growing anxiety was evident among Japanese residents. Because of the constant stream of applicants for passage aboard ships bound for Japan, the South Seas Shipping Company considered dispensing with cargoes until Japanese nationals could be evacuated.[1127]

296. Japanese Nationals Are Evacuated From The Netherlands Indies.

On previous occasions, at the direction of the Japanese Minister, the leaders of Japanese associations had advised Japanese residents owning firmly established enterprises to remain in the Netherlands Indies and continue their business. On July 31, 1941, however, he planned to advise many of them to return home since in the event that improvement in Japanese-Dutch relations became impossible, a disorderly evacuation would disgrace Japan. Judging from recent trends, and because of the danger of arrest for Japanese residents, it was also felt that all Japanese subjects acquainted with the situation in the Netherlands Indies and able to speak the Malayan language would be of great value to the military authorities, and should, therefore, return to Japan and register immediately.[1128]

297. East Indian Merchants Purchase Japanese Stocks.

Upon hearing rumors that the government of the Netherlands Indies would freeze Japanese funds, Chinese and Arabian merchants in the East Indies realized that Japanese merchants would encounter difficulties in future importations and would be interested, therefore, in cash

---

[1124]II, *Ibid.*
[1125]II, 1117.
[1126]II, 1118.
[1127]II, 1119.
[1128]II, 1115.

transactions. These traders attempted to buy up all the articles which Japanese firms had on hand, and in this way obtained a monopoly on many materials. The Netherlands Indies' government, fearing the increased prices that would result from such reckless buying, prohibited the transfer of woven and knitted goods, fabricated materials and other articles. Although these restrictions were designated to curb the transactions of the Chinese and other merchants, the Japanese Minister felt that inflation was now an imminent danger in the East Indies, and would cause more trouble to the Dutch themselves than to Japan.[1129]

298. Japan is Urged to Further Retaliation Against the Dutch.

On August 3, 1941 the Japanese Minister in Batavia reported to Tokyo that the Netherlands East Indies was concerned about food for the Dutch residents in Japan, and about the shipment of goods out of Japan which had been contracted and paid for by Netherlands Indies' merchants. Although Tokyo had so far been indecisive concerning these questions, Dutch firms nevertheless placed considerable reliance on the influence of Mr. Ishizawa.

Believing that Japan's delay was responsible for the issuance of the Netherlands freezing order, Mr. Ishizawa suggested again that Japan retaliate immediately when any actions contrary to her national well-being were undertaken by the Netherlands Indies. He requested, therefore, on August 3, 1941 that decisions reached by the Foreign Office concerning such action be wired to him without any delay.[1130] Furthermore, if time were wasted while he waited for specific instructions, a general embargo might be imposed by the Dutch with the result that Japan would be prevented from obtaining even those materials which were procurable. Such action on the part of the Dutch would possibly freeze Japanese assets indefinitely.[1131]

299. Japan Plans to Convert Its Frozen Funds.

Mr. Ishizawa again urged Tokyo on August 4, 1941 to buy materials from the Netherlands East Indies with Japanese funds available in Batavia. Since the attitude of the Dutch authorities had grown more hostile toward Japan because of the occupation of French Indo-China and the Japanese threat of moving into Thailand, he reiterated that speedy measures should be taken to procure the immediate export of vital materials.[1132] In view of the fact that the Japanese retaliatory order froze both the funds and the assets of the Netherlands, Mr. Ishizawa expected the Dutch to take even more drastic steps in return. He suggested, therefore, that the guilder funds be released without delay to be applied as payment for exports to Japan. Furthermore, Tokyo was requested to inform Ambassador Pabst that the Japanese order as well as the Netherlands measure, was to freeze only the funds, not the assets, of the other country.[1133]

Although the freezing regulations of both countries were comprehensive measures, having no bearing on individual cases, nevertheless, on August 4, 1941 the Netherlands government filed a special request for the transfer of 500,000 yen to the managers of the guild's branches in Japan. In order to preclude the Dutch from retaliating against Japanese banks in the Netherlands Indies, Mr. Ishizawa advised Tokyo to comply with their wishes regarding this transfer. Thus, in the future, when Japan was attempting the conversion of her frozen funds into exportable goods, such action would furnish a precedent for the Netherlands officials.[1134]

[1129]II, 1120.
[1130]II, 1121.
[1131]II, 1122.
[1132]II, *Ibid.*
[1133]II, 1123.
[1134]II, 1124.

PART C—JAPANESE DIPLOMATIC ACTIVITIES THROUGHOUT THE WORLD

(k) Japanese-Thaiese Relations.

300. Japanese Intelligence Reports on Thailand.

On May 23, 1941 Tokyo was informed that Chinese residents in Thailand were still pro-American and pro-British. For this reason, Mr. Shunsuke Asada, a Japanese Consul General in Bangkok, and the first secretary of the Japanese Legation in Thailand, advised Tokyo to send men acting as business agents, rather than representatives from the Nanking government, on a tour of inspection to win over the Thaiese.[1135]

301. Japan Attempts to Acquire Most of Thailand's Exports.

Since Japan was interested in Thailand's resources, reports in connection with Japan's prospects for acquiring various Thaiese mines were sent to Tokyo.[1136] On June 6, 1941 Mr. Asada suggested that inactive rice refineries belonging to Chinese operators be purchased with the view of forming a guild to secure a comprehensive export permit. This would be a means of reconciling the Chinese dealers in Thailand who would be allowed to do business with Chinese within Japanese occupied territories.[1137]

Foreign Minister Matsuoka on June 9, 1941 inquired as to Thailand's views concerning the subsidizing by Japan of a jointly-managed Thai-Japanese company which would ensure regular uninterrupted shipments of tin to Japan.[1138] Mr. Matsuoka was also maneuvering to obtain most of the tin ore mined in Thailand, and, with this in view, was attempting to purchase a two-months' prospecting contract, with an arrangement that all the tin ore mined during that time would be sent to Japan.[1139]

Since it was necessary that Japan obtain guarantees for three staples, tungsten, tin, and rubber, Mr. Asada suggested on June 6, 1941 that the Mitsui organization, which was currently negotiating for the purchase of tin mines in Thailand, be encouraged by the Foreign Office to obtain an option for these mines.[1140]

302. Japan Sends Oil Experts to Thailand in Guise of Diplomats.

To investigate the current consumption of petroleum in Thailand, a member of the Japanese Government Planning Board, Juro Suzuki, and an official of the Fuel Bureau, Yosio Yosida, were sent in early June, 1941 to Bangkok with the official titles of Foreign Office Secretary and General Affairs Official. These men were also to instruct secretly other Japanese in the methods of petroleum consumption. However, Japan was uncertain as to Thailand's reception of its "experts" and directed Mr. Yasusato Futami, Japanese Minister to Thailand, to sound out Thaiese officials in this matter.[1141]

[1135]II, 1125.
[1136]II, 1126.
[1137]II, 1127.
[1138]II, 1128.
[1139]II, 1129.
[1140]II, 1130–1131.
[1141]II, 1132.

303. Japanese-Thaiese Petroleum Negotiations.

As for petroleum, on June 6, 1941 Foreign Minister Matsuoka agreed to supply the amount needed by Thailand, but declared that in the future Japan would demand the entire amount of Thaiese rubber and tin. Japan would agree to British-Thailand petroleum negotiations only if these were on a small scale, and if Thailand would furnish Japan with as much as possible of 15,000 tons of tin ore a year. It was Japan's intention at this time to secure forty per cent of Thailand's tin production, and eventually the entire output. The amount of petroleum to be supplied by Japan for the month of June, 1941 would be decided later in view of the British-Thaiese negotiations.[1142]

304. Britain Supplies Oil to Thailand.

It was confidentially reported to Tokyo on June 6, 1941 that Great Britain had decided to furnish 6,000 tons of petroleum to Thailand.[1143] However, since business was suspended at this time, the British supply would be accepted by the Asia Petroleum Company and later reloaded.[1144]

Despite a Japanese decision that all matters pertaining to the supplying of petroleum to Thailand should be under the jurisdiction of the Foreign Office, Mr. Matsuoka informed Minister Futami that Thailand had submitted a request to the Japanese navy for 12,000 tons of crude oil. The Thaiese government was to be advised that such requests, when not submitted to the Foreign Office, would not be considered by Japan.[1145]

305. Japan Mediates a Thailand-French Indo-China Dispute.

In January, 1941 Japan had offered to mediate hostilities between Thailand and French Indo-China concerning the cessation of border territories, which Thailand had demanded. After several prolongations of the armistice, an agreement was signed in Tokyo on March 11, 1941, and later a treaty and two protocols were drafted. France was to cede some 25,000 miles of territory in French Indo-China, including the districts of Paklay and Bassac, and a large part of Cambodia, which were to be demilitarized.

During the negotiations for the ratification of the treaty, Japan asked on June 13, 1941 that Luang Songram Pibul, Prime Minister of Thailand, send Nai Pananow Wanitto, Chief of the Thaiese Trade Bureau, to Japan to assist the Foreign Office.[1146] As soon as Mr. Andre Roban, the French Plenipotentiary in French Indo-China, returned to his post, proceedings were to begin,[1147] since Thailand was anxious to have the ratification take place by June 27, 1941 at the very latest.[1148] The mediation treaty was to be presented to the Japanese Privy Council in Tokyo on June 18, 1941. Eventually, the Thailand-French Indo-China treaty was signed on June 21, 1941 and the exchange of official documents was scheduled to take place on July 1, 1941.[1149]

[1142]II, 1130–1131.
[1143]II, 1133.
[1144]II, 1134.
[1145]II, 1135.
[1146]II, 1136.
[1147]II, 1137.
[1148]II, 1138.
[1149]II, 1139.

306. Thailand Desires Continuation of Japanese Pressure on French Indo-China.

In a conversation with Mr. Futami a few days before the ratification by the French took place, Minister Pibul of Thailand had remarked that he would like to ascertain the Japanese attitude toward French Indo-China. Though he had assured the Prime Minister that there would be no change in the future policy of the Japanese government, the Japanese Minister believed that Mr. Pibul still was concerned lest Japan would weaken in exerting pressure on French Indo-China, and especially in its independent attitude toward Britain. However, on July 11, 1941 Mr. Futami informed Tokyo that the Prime Minister of Thailand, in a conversation with the Italian Minister, had raised a question as to why Japan did not advance to the north, since the pressure on the south had been alleviated.[1150]

307. Details of Japanese-Thaiese Agreement.

Mr. Futami also reported that both Ambassador Hajime Matsumiya's proposal regarding political and economical cooperation between Japan and Thailand, and the understanding between Itaro Mizuno, of the Commercial Affairs Bureau of the Foreign Ministry, and Nai Wanitto, Acting Minister of Finance of Thailand, urged that economic problems be submitted for consideration by the various firms engaged in the business concerned. However, political problems still seemed to be under the jurisdiction of Nai Wanitto.[1151]

308. Japanese Interest in Survey of Thailand's Border.

On June 20, 1941 Mr. Futami inquired of Tokyo regarding the organization by Thailand of five scientific groups, two of which were being formed for land survey, one for meteorological observation, and two for surveying the Mekong and Mei Rivers. Suggesting an increase in Japanese representation in the groups, Mr. Futami asked for a declaration of policy in order that he might negotiate the matter with the Thaiese government.[1152]

309. Japanese Propaganda Activities in Thailand.

Plans were under way to establish a Japanese printing office in Bangkok,[1153] and 4,400 baht (Thaiese monetary unit) had been appropriated from secret intelligence funds for purchasing the *Bangkok Chronicle*.[1154] The proposed visit of the editor of the *Bangkok Chronicle* to Japan was viewed with suspicion by Minister Futami in a report of July 3, 1941, since the Japanese Minister felt that the editor was making the trip to collect information for the local British Minister from whom he had received 5,000 bahts. While admitting that the accuracy of this report was questionable, Minister Futami advised that great care should be exercised.[1155]

As to the purchase of the *Bangkok Chronicle*, Mr. Futami pointed out that the paper had only a very small circulation and not much influence among the Thaiese. As an organ or propaganda, the paper's effectiveness was uncertain. Furthermore, it would be necessary to study carefully the means and methods of controlling the news in the paper as well as supervising its editorial policy.[1156]

[1150]II, 1140.
[1151]II, 1141–1142.
[1152]II, 1143.
[1153]II, 1144.
[1154]II, 1145–1146.
[1155]II, 1147.
[1156]II, 1148.

310. British Opposition to Japanese Control of Thailand's Exports.

In a dispatch to Tokyo on June 23, 1941 Mr. Futami revealed that the British had suggested to Thailand that the amount of rubber to be furnished to Japan should be reduced to 25,000 tons a year. Although he had no intention of considering this proposal, Prime Minister Pibul had asked Minister Futami whether the Japanese government could be satisfied with 35,000 tons yearly.

Mr. Wanitto informed the Japanese Minister on June 21, 1941 that the British had no objection to Japan's having up to 2,000 tons of tin ore, to which Mr. Futami had replied that this would not be half the amount which Japan needed. Reference was also made at this time to the establishment of tin refining plants, but there was no indication of Thailand's making any definite proposal. Mr. Wanitto pointed out that, considering the nature of the tin industry in Thailand and the fact that the ore was secured from tin mines affiliated with British capital, there would be opposition to a joint Japanese-Thaiese organization.[1157] Reports concerning the purchases of Thailand rubber by Germany, Britain and the United States continued to disturb Tokyo which desired these exports for its own use.[1158]

311. Estimated Value of Japanese-Thaiese Exports.

Referring to previous Japanese-Thaiese economic agreements, Mr. Futami estimated that according to the Japanese plan, Japanese products worth 130,000,000 yen would be exported to Thailand whereas Thailand's exports to Japan would reach the enormous sum of 208,000,000 yen. In view of this prospective unfavorable balance of trade, the Japanese Minister advised that Tokyo consider carefully how Japan would pay for all of these products.[1159]

312. British-Thaiese Economic Agreement.

A resume of the prospective British-Thailand agreement was sent to Tokyo on July 14, 1941. The minimum quantity of rubber to be sent to England was 18,000 tons, and although up to 30,000 tons in addition could be supplied, in no event was a total of 48,000 tons to be exceeded. In return, the Thailand government agreed not to use for re-exportation any of the petroleum furnished by Britain.[1160] Although Britain had requested the Thailand government to withdraw the currency it now had in America, no definite conclusion had been reached.

313. Japan Fears British Influence in Thailand.

Although at the time of the Wanitto conversations in Tokyo, the Thaiese people had started celebrations and demonstrations, Minister Futami reported on July 12, 1941 that this excitement had abated. Because of the resumption of relations with Great Britain, Japan feared that Thailand would revive her principle of good will for all nations, and as a result, the relations between Japan and Thailand would suffer a setback. Mr. Futami pointed out that when Mr. Wanitto had first returned from Tokyo, Thaiese authorities had expected Japan to seize Singapore in the near future. But since that time, Thailand's offer of rubber to Japan had decreased in size from 38,400 tons to 30,000.[1161]

[1157]II, 1142.
[1158]II, 1149–1151.
[1159]II, 1152.
[1160]II, 1153.
[1161]II, 1154.

314. American-Thaiese Proposals.

Minister Futami reported that Thailand had proposed to America that payment for its orders for several American-made freighters and bombers, as well as the oil purchased from Britain, be made from funds Thailand had in America. In considering this proposal, the American government had in turn requested that Thailand not exclude Christianity, form no secret foreign trade agreement with a third country, and exchange intelligence with the United States. However, the American request had not been accepted by July 15, 1941.[1162]

315. Japan Plans to Offset British Influence.

Fearing that Thailand might resume her talks with Great Britain, Japan proposed to organize immediately a Japanese-Thaiese commission. Mr. Futami was asked on July 16, 1941 to negotiate personally with Mr. Pibul with the view of working out a prospectus for joint Japanese-Thaiese rights and interests. The Japanese commission was to consist of Mr. Futami as Chairman, the Military and Naval Attaches, and two first-class diplomatic secretaries. Tokyo requested that Minister Pibul be made the chief Thailand negotiator, or that someone else amenable to Japanese influence be appointed.[1163]

316. Japan Expands Its Communications System in Thailand.

In conjunction with the Japanese policy of preparing communications facilities for use in case of emergency, Japanese representatives inquired on May 16, 1941 concerning the possibility of placing a radio transmitter in the consulate at Singora,[1164] but Tokyo decided at this time that the establishment of two-way radio communication with Canton was impracticable from the viewpoint of secrecy.[1165] However, on July 21, 1941 negotiations for the expansion of Japanese communication were under way with the Thailand Communications Bureau.[1166]

317. Japan Informs Thailand of the Japanese-French Agreement.

Realizing that Thailand would be concerned as to the purpose of the Japanese-French Joint Agreement, Japan informed its Minister at Bangkok concerning the negotiations at Vichy. Prime Minister Pibul was to be informed of the agreement at 6:00 P.M. on July 24, 1941, two days prior to the publication of a statement announcing the agreement on July 26, 1941.

Because the people of Thailand would be very much affected by the publishing of the Japanese-French Joint Agreement, Japan felt that the significance of the pact should be minimized as much as possible by Prime Minister Pibul, who was to be assured that the joint understanding was not aimed at Thailand, and that the traditional friendship between Bangkok and Tokyo would not be affected. Furthermore, Japan had not lost its eagerness to cooperate in the economic development of Thailand, for it was giving Mr. Pibul advance information concerning the Japanese-French Agreement as an indication of the intimacy of Japanese-Thaiese relations.[1167]

According to Mr. Futami's report of his interview with the Prime Minister, Mr. Pibul expressed his deep appreciation at being privately informed of the Japanese-French Agreement, which was acceptable to him, but had showed no surprise upon hearing the news.[1168]

[1162]II, 1155.
[1163]II, 1156.
[1164]II, 1157.
[1165]II, 1158.
[1166]II, 1159.
[1167]II, 1160.
[1168]II, 1161.

318. Japan Decides Not to Stop British-Thaiese Agreement.

On July 26, 1941 it was learned that Britain had agreed to supply Thailand with petroleum in return for rubber, tin, and other products, and, thus, Japan's demands upon Thailand could not be carried out. If Japan insisted on the accomplishment of her original demands, however, it would be impossible for the British-Thaiese negotiations to go through, and this would result in Thailand's calling on Japan for all of her requirements. For this reason Minister Futami thought it advisable not to hamper the negotiations between Great Britain and Thailand, although Japan would have to be satisfied with the 30,000 kilotons of rubber which Thailand was reserving for it, and would have to supply the deficiency by increasing the amount from French Indo-China. However, since the British-Thaiese agreement was to apply for one year only, Japan was to reserve the right to demand Thailand's entire output of rubber and tin in the future.[1169] Tokyo replied that Mr. Futami could handle the matter as he desired, but that Tokyo must have at least 35,000 tons of rubber and at least 6,000 tons of tin. This was to be demanded without any compromise.[1170]

On July 15, 1941 Japan reiterated its demand that she be supplied with rubber and tin in exchange for the oil which Thailand needed. Japan also asked that definite assurance of a change of attitude on the part of the Thaiese government be made,[1171] and that Japan be guaranteed 35,000 tons of rubber and 6,000 tons of tin ore each year.

Pointing out discrepancies in the representations of Nai Wanitto, as compared with Japanese findings in regard to the amounts of tin ore and tin concentrate produced in Thailand, Foreign Minister Toyoda asked that an investigation be made. In any event, the Japanese were to demand at least forty per cent of the total amount.[1172]

319. Implementation of French-Thaiese Treaty.

In answer to an inquiry from Tokyo on July 26, 1941 regarding a recent economic pact between Thailand and France, Minister Futami reported that an agreement, ratified at Saigon on July 19, 1941, was concerned with the circulation of money and the transfer of negotiable documents which had been provided for in the treaty signed in Tokyo between Thailand and French Indo-China.[1173]

320. Japanese Interests in Thailand Affected by American-British Freezing of Funds.

Another diplomatic economic problem arose for the Japanese with the freezing of their funds in America on July 26, 1941. Regarded merely as an aspect of Thaiese diplomacy, rather than having been prompted by British authorities, was the guarantee of payment which the Thaiese National Bank demanded of the Japanese for shipment of certain materials to England. In case the British bank refused to purchase the material, the Yokohama Specie Bank was to be responsible for payment.[1174]

[1169]II, 1162–1163.
[1170]II, 1164.
[1171]II, 1165.
[1172]II, 1166.
[1173]II, 1167–1168.
[1174]II, 1169.

On July 28, 1941 Minister Toyoda replied that because of the recent fund-freezing by England and the United States, he feared that Japan would be unable to purchase Thaiese products either in pounds or dollars. Since the need for Thaiese products was imperative, Thailand was to be asked to accept free yen as a provisional payment until the conclusion of the pending agreement on methods of payment.[1175]

Since the use of free yen might be prohibited, Minister Futami inquired concerning the possibility of bartering with Thailand.[1176] On July 30, 1941 he was instructed by Tokyo to settle for Thaiese goods in gold yen, and he was informed that Japanese proposals for methods of payment would be submitted later.[1177]

According to a report from the Japanese Minister in Bangkok on July 30, 1941, the National Bank of Thailand had disapproved any loans in bahts after the freezing of funds by Britain and the United States. Consequently, the Yokohama Specie Bank had been forced to postpone payment to banks in Hongkong, Shanghai, and other points. Calling on Minister Pibul, Mr. Futami warned that if this state of affairs were not remedied, a cessation of trade between Japan and Thailand would result.

The Japanese Minister reported to Tokyo that Thailand was tending to act in unison with Britain and the United States, and would eventually share in setting up a blockade against Japan.[1178] However, Minister Pibul agreed to a Japanese suggestion that there be an immediate revision of the Thailand currency law and a Japanese-Thaiese agreement for payments. Stating that the cessation of Japanese-Thaiese trade relations should be avoided, no matter what Great Britain did, on July 26, 1941 Prime Minister Pibul ordered his Finance Minister to devise a method of solution.

After several conferences with Japanese experts, it was agreed that Thaiese authorities would organize a secret loan association, comprised of three banks, which would grant to the Yokohama Specie Bank a credit amounting to 10,000,000 bahts.[1179] The period of the loan and the interest on it were to be decided on August 1, 1941 by Mon Chao Bibba, advisor to the Thaiese Finance Ministry, and Mr. Yoichi Fukuda, manager of the Yokohama Specie Bank.[1180] It appeared, however, that Thailand's Finance Minister had no intention of revising the currency law in carrying out the terms of payment, since he believed that it would be difficult to achieve uniformity of opinion within the Thaiese government, and revision would require a considerable length of time.[1181]

Another conference on the morning of August 1, 1941 ended inconclusively since an agreement in regard to the rate of interest and a time limit on the loan could not be reached,[1182] but on August 2, 1941 Mr. Futami was able to report that an agreement for credit of 10,000,000 bahts had been reached during the afternoon.[1183]

[1175]II, 1170.

[1176]II, 1171.

[1177]II, 1172.

[1178]II, 1173.

[1179]10,000,000 bahts was the equivalent at this time of approximately 3,600,000 dollars.

[1180]II, 1174.

[1181]II, 1175.

[1182]II, 1176.

[1183]II, 1177.

321. Japanese-Thaiese Rice Negotiations.

Following the completion of the Japanese-Thaiese economic treaty, Mr. Rijuta Ono, Japanese financial advisor, informed his Finance Minister in Tokyo that the situation concerning the purchase of Thaiese rice was a bit confused. Since he felt the negotiations should be completed at once, he asked that instructions be sent to him.[1184] However, on the same day Minister Futami advised Tokyo against the sending of a technical expert to look over the rice, rice bran, oil and iron ore situation, since there was now no need to hurry negotiations with Thailand. He promised that Secretary Teiichi Suzuki would amplify this advice on his return to Japan on August 9, 1941.[1185]

322. Thailand Plans to Recognize Manchukuo.

The Japanese Foreign Office reported on July 29, 1941 that Thailand would recognize the Japanese-sponsored government of Manchukuo on August 1, 1941.[1186] Since this did not take place as planned, Foreign Minister Toyoda, on August 2, 1941, asked that information relating to Thailand's recognition be forwarded from Bangkok.[1187]

Minister Futami replied on August 4, 1941 that recognition was being delayed because of the necessity of obtaining the Emperor's approval. The Ministers of Great Britain and the Netherlands had already asked the Thaiese authorities if there were any truth in newspaper reports concerning the recognition of Manchukuo, and they had been told that Thailand's action was nothing more than a friendly gesture toward Japan. The inquiries of the diplomatic representatives, according to Minister Futami, were not in the form of protests.[1188]

323. Japan Requests a Mutual Exchange of Ambassadors.

As early as June 13, 1941, it had been learned that the Japanese Legation in Thailand was soon to be raised in status to an Embassy. To strengthen the Japanese representation in Thailand, Japan ordered Mr. Ichihashi in London to start for his new post immediately.[1189] In addition, a new Japanese consulate was to be established in Singora, located on the Kra Peninsula near British Malay, for on July 17, 1941 Vice-Consul Katsuno was instructed to look in Singora for suitable office and residence buildings.[1190]

A Japanese army officer, Major Voshihiko Osone, planned to operate from this consulate under the pseudonym of Saburo Goto, a fourth-class diplomatic clerk.[1191] Keisuke Ito, a member of the Far Eastern Economic Research Bureau, was also slated to do intelligence work at Singora.[1192]

Since the matter of raising the status of the Thailand Legation to an Embassy was to be approved at the next regular meeting of the Japanese Privy Council, and was to be put into effect immediately thereafter, Mr. Futami was directed on July 3, 1941 to ask Prime Minister Pibul to

---

[1184]II, 1178.
[1185]II, 1179.
[1186]II, 1180.
[1187]II, 1181.
[1188]II, 1182.
[1189]II, 1183.
[1190]II, 1184.
[1191]II, 1185.
[1192]II, 1186.

raise the status of the Thailand Legation in Tokyo to an Embassy at the same time. As soon as the Prime Minister acceded, Mr. Futami was to inform Tokyo immediately. In case of difficulty in finding a suitable ambassador, it was suggested that Thailand appoint its Minister to act as Charge d'Affairs at the same time that the Legation was raised to an Embassy.[1193]

Having already talked with the Prime Minister and having received his approval of the plan, Mr. Futami on July 14, 1941 reported that the Thaiese Departments of the Interior and Foreign Affairs were willing to accept the simultaneous and mutual elevation of Ministries to Embassies through an aide-memoire.[1194] On July 23, 1941 Thailand was advised to make the necessary preparations, since the Japanese Privy Council had just approved the raising of the status of the Japanese Legation in Thailand and Japan wished to effect the change immediately.[1195] A week later the appointment as Japanese Ambassador of Mr. Teiji Tsubokami, who had previously been associated with the Foreign Office, was approved by Thailand.[1196]

Confidentially informing Minister Futami on August 4, 1941 that the Thaiese were delaying too long in selecting an ambassador, and advising him that Tokyo had postponed the appointment of Ambassador Tsubokami until reciprocal arrangements were made, Mr. Toyoda suggested that the Vice-Minister of Defense, or some other appropriate person of high repute, be appointed to the Embassy in Japan.[1197] For various reasons, including the opportunity of removing a popular rival of Prime Minister Pibul from Thailand, Foreign Minister Toyoda thought it best to have the Defense Vice Minister sent as the first Thaiese Ambassador to Japan. Admiral Toyoda pointed out that if conditions in Thailand were such that he could not be spared for a long period, the Defense Minister could serve for as little as half a year until a relief could be selected.[1198]

[1193]II, 1187–1188.

[1194]II, 1189.

[1195]II, 1190.

[1196]II, 1191–1192.

[1197]II, 1193.

[1198]II, 1194.

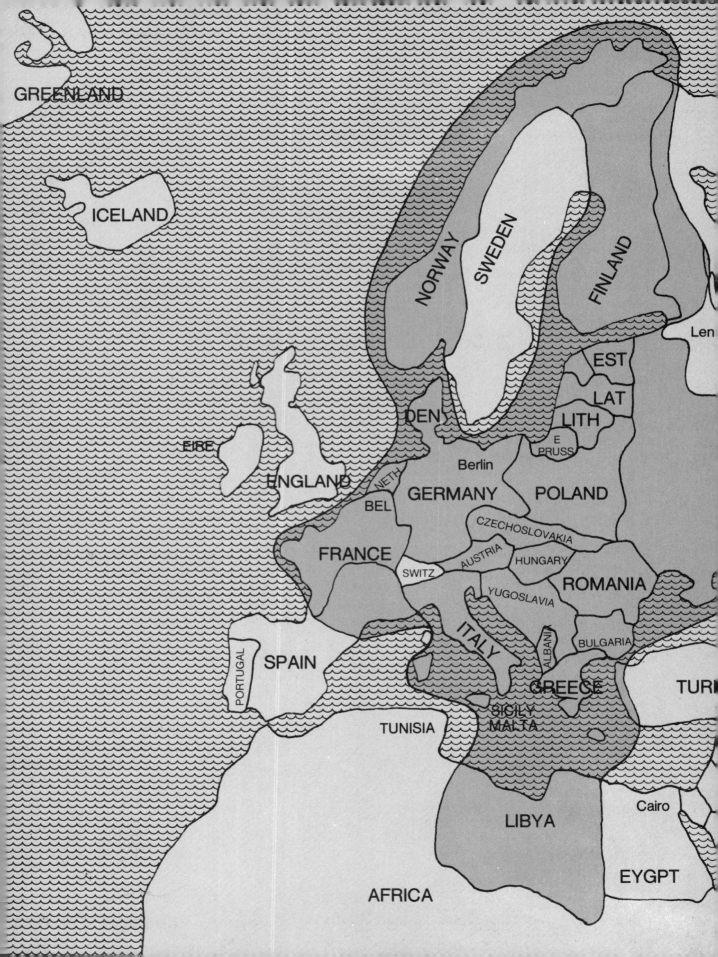